Data Mining

Data Mining
Know It All

Soumen Chakrabarti

Earl Cox

Eibe Frank

Ralf Hartmut Güting

Jaiwei Han

Xia Jiang

Micheline Kamber

Sam S. Lightstone

Thomas P. Nadeau

Richard E. Neapolitan

Dorian Pyle

Mamdouh Refaat

Markus Schneider

Toby J. Teorey

Ian H. Witten

ELSEVIER

AMSTERDAM • BOSTON • HEIDELBERG • LONDON
NEW YORK • OXFORD • PARIS • SAN DIEGO
SAN FRANCISCO • SINGAPORE • SYDNEY • TOKYO

Morgan Kaufmann is an imprint of Elsevier

MK®

MORGAN KAUFMANN PUBLISHERS

Morgan Kaufmann Publishers is an imprint of Elsevier.
30 Corporate Drive, Suite 400
Burlington, MA 01803

This book is printed on acid-free paper. ∞

Library of Congress Cataloging-in-Publication Data
Chakrabarti, Soumen.
  Data mining: know it all / Soumen Chakrabarti et al.
      p.   cm. — (Morgan Kaufmann know it all series)
  Includes bibliographical references and index.
  ISBN 978-0-12-374629-0 (alk. paper)
  1. Data mining. I. Title.
QA76.9.D343C446 2008
005.74—dc22   2008040367

For information on all Morgan Kaufmann publications,
visit our Website at *www.mkp.com or www.books.elsevier.com*

Printed and bound by CPI Group (UK) Ltd, Croydon, CR0 4YY

Transferred to Digital Print 2011

Contents

About This Book

All of the elements about data mining are here together in a single resource written by the best and brightest experts in the field! This book consolidates both introductory and advanced topics, thereby covering the gamut of data mining and machine learning tactics—from data integration and preprocessing to fundamental algorithms to optimization techniques and web mining methodology.

Data Mining: Know It All expertly combines the finest data mining material from the Morgan Kaufmann portfolio with individual chapters contributed by a select group of authors. They have been combined into one comprehensive book in a way that allows it to be used as a reference work for those interested in new and developing aspects of data mining. This book represents a quick and efficient way to unite valuable content from leaders in the data mining field, thereby creating a definitive, one-stop-shopping opportunity to access information you would otherwise need to round up from disparate sources.

Contributing Authors

Soumen Chakrabarti (Chapter 10) is an associate professor of computer science and engineering at the Indian Institute of Technology in Bombay. He is also a popular speaker at industry conferences, the associate editor for ACM "Transactions on the Web," as well as serving on other editorial boards. He is also the author of *Mining the Web,* published by Elsevier, 2003.

Earl Cox (Chapter 7) is the founder and president of Scianta Intelligence, a next-generation machine intelligence and knowledge exploration company. He is a futurist, author, management consultant, and educator dedicated to the epistemology of advanced intelligent systems, the redefinition of the machine mind, and the ways in which evolving and interconnected virtual worlds affect the sociology of business and culture. He is a recognized expert in fuzzy logic and adaptive fuzzy systems and a pioneer in the integration of fuzzy neural systems with genetic algorithms and case-based reasoning. He is also the author of *Fuzzy Modeling and Genetic Algorithms for Data Mining Exploration,* published by Elsevier, 2005.

Eibe Frank (Chapters 1 and 5) is a senior lecturer in computer science at the University of Waikato in New Zealand. He has published extensively in the area of machine learning and sits on editorial boards of the *Machine Learning Journal* and the *Journal of Artificial Intelligence Research.* He has also served on the programming committees of many data mining and machine learning conferences. He is the coauthor of *Data Mining,* published by Elsevier, 2005.

Ralf Hartmut Güting (Chapter 8) is a professor of computer science at the University of Hagen in Germany. After a one-year visit to the IBM Almaden Research Center in 1985, extensible and spatial database systems became his major research interests. He is the author of two German textbooks on data structures and algorithms and on compilers, and he has published nearly 50 articles on computational geometry and database systems. Currently, he is an associate editor of *ACM Transactions on Database Systems.* He is also a coauthor of Moving Objects Database, published by Elsevier, 2005.

Jaiwei Han (Chapter 3) is director of the Intelligent Database Systems Research Laboratory and a professor at the School of Computing Science at Simon Fraser University in Vancouver, BC. Well known for his research in the areas of data mining and database systems, he has served on program committees for dozens of international conferences and workshops and on editorial boards for several journals, including *IEEE Transactions on Knowledge and Data Engineering* and *Data Mining and Knowledge Discovery*. He is also the coauthor of *Data Mining: Concepts and Techniques*, published by Elsevier, 2006.

Xia Jiang (Chapter 6) received an M.S. in mechanical engineering from Rose Hulman University and is currently a Ph.D. candidate in the Biomedical Informatics Program at the University of Pittsburgh. She has published theoretical papers concerning Bayesian networks, along with applications of Bayesian networks to biosurveillance. She is also the coauthor of *Probabilistic Methods for Financial and Marketing Informatics*, published by Elsevier, 2007.

Micheline Kamber (Chapter 3) is a researcher and freelance technical writer with an M.S. in computer science with a concentration in artificial intelligence. She is a member of the Intelligent Database Systems Research Laboratory at Simon Fraser University in Vancouver, BC. She is also the coauthor of *Data Mining: Concepts and Techniques*, published by Elsevier, 2006.

Sam S. Lightstone (Chapter 4) is the cofounder and leader of DB2's autonomic computing R&D effort and has been with IBM since 1991. His current research interests include automatic physical database design, adaptive self-tuning resources, automatic administration, benchmarking methodologies, and system control. Mr. Lightstone is an IBM Master Inventor. He is also one of the coauthors of *Physical Database Design*, published by Elsevier, 2007.

Thomas P. Nadeau (Chapter 4) is a senior technical staff member of Ubiquiti Inc. and works in the area of data and text mining. His technical interests include data warehousing, OLAP, data mining, and machine learning. He is also one of the coauthors of *Physical Database Design*, published by Elsevier, 2007.

Richard E. Neapolitan (Chapter 6) is professor and Chair of Computer Science at Northeastern Illinois University. He is the author of *Learning Bayesian Networks* (Prentice Hall, 2004), which ha been translated into three languages; it is one of the most widely used algorithms texts worldwide. He is also the coauthor of *Probabilistic Methods for Financial and Marketing Informatics*, published by Elsevier, 2007.

Dorian Pyle (Chapter 9) has more than 25 years of experience is data mining and is currently a consultant for Data Miners Inc. He has developed a number of proprietary modeling and data mining technologies, including data preparation and data surveying tools, and a self-adaptive modeling technology used in direct marketing applications. He is also a popular speaker at industry conferences, the associate editor for ACM "Transactions on Internet Technology," and the author of *Business Modeling and Data Mining* (Morgan Kaufman, 2003).

Mamdouh Refaat (Chapter 2) is the director of Professional Services at ANGOSS Software Corporation. During the past 20 years, he has been an active member in the community, offering his services for consulting, researching, and training in various areas of information technology. He is also the author of *Data Preparation for Data Mining Using SAS,* published by Elsevier, 2007.

Markus Schneider (Chapter 8) is an assistant professor of computer science at the University of Florida, Gainesville, and holds a Ph.D. in computer Science from the University of Hagen in Germany. He is author of a monograph in the area of spatial databases, a German textbook on implementation concepts for database systems, coauthor of *Moving Objects Databases* (Morgan Kaufmann, 2005), and has published nearly 40 articles on database systems. He is on the editorial board of *GeoInformatica.*

Toby J. Teorey (Chapter 4) is a professor in the Electrical Engineering and Computer Science Department at the University of Michigan, Ann Arbor; his current research focuses on database design and performance of computing systems. He is also one of the coauthors of *Physical Database Design,* published by Elsevier, 2007.

Ian H. Witten (Chapters 1 and 5) is a professor of computer science at the University of Waikato in New Zealand and is a fellow of the ACM and the Royal Society in New Zealand. He received the 2004 IFIP Namur Award, a biennial honor accorded for outstanding contributions with international impact to the awareness of social implications of information and communication technology. He is also the coauthor of *Data Mining,* published by Elsevier, 2005.

Data Mining

What's It All About?

Human *in vitro* fertilization involves collecting several eggs from a woman's ovaries, which, after fertilization with partner or donor sperm, produce several embryos. Some of these are selected and transferred to the woman's uterus. The problem is to select the "best" embryos to use—the ones that are most likely to survive. Selection is based on around 60 recorded features of the embryos—characterizing their morphology, oocyte, follicle, and the sperm sample. The number of features is sufficiently large that it is difficult for an embryologist to assess them all simultaneously and correlate historical data with the crucial outcome of whether that embryo did or did not result in a live child. In a research project in England, machine learning is being investigated as a technique for making the selection, using as training data historical records of embryos and their outcome.

Every year, dairy farmers in New Zealand have to make a tough business decision: which cows to retain in their herd and which to sell off to an abattoir. Typically, one-fifth of the cows in a dairy herd are culled each year near the end of the milking season as feed reserves dwindle. Each cow's breeding and milk production history influences this decision. Other factors include age (a cow is nearing the end of its productive life at 8 years), health problems, history of difficult calving, undesirable temperament traits (kicking or jumping fences), and not being in calf for the following season. About 700 attributes for each of several million cows have been recorded over the years. Machine learning is being investigated as a way of ascertaining which factors are taken into account by successful farmers—not to automate the decision but to propagate their skills and experience to others.

Life and death. From Europe to the antipodes. Family and business. Machine learning is a burgeoning new technology for mining knowledge from data, a technology that a lot of people are starting to take seriously.

1.1 DATA MINING AND MACHINE LEARNING

We are overwhelmed with data. The amount of data in the world, in our lives, continues to increase—and there's no end in sight. Omnipresent personal computers make it too easy to save things that previously we would have trashed. Inexpensive multigigabyte disks make it too easy to postpone decisions about what to do with all this stuff—we simply buy another disk and keep it all. Ubiquitous electronics record our decisions, our choices in the supermarket, our financial habits, our comings and goings. We swipe our way through the world, every swipe a record in a database. The World Wide Web overwhelms us with information; meanwhile, every choice we make is recorded. And all these are just personal choices: they have countless counterparts in the world of commerce and industry. We would all testify to the growing gap between the *generation* of data and our *understanding* of it. As the volume of data increases, inexorably, the proportion of it that people understand decreases, alarmingly. Lying hidden in all this data is information, potentially useful information, that is rarely made explicit or taken advantage of.

This book is about looking for patterns in data. There is nothing new about this. People have been seeking patterns in data since human life began. Hunters seek patterns in animal migration behavior, farmers seek patterns in crop growth, politicians seek patterns in voter opinion, and lovers seek patterns in their partners' responses. A scientist's job (like a baby's) is to make sense of data, to discover the patterns that govern how the physical world works and encapsulate them in theories that can be used for predicting what will happen in new situations. The entrepreneur's job is to identify opportunities, that is, patterns in behavior that can be turned into a profitable business, and exploit them.

In *data mining,* the data is stored electronically and the search is automated—or at least augmented—by computer. Even this is not particularly new. Economists, statisticians, forecasters, and communication engineers have long worked with the idea that patterns in data can be sought automatically, identified, validated, and used for prediction. What is new is the staggering increase in opportunities for finding patterns in data. The unbridled growth of databases in recent years, databases on such everyday activities as customer choices, brings data mining to the forefront of new business technologies. It has been estimated that the amount of data stored in the world's databases doubles every 20 months, and although it would surely be difficult to justify this figure in any quantitative sense, we can all relate to the pace of growth qualitatively. As the flood of data swells and machines that can undertake the searching become commonplace, the opportunities for data mining increase. As the world grows in complexity, overwhelming us with the data it generates, data mining becomes our only hope for elucidating the patterns that underlie it. Intelligently analyzed data is a valuable resource. It can lead to new insights and, in commercial settings, to competitive advantages.

Data mining is about solving problems by analyzing data already present in databases. Suppose, to take a well-worn example, the problem is fickle customer loyalty in a highly competitive marketplace. A database of customer choices, along with customer profiles, holds the key to this problem. Patterns of behavior of former customers can be analyzed to identify distinguishing characteristics of those likely to switch products and those likely to remain loyal. Once such characteristics are found, they can be put to work to identify present customers who are likely to jump ship. This group can be targeted for special treatment, treatment too costly to apply to the customer base as a whole. More positively, the same techniques can be used to identify customers who might be attracted to another service the enterprise provides, one they are not presently enjoying, to target them for special offers that promote this service. In today's highly competitive, customer-centered, service-oriented economy, data is the raw material that fuels business growth—if only it can be mined.

Data mining is defined as the process of discovering patterns in data. The process must be automatic or (more usually) semiautomatic. The patterns discovered must be meaningful in that they lead to some advantage, usually an economic advantage. The data is invariably present in substantial quantities.

How are the patterns expressed? Useful patterns allow us to make nontrivial predictions on new data. There are two extremes for the expression of a pattern: as a black box whose innards are effectively incomprehensible and as a transparent box whose construction reveals the structure of the pattern. Both, we are assuming, make good predictions. The difference is whether or not the patterns that are mined are represented in terms of a structure that can be examined, reasoned about, and used to inform future decisions. Such patterns we call *structural* because they capture the decision structure in an explicit way. In other words, they help to explain something about the data.

Now, finally, we can say what this book is about. It is about techniques for finding and describing structural patterns in data. Most of the techniques that we cover have developed within a field known as *machine learning*. But first let us look at what structural patterns are.

1.1.1 Describing Structural Patterns

What is meant by *structural patterns?* How do you describe them? And what form does the input take? We will answer these questions by way of illustration rather than by attempting formal, and ultimately sterile, definitions. We will present plenty of examples later in this chapter, but let's examine one right now to get a feeling for what we're talking about.

Look at the contact lens data in Table 1.1. This gives the conditions under which an optician might want to prescribe soft contact lenses, hard contact lenses, or no contact lenses at all; we will say more about what the individual features mean later. Each line of the table is one of the examples. Part of a structural description of this information might be as follows:

```
If tear production rate = reduced then recommendation = none
Otherwise, if age = young and astigmatic = no
          then recommendation = soft
```

Structural descriptions need not necessarily be couched as rules such as these. Decision trees, which specify the sequences of decisions that need to

Table 1.1 The Contact Lens Data

Age	Spectacle Prescription	Astigmatism	Tear Production Rate	Recommended Lenses
Young	Myope	No	Reduced	None
Young	Myope	No	Normal	Soft
Young	Myope	Yes	Reduced	None
Young	Myope	Yes	Normal	Hard
Young	Hypermetrope	No	Reduced	None
Young	Hypermetrope	No	Normal	Soft
Young	Hypermetrope	Yes	Reduced	None
Young	Hypermetrope	Yes	Normal	Hard
Pre-presbyopic	Myope	No	Reduced	None
Pre-presbyopic	Myope	No	Normal	Soft
Pre-presbyopic	Myope	Yes	Reduced	None
Pre-presbyopic	Myope	Yes	Normal	Hard
Pre-presbyopic	Hypermetrope	No	Reduced	None
Pre-presbyopic	Hypermetrope	No	Normal	Soft
Pre-presbyopic	Hypermetrope	Yes	Reduced	None
Pre-presbyopic	Hypermetrope	Yes	Normal	None
Presbyopic	Myope	No	Reduced	None
Presbyopic	Myope	No	Normal	None
Presbyopic	Myope	Yes	Reduced	None
Presbyopic	Myope	Yes	Normal	Hard
Presbyopic	Hypermetrope	No	Reduced	None
Presbyopic	Hypermetrope	No	Normal	Soft
Presbyopic	Hypermetrope	Yes	Reduced	None
Presbyopic	Hypermetrope	Yes	Normal	None

be made and the resulting recommendation, are another popular means of expression.

This example is a simplistic one. First, all combinations of possible values are represented in the table. There are 24 rows, representing three possible values of age and two values each for spectacle prescription, astigmatism, and tear production rate ($3 \times 2 \times 2 \times 2 = 24$). The rules do not really generalize from the data; they merely summarize it. In most learning situations, the set of examples given as input is far from complete, and part of the job is to generalize to other, new examples. You can imagine omitting some of the rows in the table for which tear production rate is *reduced* and still coming up with the rule

```
If tear production rate = reduced then recommendation = none
```

which would generalize to the missing rows and fill them in correctly. Second, values are specified for all the features in all the examples. Real-life datasets invariably contain examples in which the values of some features, for some reason or other, are unknown—for example, measurements were not taken or were lost. Third, the preceding rules classify the examples correctly, whereas often, because of errors or *noise* in the data, misclassifications occur even on the data that is used to train the classifier.

1.1.2 Machine Learning

Now that we have some idea about the inputs and outputs, let's turn to machine learning. What is learning, anyway? What is machine learning? These are philosophic questions, and we will not be much concerned with philosophy in this book; our emphasis is firmly on the practical. However, it is worth spending a few moments at the outset on fundamental issues, just to see how tricky they are, before rolling up our sleeves and looking at machine learning in practice. Our dictionary defines "to learn" as follows:

- To get knowledge of by study, experience, or being taught.
- To become aware by information or from observation.
- To commit to memory.
- To be informed of, ascertain.
- To receive instruction.

These meanings have some shortcomings when it comes to talking about computers. For the first two, it is virtually impossible to test whether learning has been achieved or not. How do you know whether a machine has got knowledge of something? You probably can't just ask it questions; even if you could, you wouldn't be testing its ability to learn but would be testing its ability to answer questions. How do you know whether it has become aware of something? The whole question of whether computers can be aware, or conscious, is a burning philosophic issue. As for the last three meanings, although we can see what they denote in human terms, merely "committing to memory" and "receiving instruction" seem to fall far short of what we might mean by machine learning. They are too passive, and we know that computers find these tasks trivial. Instead, we are interested in improvements in performance, or at least in the potential for performance, in new situations. You can "commit something to memory" or "be informed of something" by rote learning without being able to apply the new knowledge to new situations. You can receive instruction without benefiting from it at all.

Earlier we defined data mining operationally as the process of discovering patterns, automatically or semiautomatically, in large quantities of data—and the patterns must be useful. An operational definition can be formulated in the same way for learning:

> Things learn when they change their behavior in a way that makes them perform better in the future.

This ties learning to performance rather than knowledge. You can test learning by observing the behavior and comparing it with past behavior. This is a much more objective kind of definition and appears to be far more satisfactory.

But there's still a problem. Learning is a rather slippery concept. Lots of things change their behavior in ways that make them perform better in the future, yet we wouldn't want to say that they have actually *learned.* A good example is a comfortable slipper. Has it *learned* the shape of your foot? It has certainly changed its behavior to make it perform better as a slipper! Yet we would hardly want to call this *learning.* In everyday language, we often use the word "training" to denote a mindless kind of learning. We train animals and even plants, although it would be stretching the word a bit to talk of training objects such as slippers that are not in any sense alive. But learning is different. Learning implies thinking. Learning implies purpose. Something that learns has to do so intentionally. That is why we wouldn't say that a vine has learned to grow round a trellis in a vineyard—we'd say it has been *trained.* Learning without purpose is merely training. Or, more to the point, in learning the purpose is the learner's, whereas in training it is the teacher's.

Thus, on closer examination the second definition of learning, in operational, performance-oriented terms, has its own problems when it comes to talking about computers. To decide whether something has actually learned, you need to see whether it intended to or whether there was any purpose involved. That makes the concept moot when applied to machines because whether artifacts can behave purposefully is unclear. Philosophic discussions of what is *really* meant by "learning," like discussions of what is *really* meant by "intention" or "purpose," are fraught with difficulty. Even courts of law find intention hard to grapple with.

1.1.3 Data Mining

Fortunately, the kind of learning techniques explained in this book do not present these conceptual problems—they are called machine learning without really presupposing any particular philosophic stance about what learning actually is. Data mining is a practical topic and involves learning in a practical, not a theoretic, sense. We are interested in techniques for finding and describing structural patterns in data as a tool for helping to explain that data and make predictions from it. The data will take the form of a set of examples—examples of customers who have switched loyalties, for instance, or situations in which certain kinds of contact lenses can be prescribed. The output takes the form of predictions about new examples—a prediction of whether a particular customer will switch or a prediction of what kind of lens will be prescribed under given circumstances. But because this book is about finding *and describing* patterns in data, the output may also include an actual description of a structure that can be used to classify unknown examples to explain the decision. As well as performance, it is helpful to supply an explicit representation of the knowledge that is acquired. In essence, this reflects both definitions of learning considered previously: the acquisition of knowledge and the ability to use it.

Many learning techniques look for structural descriptions of what is learned, descriptions that can become fairly complex and are typically expressed as sets of rules such as the ones described previously or the decision trees described later in this chapter. Because people can understand them, these descriptions explain what has been learned and explain the basis for new predictions. Experience shows that in many applications of machine learning to data mining, the explicit knowledge structures that are acquired, the structural descriptions, are at least as important, and often much more important, than the ability to perform well on new examples. People frequently use data mining to gain knowledge, not just predictions. Gaining knowledge from data certainly sounds like a good idea if you can do it. To find out how, read on!

1.2 SIMPLE EXAMPLES: THE WEATHER PROBLEM AND OTHERS

We use a lot of examples in this book, which seems particularly appropriate considering that the book is all about learning from examples! There are several standard datasets that we will come back to repeatedly. Different datasets tend to expose new issues and challenges, and it is interesting and instructive to have in mind a variety of problems when considering learning methods. In fact, the need to work with different datasets is so important that a corpus containing around 100 example problems has been gathered together so that different algorithms can be tested and compared on the same set of problems.

The illustrations used here are all unrealistically simple. Serious application of data mining involves thousands, hundreds of thousands, or even millions of individual cases. But when explaining what algorithms do and how they work, we need simple examples that capture the essence of the problem but are small enough to be comprehensible in every detail. The illustrations we will be working with are intended to be "academic" in the sense that they will help us to understand what is going on. Some actual fielded applications of learning techniques are discussed in Section 1.3, and many more are covered in the books mentioned in the Further Reading section at the end of the chapter.

Another problem with actual real-life datasets is that they are often proprietary. No corporation is going to share its customer and product choice database with you so that you can understand the details of its data mining application and how it works. Corporate data is a valuable asset, one whose value has increased enormously with the development of data mining techniques such as those described in this book. Yet we are concerned here with understanding how the methods used for data mining work and understanding the details of these methods so that we can trace their operation on actual data. That is why our illustrations are simple ones. But they are not *simplistic:* they exhibit the features of real datasets.

1.2.1 The Weather Problem

The weather problem is a tiny dataset that we will use repeatedly to illustrate machine learning methods. Entirely fictitious, it supposedly concerns the conditions that are suitable for playing some unspecified game. In general, instances in a dataset are characterized by the values of features, or *attributes,* that measure different aspects of the instance. In this case there are four attributes: *outlook, temperature, humidity,* and *windy.* The outcome is whether or not to play.

In its simplest form, shown in Table 1.2, all four attributes have values that are symbolic categories rather than numbers. Outlook can be *sunny, overcast,* or *rainy;* temperature can be *hot, mild,* or *cool;* humidity can be *high* or *normal;* and windy can be *true* or *false.* This creates 36 possible combinations (3 × 3 × 2 × 2 = 36), of which 14 are present in the set of input examples.

A set of rules learned from this information—not necessarily a very good one—might look as follows:

```
If outlook = sunny and humidity = high    then play = no
If outlook = rainy and windy = true       then play = no
If outlook = overcast                     then play = yes
If humidity = normal                      then play = yes
If none of the above                      then play = yes
```

These rules are meant to be interpreted in order: the first one; then, if it doesn't apply, the second; and so on.

A set of rules intended to be interpreted in sequence is called a *decision list.* Interpreted as a decision list, the rules correctly classify all of the examples in the table, whereas taken individually, out of context, some of the rules are incorrect. For example, the rule if humidity = normal, then play = yes gets one of the examples wrong (check which one). The meaning of a set of rules depends on how it is interpreted—not surprisingly!

In the slightly more complex form shown in Table 1.3, two of the attributes—temperature and humidity—have numeric values. This means that any learning method must create inequalities involving these attributes rather than simple

Table 1.2 The Weather Data

Outlook	Temperature	Humidity	Windy	Play
Sunny	Hot	High	False	No
Sunny	Hot	High	True	No
Overcast	Hot	High	False	Yes
Rainy	Mild	High	False	Yes
Rainy	Cool	Normal	False	Yes
Rainy	Cool	Normal	True	No
Overcast	Cool	Normal	True	Yes
Sunny	Mild	High	False	No
Sunny	Cool	Normal	False	Yes
Rainy	Mild	Normal	False	Yes
Sunny	Mild	Normal	True	Yes
Overcast	Mild	High	True	Yes
Overcast	Hot	Normal	False	Yes
Rainy	Mild	High	True	No

equality tests, as in the former case. This is called a *numeric-attribute problem—* in this case, a *mixed-attribute problem* because not all attributes are numeric.

Now the first rule given earlier might take the following form:

```
If outlook = sunny and humidity > 83 then play = no
```

A slightly more complex process is required to come up with rules that involve numeric tests.

The rules we have seen so far are *classification rules:* they predict the classification of the example in terms of whether or not to play. It is equally possible to disregard the classification and just look for any rules that strongly associate different attribute values. These are called *association rules.* Many association rules can be derived from the weather data in Table 1.2. Some good ones are as follows:

```
If temperature = cool              then humidity = normal
If humidity = normal and windy = false   then play = yes
If outlook = sunny and play = no   then humidity = high
If windy = false and play = no     then outlook = sunny
                                       and humidity = high.
```

Table 1.3 Weather Data with Some Numeric Attribute

Outlook	Temperature	Humidity	Windy	Play
Sunny	85	85	False	No
Sunny	80	90	True	No
Overcast	83	86	False	Yes
Rainy	70	96	False	Yes
Rainy	68	80	False	Yes
Rainy	65	70	True	No
Overcast	64	65	True	Yes
Sunny	72	95	False	No
Sunny	69	70	False	Yes
Rainy	75	80	False	Yes
Sunny	75	70	True	Yes
Overcast	72	90	True	Yes
Overcast	81	75	False	Yes
Rainy	71	91	True	No

All these rules are 100 percent correct on the given data; they make no false predictions. The first two apply to four examples in the dataset, the third to three examples, and the fourth to two examples. There are many other rules: in fact, nearly 60 association rules can be found that apply to two or more examples of the weather data and are completely correct on this data. If you look for rules that are less than 100 percent correct, then you will find many more. There are so many because unlike classification rules, association rules can "predict" any of the attributes, not just a specified class, and can even predict more than one thing. For example, the fourth rule predicts both that *outlook* will be *sunny* and that *humidity* will be *high*.

1.2.2 Contact Lenses: An Idealized Problem

The contact lens data introduced earlier tells you the kind of contact lens to prescribe, given certain information about a patient. Note that this example is intended for illustration only: it grossly oversimplifies the problem and should certainly not be used for diagnostic purposes!

The first column of Table 1.1 gives the age of the patient. In case you're wondering, *presbyopia* is a form of longsightedness that accompanies the onset of middle age. The second gives the spectacle prescription: *myope* means shortsighted and *hypermetrope* means longsighted. The third shows whether the patient is astigmatic, and the fourth relates to the rate of tear production, which is important in this context because tears lubricate contact lenses. The final column shows which kind of lenses to prescribe: *hard, soft,* or *none.* All possible combinations of the attribute values are represented in the table.

A sample set of rules learned from this information is shown in Figure 1.1. This is a large set of rules, but they do correctly classify all the examples. These rules are complete and deterministic: they give a unique prescription for every conceivable example. Generally, this is not the case. Sometimes there are situations in which no rule applies; other times more than one rule may apply, resulting in conflicting recommendations. Sometimes probabilities or weights may be associated with the rules themselves to indicate that some are more important, or more reliable, than others.

You might be wondering whether there is a smaller rule set that performs as well. If so, would you be better off using the smaller rule set and, if so, why? These are exactly the kinds of questions that will occupy us in this book. Because the examples form a complete set for the problem space, the rules do no more than summarize all the information that is given, expressing it in a different and more concise way. Even though it involves no generalization, this is often a useful

```
If tear production rate = reduced then recommendation = none
If age = young and astigmatic = no and
   tear production rate = normal then recommendation = soft
If age = pre-presbyopic and astigmatic = no and
   tear production rate = normal then recommendation = soft
If age = presbyopic and spectacle prescription = myope and
   astigmatic = no then recommendation = none
If spectacle prescription = hypermetrope and astigmatic = no and
   tear production rate = normal then recommendation = soft
If spectacle prescription = myope and astigmatic = yes and
   tear production rate = normal then recommendation = hard
If age = young and astigmatic = yes and
   tear production rate = normal then recommendation = hard
If age = pre-presbyopic and
   spectacle prescription = hypermetrope and astigmatic = yes
   then recommendation = none
If age = presbyopic and spectacle prescription = hypermetrope
   and astigmatic = yes then recommendation = none
```

FIGURE 1.1

Rules for the contact lens data.

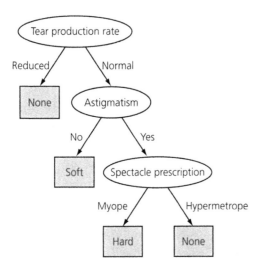

FIGURE 1.2

Decision tree for the contact lens data.

thing to do! People frequently use machine learning techniques to gain insight into the structure of their data rather than to make predictions for new cases. In fact, a prominent and successful line of research in machine learning began as an attempt to compress a huge database of possible chess endgames and their outcomes into a data structure of reasonable size. The data structure chosen for this enterprise was not a set of rules, but a decision tree.

Figure 1.2 presents a structural description for the contact lens data in the form of a decision tree, which for many purposes is a more concise and perspicuous representation of the rules and has the advantage that it can be visualized more easily. (However, this decision tree—in contrast to the rule set given in Figure 1.1—classifies two examples incorrectly.) The tree calls first for a test on *tear production rate,* and the first two branches correspond to the two possible outcomes. If *tear production rate* is *reduced* (the left branch), the outcome is *none.* If it is *normal* (the right branch), a second test is made, this time on *astigmatism.* Eventually, whatever the outcome of the tests, a leaf of the tree is reached that dictates the contact lens recommendation for that case.

1.2.3 Irises: A Classic Numeric Dataset

The iris dataset, which dates back to seminal work by the eminent statistician R. A. Fisher in the mid-1930s and is arguably the most famous dataset used in data mining, contains 50 examples each of three types of plant: *Iris setosa, Iris versicolor,* and *Iris virginica.* It is excerpted in Table 1.4. There are four attributes: *sepal length, sepal width, petal length,* and *petal width* (all measured in centimeters). Unlike previous datasets, all attributes have numeric values.

Table 1.4 The Iris Data

	Sepal Length (cm)	Sepal Width (cm)	Petal Length (cm)	Petal Width (cm)	Type
1	5.1	3.5	1.4	0.2	Iris setosa
2	4.9	3.0	1.4	0.2	Iris setosa
3	4.7	3.2	1.3	0.2	Iris setosa
4	4.6	3.1	1.5	0.2	Iris setosa
5	5.0	3.6	1.4	0.2	Iris setosa
...					
51	7.0	3.2	4.7	1.4	Iris versicolor
52	6.4	3.2	4.5	1.5	Iris versicolor
53	6.9	3.1	4.9	1.5	Iris versicolor
54	5.5	2.3	4.0	1.3	Iris versicolor
55	6.5	2.8	4.6	1.5	Iris versicolor
...					
101	6.3	3.3	6.0	2.5	Iris virginica
102	5.8	2.7	5.1	1.9	Iris virginica
103	7.1	3.0	5.9	2.1	Iris virginica
104	6.3	2.9	5.6	1.8	Iris virginica
105	6.5	3.0	5.8	2.2	Iris virginica
...					

The following set of rules might be learned from this dataset:

```
If petal length < 2.45 then Iris setosa
If sepal width < 2.10 then Iris versicolor
If sepal width < 2.45 and petal length < 4.55 then Iris versicolor
If sepal width < 2.95 and petal width < 1.35 then Iris versicolor
If petal length ≥ 2.45 and petal length < 4.45 then Iris versicolor
If sepal length ≥ 5.85 and petal length < 4.75 then Iris versicolor
If sepal width < 2.55 and petal length < 4.95 and
   petal width < 1.55 then Iris versicolor
If petal length ≥ 2.45 and petal length < 4.95 and
   petal width < 1.55 then Iris versicolor
If sepal length ≥ 6.55 and petal length < 5.05 then Iris versicolor
```

```
If sepal width < 2.75 and petal width < 1.65 and
   sepal length < 6.05 then Iris versicolor
If sepal length ≥ 5.85 and sepal length < 5.95 and
   petal length < 4.85 then Iris versicolor
If petal length ≥ 5.15 then Iris virginica
If petal width ≥ 1.85 then Iris virginica
If petal width ≥ 1.75 and sepal width < 3.05 then Iris virginica
If petal length ≥ 4.95 and petal width < 1.55 then Iris virginica
```

These rules are very cumbersome; more compact rules can be expressed that convey the same information.

1.2.4 **CPU Performance: Introducing Numeric Prediction**

Although the iris dataset involves numeric attributes, the outcome—the type of iris—is a category, not a numeric value. Table 1.5 shows some data for which the outcome and the attributes are numeric. It concerns the relative performance of computer processing power on the basis of a number of relevant attributes; each row represents 1 of 209 different computer configurations.

The classic way of dealing with continuous prediction is to write the outcome as a linear sum of the attribute values with appropriate weights, for example:

$$PRP = -55.9 + 0.0489 \ MYCT + 0.0153 \ MMIN + 0.0056 \ MMAX + 0.6410 \ CACH$$
$$- 0.2700 \ CHMIN + 1.480 \ CHMAX$$

Table 1.5 The CPU Performance Data

	Cycle Time (ns) MYCT	Main Memory (KB)		Cache (KB) CACH	Channels		Performance PRP
		Minimum MMIN	Maximum MMAX		Minimum CHMIN	Maximum CHMAX	
1	125	256	6000	256	16	128	198
2	29	8000	32000	32	8	32	269
3	29	8000	32000	32	8	32	220
4	29	8000	32000	32	8	32	172
5	29	8000	16000	32	8	16	132
...							
207	125	2000	8000	0	2	14	52
208	480	512	8000	32	0	0	67
209	480	1000	4000	0	0	0	45

(The abbreviated variable names are given in the second row of the table.) This is called a *regression equation,* and the process of determining the weights is called *regression,* a well-known procedure in statistics. However, the basic regression method is incapable of discovering nonlinear relationships (although variants do exist).

In the iris and central processing unit (CPU) performance data, all the attributes have numeric values. Practical situations frequently present a mixture of numeric and nonnumeric attributes.

1.2.5 **Labor Negotiations: A More Realistic Example**

The labor negotiations dataset in Table 1.6 summarizes the outcome of Canadian contract negotiations in 1987 and 1988. It includes all collective agreements

Table 1.6 The Labor Negotiations Data

Attribute	Type	1	2	3	...	40
Duration	Years	1	2	3		2
Wage increase first year	Percentage	2%	4%	4.3%		4.5
Wage increase second year	Percentage	?	5%	4.4%		4.0
Wage increase third year	Percentage	?	?	?		?
Cost of living adjustment	{none, tcf, tc}	None	Tcf	?		None
Working hours per week	Hours	28	35	38		40
Pension	{none, ret-allw, empl-cntr}	None	?	?		?
Standby pay	Percentage	?	13%	?		?
Shift-work supplement	Percentage	?	5%	4%		4
Education allowance	{yes, no}	Yes	?	?		?
Statutory holidays	Days	11	15	12		12
Vacation	{below-avg, avg, gen}	Avg	Gen	Gen		Avg
Long-term disability assistance	{yes, no}	No	?	?		Yes
Dental plan contribution	{none, half, full}	None	?	Full		Full
Bereavement assistance	{yes, no}	No	?	?		Yes
Health plan contribution	{none, half, full}	None	?	Full		Half
Acceptability of contract	{good, bad}	Bad	Good	Good		Good

reached in the business and personal services sector for organizations with at least 500 members (teachers, nurses, university staff, police, etc.). Each case concerns one contract, and the outcome is whether the contract is deemed *acceptable* or *unacceptable*. The acceptable contracts are ones in which agreements were accepted by both labor and management. The unacceptable ones are either known offers that fell through because one party would not accept them or acceptable contracts that had been significantly perturbed to the extent that, in the view of experts, they would not have been accepted.

There are 40 examples in the dataset (plus another 17 that are normally reserved for test purposes). Unlike the other tables here, Table 1.6 presents the examples as columns rather than as rows; otherwise, it would have to be stretched over several pages. Many of the values are unknown or missing, as indicated by question marks.

This is a much more realistic dataset than the others we have seen. It contains many missing values, and it seems unlikely that an exact classification can be obtained.

Figure 1.3 shows two decision trees that represent the dataset. Figure 1.3(a) is simple and approximate: it doesn't represent the data exactly. For example, it will predict *bad* for some contracts that are actually marked *good*. But it does make intuitive sense: a contract is bad (for the employee!) if the wage increase in the first year is too small (less than 2.5 percent). If the first-year wage increase is larger than this, it is good if there are lots of statutory holidays (more than 10 days). Even if there are fewer statutory holidays, it is good if the first-year wage increase is large enough (more than 4 percent).

Figure 1.3(b) is a more complex decision tree that represents the same dataset. In fact, this is a more accurate representation of the actual dataset that was used to create the tree. But it is not necessarily a more accurate representation of the underlying concept of good versus bad contracts. Look down the left branch. It doesn't seem to make sense intuitively that, if the working hours exceed 36, a contract is bad if there is no health-plan contribution or a full health-plan contribution but is good if there is a half health-plan contribution. It is certainly reasonable that the health-plan contribution plays a role in the decision but not if half is good and both full and none are bad. It seems likely that this is an artifact of the particular values used to create the decision tree rather than a genuine feature of the good versus bad distinction.

The tree in Figure 1.3(b) is more accurate on the data that was used to train the classifier but will probably perform less well on an independent set of test data. It is "overfitted" to the training data—it follows it too slavishly. The tree in Figure 1.3(a) is obtained from the one in Figure 1.3(b) by a process of pruning.

1.2.6 Soybean Classification: A Classic Machine Learning Success

An often-quoted early success story in the application of machine learning to practical problems is the identification of rules for diagnosing soybean diseases.

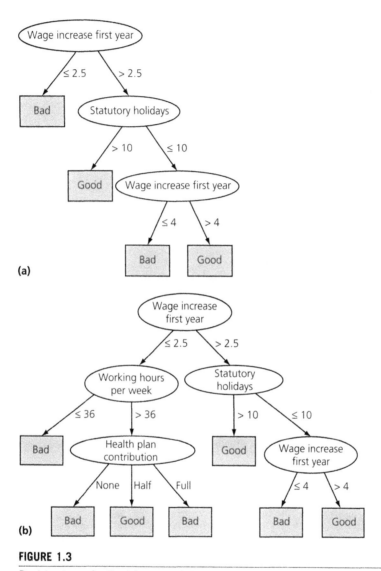

(a)

(b)

FIGURE 1.3

Decision trees for the labor negotiations data.

The data is taken from questionnaires describing plant diseases. There are about 680 examples, each representing a diseased plant. Plants were measured on 35 attributes, each one having a small set of possible values. Examples are labeled with the diagnosis of an expert in plant biology: there are 19 disease categories altogether—horrible-sounding diseases, such as diaporthe stem canker, rhizoctonia root rot, and bacterial blight, to mention just a few.

Table 1.7 gives the attributes, the number of different values that each can have, and a sample record for one particular plant. The attributes are placed into different categories just to make them easier to read.

Here are two example rules, learned from this data:

```
If      [leaf condition is normal and
        stem condition is abnormal and
        stem cankers is below soil line and
        canker lesion color is brown]
then
        diagnosis is rhizoctonia root rot

If      [leaf malformation is absent and
        stem condition is abnormal and
        stem cankers is below soil line and
        canker lesion color is brown]
then
        diagnosis is rhizoctonia root rot
```

These rules nicely illustrate the potential role of prior knowledge—often called *domain knowledge*—in machine learning, because the only difference between the two descriptions is leaf condition is normal versus leaf malformation is absent. In this domain, if the leaf condition is normal, then leaf malformation is necessarily absent, so one of these conditions happens to be a special case of the other. Thus, if the first rule is true, the second is necessarily true as well. The only time the second rule comes into play is when leaf malformation is absent

	Attribute	Number of Values	Sample Value
Table 1.7 The Soybean Data			
Environment	Time of occurrence	7	July
	Precipitation	3	Above normal
	Temperature	3	Normal
	Cropping history	4	Same as last year
	Hail damage	2	Yes
	Damaged area	4	Scattered
	Severity	3	Severe
	Plant height	2	Normal
	Plant growth	2	Abnormal
	Seed treatment	3	Fungicide
	Germination	3	Less than 80%

Table 1.7 *Continued*

	Attribute	Number of Values	Sample Value
Seed	Condition	2	Normal
	Mold growth	2	Absent
	Discoloration	2	Absent
	Size	2	Normal
	Shriveling	2	Absent
Fruit	Condition of fruit pods	3	Normal
	Fruit spots	5	–
Leaf	Condition	2	Abnormal
	Leaf spot size	3	–
	Yellow leaf spot halo	3	Absent
	Leaf spot margins	3	–
	Shredding	2	Absent
	Leaf malformation	2	Absent
	Leaf mildew growth	3	Absent
Stem	Condition	2	Abnormal
	Stem lodging	2	Yes
	Stem cankers	4	Above soil line
	Canker lesion color	3	–
	Fruiting bodies on stems	2	Present
	External decay of stem	3	Firm and dry
	Mycelium on stem	2	Absent
	Internal discoloration	3	None
	Sclerotia	2	Absent
Root	Condition	3	Normal
Diagnosis			Diaporthe stem
		19	Canker

but leaf condition is *not* normal—that is, when something other than malformation is wrong with the leaf. This is certainly not apparent from a casual reading of the rules.

Research on this problem in the late 1970s found that these diagnostic rules could be generated by a machine learning algorithm, along with rules for every other disease category, from about 300 training examples. The examples were carefully selected from the corpus of cases as being quite different from one another—"far apart" in the example space. At the same time, the plant pathologist who had produced the diagnoses was interviewed, and his expertise was translated into diagnostic rules. Surprisingly, the computer-generated rules outperformed the expert's rules on the remaining test examples. They gave the correct disease top ranking 97.5 percent of the time compared with only 72 percent for the expert-derived rules. Furthermore, not only did the learning algorithm find rules that outperformed those of the expert collaborator, but the same expert was so impressed that he allegedly adopted the discovered rules in place of his own!

1.3 FIELDED APPLICATIONS

The examples that we opened with are speculative research projects, not production systems. And the preceding illustrations are toy problems: they are deliberately chosen to be small so that we can use them to work through algorithms later in the book. Where's the beef? Here are some applications of machine learning that have actually been put into use.

Because they are fielded applications, the illustrations that follow tend to stress the use of learning in performance situations, in which the emphasis is on ability to perform well on new examples. This book also describes the use of learning systems to gain knowledge from decision structures that are inferred from the data. We believe that this is as important—probably even more important in the long run—a use of the technology as merely making high-performance predictions. Still, it will tend to be underrepresented in fielded applications because when learning techniques are used to gain insight, the result is not normally a system that is put to work as an application in its own right. Nevertheless, in three of the examples that follow, the fact that the decision structure is comprehensible is a key feature in the successful adoption of the application.

1.3.1 Decisions Involving Judgment

When you apply for a loan, you have to fill out a questionnaire that asks for relevant financial and personal information. The loan company uses this information as the basis for its decision as to whether to lend you money. Such decisions are typically made in two stages. First, statistical methods are used to determine clear "accept" and "reject" cases. The remaining borderline cases are more difficult and call for human judgment. For example, one loan company uses a statistical decision procedure to calculate a numeric parameter based on the information supplied in the questionnaire. Applicants are accepted if this parameter exceeds a preset threshold and rejected if it falls below a second threshold. This accounts for 90 percent of cases, and the remaining 10 percent are referred to loan officers for a decision. On examining historical data on whether applicants did indeed repay their loans, however, it turned out that half of the borderline applicants who were granted loans actually defaulted. Although it would be tempting simply to deny credit to borderline customers, credit industry professionals pointed out that if only their repayment future could be reliably determined it is precisely these customers whose business should be wooed; they tend to be active customers of a credit institution because their finances remain in a chronically volatile condition. A suitable compromise must be reached between the viewpoint of a company accountant, who dislikes bad debt, and that of a sales executive, who dislikes turning business away.

Enter machine learning. The input was 1000 training examples of borderline cases for which a loan had been made that specified whether the borrower had finally paid off or defaulted. For each training example, about 20 attributes were extracted from the questionnaire, such as age, years with current employer, years at current address, years with the bank, and other credit cards possessed. A machine learning procedure was used to produce a small set of classification rules that made correct predictions on two-thirds of the borderline cases in an independently chosen test set. Not only did these rules improve the success rate of the loan decisions, but the company also found them attractive because they could be used to explain to applicants the reasons behind the decision. Although the project was an exploratory one that took only a small development effort, the loan company was apparently so pleased with the result that the rules were put into use immediately.

1.3.2 Screening Images

Since the early days of satellite technology, environmental scientists have been trying to detect oil slicks from satellite images to give early warning of ecologic disasters and deter illegal dumping. Radar satellites provide an opportunity for monitoring coastal waters day and night, regardless of weather conditions. Oil slicks appear as dark regions in the image whose size and shape evolve depending on weather and sea conditions. However, other look-alike dark regions can be caused by local weather conditions such as high wind. Detecting oil slicks is an expensive manual process requiring highly trained personnel who assess each region in the image.

A hazard detection system has been developed to screen images for subsequent manual processing. Intended to be marketed worldwide to a wide variety of users—government agencies and companies—with different objectives, applications, and geographic areas, it needs to be highly customizable to individual circumstances. Machine learning allows the system to be trained on examples of spills and nonspills supplied by the user and lets the user control the trade-off between undetected spills and false alarms. Unlike other machine learning applications, which generate a classifier that is then deployed in the field, here it is the learning method itself that will be deployed.

The input is a set of raw pixel images from a radar satellite, and the output is a much smaller set of images with putative oil slicks marked by a colored border. First, standard image processing operations are applied to normalize the image. Then, suspicious dark regions are identified. Several dozen attributes are extracted from each region, characterizing its size, shape, area, intensity, sharpness and jaggedness of the boundaries, proximity to other regions, and information about the background in the vicinity of the region. Finally, standard learning techniques are applied to the resulting attribute vectors.

Several interesting problems were encountered. One is the scarcity of training data. Oil slicks are (fortunately) very rare, and manual classification is extremely costly. Another is the unbalanced nature of the problem: of the many dark regions in the training data, only a small fraction are actual oil slicks. A third is that the examples group naturally into batches, with regions drawn from each image forming a single batch, and background characteristics vary from one batch to another. Finally, the performance task is to serve as a filter, and the user must be provided with a convenient means of varying the false-alarm rate.

1.3.3 Load Forecasting

In the electricity supply industry, it is important to determine future demand for power as far in advance as possible. If accurate estimates can be made for the maximum and minimum load for each hour, day, month, season, and year, utility companies can make significant economies in areas such as setting the operating reserve, maintenance scheduling, and fuel inventory management.

An automated load forecasting assistant has been operating at a major utility supplier over the past decade to generate hourly forecasts 2 days in advance. The first step was to use data collected over the previous 15 years to create a sophisticated load model manually. This model had three components: base load for the year, load periodicity over the year, and the effect of holidays. To normalize for the base load, the data for each previous year was standardized by subtracting the average load for that year from each hourly reading and dividing by the standard deviation over the year. Electric load shows periodicity at three fundamental frequencies: diurnal, where usage has an early morning minimum and midday and afternoon maxima; weekly, where demand is lower at weekends; and seasonal, where increased demand during winter and summer for heating and cooling, respectively, creates a yearly cycle. Major holidays such as Thanksgiving, Christmas, and New Year's Day show significant variation from the normal load and are each modeled separately by averaging hourly loads for that day over the past 15 years. Minor official holidays, such as Columbus Day, are lumped together as school holidays and treated as an offset to the normal diurnal pattern. All of these effects are incorporated by reconstructing a year's load as a sequence of typical days, fitting the holidays in their correct position, and denormalizing the load to account for overall growth.

Thus far, the load model is a static one, constructed manually from historical data, and implicitly assumes "normal" climatic conditions over the year. The final step was to take weather conditions into account using a technique that locates the previous day most similar to the current circumstances and uses the historical information from that day as a predictor. In this case the prediction is treated as an additive correction to the static load model. To guard against outliers, the 8 most similar days are located and their additive corrections averaged. A database was constructed of temperature, humidity, wind speed, and cloud cover at three local weather centers for each hour of the 15-year historical record, along with the difference between the actual load and that predicted by the static model. A linear regression analysis was performed to determine the relative effects of these parameters on load, and the coefficients were used to weight the distance function used to locate the most similar days.

The resulting system yielded the same performance as trained human forecasters but was far quicker—taking seconds rather than hours to generate a daily forecast. Human operators can analyze the forecast's sensitivity to simulated changes in weather and bring up for examination the "most similar" days that the system used for weather adjustment.

1.3.4 Diagnosis

Diagnosis is one of the principal application areas of expert systems. Although the handcrafted rules used in expert systems often perform well, machine learning can be useful in situations in which producing rules manually is too labor intensive.

Preventative maintenance of electromechanical devices such as motors and generators can forestall failures that disrupt industrial processes. Technicians regularly inspect each device, measuring vibrations at various points to determine whether the device needs servicing. Typical faults include shaft misalignment, mechanical loosening, faulty bearings, and unbalanced pumps. A particular chemical plant uses more than 1000 different devices, ranging from small pumps to very large turbo-alternators, which until recently were diagnosed by a human expert with 20 years of experience. Faults are identified by measuring vibrations at different places on the device's mounting and using Fourier analysis to check the energy present in three different directions at each harmonic of the basic rotation speed. The expert studies this information, which is noisy because of limitations in the measurement and recording procedure, to arrive at a diagnosis. Although handcrafted expert system rules had been developed for some situations, the elicitation process would have to be repeated several times for different types of machinery; so a learning approach was investigated.

Six hundred faults, each comprising a set of measurements along with the expert's diagnosis, were available, representing 20 years of experience in the field. About half were unsatisfactory for various reasons and had to be discarded; the remainder were used as training examples. The goal was not to determine whether or not a fault existed but to diagnose the kind of fault, given that one was there. Thus, there was no need to include fault-free cases in the training set. The measured attributes were rather low level and had to be augmented by intermediate concepts, that is, functions of basic attributes, which were defined in consultation with the expert and embodied some causal domain knowledge. The derived attributes were run through an induction algorithm to produce a set of diagnostic rules. Initially, the expert was not satisfied with the rules because he could not relate them to his own knowledge and experience. For him, mere statistical evidence was not, by itself, an adequate explanation. Further background knowledge had to be used before satisfactory rules were generated. Although the resulting rules were complex, the expert liked them because he could justify them in light of his mechanical knowledge. He was pleased that a third of the rules coincided with ones he used himself and was delighted to gain new insight from some of the others.

Performance tests indicated that the learned rules were slightly superior to the handcrafted ones that the expert had previously elicited, and subsequent use in the chemical factory confirmed this result. It is interesting to note, however, that the system was put into use not because of its good performance but because the domain expert approved of the rules that had been learned.

1.3.5 Marketing and Sales

Some of the most active applications of data mining have been in the area of marketing and sales. These are domains in which companies possess massive volumes of precisely recorded data, data that—it has only recently been realized—is potentially extremely valuable. In these applications, predictions themselves are the chief interest: the structure of how decisions are made is often completely irrelevant.

We have already mentioned the problem of fickle customer loyalty and the challenge of detecting customers who are likely to defect so that they can be wooed back into the fold by giving them special treatment. Banks were early adopters of data mining technology because of their successes in the use of machine learning for credit assessment. Data mining is now being used to reduce customer attrition by detecting changes in individual banking patterns that may herald a change of bank or even life changes, such as a move to another city, that could result in a different bank being chosen. It may reveal, for example, a group of customers with above-average attrition rate who do most of their banking by phone after hours when telephone response is slow. Data mining may determine groups for whom new services are appropriate, such as a cluster of profitable, reliable customers who rarely get cash advances from their credit card except in November and December, when they are prepared to pay exorbitant interest rates to see them through the holiday season. In another domain, cellular phone companies fight *churn* by detecting patterns of behavior that could benefit from new services and then advertise such services to retain their customer base. Incentives provided specifically to retain existing customers can be expensive, and successful data mining allows them to be precisely targeted to those customers where they are likely to yield maximum benefit.

Market basket analysis is the use of association techniques to find groups of items that tend to occur together in transactions, typically supermarket checkout data. For many retailers, this is the only source of sales information that is available for data mining. For example, automated analysis of checkout data may uncover the fact that customers who buy beer also buy chips, a discovery that could be significant from the supermarket operator's point of view (although rather an obvious one that probably does not need a data mining exercise to discover). Or it may come up with the fact that on Thursdays, customers often purchase diapers and beer together, an initially surprising result that, on reflection, makes some sense as young parents stock up for a weekend at home. Such information could be used for many purposes: planning store layouts, limiting special discounts to just one of a set of items that tend to be purchased together, offering coupons for a matching product when one of them is sold alone, and so on. There is enormous added value in being able to identify individual customer's sales histories. In fact, this value is leading to a proliferation of discount cards or "loyalty" cards that allow retailers to identify individual customers whenever they make a purchase; the personal data that results will be far more valuable than the cash value of the discount. Identification of individual customers not only allows historical analysis of purchasing patterns but also permits precisely targeted special offers to be mailed out to prospective customers.

This brings us to direct marketing, another popular domain for data mining. Promotional offers are expensive and have an extremely low—but highly profitable—response rate. Any technique that allows a promotional mailout to be more tightly focused, achieving the same or nearly the same response from a much smaller sample, is valuable. Commercially available databases containing demographic information based on ZIP codes that characterize the associated neighborhood can be correlated with information on existing customers to find a socioeconomic model that predicts what kind of people will turn out to be actual customers. This model can then be used on information gained in response to an initial mailout, where people send back a response card or call an 800 number for more information, to predict likely future customers. Direct mail companies have the advantage over shopping mall retailers of having complete purchasing histories for each individual customer and can use data mining to determine those likely to respond to special offers. Targeted campaigns are cheaper than mass-marketed campaigns because companies save money by sending offers only to those likely to want the product. Machine learning can help companies to find the targets.

1.3.6 Other Applications

There are countless other applications of machine learning. We briefly mention a few more areas to illustrate the breadth of what has been done.

Sophisticated manufacturing processes often involve tweaking control parameters. Separating crude oil from natural gas is an essential prerequisite to oil refinement, and controlling the separation process is a tricky job. British Petroleum used machine learning to create rules for setting the parameters. This now takes just 10 minutes, whereas previously human experts took more than a day. Westinghouse faced problems in its process for manufacturing nuclear fuel pellets and used machine learning to create rules to control the process. This was reported to save the company more than $10 million per year (in 1984). The Tennessee printing company R. R. Donnelley applied the same idea to control rotogravure printing presses to reduce artifacts caused by inappropriate parameter settings, reducing the number of artifacts from more than 500 each year to fewer than 30.

In the realm of customer support and service, we have already described adjudicating loans and marketing and sales applications. Another example arises when a customer reports a telephone problem and the company must decide what kind of technician to assign to the job. An expert system developed by Bell Atlantic in 1991 to make this decision was replaced in 1999 by a set of rules acquired using machine learning, which saved more than $10 million per year by making fewer incorrect decisions.

There are many scientific applications. In biology, machine learning is used to help identify the thousands of genes within each new genome. In biomedicine, it is used to predict drug activity by analyzing not just the chemical properties of drugs but also their three-dimensional structure. This accelerates drug discovery and reduces its cost. In astronomy, machine learning has been used to develop a fully automatic cataloging system for celestial objects that are too faint to be seen by visual inspection. In chemistry, it has been used to predict the structure of certain organic compounds from magnetic resonance spectra. In all these applications, machine learning techniques have attained levels of performance—or should we say skill?—that rival or surpass human experts.

Automation is especially welcome in situations involving continuous monitoring, a job that is time consuming and exceptionally tedious for humans. Ecologic applications include the oil spill monitoring described earlier. Some other applications are rather less consequential—for example, machine learning is being used to predict preferences for TV programs based on past choices and advise viewers about the available channels. Still others may save lives. Intensive care patients may be monitored to detect changes in variables that cannot be explained by circadian rhythm, medication, and so on, raising an alarm when appropriate.

Finally, in a world that relies on vulnerable networked computer systems and is increasingly concerned about cyber security, machine learning is used to detect intrusion by recognizing unusual patterns of operation.

1.4 MACHINE LEARNING AND STATISTICS

What's the difference between machine learning and statistics? Cynics, looking wryly at the explosion of commercial interest (and hype) in this area, equate data mining to statistics plus marketing. In truth, you should not look for a dividing line between machine learning and statistics because there is a continuum—and a multidimensional one at that—of data analysis techniques. Some derive from the skills taught in standard statistics courses, and others are more closely associated with the kind of machine learning that has arisen out of computer science. His-torically, the two sides have had rather different traditions. If forced to point to a single difference of emphasis, it might be that statistics has been more concerned with testing hypotheses, whereas machine learning has been more concerned with formulating the process of generalization as a search through possible hypoth-eses. But this is a gross oversimplification: statistics is far more than hypothesis testing, and many machine learning techniques do not involve any searching at all.

In the past, similar methods have developed in parallel in machine learning and statistics. One is decision tree induction. Four statisticians (Breiman et al. 1984) published a book, *Classification and Regression Trees,* in the mid-1980s, and throughout the 1970s and early 1980s a prominent machine learning researcher, J. Ross Quinlan, was developing a system for inferring classification trees from examples. These two independent projects produced similar methods for generating trees from examples, and the researchers only became aware of one another's work much later. A second area in which similar methods have arisen involves the use of nearest-neighbor methods for classification. These are standard statistical techniques that have been extensively adapted by machine learning researchers, both to improve classification performance and to make the procedure more efficient computationally.

But now the two perspectives have converged. The techniques we will examine in this book incorporate a great deal of statistical thinking. From the beginning, when constructing and refining the initial example set, standard statistical methods apply: visualization of data, selection of attributes, discarding outliers, and so on. Most learning algorithms use statistical tests when constructing rules or trees and for correcting models that are "overfitted," in that they depend too strongly on the details of the particular examples used to produce them (we have already seen an example of this in the two decision trees of Figure 1.3 for the labor negotia-tions problem). Statistical tests are used to validate machine learning models and to evaluate machine learning algorithms. In our study of practical techniques for data mining, we will learn a great deal about statistics.

1.5 GENERALIZATION AS SEARCH

One way of visualizing the problem of learning—and one that distinguishes it from statistical approaches—is to imagine a search through a space of possible concept descriptions for one that fits the data. Although the idea of generalization as search is a powerful conceptual tool for thinking about machine learning, it is not essential for understanding the practical methods described here. That is why this section is considered optional.

Suppose, for definiteness, that *concepts*—the result of learning—are expressed as rules such as the ones given for the weather problem in Section 1.2 (although other concept description languages would do just as well). Suppose that we list all possible sets of rules and then look for ones that satisfy a given set of examples. A big job? Yes. An *infinite* job? At first glance it seems so because there is no limit to the number of rules there might be. But actually the number of possible rule sets is finite. Note first that each individual rule is no greater than a fixed maximum size, with at most one term for each attribute: for the weather data of Table 1.2 this involves four terms in all. Because the number of possible rules is finite, the number of possible rule *sets* is finite, too, although extremely large. However, we'd hardly be interested in sets that contained a very large number of rules. In fact, we'd hardly be interested in sets that had more rules than there are examples because it is difficult to imagine needing more than one rule for each example. So if we were to restrict consideration to rule sets smaller than that, the problem would be substantially reduced, although still very large.

The threat of an infinite number of possible concept descriptions seems more serious for the second version of the weather problem in Table 1.3 because these rules contain numbers. If they are real numbers, you can't enumerate them, even in principle. However, on reflection, the problem again disappears because the numbers really just represent breakpoints in the numeric values that appear in the examples. For instance, consider the *temperature* attribute in Table 1.3. It involves the numbers 64, 65, 68, 69, 70, 71, 72, 75, 80, 81, 83, and 85—12 different numbers. There are 13 possible places in which we might want to put a breakpoint for a rule involving temperature. The problem isn't infinite after all.

So the process of generalization can be regarded as a search through an enormous, but finite, search space. In principle, the problem can be solved by enumerating descriptions and striking out those that do not fit the examples presented. A positive example eliminates all descriptions that it does not match, and a negative one eliminates those it does match. With each example, the set of remaining descriptions shrinks (or stays the same). If only one is left, it is the target description—the target concept.

If several descriptions are left, they may still be used to classify unknown objects. An unknown object that matches all remaining descriptions should be classified as matching the target; if it fails to match any description, it should be classified as being outside the target concept. Only when it matches some descriptions, but not others, is there ambiguity. In this case, if the classification of the unknown object were revealed, it would cause the set of remaining descriptions to shrink because rule sets that classified the object the wrong way would be rejected.

1.5.1 **Enumerating the Concept Space**

Regarding it as search is a good way of looking at the learning process. However, the search space, although finite, is extremely big, and it is generally impractical to enumerate all possible descriptions and then see which ones fit. In the weather problem there are $4 \times 4 \times 3 \times 3 \times 2 = 288$ possibilities for each rule. There are four possibilities for the *outlook* attribute: *sunny, overcast, rainy,* or it may not participate in the rule at all. Similarly, there are four for *temperature,* three for *weather* and *humidity,* and two for the class. If we restrict the rule set to contain no more than 14 rules (because there are 14 examples in the training set), there are around 2.7×10^{34} possible different rule sets. That's a lot to enumerate, especially for such a patently trivial problem.

Although there are ways of making the enumeration procedure more feasible, a serious problem remains: in practice, it is rare for the process to converge on a unique acceptable description. Either many descriptions are still in the running after the examples are processed or the descriptors are all eliminated. The first case arises when the examples are not sufficiently comprehensive to eliminate all possible descriptions except for the "correct" one. In practice, people often want a single "best" description, and it is necessary to apply some other criteria to select the best one from the set of remaining descriptions. The second problem arises either because the description language is not expressive enough to capture the actual concept or because of noise in the examples. If an example comes in with the "wrong" classification because of an error in some of the attribute values or in the class that is assigned to it, this will likely eliminate the correct description from the space. The result is that the set of remaining descriptions becomes empty. This situation is very likely to happen if the examples contain any noise at all, which inevitably they do except in artificial situations.

Another way of looking at generalization as search is to imagine it, not as a process of enumerating descriptions and striking out those that don't apply, but as a kind of hill-climbing in description space to find the description that best matches the set of examples according to some prespecified matching criterion. This is the way that most practical machine learning methods work. However, except in the most trivial cases, it is impractical to search the whole space exhaustively; most practical algorithms involve heuristic search and cannot guarantee to find the optimal description.

1.5.2 **Bias**

Viewing generalization as a search in a space of possible concepts makes it clear that the following are most important decisions in a machine learning system.

- The concept description language.
- The order in which the space is searched.
- The way that overfitting to the particular training data is avoided.

These three properties are generally referred to as the *bias* of the search and are called *language bias, search bias,* and *overfitting-avoidance bias.* You bias the learning scheme by choosing a language in which to express concepts, by searching in a particular way for an acceptable description, and by deciding when the concept has become so complex that it needs to be simplified.

Language Bias

The most important question for language bias is whether the concept description language is universal, or whether it imposes constraints on what concepts can be learned. If you consider the set of all possible examples, a concept is really just a division of it into subsets. In the weather example, if you were to enumerate all possible weather conditions, the *play* concept is a subset of possible weather conditions. A "universal" language is one that is capable of expressing every possible subset of examples. In practice, the set of possible examples is generally huge, and in this respect our perspective is a theoretic, not a practical, one.

If the concept description language permits statements involving logical *or*, that is, *disjunctions*, then any subset can be represented. If the description language is rule based, disjunction can be achieved by using separate rules. For example, one possible concept representation is just to enumerate the examples:

```
If outlook = overcast and temperature = hot and humidity = high
   and windy = false then play = yes
If outlook = rainy and temperature = mild and humidity = high
   and windy = false then play = yes
If outlook = rainy and temperature = cool and humidity = normal
   and windy = false then play = yes
If outlook = overcast and temperature = cool and humidity = normal
   and windy = true then play = yes
 . . .
If none of the above then play = no
```

This is not a particularly enlightening concept description; it simply records the positive examples that have been observed and assumes that all the rest are negative. Each positive example is given its own rule, and the concept is the disjunction of the rules. Alternatively, you could imagine having individual rules for each of the negative examples, too—an equally uninteresting concept. In either case, the concept description does not perform any generalization; it simply records the original data.

On the other hand, if disjunction is *not* allowed, some possible concepts—sets of examples—may not be able to be represented at all. In that case, a machine learning scheme may simply be unable to achieve good performance.

Another kind of language bias is that obtained from knowledge of the particular domain being used. For example, it may be that some combinations of attribute values can never happen. This would be the case if one attribute implied another. We saw an example of this when considering the rules for the soybean problem described earlier. Then, it would be pointless to even consider concepts that involved redundant or impossible combinations of attribute values. Domain knowledge can be used to cut down the search space. Knowledge is power: a little goes a long way, and even a small hint can reduce the search space dramatically.

Search Bias

In realistic data mining problems, there are many alternative concept descriptions that fit the data, and the problem is to find the "best" one according to some criterion—usually simplicity. We use the term *fit* in a statistical sense; we seek the best description that fits the data reasonably well. Moreover, it is often computationally infeasible to search the whole space and guarantee that the description found really is the best. Consequently, the search procedure is heuristic, and no guarantees can be made about the optimality of the final result. This leaves plenty of room for bias: different search heuristics bias the search in different ways.

For example, a learning algorithm might adopt a "greedy" search for rules by trying to find the best rule at each stage and adding it in to the rule set. However, it may be that the best *pair* of rules is not just the two rules that are individually found to be the best. Or when building a decision tree, a commitment to split early on using a particular attribute might turn out later to be ill considered in light of how the tree develops below that node. To get around these problems, a *beam search* could be used in which irrevocable commitments are not made but instead a set of several active alternatives—whose number is the *beam width*—are pursued in parallel. This will complicate the learning algorithm considerably but has the potential to avoid the myopia associated with a greedy search. Of course, if the beam width is not large enough, myopia may still occur. There are more complex search strategies that help to overcome this problem.

A more general and higher-level kind of search bias concerns whether the search is done by starting with a general description and refining it or by starting with a specific example and generalizing it. The former is called a *general-to-specific* search bias, the latter a *specific-to-general* one. Many learning algorithms adopt the former policy, starting with an empty decision tree, or a very general rule, and specializing it to fit the examples. However, it is perfectly possible to work in the other direction. Instance-based methods start with a particular example and see how it can be generalized to cover nearby examples in the same class.

Overfitting-Avoidance Bias

Overfitting-avoidance bias is often just another kind of search bias. But because it addresses a rather special problem, we treat it separately. Recall the disjunction problem described previously. The problem is that if disjunction is allowed, useless concept descriptions that merely summarize the data become possible, whereas if it is prohibited, some concepts are unlearnable. To get around this problem, it is common to search the concept space starting with the simplest concept descriptions and proceeding to more complex ones: simplest-first ordering. This biases the search toward simple concept descriptions.

Using a simplest-first search and stopping when a sufficiently complex concept description is found is a good way of avoiding overfitting. It is sometimes called *forward pruning* or *prepruning* because complex descriptions are pruned away before they are reached. The alternative, *backward pruning* or *postpruning,* is also viable. Here, we first find a description that fits the data well and then prune it back to a simpler description that also fits the data. This is not as redundant as it sounds: often the only way to arrive at a simple theory is to find a complex one and then simplify it. Forward and backward pruning are both a kind of overfitting-avoidance bias.

In summary, although generalization as search is a nice way to think about the learning problem, bias is the only way to make it feasible in practice. Different learning algorithms correspond to different concept description spaces searched with different biases. This is what makes it interesting: different description languages and biases serve some problems well and other problems badly. There is no universal "best" learning method—as every teacher knows!

1.6 DATA MINING AND ETHICS

The use of data—particularly data about people—for data mining has serious ethical implications, and practitioners of data mining techniques must act responsibly by making themselves aware of the ethical issues that surround their particular application.

When applied to people, data mining is frequently used to discriminate—who gets the loan, who gets the special offer, and so on. Certain kinds of discrimination—racial, sexual, religious, and so on—are not only unethical but also illegal. However, the situation is complex: everything depends on the application. Using sexual and racial information for medical diagnosis is certainly ethical, but using the same information when mining loan payment behavior is not. Even when sensitive information is discarded, there is a risk that models will be built that rely on variables that can be shown to substitute for racial or sexual characteristics. For example, people frequently live in areas that are associated with particular ethnic identities, so using an area code in a data mining study runs the risk of building models that are based on race—even though racial information has been explicitly excluded from the data.

It is widely accepted that before people make a decision to provide personal information they need to know how it will be used and what it will be used for, what steps will be taken to protect its confidentiality and integrity, what the consequences of supplying or withholding the information are, and any rights of redress they may have. Whenever such information is collected, individuals should be told these things—not in legalistic small print but straightforwardly in plain language they can understand.

The potential use of data mining techniques means that the ways in which a repository of data can be used may stretch far beyond what was conceived when the data was originally collected. This creates a serious problem: it is necessary to determine the conditions under which the data was collected and for what purposes it may be used. Does the ownership of data bestow the right to use it in ways other than those purported when it was originally recorded? Clearly in the case of explicitly collected personal data it does not. But in general the situation is complex.

Surprising results emerge from data mining. For example, it has been reported that one of the leading consumer groups in France has found that people with red cars are more likely to default on their car loans. What is the status of such a "discovery"? What information is it based on? Under what conditions was that information collected? In what ways is it ethical to use it? Clearly, insurance companies are in the business of discriminating among people based on stereotypes—young males pay heavily for automobile insurance—but such stereotypes are not based solely on statistical correlations; they also involve commonsense knowledge about the world. Whether the preceding finding says something about the kind of person who chooses a red car, or whether it should be discarded as an irrelevancy is a matter for human judgment based on knowledge of the world, rather than on purely statistical criteria.

When presented with data, you need to ask who is permitted to have access to it, for what purpose it was collected, and what kind of conclusions is it legitimate to draw from it. The ethical dimension raises tough questions for those involved in practical data mining. It is necessary to consider the norms of the community that is used to dealing with the kind of data involved, standards that may have evolved over decades or centuries but ones that the information specialist may not know. For example, did you know that in the library community, it is taken for granted that the privacy of readers is a right that is jealously protected? If you call your university library and ask who has such-and-such a textbook out on loan, they will not tell you. This prevents a student from being subjected to pressure from an irate professor to yield access to a book that she desperately needs for her latest grant application. It also prohibits inquiry into the dubious recreational reading tastes of the university ethics committee chairperson. Those who build, say, digital libraries may not be aware of these sensitivities and might incorporate data mining systems that analyze and compare individuals' reading habits to recommend new books—perhaps even selling the results to publishers!

In addition to community standards for the use of data, logical and scientific standards must be adhered to when drawing conclusions from it. If you do come up with conclusions (such as red car owners being greater credit risks), you need to attach caveats to them and back them up with arguments other than purely statistical ones. The point is that data mining is just a tool in the whole process: It is people who take the results, along with other knowledge, and decide what action to apply.

Data mining prompts another question, which is really a political one: To what use are society's resources being put? We mentioned previously the application of data mining to basket analysis, where supermarket checkout records are analyzed to detect associations among items that people purchase. What use should be made of the resulting information? Should the supermarket manager place the beer and chips together, to make it easier for shoppers, or farther apart, making it less convenient for them, maximizing their time in the store, and therefore increasing their likelihood of being drawn into unplanned further purchases? Should the manager move the most expensive, most profitable diapers near the beer, increasing sales to harried fathers of a high-margin item and add further luxury baby products nearby?

Of course, those who use advanced technologies should consider the wisdom of what they are doing. If *data* is characterized as recorded facts, then *information* is the set of patterns, or expectations, that underlie the data. You could go on to define *knowledge* as the accumulation of your set of expectations and *wisdom* as the value attached to knowledge. Although we will not pursue it further here, this issue is worth pondering.

As we saw at the very beginning of this chapter, the techniques described in this book may be called on to help make some of the most profound and intimate decisions that life presents. Data mining is a technology that we need to take seriously.

1.7 RESOURCES

This section describes papers, books, and other resources relevant to the material covered in this chapter. The human *in vitro* fertilization research mentioned in the opening of this chapter was undertaken by the Oxford University Computing Laboratory, and the research on cow culling was performed in the Computer Science Department at the University of Waikato, New Zealand.

The example of the weather problem is from Quinlan (1986) and has been widely used to explain machine learning schemes. The corpus of example problems mentioned in the introduction to Section 1.2 is available from Blake et al. (1998). The contact lens example is from Cendrowska (1998), who introduced the PRISM rule-learning algorithm. The iris dataset was described in a classic early paper on statistical inference (Fisher 1936). The labor negotiations data is from the *Collective Bargaining Review,* a publication of Labour Canada issued by the Industrial Relations Information Service (BLI 1988), and the soybean problem was first described by Michalski and Chilausky (1980).

Some of the applications in Section 1.3 are covered in an excellent paper that gives plenty of other applications of machine learning and rule induction (Langley

& Simon 1995); another source of fielded applications is a special issue of the *Machine Learning Journal* (Kohavi & Provost 1998). The loan company application is described in more detail by Michie (1989), the oil slick detector is from Kubat et al. (1998), the electric load forecasting work is by Jabbour et al. (1988), and the application to preventative maintenance of electromechanical devices is from Saitta and Neri (1998). Fuller descriptions of some of the other projects mentioned in Section 1.3 (including the figures of dollars saved and related literature references) appear at the websites of the Alberta Ingenuity Centre for Machine Learning and MLnet, a European network for machine learning.

The book *Classification and Regression Trees* mentioned in Section 1.4 is by Breiman et al. (1984), and the independently derived but similar scheme of Quinlan was described in a series of papers that eventually led to a book (Quinlan 1993).

The first book on data mining appeared in 1991 (Piatetsky-Shapiro & Frawley 1991), a collection of papers presented at a workshop on knowledge discovery in databases in the late 1980s. Another book from the same stable has appeared since (Fayyad et al. 1996) from a 1994 workshop. There followed a rash of business-oriented books on data mining, focusing mainly on practical aspects of how it can be put into practice with only superficial descriptions of the technology that underlies the methods used. They are valuable sources of applications and inspiration. For example, Adriaans and Zantige (1996) from Syllogic, a European systems and database consultancy, provide an early introduction to data mining. Berry and Linoff (1997), from a Pennsylvania-based company specializing in data warehousing and data mining, give an excellent and example-studded review of data mining techniques for marketing, sales, and customer support. The work of Cabena et al. (1998), written by people from five international IBM laboratories, presents an overview the data mining process with many examples of real-world applications. Dhar and Stein (1997) give a business perspective on data mining and include broad-brush, popularized reviews of many of the technologies involved. Groth (1998), working for a provider of data mining software, gives a brief introduction to data mining and then a fairly extensive review of data mining software products; the book includes a CD containing a demo version of his company's product. Weiss and Indurkhya (1998) look at a wide variety of statistical techniques for making predictions from what they call "big data." Han and Kamber (2001) cover data mining from a database perspective, focusing on the discovery of knowledge in large corporate databases. Finally, Hand et al. (2001) produced an interdisciplinary book on data mining from an international group of authors who are well respected in the field.

Books on machine learning, on the other hand, tend to be academic texts suited for use in university courses rather than practical guides. Mitchell (1997) wrote an excellent book that covers many techniques of machine learning, including some—notably genetic algorithms and reinforcement learning—that are not covered here. Langley (1996) offers another good text. Although the previously mentioned book by Quinlan (1993) concentrates on a particular learning algorithm, C4.5, it is a good introduction to some of the problems and techniques of machine learning. An excellent book on machine learning from a statistical perspective is from Hastie et al. (2001). This is a theoretically oriented work and is beautifully produced with apt and telling illustrations.

Pattern recognition is a topic that is closely related to machine learning, and many of the same techniques apply. Duda et al. (2001) offer the second edition of a classic and successful book on pattern recognition (Duda & Hart 1973). Ripley (1996) and Bishop (1995) describe the use of neural networks for pattern recognition. Data mining with neural networks is the subject of a book by Bigus (1996) of IBM, which features the IBM Neural Network Utility Product that he developed.

There is a great deal of current interest in support vector machines. Cristianini and Shawe-Taylor (2000) give a nice introduction, and a follow-up work generalizes this to cover additional algorithms, kernels, and solutions with applications to pattern discovery problems in fields such as bioinformatics, text analysis, and image analysis (Shawe-Taylor & Cristianini 2004). Schölkopf and Smola (2002) provide a comprehensive introduction to support vector machines and related kernel methods by two young researchers who did their PhD research in this rapidly developing area.

Data Acquisition and Integration

2.1 INTRODUCTION

This chapter first provides a brief review of data sources and types of variables from the point of view of data mining. Then it presents the most common procedures of data rollup and aggregation, sampling, and partitioning.

2.2 SOURCES OF DATA

In most organizations today, data is stored in relational databases. The quality and utility of the data, as well as the amount of effort needed to transform the data to a form suitable for data mining, depends on the types of the applications the databases serve. These relational databases serve as data repositories for the following applications.

2.2.1 Operational Systems

Operational systems process the transactions that make an organization work. The data from these systems is, by nature, transient and keeps accumulating in the repository. A typical example of these systems is any banking transaction processing system that keeps records of opened and closed accounts, deposits, withdrawals, balances, and all other values related to the money moving among accounts, clients, and the outside world. Data extracted from such operational systems is the most *raw* form of data, in the sense that it has not been transformed, cleansed, or changed. It may contain errors as a result of data entry procedures or applications and usually has many missing values. It is also usually scattered over several tables and files. However, it is the most honest representation of the status of any business.

2.2.2 **Data Warehouses and Data Marts**

Data warehouses and data marts were conceived as a means to facilitate the compilation of regular reports on the status of the business by continuously collecting, cleaning, and summarizing the core data of the organization. Data warehouses provide a clean and organized source of data for data mining. In most cases, however, data warehouses were not created to prepare data for data modelers; they were rather created with a certain set of reporting functions in mind. Therefore, data residing in them might have been augmented or processed in a special way to facilitate those functions. Ideally, a specialized data mart should be created to house the data needed for data mining modeling and scoring processes.

2.2.3 **Online Analytical Processing Applications**

Online analytical processing (OLAP) and similar software are often given the name *business intelligence* tools. These applications reside in the data warehouse, or have their own data warehouse, and provide a graphical interface to navigate, explore, and "slice and dice" the data. The data structures that OLAP applications operate on are called *cubes.* They also provide comprehensive reporting capabilities. OLAP systems could be a source of data for data mining because of the interactive exploration capabilities that they offer the user. Therefore, the user would find the interesting data elements related to the problem through OLAP applications and then apply data mining modeling for prediction.

Alternatively, data mining can offer the identification of the significant variables that govern the behavior of some business measure (such as profit), and then OLAP can use these variables (as dimensions) to navigate and get qualitative insight into existing relationships. Data extracted from OLAP cubes may not be granular enough for data mining. This is because continuous variables are usually *binned* before they can be used as dimensions in OLAP cubes. This binning process results in the loss of some information, which may have a significant impact on the performance of data mining algorithms.

2.2.4 **Surveys**

Surveys are perhaps the most expensive source of data because they require direct interaction with customers. Surveys collect data through different communication channels with customers, such as mail, email, interviews, and forms on websites. There are many anecdotes about the accuracy and validity of the data collected from the different forms of surveys. However, they all share the following two common features:

1. The number of customers who participate in the survey is usually limited because of the cost and the number of customers willing to participate.

2. The questions asked in the survey can be designed to directly address the objective of the planned model. For example, if the objective is to market new

products, the survey would ask customers about their preferences in these products, whether they would buy them, and what price would they pay for them.

These two points highlight the fact that, if well designed and executed, surveys are indeed the most accurate representation of possible customer behavior. However, they usually generate a limited amount of data because of the cost involved.

2.2.5 Household and Demographic Databases

In most countries, databases are commercially available that contain detailed information on consumers of different products and services. The most common type is demographic databases based on a national census, where the general demographic profile of each residential area is surveyed and summarized. Data obtained from such database providers is usually clean and information rich. Their only limitation is that data is not provided on the individual customer or record level but rather is averaged over a group of customers, for example, on the level of a postal (ZIP) code. Such limitations are usually set by privacy laws aimed at protecting individuals from abuse of such data.

The use of averaged data in models could lead to *diluting* the model's ability to accurately define a target group. For example, extensive use of census-like variables in a customer segmentation model would eventually lead to a model that clusters the population on the basis of the used census demographics and not in relation to the originally envisaged rate of usage or buying habits of the planned products or services.

It is not uncommon that analysts collect data from more than one source to form the initial mining view and for the scoring of mining models.

2.3 VARIABLE TYPES

Designers of applications that use databases and different file systems attempt to optimize their applications in terms of the space required to keep the data and the speed of processing and accessing the data. Because of these considerations, the data extracted from databases is often not in optimal form from the point of view of data mining algorithms. To appreciate this issue, we provide the following discussion of the types of variables that most data mining algorithms deal with.

2.3.1 Nominal Variables

Nominal, or *categorical*, variables describe values that lack the properties of order, scale, or distance between them. For example, the variables representing the type of a housing unit can take the categories House, Apartment, or Shared Accommodation. One cannot enforce any meaning of order or scale on these values. Other examples include Gender (Male, Female), Account Type (Savings, Checking), and type of Credit Card (VISA, MasterCard, American Express, Diners Club, EuroCard, Discover, etc.).

From the point of view of data mining algorithms, it is important to retain the *lack* of order or scale in categorical variables. Therefore, it is not desirable that a category be represented in the data by a series of integers. For example, if the type of a house variable is represented by the integers 1 to 4 (1 = Detached, 2 = Semidetached, 3 = Townhome, 4 = Bungalow), a numeric algorithm may inadvertently add the numbers 1 and 2, resulting implicitly in the erroneous and meaningless statement of "Detached + Semidetached = Townhome"! Other erroneous, and equally meaningless, implications that "Bungalow > Detached" or "Bungalow − Semidetached = Townhome − Detached." The most convenient method of storing categorical variables in software applications is to use strings. This should force the application to interpret them as nominal variables.

2.3.2 Ordinal Variables

Ordinal, or *rank* or *ordered scalar*, variables are categorical variables with the notion of order added to them. For example, we may define the risk levels of defaulting on a credit card payment into three levels (Low, Medium, High). We can assert the order relationships High ≥ Medium ≥ Low. However, we cannot establish the notion of scale. In other words, we cannot accurately say that the difference between *High* and *Medium* is the same as the difference between *Medium* and *Low* levels of risk.

Based on the definition of ordinal variables, we can realize the problem that would arise when such variables are represented by a series of integers. For example, in the case of the risk level variable, representing these levels with numbers from 1 to 3 such that (Low = 1, Medium = 2, High = 3) would result in the imposition of an invalid notion of distance between the different values. In addition, this definition would impose the definition of scale on the values by implying that Medium risk is double the risk of Low, and High risk is three times the risk of Low.

Some ordinal variables come with the scale and distance notions added to them. These are best represented by a series of positive integers. They usually measure the frequency of occurrence of an event. Examples of such ordinal measures are number of local telephone calls within a month, number of people using a credit card in a week, and number of cars purchased by a prospective customer in her or his lifetime.

A typical problem, especially in data warehouses, exists in the representation of ordinal measures. Some ordinal measures are often subjected to binning to reduce the values we need to store and deal with. For example, a data warehouse may bin the number of times a customer uses a credit card per month to the representation 0-5 → 1, 6-10 → 2, 11-20 → 3, more than 20 → 4. Although this leads to a more compact representation of the variables, it may be detrimental to data mining algorithms for two reasons: (1) it reduces the granularity level of the data, which may result in a reduction in the predictive model accuracy, and (2) it distorts the ordinal nature of the original quantity being measured.

2.3.3 Real Measures

Real measures, or *continuous variables*, are the easiest to use and interpret. Continuous variables have all the desirable properties of variables: order, scale, and distance. They also have the meanings of zero and negative values defined. There could be some constraints imposed on the definition of continuous variables. For example, the age of a person cannot be negative and the monthly bill of a telephone line cannot be less than the subscription fees. Real measures are represented by real numbers, with any reasonably required precision.

The use of ratios in constrained continuous variables is sometimes troublesome. For example, if we allow the balance of a customer to be negative or positive, then the ratio between $ −10,000.00 and $ −5,000.00 is the same as that between $ +10,000.00 and $ +5,000.00. Therefore, some analysts like to distinguish between the so-called interval and ratio variables. We do not make that distinction here because in most cases the context of the implementation is clear. For example, if we wished to use the ratio of balances, we would restrict the balances to positive values only; if negative values occurred, we would devise another measure to signify that fact.

With the three types of variable from the mining point of view, the first task the analyst should consider, when acquiring the data, is to decide on the type of data to be used for each variable depending on its meaning. Of special interest are variables that represent *dates* and *times*. With the exception of time series analysis, dates and times are not useful in their raw form. One of the most effective methods of dealing with date and time values is to convert them to a *period* measure, that is, to calculate the *difference* between the values and a fixed *reference* value. For example, instead of dealing with the date of opening an account, we deal with total tenure as the difference between today's date and the date of opening the account. In fact, we use this method every day by referring to the age of a person instead of her or his birth date. In this way, we convert dates and times to real measures, with some constraint if necessary, as in the case of a person's age. (Negative age is not well defined!)

2.4 DATA ROLLUP

The simplest definition of data rollup is that we convert categories to variables. Let us consider an illustrative example.

Table 2.1 shows some records from the transaction table of a bank where deposits are denoted by positive amounts and withdrawals are shown as negative

Table 2.1 A Sample of Banking Transactions

Customer ID	Date	Amount	Account Type
1100-55555	11Jun2003	114.56	Savings
1100-55555	21Jun2003	−56.78	Checking
1100-55555	07Jul2003	359.31	Savings
1100-55555	19Jul2003	89.56	Checking
1100-55555	03Aug2003	1000.00	Savings
1100-55555	17Aug2003	−1200.00	Checking
1100-88888	14June2003	122.51	Savings
1100-88888	27June2003	42.07	Checking
1100-88888	09July2003	−146.30	Savings
1100-88888	09July2003	−1254.48	Checking
1100-88888	10Aug2003	400.00	Savings
1100-88888	11Aug 2003	500.00	Checking
. . .			

amounts. We further assume that we are building the mining view as a *customer view*. Because the first requirement is to have one, and only one, row per customer, we create a new view such that each unique customer ID appears in one and only one row. To *roll up* the multiple records on the customer level, we create a set of new variables to represent the combination of the account type and the month of the transaction. This is illustrated in Figure 2.1. The result of the rollup is shown in Table 2.2.

Table 2.1 shows that we managed to aggregate the values of the transactions in the different accounts and months into new variables. The only issue is what to do when we have more than one transaction per account per month. In this case, which is the more realistic one, we have to summarize the data in some form. For example, we can calculate the sum of the transactions values, or their average, or even create a new set of variables giving the count of such transactions for each month–account type combination.

It is obvious that this process will lead to the generation of possibly hundreds, if not thousands, of variables in any data-rich business applications. Dealing with such a large number of fields could present a challenge for the data preparation and data mining software tools. It is therefore required that we keep the number

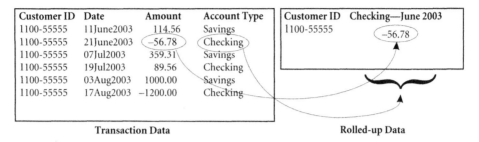

Customer ID	Date	Amount	Account Type
1100-55555	11June2003	114.56	Savings
1100-55555	21June2003	−56.78	Checking
1100-55555	07Jul2003	359.31	Savings
1100-55555	19Jul2003	89.56	Checking
1100-55555	03Aug2003	1000.00	Savings
1100-55555	17Aug2003	−1200.00	Checking

Customer ID	Checking—June 2003
1100-55555	−56.78

Transaction Data   Rolled-up Data

FIGURE 2.1

Data rollup.

Table 2.2 Result of Rolling up the Data of Table 2.1

Cust. ID	C-6	C-7	C-8	S-6	S-7	S-8
1100-55555	−56.78	89.56	−1200.00	114.56	359.30	1000.00
1100-88888	42.07	−1254.00	500.00	122.51	−146.30	400.00

of these new fields to a minimum while keeping as much information about the nature of the data as possible. Unfortunately, there is no magic recipe to achieve this balance. However, a closer look at the preceding data reveals that the key to controlling the number of new variables is to decide on the level of granularity required to perform the rollup. For example, is it necessary to roll up the transactions of each month, or is it enough to roll up the data per quarter? Similarly, in our simplified case, we had only two categories for the account type, but typically, there would be many more categories. Then comes the question of which categories we can group together, or even ignore, to reduce the number of new variables.

In the end, even with careful selection of the categories and resolution of combining the different categories to form new variables, we usually end up with a relatively large number of variables, which most implementations of data mining algorithms cannot handle adequately. However, we should not worry too much about this problem for the moment because data reduction is a basic step in our planned approach. In later chapters, we will investigate techniques to reduce the number of variables.

In the last example demonstrating the rollup process, we performed the rollup on the level of two variables: the account type and the transaction month. This is usually called *multilevel rollup*. On the other hand, if we had had only one type of account, say only savings, then we could have performed a simpler rollup using only the transaction month as the summation variable. This type of rollup is called *simple rollup*. In fact, multilevel rollup is only an aggregation of several simple rollups on the row level, which is the customer ID in our example. Therefore, data preparation procedures, in either SAS or SQL, can use this property to simplify the implementation by performing several simple rollups for each combination of the summarization variables and combining them. This is the approach we will adopt in developing our macro to demonstrate the rollup of our sample dataset.

Now let us describe how to perform the rollup operation using SAS. We will do this using our simple example first and then generalize the code using macros to facilitate its use with other datasets. We stress again that in writing the code we preferred to keep the code simple and readable at the occasional price of efficiency of execution, and the use of memory resources. You are welcome to modify the code to make it more efficient or general as required.

We use Table 2.1 to create the dataset as follows:

```
Data Transaction;
Informat CustID $10.;
Informat TransDate date9.;
format TransDate Date9.;
input CustID $ TransDate Amount AccountType$; Cards;
55555       11Jun2003        114.56      Savings
55555       12Jun2003        119.56      Savings
55555       21Jun2003        -56.78      Checking
55555       07Jul2003        359.31      Savings
55555       19Jul2003         89.56      Checking
55555       03Aug2003       1000.00      Savings
66666       22Feb2003        549.56      Checking
77777       03Dec2003        645.21      Savings
55555       17Aug2003      -1200.00      Checking
88888       14Jun2003        122.51      Savings
88888       27Jun2003         42.07      Checking
88888       09Jul2003       -146.30      Savings
88888       09Jul2003      -1254.48      Checking
88888       10Aug2003        400.00      Savings
88888       11Aug2003        500.00      Checking
;
run;
```

The next step is to create the month field using the SAS Month function:

```
data Trans;
 set Transaction;
  Month = month(TransDate);
run;
```

Then we accumulate the transactions into a new field to represent the balance in each account:

```
proc sort data=Trans;
     by CustID month AccountType;
run;
```

```
/* Create cumulative balances for each of the accounts */
data Trans2;
 retain Balance 0;
 set Trans;
  by CustID month AccountType;
  if first.AccountType then Balance=0;
   Balance = Balance + Amount;
   if last.AccountType then output;
   drop amount;
run;
```

Finally, we use PROC TRANSPOSE to roll up the data in each account type and merge the two resulting datasets into the final file:

```
/* Prepare for the transpose */
proc sort data=trans2;
  by CustID accounttype;
  run;

proc transpose data =Trans2 out=rolled_C prefix=C_;
  by CustID accounttype;
ID month ;
var balance ;
where AccountType='Checking';
run;

proc transpose data =Trans2 out=rolled_S prefix=S_;
by CustID accounttype;
ID month ;
var balance ;
where AccountType='Savings';
run;

data Rollup;
 merge Rolled_S Rolled_C;
 by CustID;
 drop AccountType _Name_;
run;
```

To pack this procedure in a general macro using the combination of two variables, one for transaction categories and one for time, we simply replace the Month variable with a TimeVar, the customer ID with IDVar, and the AccountType with TypeVar. We also specify the number of characters to be used from the category variable to prefix the time values. Finally, we replace the two repeated TRANSPOSE code segments with a %do loop that iterates over the categories of the TypeVar (which requires extracting these categories and counting them). The following steps detail the resulting macro.

Table 2.3 Parameters of TBRollup() Macro

Header Parameter	TBRollup (TDS, IDVar, TimeVar, TypeVar, Nchars, Value, RDS) Description
TDS	Input transaction dataset
IDVar	ID variable
TimeVar	Time variable
TypeVar	Quantity being rolled up
Nchars	Number of characters to be used in rollup
Value	Values to be accumulated
RDS	The output rolled up dataset

Step 1

Sort the transaction file using the ID, Time, and Type variables:

```
proc sort data=&TDS;
by &IDVar &TimeVar &TypeVar;
run;
```

Step 2

Accumulate the values over time to a temporary _Tot variable in the temporary table Temp1 (see Table 2.3). Then sort Temp1 using the ID and the Type variables:

```
data Temp1;
retain _TOT 0;
set &TDS;
by &IDVar &TimeVar &TypeVar;
if first.&TypeVar then _TOT=0;
_TOT = _TOT + &Value;
if last.&TypeVar then output;
drop &Value;
   run;
proc sort data=Temp1;
by &IDVar &TypeVar;
run;
```

Step 3

Extract the categories of the Type variable, using PROC FREQ, and store them in macro variables:

```
proc freq data =Temp1 noprint;
tables &TypeVar /out=Types ;
run;
```

```
data _null_;
set Types nobs=Ncount;
if &typeVar ne " then
call symput('Cat_'||left(_n_), &TypeVar);
if _N_=Ncount then call symput('N', Ncount);
run;
```

Step 4

Loop over these N categories and generate their rollup part:

```
%do i=1 %to &N;
proc transpose
data =Temp1
out=_R_&i
prefix=%substr(&&Cat_&i, 1, &Nchars)_;
by &IDVar &TypeVar;
ID &TimeVar ;
var _TOT ;
where &TypeVar="&&Cat_&i";
run;
%end;
```

Step 5

Finally, assemble the parts using the ID variable:

```
data &RDS;
merge %do i=1 %to &N; _R_&i %end ; ;
by &IDVar;
drop &TypeVar _Name_;
run;
```

Step 6

Clean the workspace and finish the macro:

```
proc datasets library=work nodetails;
delete Temp1 Types %do i=1 %to &N; _R_&I %end; ;
run;
quit;

%mend;
```

We can now call this macro to roll up the previous example Transaction dataset using the following code:

```
data Trans;
set Transaction;
Month = month(TransDate);
drop transdate;
run;
```

```
%let IDVar   = CustID;      /* The row ID variable */
%let TimeVar = Month;       /* The time variable */
%let TypeVar = AccountType; /* The Type variable */
%let Value   = Amount;      /* The time measurement variable */
%let Nchars  = 1;           /* Number of letters in Prefix */
%let TDS      = Trans;      /* The value variable */
%let RDS      = Rollup;     /* the rollup file */
%TBRollup(&TDS, &IDVar, &TimeVar, &TypeVar, &Nchars, &Value,
&RDS);
```

The result of this call is shown in Table 2.4.

Table 2.4 Result of Rollup Macro

CustID	C_6	C_7	C_8	C_{12}	S_6	S_7	S_8	S_{12}
5555	−56.78	89.56	−1200	.	234.12	359.31	1000	.
6666	.	.	.	549.56	.	.	.	.
7777	.	.	.	.	.	.	.	645.21
8888	42.07	−1254.48	500	.	122.51	−146.3	400	.

2.5 ROLLUP WITH SUMS, AVERAGES, AND COUNTS

In addition to finding the sum of a value variable during the rollup, it may also be more meaningful sometimes to calculate average value or the number of records that represent certain events—for example, number of deposits, number of withdrawals, or number of mailings a customer received responding to an offer.

In our rollup macro, these requirements would alter only the middle part of our code, where we calculated the cumulative value of the Value variable. The following code segment would modify the macro to calculate the average value and the number of transactions for each account type instead of the total:

Step 2

```
data _Temp1;
retain _TOT 0;
retain _NT 0;
set &TDS;
by &IDVar &TimeVar &TypeVar;
if first.&TypeVar then _TOT=0;
_TOT = _TOT + &Value;
if &Value ne . then _NT=_NT+1;
if last.&TypeVar then
do;
```

```
_AVG=_TOT/_NT;
output;
_NT=0;
end;
drop &Value;
run;
```

Furthermore, the code inside the %do loop should also reflect our interest in transposing the values of the average variable, _AVG. Therefore, the code will be as follows:

Step 4

```
%do i=1 %to &N;
0proc transpose
data =_Temp1
out=_R_&i
prefix=%substr(&&Cat_&i, 1, &Nchars)_;
by &IDVar &TypeVar;
ID &TimeVar;
var _AVG;
where &TypeVar="&&Cat_&i";
run;
%end;
```

The complete code for the modified code to roll up the average value is included in the macro ABRollup().

2.6 CALCULATION OF THE MODE

Another useful summary statistic is the mode, which is used in both the rollup stage and the event-driven architecture (EDA). The mode is the most common category of transaction. The mode for nominal variables is equivalent to the use of the average or the sum for the continuous case. For example, when customers use different payment methods, it may be beneficial to identify the payment method most frequently used by each customer.

The computation of the mode on the mining view entity level from a transaction dataset is a demanding task because we need to search for the frequencies of the different categories for *each* unique value of the entity variable. The macro shown in Table 2.5 is based on a *classic* SQL query for finding the mode on the entity level from a transaction table. The variable being searched is XVar, and the entity level is identified through the unique value of the variable IDVar:

```
%macro VarMode(TransDS, XVar, IDVar, OutDS);
/* A classic implementation of the mode of transactional
   data using SQL */
proc sql noprint;
create table &OutDS as
```

Table 2.5 Parameters of VarMode() Macro

Header Parameter	VarMode (TransDS, XVar, IDVar, OutDS) Description
TransDS	Input transaction dataset
XVar	Variable for which the mode is to be calculated
IDVar	ID variable
OutDS	The output dataset with the mode for unique IDs

```
SELECT &IDVar , MIN(&XVar ) AS mode
FROM (
            SELECT &IDVar, &XVar
            FROM &TransDS p1
            GROUP BY &IDVar, &XVar
            HAVING COUNT( * ) =
                (SELECT MAX(CNT )
                FROM (SELECT COUNT( * ) AS CNT
                    FROM &TransDS p2
                    WHERE p2.&IDVar= p1.&IDVar
                    GROUP BY p2.&XVar
                    ) AS p3
                )
            ) AS p
        GROUP BY p.&IDVar;
quit;
%mend;
```

The query works by calculating a list holding the frequency of the XVar categories, identified as CNT, then using the maximum of these counts as the mode. The query then creates a new table containing IDVar and XVar where the XVar category frequency is equal to the maximum count, that is, the mode.

The preceding compound SELECT statement is computationally demanding because of the use of several layers of GROUP BY and HAVING clauses. Indexing should always be considered when dealing with large datasets. Sometimes it is even necessary to partition the transaction dataset into smaller datasets before applying such a query to overcome memory limitations.

2.7 DATA INTEGRATION

The data necessary to compile the mining view usually comes from many different tables. The rollup and summarization operations described in the last two sections can be performed on the data coming from each of these data sources independently. Finally, we would be required to assemble all these segments in one mining view. The most used assembly operations are *merging* and *concatenation*. Merging is used to collect data for the same key variable (e.g., customer ID) from different sources. Concatenation is used to assemble different portions of the same data fields for different segments of the key variable. It is most useful when preparing the scoring view with a very large number of observations (many millions). In this case, it is more efficient to partition the data into smaller segments, prepare each segment, and finally concatenate them together.

2.7.1 **Merging**

SAS provides several options for merging and concatenating tables together using DATA step commands. However, we could also use SQL queries, through PROC SQL, to perform the same operations. In general, SAS DATA step options are more efficient in merging datasets than PROC SQL is. However, DATA step merging may require sorting of the datasets before merging them, which could be a slow process for large datasets. On the other hand, the performance of SQL queries can be enhanced significantly by creating indexes on the key variables used in merging.

Because of the requirement that the mining view have a unique record per category of key variable, most merging operations required to integrate different pieces of the mining view are of the type called *match-merge with nonmatched observations*. We demonstrate this type of merging with a simple example.

EXAMPLE 2.1

We start with two datasets, Left and Right, as shown in Table 2.6.

The two tables can be joined using the MERGE-BY commands within a DATA step operation as follows:

```
DATA Left;
 INPUT ID Age Status $;
 datalines;
 1  30  Gold
 2  20  .
 4  40  Gold
 5  50  Silver
 ;
RUN;

DATA Right;
 INPUT ID Balance Status $;
 datalines;
 2  3000  Gold
 4  4000  Silver
 ;
RUN;
```

Table 2.6 Two Sample Tables: Left and Right

	Table: Left			Table: Right	
ID	Age	Status	ID	Balance	Status
1	30	Gold	2	3000	Gold
2	20	.	4	4000	Silver
4	40	Gold			
5	50	Silver			

Table 2.7 Result of Merging: Dataset Both

Obs	ID	Age	Status	Balance
1	1	30	Gold	.
2	2	20	Gold	3000
3	4	40	Silver	4000
4	5	50	Silver	.

```
DATA Both;
 MERGE Left Right;
 BY ID;
RUN;

PROC PRINT DATA=Both;
RUN;
```

The result of the merging is the dataset Both given in Table 2.7, which shows that the MERGE-BY commands did merge the two datasets as needed using ID as the key variable. We also notice that the common file Status was overwritten by values from the Right dataset. Therefore, we have to be careful about this possible side effect. In most practical cases, common fields should have identical values. In our case, where the variable represented some customer designation status (Gold or Silver), the customer should have had the same status in different datasets. Therefore, checking these status values should be one of the data integrity tests to be performed before performing the merging.

Merging datasets using this technique is very efficient. It can be used with more than two datasets as long as all the datasets in the MERGE statement have the common variable used in the BY statement. The only possible difficulty is that SAS requires that *all* the datasets be sorted by the BY variable. Sorting very large datasets can sometimes be slow.

You have probably realized by now that writing a general macro to merge a *list* of datasets using an ID variable is a simple task. Assuming that all the datasets have been sorted using ID before attempting to merge them, the macro would simply be given as follows:

```
%macro MergeDS(List, IDVar, ALL);
DATA &ALL;
    MERGE &List; by
    &IDVar;
run;
%mend;
```

Finally, calling this macro to merge the two datasets in Table 2.6 would simply be as follows:

```
%let List=Left Right;
%let IDVar=ID;
%let ALL = Both;
%MergeDS(&List, &IDVar, &ALL);
```

2.7.2 Concatenation

Concatenation is used to attach the contents of one dataset to the end of another dataset without duplicating the common fields. Fields unique to one of the two files would be filled with missing values. Concatenating datasets in this fashion does not check on the uniqueness of the ID variable. However, if the data acquisition and rollup procedures were correctly performed, such a problem should not exist.

Performing concatenation in SAS is straightforward. We list the datasets to be concatenated in a SET statement within the destination dataset. This is illustrated in the following example.

EXAMPLE 2.2

Start with two datasets TOP and BOTTOM, as shown in Tables 2.8 and 2.9.

We then use the following code to implement the concatenation of the two datasets into a new dataset:

```
DATA TOP;
 input ID Age Status $;
 datalines;
 1  30  Gold
 2  20  .
 3  30  Silver
 4  40  Gold
 5  50  Silver
 ;
 run;
```

Table 2.8 Table: TOP

Obs	ID	Age	Status
1	1	30	Gold
2	2	20	.
3	3	30	Silver
4	4	40	Gold
5	5	50	Silver

Table 2.9 Table: BOTTOM

Obs	ID	Balance	Status
1	6	6000	Gold
2	7	7000	Silver

```
DATA BOTTOM;
input ID Balance Status $;
datalines;
6  6000  Gold
7  7000  Silver
;
run;

DATA BOTH;
SET TOP BOTTOM;
run;

DATA BOTH;
SET TOP BOTTOM;
run;
```

The resulting dataset is shown in Table 2.10.

As in the case of merging datasets, we may include a list of several datasets in the SET statement to concatenate. The resulting dataset will contain all the records of the contributing datasets in the same order in which they appear in the SET statement.

Table 2.10 Table: BOTH

Obs	ID	Age	Status	Balance
1	1	30	Gold	.
2	2	20	.	.
3	3	30	Silver	.
4	4	40	Gold	.
5	5	50	Silver	.
6	6	.	Gold	6000
7	7	.	Silver	7000

The preceding process can be packed into the following macro:

```
%macro ConcatDS(List, ALL);
DATA &ALL;
 SET &List;
run;
%mend;
```

To use this macro to achieve the same result as in the previous example, we use the following calling code:

```
%let List=TOP BOTTOM;
%let ALL = BOTH;
%ConcatDS(&List, &ALL);
```

Data Preprocessing

Today's real-world databases are highly susceptible to noisy, missing, and inconsistent data because of their typically huge size (often several gigabytes or more) and their likely origin from multiple, heterogenous sources. Low-quality data will lead to low-quality mining results.

How can the data be preprocessed in order to help improve the quality of the data and, consequently, of the mining results? How can the data be preprocessed so as to improve the efficiency and ease of the mining process?

There are a number of data preprocessing techniques. Data cleaning can be applied to remove noise and correct inconsistencies in the data. Data integration merges data from multiple sources into a coherent data store, such as a data warehouse. Data transformations, such as normalization, may be applied. For example, normalization may improve the accuracy and efficiency of mining algorithms involving distance measurements. Data reduction can reduce the data size by aggregating, eliminating redundant features, or clustering, for instance. These techniques are not mutually exclusive; they may work together. For example, data cleaning can involve transformations to correct wrong data, such as by transforming all entries for a date field to a common format. Data processing techniques, when applied before mining, can substantially improve the overall quality of the patterns mined or the time required for the actual mining.

In Section 3.1 of this chapter, we introduce the basic concepts of data preprocessing. Section 3.2 presents *descriptive data summarization*, which serves as a foundation for data preprocessing. Descriptive data summarization helps us study the general characteristics of the data and identify the presence of noise or outliers, which is useful for successful data cleaning and data integration. The methods for data preprocessing are organized into the following categories: *data cleaning* (Section 3.3), *data integration and transformation* (Section 3.4), and *data reduction* (Section 3.5). Concept hierarchies can be used in an alternative form of data reduction where we replace low-level data (such as raw values for *age*) with higher-level concepts (such as *youth, middle-aged*, or *senior*). This form of data reduction is the topic of Section 3.6, wherein we discuss the automatic generation of concept hierarchies from numeric data using data discretization techniques. The automatic generation of concept hierarchies from categorical data is also described.

3.1 WHY PREPROCESS THE DATA?

Imagine that you are a manager at *AllElectronics* and have been charged with analyzing the company's data with respect to the sales at your branch. You immediately set out to perform this task. You carefully inspect the company's database and data warehouse, identifying and selecting the attributes or dimensions to be included in your analysis, such as *item, price*, and *units_sold*. Alas! You notice that several of the attributes for various tuples have no recorded value. For your analysis, you would like to include information as to whether each item purchased was advertised as on sale, yet you discover that this information has not been recorded. Furthermore, users of your database system have reported errors, unusual values, and inconsistencies in the data recorded for some transactions. In other words, the data you wish to analyze by data mining techniques are **incomplete** (lacking attribute values or certain attributes of interest, or containing only aggregate data), **noisy** (containing errors, or *outlier* values that deviate from the expected), and **inconsistent** (e.g., containing discrepancies in the department codes used to categorize items). Welcome to the real world!

Incomplete, noisy, and inconsistent data are commonplace properties of large real-world databases and data warehouses. Incomplete data can occur for a number of reasons. Attributes of interest may not always be available, such as customer information for sales transaction data. Other data may not be included simply because it was not considered important at the time of entry. Relevant data may not be recorded because of a misunderstanding or because of equipment malfunctions. Data that were inconsistent with other recorded data may have been deleted. Furthermore, the recording of the history or modifications to the data may have been overlooked. Missing data, particularly for tuples with missing values for some attributes, may need to be inferred.

There are many possible reasons for noisy data (having incorrect attribute values). The data collection instruments used may be faulty. There may have been human or computer errors occurring at data entry. Errors in data transmission can also occur. There may be technology limitations, such as limited buffer size for coordinating synchronized data transfer and consumption. Incorrect data may also result from inconsistencies in naming conventions or data codes used, or inconsistent formats for input fields, such as *date*. Duplicate tuples also require data cleaning.

Data cleaning routines work to "clean" the data by filling in missing values, smoothing noisy data, identifying or removing outliers, and resolving inconsistencies. If users believe the data are dirty, they are unlikely to trust the results of any data mining that has been applied to it. Furthermore, dirty data can cause confusion for the mining procedure, resulting in unreliable output. Although most mining routines have some procedures for dealing with incomplete or noisy data, they are not always robust. Instead, they may concentrate on avoiding overfitting the data to the function being modeled. Therefore, a useful preprocessing step is to run your data through some data cleaning routines. Section 3.3 discusses methods for cleaning up your data.

Getting back to your task at *AllElectronics*, suppose that you would like to include data from multiple sources in your analysis. This would involve integrating multiple databases, data cubes, or files, that is, **data integration**. Yet some attributes representing a given concept may have different names in different databases, causing inconsistencies and redundancies. For example, the attribute for customer identification may be referred to as *customer_id* in one data store and *cust_id* in another. Naming inconsistencies may also occur for attribute values. For example, the same first name could be registered as "Bill" in one database but "William" in another, and "B." in the third. Furthermore, you suspect that some attributes may be inferred from others (e.g., annual revenue). Having a large amount of redundant data may slow down or confuse the knowledge discovery process. Clearly, in addition to data cleaning, steps must be taken to help avoid redundancies during data integration. Typically, data cleaning and data integration are performed as a preprocessing step when preparing the data for a data warehouse. Additional data cleaning can be performed to detect and remove redundancies that may have resulted from data integration.

Getting back to your data, you have decided, say, that you would like to use a distance-based mining algorithm for your analysis, such as neural networks, nearest-neighbor classifiers, or clustering. Such methods provide better results if the data to be analyzed have been *normalized*, that is, scaled to a specific range such as (0.0, 1.0). Your customer data, for example, contain the attributes *age* and *annual salary*. The *annual salary* attribute usually takes much larger values than *age*. Therefore, if the attributes are left unnormalized, the distance measurements taken on *annual salary* will generally outweigh distance measurements taken on *age*. Furthermore, it would be useful for your analysis to obtain aggregate information as to the sales per customer region—something that is not part of any precomputed data cube in your data warehouse. You soon realize that **data transformation** operations, such as normalization and aggregation, are additional data preprocessing procedures that would contribute toward the success of the mining process. Data integration and data transformation are discussed in Section 3.4.

"Hmmm," you wonder, as you consider your data even further. "The dataset I have selected for analysis is *huge*, which is sure to slow down the mining process. Is there any way I can reduce the size of my dataset without jeopardizing the data mining results?" **Data reduction** obtains a reduced representation of the dataset that is much smaller in volume yet produces the same (or almost the same) analytical results. There are a number of strategies for data reduction. These include *data aggregation* (e.g., building a data cube), *attribute subset selection* (e.g., removing irrelevant attributes through correlation analysis), *dimensionality reduc-*

tion (e.g., using encoding schemes such as minimum length encoding or wavelets), and *numerosity reduction* (e.g., "replacing" the data by alternative, smaller representations such as clusters or parametric models). Data reduction is the topic of Section 3.5. Data can also be "reduced" by *generalization* with the use of concept hierarchies, where low-level concepts, such as *city* for customer location, are replaced with higher-level concepts, such as *region* or *province_or_state*. A concept hierarchy organizes the concepts into varying levels of abstraction. *Data discretization* is a form of data reduction that is very useful for the automatic generation of concept hierarchies from numeric data. This is described in Section 3.6, along with the automatic generation of concept hierarchies for categorical data.

Figure 3.1 summarizes the data preprocessing steps described here. Note that the categorization just described is not mutually exclusive. For example, the

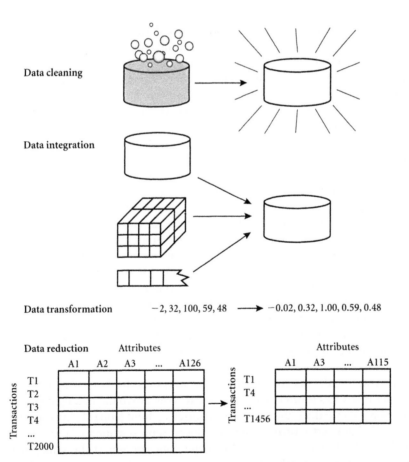

FIGURE 3.1

Forms of data preprocessing.

removal of redundant data may be seen as a form of data cleaning, as well as data reduction.

In summary, real-world data tend to be dirty, incomplete, and inconsistent. Data preprocessing techniques can improve the quality of the data, thereby helping to improve the accuracy and efficiency of the subsequent mining process. Data preprocessing is an important step in the knowledge discovery process, because quality decisions must be based on quality data. Detecting data anomalies, rectifying them early, and reducing the data to be analyzed can lead to huge payoffs for decision making.

3.2 DESCRIPTIVE DATA SUMMARIZATION

For data preprocessing to be successful, it is essential to have an overall picture of your data. Descriptive data summarization techniques can be used to identify the typical properties of your data and highlight which data values should be treated as noise or outliers. Thus, we first introduce the basic concepts of descriptive data summarization before getting into the concrete workings of data preprocessing techniques.

For many data preprocessing tasks, users would like to learn about data characteristics regarding both central tendency and dispersion of the data. Measures of central tendency include *mean, median, mode*, and *midrange*, whereas measures of data dispersion include *quartiles, interquartile range (IQR)*, and *variance*. These descriptive statistics are of great help in explaining the distribution of the data. Such measures have been studied extensively in the statistical literature. From the data mining point of view, we need to examine how they can be computed efficiently in large databases. In particular, it is necessary to introduce the notions of *distributive measure, algebraic measure*, and *holistic measure*. Knowing what kind of measure we are dealing with can help us choose an efficient implementation for it.

3.2.1 Measuring the Central Tendency

In this section, we look at various ways to measure the central tendency of data. The most common and most effective numeric measure of the "center" of a set of data is the *(arithmetic) mean*. Let $x_1, x_2, \ldots x_N$ be a set of N values or observations, such as for some attribute, like *salary*. The **mean** of this set of values is

$$\bar{x} = \frac{\sum_{i=1}^{N} x_i}{N} = \frac{x_1 + x_2 + \cdots + x_N}{N} \tag{3.1}$$

This corresponds to the built-in aggregate function, *average* (avg() in SQL), provided in relational database systems.

A **distributive measure** is a measure (i.e., function) that can be computed for a given dataset by partitioning the data into smaller subsets, computing the measure for each subset, and then merging the results in order to arrive at the measure's value for the original (entire) dataset. Both sum() and count() are distributive measures because they can be computed in this manner. Other examples include max() and min(). An **algebraic measure** is a measure that can be computed by applying an algebraic function to one or more distributive measures. Hence, *average* (or mean()) is an algebraic measure because it can be computed by sum()/count(). When computing data cubes, sum() and count() are typically saved in precomputation. Thus, the derivation of *average* for data cubes is straightforward.

Sometimes, each value x_i in a set may be associated with a weight w_i, for $i = 1, \ldots, N$. The weights reflect the significance, importance, or occurrence frequency attached to their respective values. In this case, we can compute

$$\bar{x} = \frac{\sum_{i=1}^{N} w_i x_i}{\sum_{i=1}^{N} w_i} = \frac{w_1 x_1 + w_2 x_2 + \cdots + w_N x_N}{w_1 + w_2 + \cdots + w_N} \tag{3.2}$$

This is called the **weighted arithmetic mean** or the **weighted average**. Note that the weighted average is another example of an algebraic measure.

Although the mean is the single most useful quantity for describing a dataset, it is not always the best way of measuring the center of the data. A major problem with the *mean* is its sensitivity to extreme (e.g., outlier) values. Even a small number of extreme values can corrupt the mean. For example, the salary of a few highly paid managers may substantially push up the mean salary at a company. Similarly, the average score of a class in an exam could be pulled down quite a bit by a few very low scores. To offset the effect caused by a small number of extreme values, we can instead use the **trimmed mean**, which is the mean obtained after chopping off values at the high and low extremes. For example, we can sort the values observed for *salary* and remove the top and bottom 2 percent before computing the mean. We should avoid trimming too large a portion (such as 20 percent) at both ends as this can result in the loss of valuable information.

For skewed (asymmetric) data, a better measure of the center of data is the *median*. Suppose that a given dataset of N distinct values is sorted in numeric order. If N is odd, then the median is the *middle value* of the ordered set; otherwise (i.e., if N is even), the median is the average of the middle two values.

A **holistic measure** is a measure that must be computed on the entire dataset as a whole. It cannot be computed by partitioning the given data into subsets and merging the values obtained for the measure in each subset. The median is an example of a holistic measure. Holistic measures are much more expensive to compute than distributive measures such as those listed previously.

We can, however, easily *approximate* the median value of a dataset. Assume that data are grouped in intervals according to their x_i data values and that the frequency (i.e., number of data values) of each interval is known. For example, people may be grouped according to their annual salary in intervals such as 10 to 20 K, 20 to 30 K, and so on. Let the interval that contains the median frequency be the *median interval*. We can approximate the median of the entire dataset (e.g., the median salary) by interpolation using the formula:

$$median = L_1 + \left(\frac{N/2 - \left(\sum freq \right)_l}{freq_{median}} \right) width \qquad (3.3)$$

where L_1 is the lower boundary of the median interval, N is the number of values in the entire dataset, $\left(\sum freq \right)_l$ is the sum of the frequencies of all of the intervals that are lower than the median interval, $freq_{median}$ is the frequency of the median interval, and *width* is the width of the median interval.

Another measure of central tendency is the *mode*. The **mode** for a set of data is the value that occurs most frequently in the set. It is possible for the greatest frequency to correspond to several different values, which results in more than one mode. Datasets with one, two, or three modes are respectively called **unimodal**, **bimodal**, and **trimodal**. In general, a dataset with two or more modes is **multimodal**. At the other extreme, if each data value occurs only once, then there is no mode.

For unimodal frequency curves that are moderately skewed (asymmetric), we have the following empirical relation:

$$mean - mode = 3 \times (mean \times median) \qquad (3.4)$$

This implies that the mode for unimodal frequency curves that are moderately skewed can easily be computed if the mean and median values are known.

In a unimodal frequency curve with perfect symmetric data distribution, the mean, median, and mode are all at the same center value, as shown in Figure 3.2(a). However, data in most real applications are not symmetric. They may instead be either positively skewed, where the mode occurs at a value that is smaller than the median (Figure 3.2(b)), or negatively skewed, where the mode occurs at a value greater than the median (Figure 3.2(c)).

The **midrange** can also be used to assess the central tendency of a dataset. It is the average of the largest and smallest values in the set. This algebraic measure is easy to compute using the SQL aggregate functions, `max()` and `min()`.

3.2.2 Measuring the Dispersion of Data

The degree to which numeric data tend to spread is called the **dispersion**, or **variance** of the data. The most common measures of data dispersion are *range*, the *five-number summary* (based on *quartiles*), the *interquartile range*, and the *standard deviation*. Boxplots can be plotted based on the five-number summary and are a useful tool for identifying outliers.

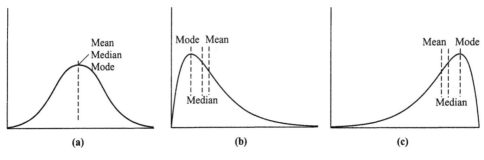

FIGURE 3.2

Mean, median, and mode of symmetric (a) versus positively (b) and (c) negatively skewed data.

Range, Quartiles, Outliers, and Boxplots

Let $x_1, x_2, \ldots x_N$ be a set of observations for some attribute. The **range** of the set is the difference between the largest (max( )) and smallest (min( )) values. For the remainder of this section, let's assume that the data are sorted in increasing numeric order.

The **kth percentile** of a set of data in numeric order is the value x_i having the property that k percent of the data entries lie at or below x_i. The *median* (discussed in the previous subsection) is the 50th percentile.

The most commonly used percentiles other than the median are **quartiles**. The **first quartile**, denoted by Q_1, is the 25th percentile; the **third quartile**, denoted by Q_3, is the 75th percentile. The quartiles, including the median, give some indication of the center, spread, and shape of a distribution. The distance between the first and third quartiles is a simple measure of spread that gives the range covered by the middle half of the data. This distance is called the **interquartile range** (*IQR*) and is defined as

$$IQR = Q_3 - Q_1 \qquad (3.5)$$

Based on reasoning similar to that in our analysis of the median in Section 3.2.1, we can conclude that Q_1 and Q_3 are holistic measures, as is *IQR*.

No single numeric measure of spread, such as *IQR*, is useful for describing skewed distributions. The spreads of two sides of a skewed distribution are unequal (Figure 3.2). Therefore, it is more informative to also provide the two quartiles Q_1 and Q_3, along with the median. A common rule of thumb for identifying suspected **outliers** is to single out values falling at least $1.5 \times IQR$ above the third quartile or below the first quartile.

Because Q_1, the median, and Q_3 together contain no information about the endpoints (e.g., tails) of the data, a fuller summary of the shape of a distribution can be obtained by providing the lowest and highest data values as well. This is known as the *five-number summary*. The **five-number summary** of a distribution consists of the median, the quartiles Q_1 and Q_3, and the smallest and the largest individual observations, written in the order *Minimum, Q_1, Median, Q_3, Maximum.*

Boxplots are a popular way of visualizing a distribution. A boxplot incorporates the five-number summary as follows:

- Typically, the ends of the box are at the quartiles, so that the box length is the interquartile range, *IQR.*
- The median is marked by a line within the box.
- Two lines (called *whiskers*) outside the box extend to the smallest (*Minimum*) and largest (*Maximum*) observations.

When dealing with a moderate number of observations, it is worthwhile to plot potential outliers individually. To do this in a boxplot, the whiskers are extended to the extreme low and high observations *only if* these values are less than $1.5 \times IQR$ beyond the quartiles. Otherwise, the whiskers terminate at the most extreme observations occurring within $1.5 \times IQR$ of the quartiles. The remaining cases are plotted individually. Boxplots can be used in the comparisons of several sets of compatible data. Figure 3.3 shows boxplots for unit price data for items sold at four branches of *AllElectronics* during a given time period. For branch 1, we see that the median price of items sold is $80, Q_1 is $60, Q_3 is $100. Notice that two outlying observations for this branch were plotted individually,

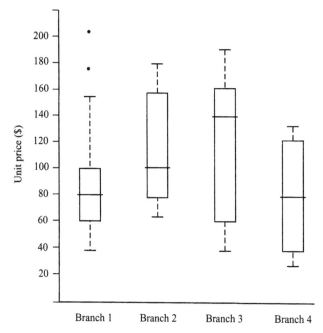

FIGURE 3.3

Boxplot for the unit price data for items sold at four branches of *AllElectronics* during a given time period.

as their values of 175 and 202 are more than 1.5 times the IQR here of 40. The efficient computation of boxplots, or even *approximate boxplots* (based on approximates of the five-number summary), remains a challenging issue for the mining of large datasets.

Variance and Standard Deviation

The **variance** of N observations, $x_1, x_2, \ldots x_N$, is

$$\sigma^2 = \frac{1}{N}\sum_{i=1}^{N}(x_i - \bar{x})^2 = \frac{1}{N}\left[\sum x_i^2 - \frac{1}{N}\left(\sum x_i\right)^2\right] \tag{3.6}$$

where $\bar{x}$ is the mean value of the observations, as defined in Equation 3.1. The **standard deviation**, σ, of the observations is the square root of the variance, σ^2.

The basic properties of the standard deviation, σ, as a measure of spread are

- σ measures spread about the mean and should be used only when the mean is chosen as the measure of center.
- $\sigma = 0$ only when there is no spread, that is, when all observations have the same value. Otherwise $\sigma > 0$.

The variance and standard deviation are algebraic measures because they can be computed from distributive measures. That is, N (which is count() in SQL), $\sum x_i$ (which is the sum() of x_i), and $\sum x_i^2$ (which is the sum() of x_i^2) can be computed in any partition and then merged to feed into the algebraic Equation 3.6. Thus, the computation of the variance and standard deviation is scalable in large databases.

3.2.3 Graphic Displays of Basic Descriptive Data Summaries

Aside from the bar charts, pie charts, and line graphs used in most statistical or graphical data presentation software packages, there are other popular types of graphs for the display of data summaries and distributions. These include *histograms, quantile plots, q-q plots, scatter plots*, and *loess curves*. Such graphs are very helpful for the visual inspection of your data.

Plotting **histograms**, or **frequency histograms**, is a graphical method for summarizing the distribution of a given attribute. A histogram for an attribute A partitions the data distribution of A into disjoint subsets, or *buckets*. Typically, the width of each bucket is uniform. Each bucket is represented by a rectangle whose height is equal to the count or relative frequency of the values at the bucket. If A is categorical, such as *automobile_model* or *item_type*, then one rectangle is drawn for each known value of A, and the resulting graph is more commonly referred to as a **bar chart**. If A is numeric, the term *histogram* is preferred. Partitioning rules for constructing histograms for numeric attributes are discussed in Section 3.5.4. In an equal-width histogram, for example, each bucket represents an equal-width range of numeric attribute A.

Figure 3.4 shows a histogram for the dataset of Table 3.1, where buckets are defined by equal-width ranges representing $20 increments and frequency is the count of items sold. Histograms are at least a century old and a widely used univariate graphical method. However, they may not be as effective as quantile plot, q-q plot, and boxplot methods for comparing groups of univariate observations.

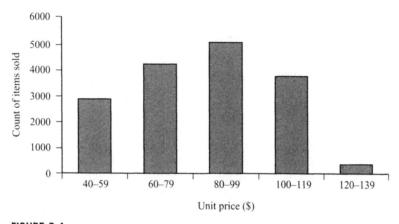

FIGURE 3.4

A histogram for the dataset of Table 3.1.

Table 3.1 A Set of Unit Price Data for Items Sold at a Branch of *AllElectronics*

Unit Price ($)	Count of Items Sold
40	275
43	300
47	250
...	...
74	360
75	515
78	540
...	...
115	320
117	270
120	350

A **quantile plot** is a simple and effective way to have a first look at a univariate data distribution. First, it displays all of the data for the given attribute (allowing the user to assess both the overall behavior and unusual occurrences). Second, it plots quantile information. The mechanism used in this step is slightly different from the percentile computation discussed in Section 3.2.2. Let x_i, for $i = 1$ to N, be the data sorted in increasing order so that x_1 is the smallest observation and x_N is the largest. Each observation, x_i, is paired with a percentage, f_i, which indicates that approximately $100 f_i$ percent of the data are below or equal to the value x_i. We say "approximately" because there may not be a value with exactly a fraction, f_i, of the data below or equal to x_i. Note that the 0.25 quantile corresponds to quartile Q_1, the 0.50 quantile is the median, and the 0.75 quantile is Q_3.

Let

$$f_i = \frac{i - 0.5}{N} \tag{3.7}$$

These numbers increase in equal steps of $1/N$, ranging from $1/2N$ (which is slightly above zero) to $1 - 1/2N$ (which is slightly below one). On a quantile plot, x_i is graphed against f_i. This allows us to compare different distributions based on their quantiles. For example, given the quantile plots of sales data for two different time periods, we can compare their Q_1, median, Q_3, and other f_i values at a glance. Figure 3.5 shows a quantile plot for the *unit price* data of Table 3.1.

A **quantile-quantile plot**, or **q-q plot**, graphs the quantiles of one univariate distribution against the corresponding quantiles of another. It is a powerful visualization tool in that it allows the user to view whether there is a shift in going from one distribution to another.

Suppose that we have two sets of observations for the variable *unit price*, taken from two different branch locations. Let $x_1, \ldots x_N$ be the data from the first branch and $y_1, \ldots y_M$ be the data from the second, where each dataset is sorted in increasing order. If $M = N$ (i.e., the number of points in each set is the same), then we simply plot y_i against x_i, where y_i and x_i are both $(i - 0.5)/N$ quantiles

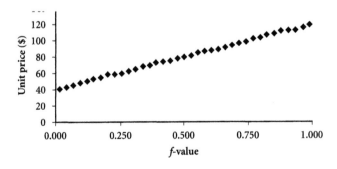

FIGURE 3.5

A quantile plot for the unit price data of Table 3.1.

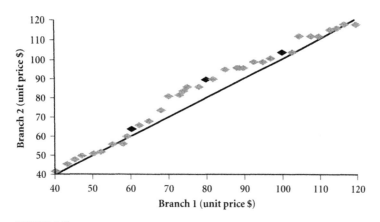

FIGURE 3.6

A quantile-quantile plot for unit price data from two different branches.

of their respective datasets. If $M < N$ (i.e., the second branch has fewer observations than the first), there can be only M points on the q-q plot. Here, y_i is the $(i - 0.5)/M$ quantile of the y data, which is plotted against the $(i - 0.5)/M$ quantile of the x data. This computation typically involves interpolation.

Figure 3.6 shows a quantile-quantile plot for *unit price* data of items sold at two different branches of *AllElectronics* during a given time period. Each point corresponds to the same quantile for each dataset and shows the unit price of items sold at branch 1 versus branch 2 for that quantile. For example, here the lowest point in the left corner corresponds to the 0.03 quantile. (To aid in comparison, we also show a straight line that represents the case of when, for each given quantile, the unit price at each branch is the same. In addition, the darker points correspond to the data for Q_1, the median, and Q_3, respectively.) We see that at this quantile, the unit price of items sold at branch 1 was slightly less than that at branch 2. In other words, 3 percent of items sold at branch 1 were less than or equal to $40, whereas 3 percent of items at branch 2 were less than or equal to $42. At the highest quantile, we see that the unit price of items at branch 2 was slightly less than that at branch 1. In general, we note that there is a shift in the distribution of branch 1 with respect to branch 2 in that the unit prices of items sold at branch 1 tend to be lower than those at branch 2.

A **scatter plot** is one of the most effective graphical methods for determining if there appears to be a relationship, pattern, or trend between two numeric attributes. To construct a scatter plot, each pair of values is treated as a pair of coordinates in an algebraic sense and plotted as points in the plane. Figure 3.7 shows a scatter plot for the set of data in Table 3.1. The scatter plot is a useful method for providing a first look at bivariate data to see clusters of points and outliers, or to explore the possibility of correlation relationships.[1] In Figure 3.8, we see

---

[1]A statistical test for correlation is given in Section 3.4.1 on data integration (Equation 3.8).

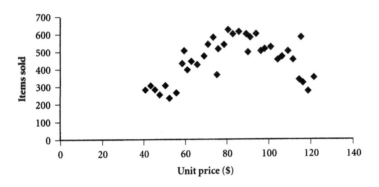

FIGURE 3.7

A scatter plot for the dataset of Table 3.1.

FIGURE 3.8

Scatter plots can be used to find (a) positive or (b) negative correlations between attributes.

examples of positive and negative correlations between two attributes in two different datasets. Figure 3.9 shows three cases for which there is no correlation relationship between the two attributes in each of the given datasets.

When dealing with several attributes, the **scatter-plot matrix** is a useful extension to the scatter plot. Given n attributes, a scatter-plot matrix is an $n \times n$ grid of scatter plots that provides a visualization of each attribute (or dimension) with every other attribute. The scatter-plot matrix becomes less effective as the number of attributes under study grows. In this case, user interactions, such as zooming and panning, become necessary to help interpret the individual scatter plots effectively.

A **loess curve** is another important exploratory graphic aid that adds a smooth curve to a scatter plot in order to provide better perception of the pattern of dependence. The word *loess* is short for "local regression." Figure 3.10 shows a loess curve for the set of data in Table 3.1.

To fit a loess curve, values need to be set for two parameters—α, a smoothing parameter, and λ, the degree of the polynomials that are fitted by the regression.

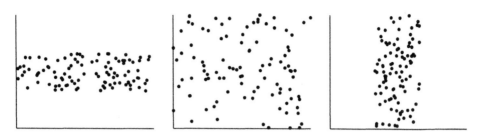

FIGURE 3.9

Three cases where there is no observed correlation between the two plotted attributes in each of the datasets.

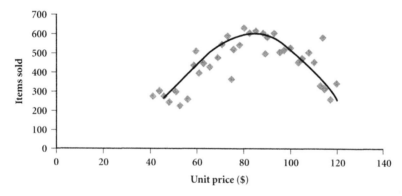

FIGURE 3.10

A loess curve for the dataset of Table 3.1.

Whereas α can be any positive number (typical values are between $\frac{1}{4}$ and 1), λ can be 1 or 2. The goal in choosing α is to produce a fit that is as smooth as possible without unduly distorting the underlying pattern in the data. The curve becomes smoother as α increases. There may be some lack of fit, however, indicating possible "missing" data patterns. If α is very small, the underlying pattern is tracked, yet overfitting of the data may occur where local "wiggles" in the curve may not be supported by the data. If the underlying pattern of the data has a "gentle" curvature with no local maxima and minima, then local linear fitting is usually sufficient ($\lambda = 1$). However, if there are local maxima or minima, then local quadratic fitting ($\lambda = 2$) typically does a better job of following the pattern of the data and maintaining local smoothness.

In conclusion, descriptive data summaries provide valuable insight into the overall behavior of your data. By helping you to identify noise and outliers, they are especially useful for data cleaning.

3.3 DATA CLEANING

Real-world data tend to be incomplete, noisy, and inconsistent. *Data cleaning* (or *data cleansing*) routines attempt to fill in missing values, smooth out noise while identifying outliers, and correct inconsistencies in the data. In this section, you will study basic methods for data cleaning. Section 3.3.1 looks at ways of handling missing values. Section 3.3.2 explains data smoothing techniques. Section 3.3.3 discusses approaches to data cleaning as a process.

3.3.1 Missing Values

Imagine that you need to analyze *AllElectronics* sales and customer data. You note that many tuples have no recorded value for several attributes, such as customer *income*. How can you go about filling in the missing values for this attribute? Let's look at the following methods.

1. *Ignore the tuple.* This is usually done when the class label is missing (that is, assuming the mining task involves classification). This method is not very effective, unless the tuple contains several attributes with missing values. It is especially poor when the percentage of missing values per attribute varies considerably.

2. *Fill in the missing value manually.* In general, this approach is time consuming and may not be feasible given a large dataset with many missing values.

3. *Use a global constant to fill in the missing value.* Replace all missing attribute values by the same constant, such as a label like "*Unknown*" or $-\infty$. If missing values are replaced by, say, "*Unknown*," then the mining program may mistakenly think that they form an interesting concept, as they all have a value in common—that of "*Unknown*." Hence, although this method is simple, it is not foolproof.

4. *Use the attribute mean to fill in the missing value.* For example, suppose that the average income of *AllElectronics* customers is $56,000. Use this value to replace the missing value for *income*.

5. *Use the attribute mean for all samples belonging to the same class as the given tuple.* For example, if classifying customers according to *credit_risk*, replace the missing value with the average *income* value for customers in the same credit-risk category as that of the given tuple.

6. *Use the most probable value to fill in the missing value.* This may be determined with regression, inference-based tools using a Bayesian formalism, or decision tree induction. For example, using the other customer attributes in your dataset, you may construct a decision tree to predict the missing values for *income*.

Methods 3 to 6 bias the data. The filled-in value may not be correct. Method 6, however, is a popular strategy. In comparison to the other methods, it uses the most information from the present data to predict missing values. By considering the values of the other attributes in its estimation of the missing value for *income*, there is a greater chance that the relationships between *income* and the other attributes are preserved.

It is important to note that, in some cases, a missing value may not imply an error in the data! For example, when applying for a credit card, candidates may be asked to supply their driver's license number. Candidates who do not have a driver's license may naturally leave this field blank. Forms should allow respondents to specify values such as "not applicable." Software routines may also be used to uncover other null values, such as "don't know," "?," or "none." Ideally, each attribute should have one or more rules regarding the *null* condition. The rules may specify whether or not nulls are allowed or how such values should be handled or transformed. Fields may also be intentionally left blank if they are to be provided in a later step of the business process. Hence, although we can try our best to clean the data after they are seized, good design of databases, and of data entry procedures, should minimize the number of missing values or errors in the first place.

3.3.2 Noisy Data

"What is noise?" **Noise** is a random error or variance in a measured variable. Given a numeric attribute such as, say, *price*, how can we "smooth" out the data to remove the noise? Let's look at the following data smoothing techniques:

Binning. Binning methods smooth a sorted data value by consulting its "neighborhood"—that is, the values around it. The sorted values are distributed into a number of "buckets," or *bins*. Because binning methods consult the neighborhood of values, they perform *local* smoothing. Figure 3.11 illustrates some binning techniques. In this example, the data for *price* are first sorted and then partitioned into *equal-frequency* bins of size 3 (i.e., each bin contains three values). In **smoothing by bin means**, each value in a bin is replaced by the mean value of the bin. For example, the mean of the values 4, 8, and 15 in Bin 1 is 9. Therefore, each original value in this bin is replaced by the value 9. Similarly, **smoothing by bin medians** can be employed, in which each bin value is replaced by the bin median. In **smoothing by bin boundaries**, the minimum and maximum values in a given bin are identified as the *bin boundaries*. Each bin value is then replaced by the closest boundary value. In general, the larger the width, the greater the smoothing's effect. Alternatively, bins may be *equal-width*, where the interval range of values in each bin is constant. Binning is also used as a discretization technique and is further discussed in Section 3.6.

Regression. Data can be smoothed by fitting the data to a function, such as with regression. *Linear regression* involves finding the "best" line to fit two attri-

Sorted data for *price* (in dollars): 4, 8, 15, 21, 21, 24, 25, 28, 34

    Partition into (equal-frequency) bins:

        Bin 1: 4, 8, 15
        Bin 2: 21, 21, 24
        Bin 3: 25, 28, 34

    Smoothing by bin means:

        Bin 1: 9, 9, 9
        Bin 2: 22, 22, 22
        Bin 3: 29, 29, 29

    Smoothing by bin boundaries:

        Bin 1: 4, 4, 15
        Bin 2: 21, 21, 24
        Bin 3: 25, 25, 34

FIGURE 3.11

Binning methods for data smoothing.

butes (or variables), so that one attribute can be used to predict the other. *Multiple linear regression* is an extension of linear regression, where more than two attributes are involved and the data are fit to a multidimensional surface. Regression is further described in Section 3.5.4.

Clustering. Outliers may be detected by clustering, where similar values are organized into groups, or "clusters." Intuitively, values that fall outside of the set of clusters may be considered outliers (Figure 3.12).

Many methods for data smoothing are also methods for data reduction involving discretization. For example, the binning techniques described previously reduce the number of distinct values per attribute. This acts as a form of data reduction for logic-based data mining methods, such as decision tree induction, which repeatedly make value comparisons on sorted data. Concept hierarchies are a form of data discretization that can also be used for data smoothing. A concept hierarchy for *price*, for example, may map real *price* values into *inexpensive, moderately priced*, and *expensive*, thereby reducing the number of data values to be handled by the mining process. Data discretization is discussed in Section 3.6. Some methods of classification, such as neural networks, have built-in data smoothing mechanisms.

3.3.3 Data Cleaning as a Process

Missing values, noise, and inconsistencies contribute to inaccurate data. So far, we have looked at techniques for handling missing data and for smoothing data.

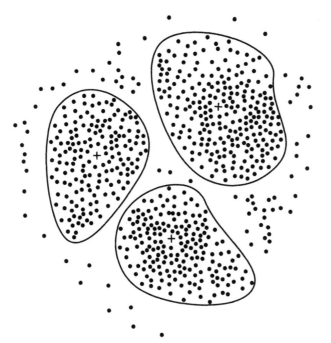

FIGURE 3.12

A 2-D plot of customer data with respect to customer locations in a city, showing three data clusters. Each cluster centroid is marked with a "+," representing the average point in space for that cluster. Outliers may be detected as values that fall outside of the sets of clusters.

"But data cleaning is a big job. What about data cleaning as a process? How exactly does one proceed in tackling this task? Are there any tools out there to help?"

The first step in data cleaning as a process is *discrepancy detection*. Discrepancies can be caused by several factors, including poorly designed data entry forms that have many optional fields, human error in data entry, deliberate errors (e.g., respondents not wanting to divulge information about themselves), and data decay (e.g., outdated addresses). Discrepancies may also arise from inconsistent data representations and the inconsistent use of codes. Errors in instrumentation devices that record data, and system errors, are another source of discrepancies. Errors can also occur when the data are (inadequately) used for purposes other than originally intended. There may also be inconsistencies caused by data integration (e.g., where a given attribute can have different names in different databases).[2]

---

[2]Data integration and the removal of redundant data that can result from such integration are further described in Section 3.4.1.

"So how can we proceed with discrepancy detection?" As a starting point, use any knowledge you may already have regarding properties of the data. Such knowledge, or "data about data," is referred to as **metadata**. For example, what are the domain and data type of each attribute? What are the acceptable values for each attribute? What is the range of the length of values? Do all values fall within the expected range? Are there any known dependencies between attributes? The descriptive data summaries presented in Section 3.2 are useful here for grasping data trends and identifying anomalies. For example, values that are more than two standard deviations away from the mean for a given attribute may be flagged as potential outliers. In this step, you may write your own scripts or use some of the tools that we discuss later. From this, you may find noise, outliers, and unusual values that need investigation.

As a data analyst, you should be on the lookout for the inconsistent use of codes and any inconsistent data representations (such as "2004/12/25" and "25/12/2004" for *date*). **Field overloading** is another source of errors that typically results when developers squeeze new attribute definitions into unused (bit) portions of already defined attributes (e.g., using an unused bit of an attribute whose value range uses only, say, 31 out of 32 bits).

The data should also be examined regarding unique rules, consecutive rules, and null rules. A **unique rule** says that each value of the given attribute must be different from all other values for that attribute. A **consecutive rule** says that there can be no missing values between the lowest and highest values for the attribute and that all values must also be unique (e.g., as in check numbers). A **null rule** specifies the use of blanks, question marks, special characters, or other strings that may indicate the null condition (e.g., where a value for a given attribute is not available) and how such values should be handled. As mentioned in Section 3.3.1, reasons for missing values may include (1) the person originally asked to provide a value for the attribute refuses, or finds that the information requested is not applicable (e.g., a *license-number* attribute left blank by nondrivers); (2) the data entry person does not know the correct value; or (3) the value is to be provided by a later step of the process. The null rule should specify how to record the null condition, for example, such as to store zero for numeric attributes, a blank for character attributes, or any other conventions that may be in use (such as that entries like "don't know" or "?" should be transformed to blank).

There are a number of different commercial tools that can aid in the step of discrepancy detection. **Data scrubbing tools** use simple domain knowledge (e.g., knowledge of postal addresses and spell-checking) to detect errors and make corrections in the data. These tools rely on parsing and fuzzy matching techniques when cleaning data from multiple sources. **Data auditing tools** find discrepancies by analyzing the data to discover rules and relationships and detecting data that violate such conditions. They are variants of data mining tools. For example, they may employ statistical analysis to find correlations, or they may use clustering to identify outliers. They may also use the descriptive data summaries that were described in Section 3.2.

Some data inconsistencies may be corrected manually using external references. For example, errors made at data entry may be corrected by performing a paper trace. Most errors, however, will require *data transformations*. This is the second step in data cleaning as a process. That is, once we find discrepancies, we typically need to define and apply (a series of) transformations to correct them.

Commercial tools can assist in the data transformation step. **Data migration tools** allow simple transformations to be specified, such as to replace the string *gender* by *sex.* **Extraction/transformation/loading (ETL) tools** allow users to specify transforms through a graphical user interface (GUI). These tools typically support only a restricted set of transforms so that, often, we may also choose to write custom scripts for this step of the data cleaning process.

The two-step process of discrepancy detection and data transformation (to correct discrepancies) iterates. This process, however, is error prone and time consuming. Some transformations may introduce more discrepancies. Some *nested discrepancies* may only be detected after others have been fixed. For example, a typo such as "20004" in a year field may only surface once all date values have been converted to a uniform format. Transformations are often done as a batch process while the user waits without feedback. Only after the transformation is complete can the user go back and check that no new anomalies have been created by mistake. Typically, numerous iterations are required before the user is satisfied. Any tuples that cannot be automatically handled by a given transformation are typically written to a file without any explanation regarding the reasoning behind their failure. As a result, the entire data cleaning process also suffers from a lack of interactivity.

New approaches to data cleaning emphasize increased interactivity. Potter's Wheel, for example, is a publicly available data cleaning tool (see *http://control. cs.berkeley.edu/abc*) that integrates discrepancy detection and transformation. Users gradually build a series of transformations by composing and debugging individual transformations, one step at a time, on a spreadsheet-like interface. The transformations can be specified graphically or by providing examples. Results are shown immediately on the records that are visible on the screen. The user can choose to undo the transformations, so that transformations that introduced additional errors can be "erased." The tool performs discrepancy checking automatically in the background on the latest transformed view of the data. Users can gradually develop and refine transformations as discrepancies are found, leading to more effective and efficient data cleaning.

Another approach to increased interactivity in data cleaning is the development of declarative languages for the specification of data transformation operators. Such work focuses on defining powerful extensions to SQL and algorithms that enable users to express data cleaning specifications efficiently.

As we discover more about the data, it is important to keep updating the metadata to reflect this knowledge. This will help speed up data cleaning on future versions of the same data store.

3.4 DATA INTEGRATION AND TRANSFORMATION

Data mining often requires data integration—the merging of data from multiple data stores. The data may also need to be transformed into forms appropriate for mining. This section describes both data integration and data transformation.

3.4.1 Data Integration

It is likely that your data analysis task will involve *data integration*, which combines data from multiple sources into a coherent data store, as in data warehousing. These sources may include multiple databases, data cubes, or flat files.

There are a number of issues to consider during data integration. *Schema integration* and *object matching* can be tricky. How can equivalent real-world entities from multiple data sources be matched up? This is referred to as the **entity identification problem**. For example, how can the data analyst or the computer be sure that *customer id* in one database and *cust number* in another refer to the same attribute? Examples of metadata for each attribute include the name, meaning, data type, and range of values permitted for the attribute, and null rules for handling blank, zero, or null values (Section 3.3). Such metadata can be used to help avoid errors in schema integration. The metadata may also be used to help transform the data (e.g., where data codes for *pay type* in one database may be *H* and *S*, and they may be *1* and *2* in another). Hence, this step also relates to data cleaning, as described earlier.

Redundancy is another important issue. An attribute (such as *annual revenue*, for instance) may be redundant if it can be "derived" from another attribute or set of attributes. Inconsistencies in attribute or dimension naming can also cause redundancies in the resulting dataset.

Some redundancies can be detected by **correlation analysis**. Given two attributes, such analysis can measure how strongly one attribute implies the other, based on the available data. For numeric attributes, we can evaluate the correlation between two attributes, *A* and *B*, by computing the **correlation coefficient** (also known as *Pearson's product moment coefficient*, named after its inventor, Karl Pearson). This is

$$r_{A,B} = \frac{\sum_{i=1}^{N}(a_i - \bar{A})(b_i - \bar{B})}{N\sigma_A\sigma_B} = \frac{\sum_{i=1}^{N}(a_ib_i) - N\bar{A}\bar{B}}{N\sigma_A\sigma_B} \tag{3.8}$$

where N is the number of tuples, a_i and b_i are the respective values of A and B in tuple i, $\bar{A}$ and $\bar{B}$ are the respective mean values of A and B, σ_A and σ_B are the respective standard deviations of A and B (as defined in Section 3.2.2), and $\Sigma(a_ib_i)$ is the sum of the AB cross-product (that is, for each tuple, the value for A is multiplied by the value for B in that tuple). Note that $-1 \leq r_{A,B} \leq +1$. If $r_{A,B}$ is greater than 0, then A and B are positively correlated, meaning that the values of A increase as the values of B increase. The higher the value, the stronger the correlation (i.e., the more each attribute implies the other). Hence, a higher value may indicate that A (or B) may be removed as a redundancy. If the resulting value is equal to 0, then A and B are independent and there is no correlation between them. If the resulting value is less than 0, then A and B are negatively correlated, where the values of one attribute increase as the values of the other attribute decrease. This means that each attribute discourages the other. Scatter plots can also be used to view correlations between attributes (Section 3.2.3).

Note that correlation does not imply causality. That is, if A and B are correlated, this does not necessarily imply that A causes B or that B causes A. For example, in analyzing a demographic database, we may find that attributes representing the number of hospitals and the number of car thefts in a region are correlated. This does not mean that one causes the other. Both are actually causally linked to a third attribute, namely, *population*.

For categorical (discrete) data, a correlation relationship between two attributes, A and B, can be discovered by a χ^2 (**chi-square**) test. Suppose A has c distinct values, namely a_1, a_2, a_c. B has r distinct values, namely b_1, b_2, b_r. The data tuples described by A and B can be shown as a **contingency table**, with the c values of A making up the columns and the r values of B making up the rows. Let (A_i, B_j) denote the event that attribute A takes on value a_i and attribute B takes on value b_j, that is, where $(A = a_i, B = b_j)$. Each and every possible (A_i, B_j) joint event has its own cell (or slot) in the table. The χ^2 value (also known as the *Pearson χ^2 statistic*) is computed as

$$\chi^2 = \sum_{i=1}^{c} \sum_{j=1}^{r} \frac{(o_{ij} - e_{ij})^2}{e_{ij}} \tag{3.9}$$

where o_{ij} is the *observed frequency* (i.e., actual count) of the joint event (A_i, B_j) and e_{ij} is the *expected frequency* of (A_i, B_j), which can be computed as

$$e_{ij} = \frac{count(A = a_i) \times count(B = b_j)}{N} \tag{3.10}$$

where N is the number of data tuples, $count(A = a_i)$ is the number of tuples having value a_i for A, and $count(B = b_j)$ is the number of tuples having value b_j for B. The sum in Equation 3.9 is computed over all of the $r \times c$ cells. Note that the cells that contribute the most to the χ^2 value are those whose actual count is very different from that expected.

The χ^2 statistic tests the hypothesis that A and B are independent. The test is based on a significance level, with $(r - 1) \times (c - 1)$ degrees of freedom. We will illustrate the use of this statistic in the example that follows. If the hypothesis can be rejected, then we say that A and B are statistically related or associated.

Let's look at a concrete example.

EXAMPLE 3.1

Correlation Analysis of Categorical Attributes Using χ^2

Suppose that a group of 1500 people was surveyed. The gender of each person was noted. Each person was polled as to whether his or her preferred type of reading material was fiction or nonfiction. Thus, we have two attributes, *gender* and *preferred reading*. The observed frequency (or count) of each possible joint event is summarized in the contingency table shown in Table 3.2, where the numbers in parentheses are the expected frequencies (calculated based on the data distribution for both attributes using Equation 3.10).

Using Equation 3.10, we can verify the expected frequencies for each cell. For example, the expected frequency for the cell (male, fiction) is

$$e_{11} = \frac{count(male) \times count(fiction)}{N} = \frac{300 \times 450}{1500} = 90$$

and so on. Notice that in any row, the sum of the expected frequencies must equal the total observed frequency for that row, and the sum of the expected frequencies in any column must also equal the total observed frequency for that column. Using Equation 3.9 for χ^2 computation, we get

$$\chi^2 = \frac{(250-90)^2}{90} + \frac{(50-210)^2}{210} + \frac{(200-360)^2}{360} + \frac{(1000-840)^2}{840}$$
$$= 284.44 + 121.90 + 71.11 + 30.48 = 507.93$$

For this 2×2 table, the degrees of freedom are $(2-1)(2-1) = 1$. For 1 degree of freedom, the χ^2 value needed to reject the hypothesis at the 0.001 significance level is 10.828 (taken from the table of upper percentage points of the χ^2 distribution, typically available from any textbook on statistics). Because our computed value is above this, we can reject the hypothesis that *gender* and *preferred_reading* are independent and conclude that the two attributes are (strongly) correlated for the given group of people.

Table 3.2 A 2×2 Contingency Table for Data in Example 3.1: Are *Gender* and *preferred_Reading* Correlated?

	Male	Female	Total
fiction	250 (90)	200 (360)	450
non-fiction	50 (210)	1000 (840)	1050
Total	300	1200	1500

In addition to detecting redundancies between attributes, duplication should also be detected at the tuple level (e.g., where there are two or more identical tuples for a given unique data entry case). The use of denormalized tables (often done to improve performance by avoiding joins) is another source of data redundancy. Inconsistencies often arise between various duplicates because of inaccurate data entry or updating some but not all of the occurrences of the data. For example, if a purchase order database contains attributes for the purchaser's name and address instead of a key to this information in a purchaser database, discrepancies can occur, such as the same purchaser's name appearing with different addresses within the purchase order database.

A third important issue in data integration is the *detection and resolution of data value conflicts*. For example, for the same real-world entity, attribute values from different sources may differ. This may be due to differences in representation, scaling, or encoding. For instance, a *weight* attribute may be stored in metric units in one system and British imperial units in another. For a hotel chain, the *price* of rooms in different cities may involve not only different currencies but also different services (such as free breakfast) and taxes. An attribute in one system may be recorded at a lower level of abstraction than the "same" attribute in another. For example, the *total sales* in one database may refer to one branch of *All_Electronics*, whereas an attribute of the same name in another database may refer to the total sales for *All_Electronics* stores in a given region.

When matching attributes from one database to another during integration, special attention must be paid to the *structure* of the data. This is to ensure that any attribute functional dependencies and referential constraints in the source system match those in the target system. For example, in one system, a *discount* may be applied to the order, whereas in another system it is applied to each individual line item within the order. If this is not caught before integration, items in the target system may be improperly discounted.

The semantic heterogeneity and structure of data pose great challenges in data integration. Careful integration of the data from multiple sources can reduce and avoid redundancies and inconsistencies in the resulting dataset. This can improve the accuracy and speed of the subsequent mining process.

3.4.2 Data Transformation

In *data transformation*, the data are transformed or consolidated into forms appropriate for mining. Data transformation can involve the following:

Smoothing, which works to remove noise from the data. Such techniques include binning, regression, and clustering.

Aggregation, where summary or aggregation operations are applied to the data. For example, the daily sales data may be aggregated so as to compute monthly and annual total amounts. This step is typically used in constructing a data cube for analysis of the data at multiple granularities.

Generalization of the data, where low-level or "primitive" (raw) data are replaced by higher-level concepts through the use of concept hierarchies. For example, categorical attributes, like *street*, can be generalized to higher-level concepts, like *city* or *country*. Similarly, values for numeric attributes, like *age*, may be mapped to higher-level concepts, like *youth*, *middle-aged*, and *senior*.

Normalization, where the attribute data are scaled so as to fall within a small specified range, such as −1.0 to 1.0, or 0.0 to 1.0.

Attribute construction (or *feature construction*), where new attributes are constructed and added from the given set of attributes to help the mining process.

Smoothing is a form of data cleaning and was addressed in Section 3.3.2. Section 3.3.3 on the data cleaning process also discussed ETL tools, where users specify transformations to correct data inconsistencies. Aggregation and generalization serve as forms of data reduction and are discussed in Sections 3.5 and 3.6, respectively. In this section, we therefore discuss normalization and attribute construction.

An attribute is normalized by scaling its values so that they fall within a small specified range, such as 0.0 to 1.0. Normalization is particularly useful for classification algorithms involving neural networks or distance measurements such as nearest-neighbor classification and clustering. If using the neural network back-propagation algorithm for classification mining, normalizing the input values for each attribute measured in the training tuples will help speed up the learning phase. For distance-based methods, normalization helps prevent attributes with initially large ranges (e.g., *income*) from outweighing attributes with initially smaller ranges (e.g., binary attributes). There are many methods for data normalization. We study three: *min-max normalization, z-score normalization*, and *normalization by decimal scaling*.

Min-max normalization performs a linear transformation on the original data. Suppose that min_A and max_A are the minimum and maximum values of an attribute, A. Min-max normalization maps a value, v, of A to v' in the range $[new\_min_A, new\_max_A]$ by computing

$$v' = \frac{v - min_A}{max_A - min_A}(new\_max_A - new\_min_A) + new\_min_A \qquad (3.11)$$

Min-max normalization preserves the relationships among the original data values. It will encounter an "out-of-bounds" error if a future input case for normalization falls outside of the original data range for A.

EXAMPLE 3.2

Min-Max Normalization

Suppose that the minimum and maximum values for the attribute *income* are $12,000 and $98,000, respectively. We would like to map *income* to the range (0.0, 1.0]. By min-max normalization, a value of $73,600 for *income* is transformed to

$$\frac{73,600 - 12,000}{98,000 - 12,000}(1.0 - 0) + 0 = 0.716$$

In **z-score normalization** (or *zero-mean normalization*), the values for an attribute, A, are normalized based on the mean and standard deviation of A. A value, v, of A is normalized to v' by computing

$$v' = \frac{v - \bar{A}}{\sigma_A} \tag{3.12}$$

where $\bar{A}$ and σ_A are the mean and standard deviation, respectively, of attribute A. This method of normalization is useful when the actual minimum and maximum of attribute A are unknown or when there are outliers that dominate the min-max normalization.

EXAMPLE 3.3

z-Score Normalization

Suppose that the mean and standard deviation of the values for the attribute *income* are $54,000 and $16,000, respectively. With z-score normalization, a value of $73,600 for *income* is transformed to

$$\frac{73,600 - 54,000}{16,000} = 1.225$$

Normalization by decimal scaling normalizes by moving the decimal point of values of attribute A. The number of decimal points moved depends on the maximum absolute value of A. A value, v, of A is normalized to v' by computing

$$v' = \frac{v}{10^j} \tag{3.13}$$

where j is the smallest integer such that $Max(|v'|) < 1$.

EXAMPLE 3.4

Decimal Scaling

Suppose that the recorded values of A range from −986 to 917. The maximum absolute value of A is 986. To normalize by decimal scaling, we therefore divide each value by 1000 (i.e., $j = 3$) so that −986 normalizes to −0.986 and 917 normalizes to 0.917.

Note that normalization can change the original data quite a bit, especially the latter two methods shown here. It is also necessary to save the normalization parameters (such as the mean and standard deviation if using z-score normalization) so that future data can be normalized in a uniform manner.

In **attribute construction**,[3] new attributes are constructed from the given attributes and added to help improve the accuracy and understanding of structure in high-dimensional data. For example, we may wish to add the attribute *area* based on the attributes *height* and *width*. By combining attributes, attribute construction can discover missing information about the relationships between data attributes that can be useful for knowledge discovery.

3.5 DATA REDUCTION

Imagine that you have selected data from the *AllElectronics* data warehouse for analysis. The dataset will likely be huge! Complex data analysis and mining on huge amounts of data can take a long time, making such analysis impractical or infeasible.

Data reduction techniques can be applied to obtain a reduced representation of the dataset that is much smaller in volume yet closely maintains the integrity of the original data. That is, mining on the reduced dataset should be more efficient yet produce the same (or almost the same) analytical results. Strategies for data reduction include the following:

1. *Data cube aggregation,* where aggregation operations are applied to the data in the construction of a data cube.

2. *Attribute subset selection,* where irrelevant, weakly relevant, or redundant attributes or dimensions may be detected and removed.

3. *Dimensionality reduction,* where encoding mechanisms are used to reduce the dataset size.

4. *Numerosity reduction,* where the data are replaced or estimated by alternative, smaller data representations such as parametric models (which need store only the model parameters instead of the actual data) or nonparametric methods such as clustering, sampling, and the use of histograms.

5. *Discretization and concept hierarchy generation,* where raw data values for attributes are replaced by ranges or higher conceptual levels. Data discretization is a form of numerosity reduction that is useful for the automatic generation of concept hierarchies. Discretization and concept hierarchy generation are powerful data mining tools, in that they allow the mining of data at mul-

---

[3]In the machine learning literature, attribute construction is known as *feature construction*.

tiple levels of abstraction. We therefore defer the discussion of discretization and concept hierarchy generation to Section 3.6, which is devoted entirely to this topic.

The remainder of this section discusses strategies 1 to 4. The computational time spent on data reduction should not outweigh or "erase" the time saved by mining on a reduced dataset size.

3.5.1 Data Cube Aggregation

Imagine that you have collected the data for your analysis. These data consist of the *AllElectronics* sales per quarter, for the years 2002 to 2004. You are, however, interested in the annual sales (total per year), rather than the total per quarter. Thus, the data can be *aggregated* so that the resulting data summarize the total sales per year instead of per quarter. This aggregation is illustrated in Figure 3.13. The resulting dataset is smaller in volume, without loss of information necessary for the analysis task.

We briefly introduce some concepts of data cubes here. Data cubes store multidimensional aggregated information. For example, Figure 3.14 shows a data cube for multidimensional analysis of sales data with respect to annual sales per item type for each *AllElectronics* branch. Each cell holds an aggregate data value, corresponding to the data point in multidimensional space. (For readability, only some cell values are shown.) Concept hierarchies may exist for each attribute, allowing the analysis of data at multiple levels of abstraction. For example, a hierarchy for *branch* could allow branches to be grouped into regions, based on their address. Data cubes provide fast access to precomputed, summarized data, thereby benefiting online analytical processing as well as data mining.

The cube created at the lowest level of abstraction is referred to as the *base cuboid*. The base cuboid should correspond to an individual entity of interest,

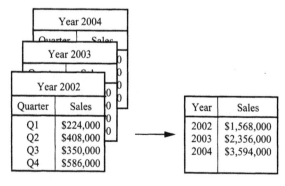

FIGURE 3.13

Sales data for a given branch of *AllElectronics* for 2002 to 2004. On the left, sales are shown per quarter. On the right, data are aggregated to provide annual sales.

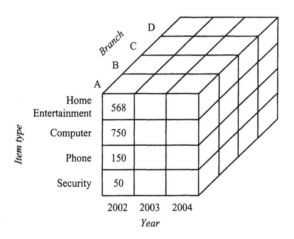

FIGURE 3.14

A data cube for sales at *AllElectronics*.

such as *sales* or *customer*. In other words, the lowest level should be usable, or useful for the analysis. A cube at the highest level of abstraction is the *apex cuboid*. For the sales data of Figure 3.14, the apex cuboid would give one total—the total *sales* for all three years, for all item types and for all branches. Data cubes created for varying levels of abstraction are often referred to as *cuboids*, so that a data cube may instead refer to a *lattice of cuboids*. Each higher level of abstraction further reduces the resulting data size. When replying to data mining requests, the *smallest* available cuboid relevant to the given task should be used.

3.5.2 Attribute Subset Selection

Datasets for analysis may contain hundreds of attributes, many of which may be irrelevant to the mining task or redundant. For example, if the task is to classify customers as to whether they are likely to purchase a popular new CD at *AllElectronics* when notified of a sale, attributes such as the customer's telephone number are likely to be irrelevant, unlike attributes such as *age* or *music-taste*. Although it may be possible for a domain expert to pick out some of the useful attributes, this can be a difficult and time-consuming task, especially when the behavior of the data is not well known (hence, a reason behind its analysis!). Leaving out relevant attributes or keeping irrelevant attributes may be detrimental, causing confusion for the mining algorithm employed. This can result in discovered patterns of poor quality. In addition, the added volume of irrelevant or redundant attributes can slow down the mining process.

Attribute subset selection[4] reduces the dataset size by removing irrelevant or redundant attributes (or dimensions). The goal of attribute subset selection is

---

[4] In machine learning, attribute subset selection is known as *feature subset selection*.

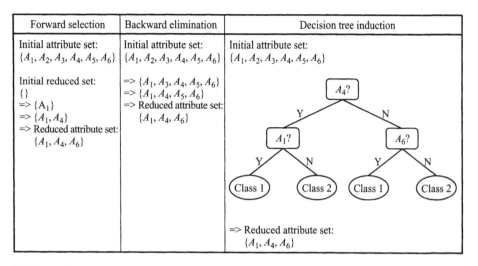

Forward selection	Backward elimination	Decision tree induction
Initial attribute set: $\{A_1, A_2, A_3, A_4, A_5, A_6\}$	Initial attribute set: $\{A_1, A_2, A_3, A_4, A_5, A_6\}$	Initial attribute set: $\{A_1, A_2, A_3, A_4, A_5, A_6\}$
Initial reduced set: $\{\}$ => $\{A_1\}$ => $\{A_1, A_4\}$ => Reduced attribute set: $\{A_1, A_4, A_6\}$	=> $\{A_1, A_3, A_4, A_5, A_6\}$ => $\{A_1, A_4, A_5, A_6\}$ => Reduced attribute set: $\{A_1, A_4, A_6\}$	

FIGURE 3.15

Greedy (heuristic) methods for attribute subset selection.

to find a minimum set of attributes such that the resulting probability distribution of the data classes is as close as possible to the original distribution obtained using all attributes. Mining on a reduced set of attributes has an additional benefit. It reduces the number of attributes appearing in the discovered patterns, helping to make the patterns easier to understand.

"How can we find a 'good' subset of the original attributes?" For n attributes, there are 2^n possible subsets. An exhaustive search for the optimal subset of attributes can be prohibitively expensive, especially as n and the number of data classes increase. Therefore, heuristic methods that explore a reduced search space are commonly used for attribute subset selection. These methods are typically **greedy** in that, while searching through attribute space, they always make what looks to be the best choice at the time. Their strategy is to make a locally optimal choice in the hope that this will lead to a globally optimal solution. Such greedy methods are effective in practice and may come close to estimating an optimal solution.

The "best" (and "worst") attributes are typically determined using tests of statistical significance, which assume that the attributes are independent of one another. Many other attribute evaluation measures can be used, such as the *information gain* measure used in building decision trees for classification.[5]

Basic heuristic methods of attribute subset selection include the following techniques, some of which are illustrated in Figure 3.15.

---

[5]The information gain measure is briefly described in Section 3.6.1 with respect to attribute discretization.

1. *Stepwise forward selection.* The procedure starts with an empty set of attributes as the reduced set. The best of the original attributes is determined and added to the reduced set. At each subsequent iteration or step, the best of the remaining original attributes is added to the set.

2. *Stepwise backward elimination.* The procedure starts with the full set of attributes. At each step, it removes the worst attribute remaining in the set.

3. *Combination of forward selection and backward elimination.* The stepwise forward selection and backward elimination methods can be combined so that, at each step, the procedure selects the best attribute and removes the worst from among the remaining attributes.

4. *Decision tree induction.* Decision tree algorithms, such as ID3, C4.5, and CART, were originally intended for classification. Decision tree induction constructs a flowchart-like structure where each internal (nonleaf) node denotes a test on an attribute, each branch corresponds to an outcome of the test, and each external (leaf) node denotes a class prediction. At each node, the algorithm chooses the "best" attribute to partition the data into individual classes.

When decision tree induction is used for attribute subset selection, a tree is constructed from the given data. All attributes that do not appear in the tree are assumed to be irrelevant. The set of attributes appearing in the tree form the reduced subset of attributes.

The stopping criteria for the methods may vary. The procedure may employ a threshold on the measure used to determine when to stop the attribute selection process.

3.5.3 Dimensionality Reduction

In *dimensionality reduction*, data encoding or transformations are applied so as to obtain a reduced or "compressed" representation of the original data. If the original data can be *reconstructed* from the compressed data without any loss of information, the data reduction is called **lossless**. If, instead, we can reconstruct only an approximation of the original data, then the data reduction is called **lossy**. There are several well-tuned algorithms for string compression. Although they are typically lossless, they allow only limited manipulation of the data. In this section, we instead focus on two popular and effective methods of lossy dimensionality reduction: *wavelet transforms* and *principal components analysis*.

Wavelet Transforms

The **discrete wavelet transform (DWT)** is a linear signal processing technique that, when applied to a data vector X, transforms it to a numerically different vector, X', of **wavelet coefficients**. The two vectors are of the same length. When applying this technique to data reduction, we consider each tuple as an

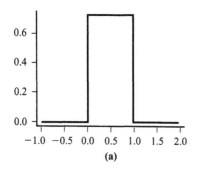
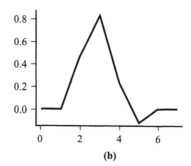

               (a)   (b)

FIGURE 3.16

Examples of wavelet families: (a) Haar-2; (b) Daubechies-4. The number next to a wavelet name is the number of *vanishing moments* of the wavelet. This is a set of mathematical relationships that the coefficients must satisfy and is related to the number of coefficients.

n-dimensional data vector, that is, $X = (x_1, x_2, \ldots x_n)$, depicting n measurements made on the tuple from n database attributes.[6]

    "How can this technique be useful for data reduction if the wavelet transformed data are of the same length as the original data?" The usefulness lies in the fact that the wavelet transformed data can be truncated. A compressed approximation of the data can be retained by storing only a small fraction of the strongest of the wavelet coefficients. For example, all wavelet coefficients larger than some user-specified threshold can be retained. All other coefficients are set to 0. The resulting data representation is therefore very sparse, so that operations that can take advantage of data sparsity are computationally very fast if performed in wavelet space. The technique also works to remove noise without smoothing out the main features of the data, making it effective for data cleaning as well. Given a set of coefficients, an approximation of the original data can be constructed by applying the inverse of the DWT used.

    The DWT is closely related to the *discrete Fourier transform (DFT)*, a signal processing technique involving sines and cosines. In general, however, the DWT achieves better lossy compression. That is, if the same number of coefficients is retained for a DWT and a DFT of a given data vector, the DWT version will provide a more accurate approximation of the original data. Hence, for an equivalent approximation, the DWT requires less space than the DFT. Unlike the DFT, wavelets are quite localized in space, contributing to conservation of local detail.

    There is only one DFT, yet there are several families of DWTs. Figure 3.16 shows some wavelet families. Popular wavelet transforms include the Haar-2, Daubechies-4, and Daubechies-6 transforms. The general procedure for applying a discrete wavelet transform uses a hierarchical *pyramid algorithm* that halves

---

[6]In our notation, any variable representing a vector is shown in bold italic font; measurements depicting the vector are shown in italic font.

the data at each iteration, resulting in fast computational speed. The method is as follows:

1. The length, L, of the input data vector must be an integer power of 2. This condition can be met by padding the data vector with zeros as necessary ($L \geq n$).

2. Each transform involves applying two functions. The first applies some data smoothing, such as a sum or weighted average. The second performs a weighted difference, which acts to bring out the detailed features of the data.

3. The two functions are applied to pairs of data points in X, that is, to all pairs of measurements (x_{2i}, x_{2i+1}). This results in two sets of data of length $L/2$. In general, these represent a smoothed or low-frequency version of the input data and the high-frequency content of it, respectively.

4. The two functions are recursively applied to the sets of data obtained in the previous loop, until the resulting datasets obtained are of length 2.

5. Selected values from the datasets obtained in the preceding iterations are designated the wavelet coefficients of the transformed data.

Equivalently, a matrix multiplication can be applied to the input data in order to obtain the wavelet coefficients, where the matrix used depends on the given DWT. The matrix must be **orthonormal**, meaning that the columns are unit vectors and are mutually orthogonal, so that the matrix inverse is just its transpose. Although we do not have room to discuss it here, this property allows the reconstruction of the data from the smooth and smooth-difference datasets. By factoring the matrix used into a product of a few sparse matrices, the resulting *"fast DWT"* algorithm has a complexity of $O(n)$ for an input vector of length n.

Wavelet transforms can be applied to multidimensional data, such as a data cube. This is done by first applying the transform to the first dimension, then to the second, and so on. The computational complexity involved is linear with respect to the number of cells in the cube. Wavelet transforms give good results on sparse or skewed data and on data with ordered attributes. Lossy compression by wavelets is reportedly better than JPEG compression, the current commercial standard. Wavelet transforms have many real-world applications, including the compression of fingerprint images, computer vision, analysis of time-series data, and data cleaning.

Principal Components Analysis

In this subsection, we provide an intuitive introduction to principal components analysis as a method of dimesionality reduction. A detailed theoretic explanation is beyond the scope of this book.

Suppose that the data to be reduced consist of tuples or data vectors described by n attributes or dimensions. **Principal components analysis**, or **PCA** (also called the Karhunen-Loeve, or K-L, method), searches for k n-dimensional orthogonal vectors that can best be used to represent the data, where $k \leq n$. The original data are thus projected onto a much smaller space, resulting in dimensionality reduction. Unlike attribute subset selection, which reduces the attribute set size by retaining a subset of the initial set of attributes, PCA "combines" the essence of attributes by creating an alternative, smaller set of variables. The initial data can then be projected onto this smaller set. PCA often reveals relationships that were not previously suspected and thereby allows interpretations that would not ordinarily result.

The basic procedure is as follows:

1. The input data are normalized, so that each attribute falls within the same range. This step helps ensure that attributes with large domains will not dominate attributes with smaller domains.

2. PCA computes k orthonormal vectors that provide a basis for the normalized input data. These are unit vectors that each point in a direction perpendicular to the others. These vectors are referred to as the *principal components*. The input data are a linear combination of the principal components.

3. The principal components are sorted in order of decreasing "significance" or strength. The principal components essentially serve as a new set of axes for the data, providing important information about variance. That is, the sorted axes are such that the first axis shows the most variance among the data, the second axis shows the next highest variance, and so on. For example, Figure 3.17 shows the first two principal components, Y_1 and Y_2, for the given set of data originally mapped to the axes X_1 and X_2. This information helps identify groups or patterns within the data.

4. Because the components are sorted according to decreasing order of "significance," the size of the data can be reduced by eliminating the weaker components, that is, those with low variance. Using the strongest principal components, it should be possible to reconstruct a good approximation of the original data.

PCA is computationally inexpensive, can be applied to ordered and unordered attributes, and can handle sparse data and skewed data. Multidimensional data of

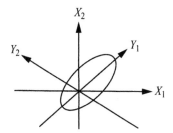

FIGURE 3.17

Principal components analysis. Y_1 and Y_2 are the first two principal components for the given data.

more than two dimensions can be handled by reducing the problem to two dimensions. Principal components may be used as inputs to multiple regression and cluster analysis. In comparison with wavelet transforms, PCA tends to be better at handling sparse data, whereas wavelet transforms are more suitable for data of high dimensionality.

3.5.4 Numerosity Reduction

"Can we reduce the data volume by choosing alternative, 'smaller' forms of data representation?" Techniques of numerosity reduction can indeed be applied for this purpose. These techniques may be parametric or nonparametric. For parametric methods, a model is used to estimate the data, so that typically only the data parameters need to be stored, instead of the actual data. (Outliers may also be stored.) Log-linear models, which estimate discrete multidimensional probability distributions, are an example. Nonparametric methods for storing reduced representations of the data include histograms, clustering, and sampling.

Let's look at each of the numerosity reduction techniques mentioned earlier.

Regression and Log-Linear Models

Regression and log-linear models can be used to approximate the given data. In (simple) linear **regression**, the data are modeled to fit a straight line. For example, a random variable, y (called a *response variable*), can be modeled as a linear function of another random variable, x (called a *predictor variable*), with the equation

$$y = wx + b \tag{3.14}$$

where the variance of y is assumed to be constant. In the context of data mining, x and y are numeric database attributes. The coefficients, w and b (called *regression coefficients*), specify the slope of the line and the y intercept, respectively. These coefficients can be solved for by the *method of least squares*, which minimizes the error between the actual line separating the data and the estimate of the line. **Multiple linear regression** is an extension of (simple) linear regression, which allows a response variable, y, to be modeled as a linear function of two or more predictor variables.

Log-linear models approximate discrete multidimensional probability distributions. Given a set of tuples in n dimensions (e.g., described by n attributes), we can consider each tuple as a point in an n-dimensional space. Log-linear models can be used to estimate the probability of each point in a multidimensional space for a set of discretized attributes, based on a smaller subset of dimensional combinations. This allows a higher-dimensional data space to be constructed from lower-dimensional spaces. Log-linear models are therefore also useful for dimensionality reduction (because the lower-dimensional points together typically occupy less space than the original data points) and data smoothing (because aggregate estimates in the lower-dimensional space are less subject to sampling variations than the estimates in the higher-dimensional space).

Regression and log-linear models can both be used on sparse data, although their application may be limited. Although both methods can handle skewed data, regression does exceptionally well. Regression can be computationally intensive when applied to high-dimensional data, whereas log-linear models show good scalability for up to ten or so dimensions.

Histograms

Histograms use binning to approximate data distributions and are a popular form of data reduction. Histograms were introduced in Section 3.2.3. A **histogram** for an attribute, A, partitions the data distribution of A into disjoint subsets, or *buckets*. If each bucket represents only a single attribute-value/frequency pair, the buckets are called *singleton buckets*. Often, buckets instead represent continuous ranges for the given attribute.

EXAMPLE 3.5

Histograms

The following data are a list of prices of commonly sold items at AllElectronics (rounded to the nearest dollar). The numbers have been sorted: 1, 1, 5, 5, 5, 5, 5, 8, 8, 10, 10, 10, 10, 12, 14, 14, 14, 15, 15, 15, 15, 15, 15, 18, 18, 18, 18, 18, 18, 18, 18, 20, 20, 20, 20, 20, 20, 20, 21, 21, 21, 21, 25, 25, 25, 25, 25, 28, 28, 30, 30, 30.

Figure 3.18 shows a histogram for the data using singleton buckets. To further reduce the data, it is common to have each bucket denote a continuous range of values for the given attribute. In Figure 3.19, each bucket represents a different $10 range for *price*.

"How are the buckets determined and the attribute values partitioned?" There are several partitioning rules, including the following:

Equal-width. In an equal-width histogram, the width of each bucket range is uniform (such as the width of $10 for the buckets in Figure 3.19).

Equal-frequency (or equidepth). In an equal-frequency histogram, the buckets are created so that, roughly, the frequency of each bucket is constant (that is, each bucket contains roughly the same number of contiguous data samples).

V-Optimal. If we consider all of the possible histograms for a given number of buckets, the V-Optimal histogram is the one with the least variance. Histogram variance is a weighted sum of the original values that each bucket represents, where bucket weight is equal to the number of values in the bucket.

MaxDiff. In a MaxDiff histogram, we consider the difference between each pair of adjacent values. A bucket boundary is established between each pair for pairs having the $\beta-1$ largest differences, where β is the user-specified number of buckets.

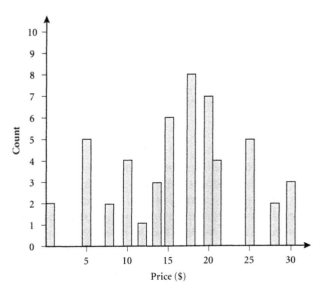

FIGURE 3.18

Histogram for price using singleton buckets—each represents one price-value/frequency pair.

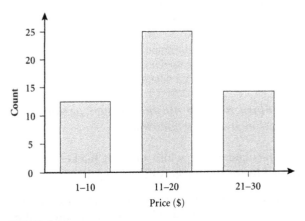

FIGURE 3.19

Equal-width histogram for *price*, where values are aggregated so that each bucket has a uniform width of $10.

V-Optimal and MaxDiff histograms tend to be the most accurate and practical. Histograms are highly effective at approximating both sparse and dense data, as well as highly skewed and uniform data. The histograms described earlier for single attributes can be extended for multiple attributes. *Multidimensional histograms* can capture dependencies between attributes. Such histograms have been found effective in approximating data with up to five attributes. More studies are needed regarding the effectiveness of multidimensional histograms for very high dimensions. Singleton buckets are useful for storing outliers with high frequency.

Clustering

Clustering techniques consider data tuples as objects. They partition the objects into groups or *clusters*, so that objects within a cluster are "similar" to one another and "dissimilar" to objects in other clusters. Similarity is commonly defined in terms of how "close" the objects are in space, based on a distance function. The "quality" of a cluster may be represented by its *diameter*, the maximum distance between any two objects in the cluster. *Centroid distance* is an alternative measure of cluster quality and is defined as the average distance of each cluster object from the cluster centroid (denoting the "average object," or average point in space for the cluster). Figure 3.12 of Section 3.3.2 shows a 2-D plot of customer data with respect to customer locations in a city, where the centroid of each cluster is shown with a "+." Three data clusters are visible.

In data reduction, the cluster representations of the data are used to replace the actual data. The effectiveness of this technique depends on the nature of the data. It is much more effective for data that can be organized into distinct clusters than for smeared data.

In database systems, **multidimensional index trees** are primarily used for providing fast data access. They can also be used for hierarchical data reduction, providing a multiresolution clustering of the data. This can be used to provide approximate answers to queries. An index tree recursively partitions the multidimensional space for a given set of data objects, with the root node representing the entire space. Such trees are typically balanced, consisting of internal and leaf nodes. Each parent node contains keys and pointers to child nodes that, collectively, represent the space represented by the parent node. Each leaf node contains pointers to the data tuples they represent (or to the actual tuples).

An index tree can therefore store aggregate and detail data at varying levels of resolution or abstraction. It provides a hierarchy of clusterings of the dataset, where each cluster has a label that holds for the data contained in the cluster. If we consider each child of a parent node as a bucket, then an index tree can be considered as a *hierarchical histogram*. For example, consider the root of a B+-tree as shown in Figure 3.20, with pointers to the data keys 986, 3396, 5411, 8392, and 9544. Suppose that the tree contains 10,000 tuples with keys ranging from 1 to 9999. The data in the tree can be approximated by an equal-frequency histogram of six buckets for the key ranges 1 to 985, 986 to 3395, 3396 to 5410, 5411 to 8391, 8392 to 9543, and 9544 to 9999. Each bucket contains roughly 10,000/6 items. Similarly, each bucket is subdivided into smaller buckets, allowing for aggregate data at a finer-detailed level. The use of multidimensional index trees as a form of data reduction relies on an ordering of the attribute values in each dimension. Two-dimensional or multidimensional index trees include R-trees,

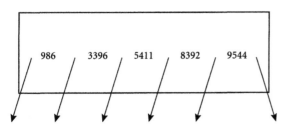

FIGURE 3.20

The root of a B+-tree for a given set of data.

quad-trees, and their variations. They are well suited for handling both sparse and skewed data.

There are many measures for defining clusters and cluster quality.

Sampling

Sampling can be used as a data reduction technique because it allows a large dataset to be represented by a much smaller random data sample (or subset). Suppose that a large dataset, D, contains N tuples. Let's look at the most common ways that we could sample D for data reduction, as illustrated in Figure 3.21:

Simple random sample without replacement (SRSWOR) of size s. This is created by drawing s of the N tuples from D ($s < N$), where the probability of drawing any tuple in D is $1/N$, that is, all tuples are equally likely to be sampled.

Simple random sample with replacement (SRSWR) of size s. This is similar to SRSWOR, except that each time a tuple is drawn from D, it is recorded and then *replaced*. That is, after a tuple is drawn, it is placed back in D so that it may be drawn again.

Cluster sample. If the tuples in D are grouped into M mutually disjoint "clusters," then an SRS of s clusters can be obtained, where $s < M$. For example, tuples in a database are usually retrieved a page at a time, so that each page can be considered a cluster. A reduced data representation can be obtained by applying, say, SRSWOR to the pages, resulting in a cluster sample of the tuples. Other clustering criteria conveying rich semantics can also be explored. For example, in a spatial database, we may choose to define clusters geographically based on how closely different areas are located.

Stratified sample. If D is divided into mutually disjoint parts called *strata*, a stratified sample of D is generated by obtaining an SRS at each stratum. This helps ensure a representative sample, especially when the data are skewed. For example, a stratified sample may be obtained from customer data, where a stratum is created for each customer age group. In this way, the age group having the smallest number of customers will be sure to be represented.

An advantage of sampling for data reduction is that the cost of obtaining a sample *is proportional to the size of the sample, s,* as opposed to N, the dataset

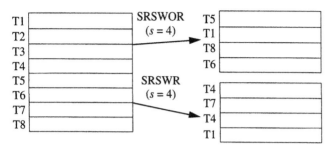

Cluster sample ($s = 2$)

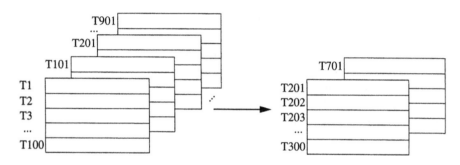

Stratified sample
(according to *age*)

T38	youth
T256	youth
T307	youth
T391	youth
T96	middle_aged
T117	middle_aged
T138	middle_aged
T263	middle_aged
T290	middle_aged
T308	middle_aged
T326	middle_aged
T387	middle_aged
T69	senior
T284	senior

T38	youth
T391	youth
T117	middle_aged
T138	middle_aged
T290	middle_aged
T326	middle_aged
T69	senior

FIGURE 3.21

Sampling can be used for data reduction.

size. Hence, sampling complexity is potentially *sublinear* to the size of the data. Other data reduction techniques can require at least one complete pass through *D*. For a fixed sample size, sampling complexity increases only linearly as the number of data dimensions, *n*, increases, whereas techniques using histograms, for example, increase exponentially in *n*.

When applied to data reduction, sampling is most commonly used to estimate the answer to an aggregate query. It is possible (using the central limit theorem) to determine a sufficient sample size for estimating a given function within a specified degree of error. This sample size, s, may be extremely small in comparison to N. Sampling is a natural choice for the progressive refinement of a reduced dataset. Simply increasing the sample size can further refine such a set.

3.6 DATA DISCRETIZATION AND CONCEPT HIERARCHY GENERATION

Data discretization techniques can be used to reduce the number of values for a given continuous attribute by dividing the range of the attribute into intervals. Interval labels can then be used to replace actual data values. Replacing numerous values of a continuous attribute by a small number of interval labels thereby reduces and simplifies the original data. This leads to a concise, easy-to-use, knowledge-level representation of mining results.

Discretization techniques can be categorized based on how the discretization is performed, such as whether it uses class information or which direction it proceeds (i.e., top-down versus bottom-up). If the discretization process uses class information, then we say it is *supervised discretization*. Otherwise, it is unsupervised. If the process starts by first finding one or a few points (called *split points* or *cut points*) to split the entire attribute range, and then repeats this recursively on the resulting intervals, it is called *top-down discretization* or *splitting*. This contrasts with *bottom-up discretization* or *merging*, which starts by considering all of the continuous values as potential split points, removes some by merging neighborhood values to form intervals, and then recursively applies this process to the resulting intervals. Discretization can be performed recursively on an attribute to provide a hierarchical or multiresolution partitioning of the attribute values, known as a concept hierarchy. Concept hierarchies are useful for mining at multiple levels of abstraction.

A concept hierarchy for a given numeric attribute defines a discretization of the attribute. Concept hierarchies can be used to reduce the data by collecting and replacing low-level concepts (such as numeric values for the attribute *age*) with higher-level concepts (such as *youth, middle-aged*, or *senior*). Although detail is lost by such data generalization, the generalized data may be more meaningful and easier to interpret. This contributes to a consistent representation of data mining results among multiple mining tasks, which is a common requirement. In addition, mining on a reduced dataset requires fewer input/output operations and is more efficient than mining on a larger, ungeneralized dataset. Because of these benefits, discretization techniques and concept hierarchies are typically applied before data mining as a preprocessing step, rather than during mining. An example of a concept hierarchy for the attribute *price* is given in Figure 3.22.

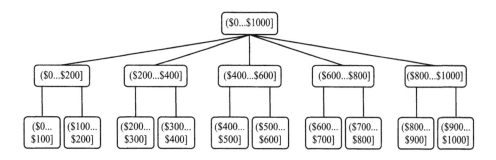

FIGURE 3.22

A concept hierarchy for the attribute *price*, where an interval ($X . . . $Y] denotes the range from $X (exclusive) to $Y (inclusive).

More than one concept hierarchy can be defined for the same attribute in order to accommodate the needs of various users.

Manual definition of concept hierarchies can be a tedious and time-consuming task for a user or a domain expert. Fortunately, several discretization methods can be used to automatically generate or dynamically refine concept hierarchies for numeric attributes. Furthermore, many hierarchies for categorical attributes are implicit within the database schema and can be automatically defined at the schema definition level.

Let's look at the generation of concept hierarchies for numeric and categorical data.

3.6.1 Discretization and Concept Hierarchy Generation for Numeric Data

It is difficult and laborious to specify concept hierarchies for numeric attributes because of the wide diversity of possible data ranges and the frequent updates of data values. Such manual specification can also be quite arbitrary.

Concept hierarchies for numeric attributes can be constructed automatically based on data discretization. We examine the following methods: *binning, histogram analysis, entropy-based discretization, χ^2-merging, cluster analysis*, and *discretization by intuitive partitioning*. In general, each method assumes that the values to be discretized are sorted in ascending order.

Binning

Binning is a top-down splitting technique based on a specified number of bins. Section 3.3.2 discussed binning methods for data smoothing. These methods are also used as discretization methods for numerosity reduction and concept hierarchy generation. For example, attribute values can be discretized by applying equal-width or equal-frequency binning and then replacing each bin value by the bin mean or median, as in *smoothing by bin means* or *smoothing by bin medians*, respectively. These techniques can be applied recursively to the resulting partitions to generate concept hierarchies. Binning does not use class information and is therefore an unsupervised discretization technique. It is sensitive to the user-specified number of bins, as well as the presence of outliers.

Histogram Analysis

Like binning, histogram analysis is an unsupervised discretization technique because it does not use class information. Histograms partition the values for an attribute, A, into disjoint ranges called *buckets*. Histograms were introduced in Section 3.2.3. Partitioning rules for defining histograms were described in Section 3.5.4. In an *equal-width* histogram, for example, the values are partitioned into equal-sized partitions or ranges (such as in Figure 3.19 for *price*, where each bucket has a width of $10). With an *equal-frequency* histogram, the values are partitioned so that, ideally, each partition contains the same number of data tuples. The histogram analysis algorithm can be applied recursively to each partition to automatically generate a multilevel concept hierarchy, with the procedure terminating once a prespecified number of concept levels has been reached. A *minimum interval size* can also be used per level to control the recursive procedure. This specifies the minimum width of a partition, or the minimum number of values for each partition at each level. Histograms can also be partitioned based on cluster analysis of the data distribution, as described next.

Entropy-Based Discretization

Entropy is one of the most commonly used discretization measures. Claude Shannon first introduced it in pioneering work on information theory and the concept of information gain. Entropy-based discretization is a supervised, top-down splitting technique. It explores class distribution information in its calculation and determination of split points (data values for partitioning an attribute range). To discretize a numeric attribute, A, the method selects the value of A that has the minimum entropy as a split point and recursively partitions the resulting intervals to arrive at a hierarchical discretization. Such discretization forms a concept hierarchy for A.

Let D consist of data tuples defined by a set of attributes and a class-label attribute. The class-label attribute provides the class information per tuple. The basic method for entropy-based discretization of an attribute A within the set is as follows:

1. Each value of A can be considered as a potential interval boundary or split point (denoted *split_point*) to partition the range of A. That is, a split point for A can partition the tuples in D into two subsets satisfying the conditions $A \leq split\_point$ and $A > split\_point$, respectively, thereby creating a binary discretization.

2. Entropy-based discretization, as mentioned previously, uses information regarding the class label of tuples. To explain the intuition behind entropy-based

discretization, we must take a glimpse at classification. Suppose we want to classify the tuples in D by partitioning on attribute A and some split point. Ideally, we would like this partitioning to result in an exact classification of the tuples. For example, if we had two classes, we would hope that all of the tuples of, say, class C_1 will fall into one partition, and all of the tuples of class C_2 will fall into the other partition. However, this is unlikely. For example, the first partition may contain many tuples of C_1, but also some of C_2. How much more information would we still need for a perfect classification, after this partitioning? This amount is called the *expected information requirement* for classifying a tuple in D based on partitioning by A. It is given by

$$Info_A(D) = \frac{|D_1|}{|D|} Entropy(D_1) + \frac{|D_2|}{|D|} Entropy(D_2) \qquad (3.15)$$

where D_1 and D_2 correspond to the tuples in D satisfying the conditions $A \leq$ *split_point* and $A >$ *split_point*, respectively; $|D|$ is the number of tuples in D, and so on. The entropy function for a given set is calculated based on the class distribution of the tuples in the set. For example, given m classes, $C_1, C_2, \ldots, C_m$, the entropy of D_1 is

$$Entropy(D_1) = -\sum_{i=1}^{m} p_i \log_2(p_i) \qquad (3.16)$$

where p_i is the probability of class C_i in D_1, determined by dividing the number of tuples of class C_i in D_1 by $|D_1|$, the total number of tuples in D_1. Therefore, when selecting a split point for attribute A, we want to pick the attribute value that gives the minimum expected information requirement (i.e., min($Info_A(D)$)). This would result in the minimum amount of expected information (still) required to perfectly classify the tuples after partitioning by $A \leq$ *split_point* and $A >$ *split_point*. This is equivalent to the attribute-value pair with the maximum information gain. Note that the value of $Entropy(D_2)$ can be computed similarly as in Equation 3.16.

"*But our task is discretization, not classification!*" you may exclaim. This is true. We use the split point to partition the range of A into two intervals, corresponding to $A \leq$ *split_point* and $A >$ *split_point*.

3. The process of determining a split point is recursively applied to each partition obtained, until some stopping criterion is met, such as when the minimum information requirement on all candidate split points is less than a small threshold, ε, or when the number of intervals is greater than a threshold, *max_interval*.

Entropy-based discretization can reduce data size. Unlike the other methods mentioned here so far, entropy-based discretization uses class information. This makes it more likely that the interval boundaries (split-points) are defined to occur in places that may improve classification accuracy. The entropy and information gain measures described here are also used for decision tree induction. These measures are revisited in greater detail in Section 3.3.2.

Interval Merging by χ^2 Analysis

ChiMerge is a χ^2-based discretization method. The discretization methods that we have studied up to this point have all employed a top-down, splitting strategy. This contrasts with ChiMerge, which employs a bottom-up approach by finding the best neighboring intervals and then merging these to form larger intervals, recursively. The method is supervised in that it uses class information. The basic notion is that for accurate discretization, the relative class frequencies should be fairly consistent within an interval. Therefore, if two adjacent intervals have a very similar distribution of classes, then the intervals can be merged. Otherwise, they should remain separate.

ChiMerge proceeds as follows. Initially, each distinct value of a numeric attribute A is considered to be one interval. χ^2 tests are performed for every pair of adjacent intervals. Adjacent intervals with the least χ^2 values are merged together, because low χ^2 values for a pair indicate similar class distributions. This merging process proceeds recursively until a predefined stopping criterion is met.

The χ^2 statistic was introduced in Section 3.4.1 on data integration, where we explained its use to detect a correlation relationship between two categorical attributes (Equation 3.9). Because ChiMerge treats intervals as discrete categories, Equation 3.9 can be applied. The χ^2 statistic tests the hypothesis that two adjacent intervals for a given attribute are independent of the class. Following the method in Example 3.1, we can construct a contingency table for our data. The contingency table has two columns (representing the two adjacent intervals) and m rows, where m is the number of distinct classes. Applying Equation 3.9 here, the cell value o_{ij} is the count of tuples in the ith interval and j^{th} class. Similarly, the expected frequency of o_{ij} is e_{ij} = (number of tuples in interval i) × (number of tuples in class j)/N, where N is the total number of data tuples. Low χ^2 values for an interval pair indicate that the intervals are independent of the class and can, therefore, be merged.

The stopping criterion is typically determined by three conditions. First, merging stops when χ^2 values of all pairs of adjacent intervals exceed some threshold, which is determined by a specified significance level. A too (or very) high value of significance level for the χ^2 test may cause overdiscretization, whereas a too (or very) low value may lead to underdiscretization. Typically, the significance level is set between 0.10 and 0.01. Second, the number of intervals cannot be over a prespecified *max-interval*, such as 10 to 15. Finally, recall that the premise behind ChiMerge is that the relative class frequencies should be fairly consistent within an interval. In practice, some inconsistency is allowed, although this should be no more than a prespecified threshold, such as 3 percent, which may be estimated from the training data. This last condition can be used to remove irrelevant attributes from the dataset.

Cluster Analysis

Cluster analysis is a popular data discretization method. A clustering algorithm can be applied to discretize a numeric attribute, A, by partitioning the values of A into clusters or groups. Clustering takes the distribution of A into consideration, as well as the closeness of data points, and therefore is able to produce high-quality discretization results. Clustering can be used to generate a concept hierarchy for A by following either a top-down splitting strategy or a bottom-up merging strategy, where each cluster forms a node of the concept hierarchy. In the former, each initial cluster or partition may be further decomposed into several subclusters, forming a lower level of the hierarchy. In the latter, clusters are formed by repeatedly grouping neighboring clusters to form higher-level concepts.

Discretization by Intuitive Partitioning

Although the preceding discretization methods are useful in the generation of numeric hierarchies, many users would like to see numeric ranges partitioned into relatively uniform, easy-to-read intervals that appear intuitive or "natural." For example, annual salaries broken into ranges like ($50,000, $60,000] are often more desirable than ranges like ($51,263.98, $60,872.34], obtained by, say, some sophisticated clustering analysis.

The **3-4-5 rule** can be used to segment numeric data into relatively uniform, natural-seeming intervals. In general, the rule partitions a given range of data into 3, 4, or 5 relatively equal-width intervals, recursively and level by level, based on the value range at the most significant digit. We will illustrate the use of the rule with an example later. The rule is as follows:

- If an interval covers 3, 6, 7, or 9 distinct values at the most significant digit, then partition the range into three intervals (three equal-width intervals for 3, 6, and 9; and three intervals in the grouping of 2-3-2 for 7).

- If it covers 2, 4, or 8 distinct values at the most significant digit, then partition the range into four equal-width intervals.

- If it covers 1, 5, or 10 distinct values at the most significant digit, then partition the range into five equal-width intervals.

The rule can be recursively applied to each interval, creating a concept hierarchy for the given numeric attribute. Real-world data often contain extremely large positive or negative outlier values, which could distort any top-down discretization method based on minimum and maximum data values. For example, the assets of a few people could be several orders of magnitude higher than those of others in the same dataset. Discretization based on the maximal asset values may lead to a highly biased hierarchy. Thus, the top-level discretization can be performed based on the range of data values representing the majority (e.g., 5th percentile to 95th percentile) of the given data. The extremely high or low values beyond the top-level discretization will form distinct interval(s) that can be handled separately, but in a similar manner.

The following example illustrates the use of the 3-4-5 rule for the automatic construction of a numeric hierarchy.

EXAMPLE 3.6

Numeric Concept Hierarchy Generation by Intuitive Partitioning

Suppose that profits at different branches of *AllElectronics* for the year 2004 cover a wide range, from –$351,976.00 to $4,700,896.50. A user desires the automatic generation of a concept hierarchy for *profit*. For improved readability, we use the notation (l . . . r] to represent the interval (l, r]. For example, (–$1,000,000 . . . $0] denotes the range from –$1,000,000 (exclusive) to $0 (inclusive).

Suppose that the data within the 5th and 95th percentiles are between $159,876 and $1,838,761. The results of applying the 3-4-5 rule are shown in Figure 3.23.

1. Based on the preceding information, the minimum and maximum values are *MIN* = –$351,976.00, and *MAX* = $4,700,896.50. The low (5th percentile) and high (95th percentile) values to be considered for the top or first level of discretization are *LOW* = –$159,876, and *HIGH* = $1,838,761.

2. Given LOW and HIGH, the most significant digit (*msd*) is at the million dollar digit position (i.e., *msd* = 1,000,000). Rounding *LOW* down to the million dollar digit, we get *LOW'* = –$1,000,000; rounding *HIGH* up to the million dollar digit, we get *HIGH'* = +$2,000,000.

3. Because this interval ranges over three distinct values at the most significant digit, that is, (2,000,000 – (–1,000,000))/1,000,000 = 3, the segment is partitioned into three equal-width subsegments according to the 3-4-5 rule: (–$1,000,000 . . . $0], ($0 . . . $1,000,000], and ($1,000,000 . . . $2,000,000]. This represents the top tier of the hierarchy.

4. We now examine the MIN and MAX values to see how they "fit" into the first-level partitions. Because the first interval (–$1,000,000 . . . $0] covers the *MIN* value, that is, *LOW'* < *MIN*, we can adjust the left boundary of this interval to make the interval smaller. The most significant digit of *MIN* is the hundred thousand digit position. Rounding *MIN* down to this position, we get *MIN'* = –$400,000. Therefore, the first interval is redefined as (–$400,000 . . . 0].

    Because the last interval, ($1,000,000 . . . $2,000,000], does not cover the *MAX* value— that is, *MAX* > *HIGH'*—we need to create a new interval to cover it. Rounding up *MAX* at its most significant digit position, the new interval is ($2,000,000 . . . $5,000,000]. Therefore, the hierarchy's topmost level contains four partitions: (–$400,000 . . . $0], ($0 . . . $1,000,000], ($1,000,000 . . . $2,000,000], and ($2,000,000 . . . $5,000,000].

5. Recursively, each interval can be further partitioned according to the 3-4-5 rule to form the next lower level of the hierarchy:
    - The first interval, (–$400,000 . . . $0], is partitioned into four subintervals: (–$400,000 . . . –$300,000], (–$300,000 . . . –$200,000], (–$200,000 . . . –$100,000], and (–$100,000 . . . $0].
    - The second interval, ($0 . . . $1,000,000], is partitioned into five subintervals: ($0 . . . $200,000], ($200,000 . . . $400,000], ($400,000 . . . $600,000], ($600,000 . . . $800,000], and ($800,000 . . . $1,000,000].

- The third interval, ($1,000,000...$2,000,000], is partitioned into five subintervals: ($1,000,000...$1,200,000], ($1,200,000...$1,400,000], ($1,400,000...$1,600,000], ($1,600,000...$1,800,000], and ($1,800,000...$2,000,000].
- The last interval, ($2,000,000...$5,000,000], is partitioned into three subintervals: ($2,000,000...$3,000,000], ($3,000,000...$4,000,000], and ($4,000,000...$5,000,000].

Similarly, the 3-4-5 rule can be carried on iteratively at deeper levels, as necessary.

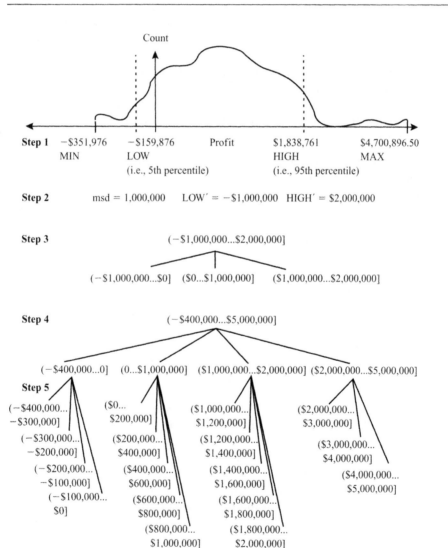

FIGURE 3.23

Automatic generation of a concept hierarchy for profit based on the 3-4-5 rule.

3.6.2 Concept Hierarchy Generation for Categorical Data

Categorical data are discrete data. Categorical attributes have a finite (but possibly large) number of distinct values, with no ordering among the values. Examples include *geographic location, job category*, and *item type*. There are several methods for the generation of concept hierarchies for categorical data:

Specification of a partial ordering of attributes explicitly at the schema level by users or experts. Concept hierarchies for categorical attributes or dimensions typically involve a group of attributes. A user or expert can easily define a concept hierarchy by specifying a partial or total ordering of the attributes at the schema level. For example, a relational database or a dimension *location* of a data warehouse may contain the following group of attributes: *street, city, province_or_state*, and *country*. A hierarchy can be defined by specifying the total ordering among these attributes at the schema level, such as *street < city < province_or_state < country*.

Specification of a portion of a hierarchy by explicit data grouping. This is essentially the manual definition of a portion of a concept hierarchy. In a large database, it is unrealistic to define an entire concept hierarchy by explicit value enumeration. On the contrary, we can easily specify explicit groupings for a small portion of intermediate-level data. For example, after specifying that *province* and *country* form a hierarchy at the schema level, a user could define some intermediate levels manually, such as "{*Alberta, Saskatchewan, Manitobag*} ⊂ *prairies_Canada*" and "{*British Columbia, prairies_Canada*} ⊂ *Western Canada*".

Specification of a set of attributes, but not of their partial ordering. A user may specify a set of attributes forming a concept hierarchy but omit to explicitly state their partial ordering. The system can then try to automatically generate the attribute ordering so as to construct a meaningful concept hierarchy. *"Without knowledge of data semantics, how can a hierarchical ordering for an arbitrary set of categorical attributes be found?"* Consider the following observation that because higher-level concepts generally cover several subordinate lower-level concepts, an attribute defining a high concept level (e.g., *country*) will usually contain a smaller number of distinct values than an attribute defining a lower concept level (e.g., *street*). Based on this observation, a concept hierarchy can be automatically generated based on the number of distinct values per attribute in the given attribute set. The attribute with the most distinct values is placed at the lowest level of the hierarchy. The lower the number of distinct values an attribute has, the higher it is in the generated concept hierarchy. This heuristic rule works well in many cases. Users or experts may apply some local-level swapping or adjustments when necessary, after examination of the generated hierarchy.

Let's examine an example of this method.

EXAMPLE 3.7

Concept Hierarchy Generation Based on the Number of Distinct
Values per Attribute

Suppose a user selects a set of location-oriented attributes, *street, country, province_or_
state*, and *city*, from the *AllElectronics* database but does not specify the hierarchical ordering among the attributes.

A concept hierarchy for *location* can be generated automatically, as illustrated in Figure
3.24. First, sort the attributes in ascending order based on the number of distinct values in
each attribute. This results in the following (where the number of distinct values per attribute
is shown in parentheses): *country* (15), *province_or_state* (365), *city* (3567), and *street*
(674,339). Second, generate the hierarchy from the top down according to the sorted order,
with the first attribute at the top level and the last attribute at the bottom level. Finally, the
user can examine the generated hierarchy and, when necessary, modify it to reflect desired
semantic relationships among the attributes. In this example, it is obvious that there is no
need to modify the generated hierarchy.

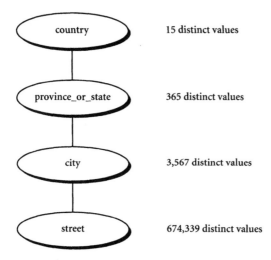

FIGURE 3.24

Automatic generation of a schema concept hierarchy based on the number of distinct
attribute values.

Note that this heuristic rule is not foolproof. For example, a time dimension
in a database may contain 20 distinct years, 12 distinct months, and 7 distinct
days. However, this does not suggest that the time hierarchy should be "*year* <
month < *days_of_the week*" with *days_of_the week* at the top of the hierarchy.

Specification of only a partial set of attributes. Sometimes a user can be sloppy
when defining a hierarchy, or have only a vague idea about what should be
included in a hierarchy. Consequently, the user may have included only a small

---

EXAMPLE 3.8

Concept Hierarchy Generation Using Prespecified Semantic Connections

Suppose that a data mining expert (serving as an administrator) has pinned together the five attributes *number, street, city, province_ or_ state*, and *country*, because they are closely linked semantically regarding the notion of *location*. If a user were to specify only the attribute *city* for a hierarchy defining *location*, the system can automatically drag in all of the preceding five semantically related attributes to form a hierarchy. The user may choose to drop any of these attributes, such as *number* and *street*, from the hierarchy, keeping *city* as the lowest conceptual level in the hierarchy.

---

subset of the relevant attributes in the hierarchy specification. For example, instead of including all of the hierarchically relevant attributes for *location*, the user may have specified only *street* and *city*. To handle such partially specified hierarchies, it is important to embed data semantics in the database schema so that attributes with tight semantic connections can be pinned together. In this way, the specification of one attribute may trigger a whole group of semantically tightly linked attributes to be "dragged in" to form a complete hierarchy. Users, however, should have the option to override this feature, as necessary.

3.7 SUMMARY

Data preprocessing is an important issue for both data warehousing and data mining, as real-world data tend to be incomplete, noisy, and inconsistent. Data preprocessing includes data cleaning, data integration, data transformation, and data reduction.

Descriptive data summarization provides the analytical foundation for data preprocessing. The basic statistical measures for data summarization include *mean, weighted mean, median*, and *mode* for measuring the central tendency of data and *range, quartiles, interquartile range, variance*, and *standard deviation* for measuring the dispersion of data. Graphical representations, such as *histograms, boxplots, quantile plots, quantile-quantile plots, scatter plots*, and *scatter-plot matrices*, facilitate visual inspection of the data and are thus useful for data preprocessing and mining.

Data cleaning routines attempt to fill in missing values, smooth out noise while identifying outliers, and correct inconsistencies in the data. Data cleaning is usually performed as an iterative two-step process consisting of discrepancy detection and data transformation.

Data integration combines data from multiple sources to form a coherent data store. Metadata, correlation analysis, data conflict detection, and the resolution of semantic heterogeneity contribute toward smooth data integration.

Data transformation routines convert the data into appropriate forms for mining. For example, attribute data may be **normalized** so as to fall between a small range, such as 0.0 to 1.0.

Data reduction techniques such as data cube aggregation, attribute subset selection, dimensionality reduction, numerosity reduction, and discretization can be used to obtain a reduced representation of the data while minimizing the loss of information content.

Data discretization and automatic generation of concept hierarchies for numeric data can involve techniques such as binning, histogram analysis, entropy-based discretization, χ^2 analysis, cluster analysis, and discretization by intuitive partitioning. For categorical data, concept hierarchies may be generated based on the number of distinct values of the attributes defining the hierarchy.

Although numerous methods of data preprocessing have been developed, data preprocessing remains an active area of research because of the huge amount of inconsistent or dirty data and the complexity of the problem.

3.8 RESOURCES

Data preprocessing is discussed in a number of textbooks, including English (1999), Pyle (1999), Loshin (2001), Redman (2001), and Dasu and Johnson (2003). More specific references to individual preprocessing techniques are given here.

Methods for descriptive data summarization have been studied in the statistics literature long before the onset of computers. Good summaries of statistical descriptive data mining methods include Freedman, Pisani, and Purves (1997) and Devore (1995). For statistics-based visualization of data using boxplots, quantile plots, quantile-quantile plots, scatter plots, and loess curves, see Cleveland (1993).

For discussion regarding data quality, see Redman (1992), Wang, Storey, and Firth (1995); Wand and Wang (1996); Ballou and Tayi (1999); and Olson (2003). Potter's Wheel (*http://control.cs.berkeley.edu/abc*), the interactive data cleaning tool described in Section 3.3.3, is presented in Raman and Hellerstein (2001). An example of the development of declarative languages for the specification of data transformation operators is given in Galhardas, Florescu, Shasha, et al. (2001). The handling of missing attribute values is discussed in Friedman (1977); Breiman, Friedman, Olshen, and Stone (1984); and Quinlan (1989). A method for the detection of outlier or "garbage" patterns in a handwritten character database is given in Guyon, Matic, and Vapnik (1996).

Binning and data normalization are treated in many texts, including Kennedy, Lee, Van Roy et al. (1998), Weiss and Indurkhya (1998), and Pyle (1999). Systems that include attribute (or feature) construction include BACON by Langley, Simon,

Bradshaw, and Zytkow (1987), Stagger by Schlimmer (1986), FRINGE by Pagallo (1989), and AQ17-DCI by Bloedorn and Michalski (1998). Attribute construction is also described in Liu and Motoda (1998). Dasu, Johnson, Muthukr-ishnan, and Shkapenyuk (2002) developed a system called Bellman wherein they propose a set of methods for building a data quality browser by mining on the structure of the database.

A good survey of data reduction techniques can be found in Barbará, Du Mouchel, Faloutos, et al. (1997). For algorithms on data cubes and their precomputation, see Sarawagi and Stonebraker (1994); Agarwal, Agrawal, Deshpande, et al. (1996); Harinarayan, Rajaraman, and Ullman (1996); Ross and Srivastava (1997); and Zhao, Deshpande, and Naughton (1997). Attribute subset selection (or *feature subset selection*) is described in many texts, such as Neter, Kutner, Nachtsheim, and Wasserman (1996); Dash and Liu (1997); and Liu and Motoda (1998a, 1998b). A combination forward selection and backward elimination method was proposed in Siedlecki and Sklansky (1988). A wrapper approach to attribute selection is described in Kohavi and John (1997). Unsupervised attribute subset selection is described in Dash, Liu, and Yao (1997).

For a description of wavelets for dimensionality reduction, see Press, Teukolosky, Vetterling, and Flannery (1996). A general account of wavelets can be found in Hubbard (1996). For a list of wavelet software packages, see Bruce, Donoho, and Gao (1996). Daubechies transforms are described in Daubechies (1992). The book by Press et al. (1996) includes an introduction to singular value decomposition for principal components analysis. Routines for PCA are included in most statistical software packages, such as SAS (*www.sas.com/SASHome. html*).

An introduction to regression and log-linear models can be found in several textbooks, such as James (1985), Dobson (1990), Johnson and Wichern (1992), Devore (1995), and Neter et al. (1996). For log-linear models (known as *multiplicative models* in the computer science literature), see Pearl (1988). For a general introduction to histograms, see Barbará et al. (1997) and Devore and Peck (1997). For extensions of single attribute histograms to multiple attributes, see Muralikrishna and DeWitt (1988) and Poosala and Ioannidis (1997).

A survey of multidimensional indexing structures is given in Gaede and Günther (1998). The use of multidimensional index trees for data aggregation is discussed in Aoki (1998). Index trees include R-trees (Guttman, 1984), quad-trees (Finkel and Bentley, 1974), and their variations. For discussion on sampling and data mining, see Kivinen and Mannila (1994) and John and Langley (1996).

There are many methods for assessing attribute relevance. Each has its own bias. The information gain measure is biased toward attributes with many values. Many alternatives have been proposed, such as gain ratio (Quinlan, 1993), which considers the probability of each attribute value. Other relevance measures include the gini index (Breiman, Friedman, Olshen, and Stone, 1984), the χ^2 contingency table statistic, and the uncertainty coefficient (Johnson and Wichern, 1992). For a comparison of attribute selection measures for decision tree induction, see

Buntine and Niblett (1992). For additional methods, see Liu and Motoda (1998b), Dash and Liu (1997), and Almuallim and Dietterich (1991).

Liu, Hussain, Tan, and Dash (2002) performed a comprehensive survey of data discretization methods. Entropy-based discretization with the C4.5 algorithm is described in Quinlan (1993). In Catlett (1991), the D-2 system binarizes a numeric feature recursively. ChiMerge by Kerber (1992) and Chi2 by Liu and Setiono (LS95) are methods for the automatic discretization of numeric attributes that both employ the χ^2 statistic. Fayyad and Irani (1993) apply the minimum description length principle to determine the number of intervals for numeric discretization. Concept hierarchies and their automatic generation from categorical data are described in Han and Fu (1994).

Physical Design for Decision Support, Warehousing, and OLAP

The concept of using a data storage area to support the calculations of a general-purpose computer date back to the mid-nineteenth century. The year 1837 is not a mistake for the above quotation! The source is a paper titled "On the Mathematical Powers of the Calculating Engine" that was published by Charles Babbage in 1837. This paper details the analytical engine, a plan for a mechanical computer. The organization of the analytical engine became the inspiration for the electronic numerical integrator and computer (ENIAC) more than one hundred years later. The ENIAC was the first general-purpose electronic computer, which in turn influenced the organization of computers in common use today.

Surprisingly, this quote from well over 150 years ago describes the current data warehousing and online analytical processing (OLAP) technologies. The original data is placed in the fact tables and dimension tables of a data warehouse. Intermediate results are often calculated and stored on disk as materialized views, also known as materialized query tables (MQTs). The materialized views can be further queried until the required results are found. We focus on two decision support technologies in this chapter: data warehousing and OLAP. We detail the physical design issues that arise relative to these decision support technologies.

4.1 WHAT IS ONLINE ANALYTICAL PROCESSING?

Online analytical processing is a service that typically sits on top of a data warehouse. The data warehouse provides the infrastructure that supplies the detailed data. Data warehouses often contain hundreds of millions of rows of historical data. Answering queries posed directly against the detailed data can consume valuable computer resources. The purpose of OLAP is to answer queries quickly from the large amount of underlying data. The queries posed against OLAP systems

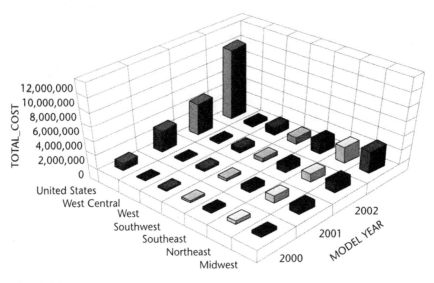

FIGURE 4.1

Graph example produced from Cognos PowerPlay.

typically "group by" certain attributes and apply aggregation functions against other attributes. For example, a manager may be interested in looking at total cost, grouped by year and region. Most OLAP systems offer a graphical representation of the results (Figure 4.1).

Figure 4.1 includes two-dimensional attributes, namely location and model year, organized orthogonally. The third axis represents the magnitude of the measure of interest—the total cost. We are looking at a subset of the possible dimensions and measures for this dataset. The database used to generate this graph contains six dimension attributes available for "group by" and four measures available for aggregation. The schema for this database is discussed further in Sections 4.2 and 4.3. The user selected the location at the region level and the model year dimensions along with the total cost in order to view the graph shown in Figure 4.1. The data space can be conceptualized as a hyperdimensional cube, with dimension values slicing across each dimension. Each cell of the cube contains values for the measures corresponding to the dimension values at that cell.

OLAP systems are organized for easy manipulation. Dimensions are easily added, replaced, or removed from the display. For example, we can replace the location dimension with the problem dimension using a simple drag-and-drop action, quickly changing the view to observe the total cost grouped by problem and model year. Likewise, we can change the measure to examine the sum of labor costs, if we decide to focus on labor. If we spot a dominant problem, we can double-click on the column of interest, and "drill down" into more detailed data. OLAP systems make exploring large amounts of data easy and quick.

How exactly is this service accomplished? Most OLAP systems rely on saving summary results in materialized views. Because the materialized views are summary data, they are usually much smaller than the tables containing the detailed information. When a query is posed, the materialized views are utilized to obtain a quick response, avoiding calculating the results from the huge amount of underlying data. An OLAP system automatically decides which views to materialize to achieve good performance.

There are three general categories of storage mechanisms in OLAP systems: relational OLAP (ROLAP), multidimensional OLAP (MOLAP), and hybrid OLAP (HOLAP). ROLAP uses standard relational tables to store data, typically using the dimensions as a composite primary key. Each row represents a cell of the data cube. Empty cells are not explicitly represented in ROLAP. MOLAP stores data on disk organized by location in the cube. Each cell is represented by a fixed, calculable location. Empty cells consume space in MOLAP representations. It is possible to utilize compression techniques to reduce the wasted space in MOLAP. It is generally recognized that ROLAP is better when the data is sparse, and MOLAP is good when the data is dense. Sparsity and density of the data can be measured in terms of the number of distinct keys in the data, compared to the number of possible key combinations. Let's illustrate with a simple example and then discuss HOLAP.

Imagine a grocery store that tracks customer sales. The customer presents a membership card and receives discounts for participating. The store tracks the customer ID, the items, and the date sold. Figure 4.2 illustrates a small portion of the data, showing the fruits bought by a single customer during one week. An X in a cell means that a transaction took place for the given combination of dimension values. The customer bought apples and bananas on Monday and bought oranges and strawberries on Wednesday. The table can be thought of as four separate views. The upper left box contains the most detailed data. The weekly subtotals for each fruit are contained in the upper right box. The fruit subtotals for each day are contained in the lower left box. The grand total is contained in

	M	Tu	W	Th	F	Week
Apples	X					X
Bananas	X					X
Oranges			X			X
Strawberries			X			X
Kiwis						
Fruits	X		X			X

FIGURE 4.2

Aggregation increases data density.

the lower right box. The data density of the most detailed data, weekly subtotals, fruit subtotals, and the grand totals, are 0.12, 0.4, 0.8, and 1.0, respectively. Generally, aggregating data from one view into another view increases the data density.

The difference in data density from the core data to summary views can be very marked. Extending our grocery store example, let's say that the store has 3000 items available, and the average customer buys 30 distinct items per visit, shopping once a week. The data density of the core data is (30/3000)(1/5) = 0.002. However, if we summarize the data across all customers, then it would not be unreasonable to have a data density of say 0.95 (i.e., most items have some units sold on any given day). Because ROLAP performs well for sparse data and MOLAP performs best for dense data, a useful strategy might be to store the sparse data using ROLAP and the dense data using MOLAP. This hybrid approach is called HOLAP. Some OLAP systems offer ROLAP, MOLAP, and HOLAP options.

4.2 DIMENSION HIERARCHIES

The ability to view different levels of detail is very useful when exploring data. OLAP systems allow "drill-down" operations to move from summary to more detailed data and "roll-up" operations to move from detailed to summary data. For example, the user viewing the graph in Figure 4.1 may be curious to find out more detail on the large amount of cost in the Midwest region. Drilling down on the Midwest region shows summary data for states in the Midwest. Perhaps Michigan dominates costs in the Midwest. The user may wish to further drill down on Michigan to view data at the city or dealership level. The location information can be stored in a dimension table named "Location." The levels of the location dimension may be represented as attributes in the location table. Figure 4.3 is a simple Unified Modeling Language (UML) class diagram, showing the attributes of the location table, supporting a location hierarchy. We indicate the primary key using the stereotype «pk».

Notice that this dimension table is not normalized. Data warehouse design is driven by efficiency of query response and simplicity. Normalization is not the

Location
«pk» loc_id dealership city state-province region country

FIGURE 4.3

Example of a dimension table with hierarchy.

«table» Date_Dimension	«view» Production_Date	«view» Repair_Date
«pk»date_id date_desc week month quarter yr	«pk»prod_date_id prod_date_desc prod_week prod_month prod_quarter prod_year	«pk»Repair_date_id Repair_date_desc Repair_week Repair_month Repair_quarter Repair_year

FIGURE 4.4

Example of date dimensions with hierarchies.

driving factor as it is in the design of databases for daily transactions. Dimensional modeling is the dominant approach utilized for designing data warehouses. The book on logical design (Teorey, Lightstone, & Nadeau 2006) includes an overview of the dimensional modeling approach. Kimball and Ross (2002) is an excellent and detailed resource covering the dimensional modeling approach for data warehousing.

Figure 4.4 illustrates two date dimensions that are implemented as views. The Production_Date dimension and the Repair_Date dimension are similarly structured, with the same underlying data. Following the recommendations of Kimball and Ross (2002), in such cases we implement one underlying table and use a view fulfilling each role, presenting separate date dimensions.

4.3 STAR AND SNOWFLAKE SCHEMAS

The dimension tables are used to group data in various ways, offering the user the freedom to explore the data at different levels. The measures to be aggregated are kept in a central table known as a *fact table*. The fact table is surrounded by the dimension tables.

The fact table is composed of dimension attributes and measures. The dimension attributes are foreign keys referencing the dimension tables. Figure 4.5 illustrates what is commonly known as a *star schema*. The Warranty_Claim table is the fact table, and the six surrounding tables are the dimension tables. Star schemas are the dominant configuration in the context of data warehousing.

The foreign keys are indicated using the «fk» stereotype. Notice also the «dd» stereotype on the claim_id attribute. This signifies a degenerate dimension. The claim_id is included to maintain the granularity at the claim level in the fact table. Degenerate dimensions do not have any associated dimension table. The dimension attributes form a superkey to the fact table, because the values of the dimension attributes uniquely identify a cell in the data cube and therefore determine the values of the measures associated with the cell. Sometimes the set of

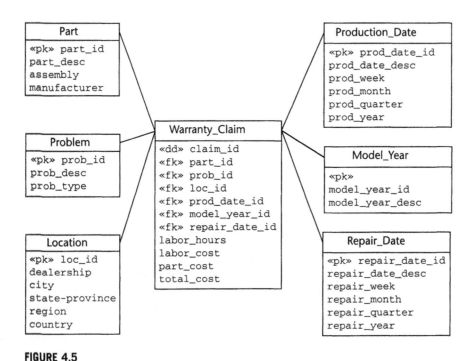

FIGURE 4.5

Example of a star schema.

dimension attributes also forms the primary key of the fact table. It is possible for a proper subset of the dimension attributes to form a candidate key. Such is the case in Figure 4.5, where claim_id by itself determines all other attributes in the table, making it a candidate key.

The star schema is an efficient design in the context of data warehousing. Performance gains are possible with a star schema when the environment is dominated by reads. This is exactly the case in a data warehouse environment. Because the data is mostly historical, the reads predominate, and the star schema is a winner.

The snowflake schema is another configuration that sometimes arises in data warehouse design. If you normalize the dimension tables in a star schema, you end up with a snowflake schema. Figure 4.6 shows the snowflake schema equivalent to the star schema of Figure 4.5. As you can see, there are many more tables. Most queries require many joins with the snowflake schema, whereas the dimension tables in the star schema are only one step away from the fact table. Most database systems implement an efficient "star join" to support the star schema configuration. The efficiency and simplicity are the primary reasons why the star schema is a common pattern in data warehouse design.

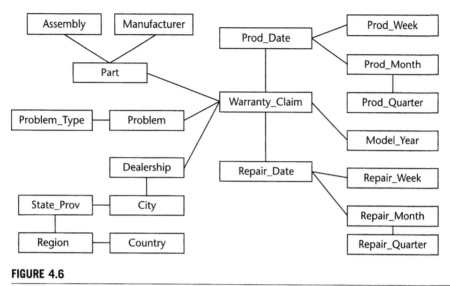

FIGURE 4.6

Example of a snowflake schema.

4.4 WAREHOUSES AND MARTS

Data warehouses typically contain large amounts of historical data. Data can feed into the data warehouse from multiple databases. For example, a large company may have many plants, each with its own database for managing day-to-day operations. The company may wish to look for overall trends across the data from all plants. Each plant may have a different database schema. The names of the tables and attributes can differ between source databases. A plant in the United States may have an attribute named "state," whereas another plant in Canada may use an attribute named "province." The values of corresponding attributes may vary from plant to plant. Maybe one plant uses "B" as an operational code specifying a "blue" widget, and another plant uses "B" to specify "black." The pertinent data needs to be extracted from the feeder database into a staging area. The data is cleaned and transformed in the staging area. Corresponding attributes are mapped to the same data warehouse attribute. Disparate operational codes are replaced with consistent surrogate IDs. Terminology is standardized across the company. Then the data is loaded into the data warehouse. Moving data from the feeder databases into the data warehouse is often referred to as an *extract, transform, and load (ETL) process*. Data in the warehouse can then be explored in a variety of ways, including OLAP, data mining, report generators, and ad hoc query tools. Figure 4.7 illustrates the overall flow of data.

Data warehouse schemas are typically arrived at through the dimensional modeling approach. The business processes of interest are determined. For example, a company may be interested in exploring data from scheduling, productivity

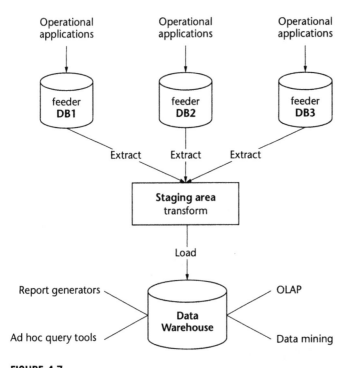

FIGURE 4.7

Basic data warehouse architecture.

tracking, and job costing. The data from each business process is destined to become a star schema. Some of the business processes may share dimensions. For example, the Cost_Center dimension is meaningful for scheduling, productivity tracking, and job costing. A useful tool for capturing the commonality of dimensions between business processes is the data warehouse bus. Table 4.1 shows a data warehouse bus where each row represents a business process and each column represents a dimension. Each X indicates that the given dimension is applicable to the business process. The dimensions that are shared across business processes should be "conformed." That is, each dimension and its levels should be known by the same names and have the same meanings across the entire enterprise; likewise for the values contained by said dimension levels. This is important so that data can be compared across business processes where meaningful, and people can discuss the data in the same terms from department to department, facilitating meaningful communication. The dimension data can be thought of as flowing through the data warehouse bus.

The data warehouse schema can contain multiple star schemas, with shared dimensions as indicated by the data warehouse bus. Figure 4.8 illustrates the data warehouse schema corresponding to the data warehouse bus shown in Table 4.1.

Table 4.1 Example of Data Warehouse Bus

	Shape	Color	Texture	Density	Size	Estimate Date	Win Date	Customer	Promotion	Cost Center	Sched Start Date	Sched Start Time	Sched Finish Date	Sched Finish Time	Actual Start Date	Actual Start Time	Actual Finish Date	Actual Finish Time	Employee	Invoice Date
Scheduling										x	x	x	x	x	x	x	x	x		
Productivity tracking										x					x	x	x	x	x	
Job costing	x	x	x	x	x			x	x	x										x

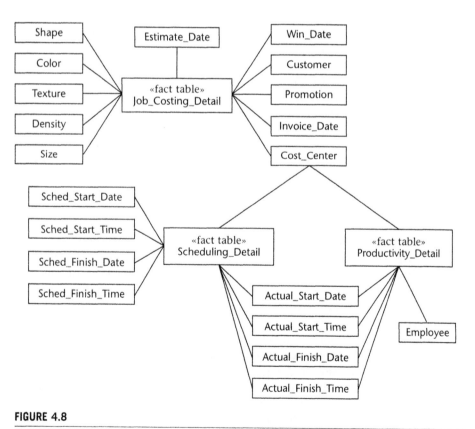

FIGURE 4.8

Example of a data warehouse constellation.

The attributes are elided because we are focusing on the fact tables and dimensions. We have marked the fact tables using a «fact table» stereotype, whereas the tables that are not marked are dimension tables. The configuration of multiple star schemas in a data warehouse forms a constellation.

Even though the constellation forms a united schema for the data warehouse, the people analyzing each business process may be interested only in their piece of the puzzle. A scheduler will naturally focus on the scheduling star schema. Each star schema can be thought of as a data mart for the corresponding business process. It is possible to deploy data marts on physically different machines. Perhaps the scheduling department has its own dedicated computer system that it prefers. When deploying data to physically distinct data marts, it is still important for the data to be conformed, so that everyone is communicating meaningfully.

4.5 SCALING UP THE SYSTEM

Horizontal table partitioning is common to many commercial systems, allowing the storage of a large table in meaningful pieces, according to the dimension values. The most common dimension for partitioning is time, but other dimensions can also be good candidates for partitioning, depending on the query processing required. For the time dimension, one option is to divide the data by month over n years and have $12 \times n$ partitions. The union of these partitions forms the whole table. One advantage of horizontal partitioning is that new data often only affects one partition, whereas the majority of the partitions remains unchanged. Partitioning can focus updates on a smaller set of data, improving update performance. Another advantage of horizontal partitioning is that the partitions can be stored on separate devices, and then a query can be processed in parallel, improving query response. Multiple CPUs can divide the work, and the system is not input/output (I/O) bound at the disks, because partitioning permits the number of disks to scale up with the amount of data. Range partitioning can be used to horizontally partition data.

To achieve parallel processing gains, many data warehouses and data marts exploit shared nothing partitioning. This is the strategy used by IBM's DB2 and NCR's Teradata products. Shared nothing partitioning horizontally partitions data into multiple logical or physical servers by hashing each table record to a partition. The technique has been massively successful, though design complexities are introduced.

Vertical table partitioning allows dividing a table physically by groups of columns. This has the advantage of putting rarely used columns out of the mainstream of query processing, and in general it helps match the processing requirements with the available columns. Some overhead is incurred because the table key must be replicated in each partition.

Pushing the query processing down toward the disks is a recent interesting innovation that allows scalability through parallelism. Netezza Corporation has

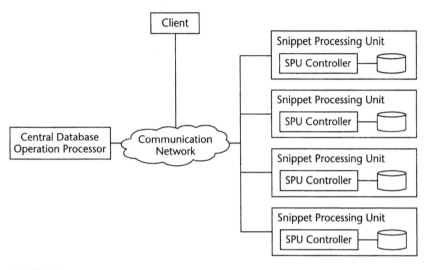

FIGURE 4.9

Netezza's asymmetric massively parallel processing architecture.

patented technology (see Hindshaw et al.) that uses active disks in a massively parallel processing (MPP) architecture. Figure 4.9 illustrates the general concept. Clients pose queries to the database over a communications network. The central database operation processor parses and optimizes the query, producing an execution plan where the query operations are broken into "snippets." Each snippet is assigned to a snippet processing unit (SPU). A SPU is composed of a SPU controller coupled with a storage device, typically a disk drive. Database tables can be distributed across the disk drives, either as redundant copies or sectioned with records assigned to specific SPUs. The SPU controller executes query processing of the snippet locally. Data can be streamed from the disk and processed without materializing the raw data in memory. Only the processed data is sent back to the central database operation processor, thereby reducing the demand on bandwidth. Netezza's approach exploits proprietary hardware. Other companies, like DATAllegro, are currently attempting to deploy similar data warehouse appliance technology using commodity components.

The Netezza approach is based on massive I/O parallelism, and one of Netezza's claims is that the technique obviates the need for index and materialized view design. After all, do you need indexes when you can scan more than a terabyte per minute? On the flip side, Netezza has no caching, no indexing. Every data request requires access to disk. The strategy is best suited to query processing needs and may not be ideal for active data warehousing, a current trend in data warehousing where data warehouses are becoming increasingly near real time. Active data warehouses include a larger and more frequent amount of inserts and update activity. This interesting technology is emerging, and the next few years will be telling in terms of its success. There are major gains in scalability from the parallelism obtained by distributing the query processing.

4.6 DSS, WAREHOUSING, AND OLAP DESIGN CONSIDERATIONS

Use the star schema approach rather than querying from normalized tables. The facts are central to the star schema, and the dimensions are only one step away. The star schema is efficient. The snowflake schema requires more joins and is less intuitive to navigate. The dimension tables of the star schema contain redundant data, but they are small compared to the fact table. Databases support efficient star joins.

Index each dimension attribute of the fact table. The dimension tables are used to select and group rows of the fact table. The dimension tables are the entrance into the fact table. Indexing each dimension attribute of the fact table is crucial for performance. Use bitmap indexes for each dimension attribute having a small cardinality of distinct values. Bitmap indexes are fast and small compared to B+tree indexes, when the number of distinct values is low. A bitmap index is implemented with a bitmap for each distinct value of the attribute. Every bitmap has one bit for each row in the table. Each bit indicates if the given row contains the given value. When the user specifies conditions on multiple dimensions, conjunction operations using the bitmaps are very fast, determining exactly which rows need to be fetched from the fact table.

Don't use views, with the exception of a dimension table fulfilling multiple roles. Views store a defining query rather than data. Every time a query is issued against a view, the underlying query for the view is run to obtain the data. This can lead to excessive processing. A web design company, unfamiliar with data warehouse and OLAP technology, attempted to design an OLAP application for one of its clients. The fact table was designed as a view built on base tables in normalized form. Every time the fact table (actually a view in this case) was accessed, the underlying query was run, leading to joins of huge tables. The OLAP system could not process the initial load of the cube. The system would hang endlessly. The gains of the data warehouse and OLAP are based on reusing results. The use of views defeats the gains by processing the same query with each use. As mentioned, there is a possible exception to the rule. If multiple dimensions have the same underlying data but are used for different roles, then views can be used to rename the underlying table and attributes. For example, the production and repair dates of Figure 4.4 both rely on the same underlying date dimension. Some designers eschew the use of views even in this case, copying the data to multiple dimension tables. Kimball and Ross (2002) recommended using one underlying table. In this instance, views reduce the resources required to maintain the dimensions. Changes only need to occur once in a single underlying dimension table. The heavier use of the single underlying table could also lead to better buffer pool performance. The cost of using views to fulfill roles is small, because renaming operations require few system resources.

4.7 USAGE SYNTAX AND EXAMPLES FOR MAJOR DATABASE SERVERS

We give a few concrete examples utilizing specific commercial products in this section to illustrate the implementation of some of the concepts we've discussed. Recommendations for more complete coverage of specific products are given in the Literature Summary section at the end of the chapter.

4.7.1 Oracle

Oracle offers many ways of partitioning data, including by range, by list, and by hash value. Each partition can reside in its own tablespace. A tablespace in Oracle is a physical location for storing data.

Partitioning by range allows data to be stored in separate tablespaces based on specified value ranges for each partition. For example, we may want to separate historical data from recent data. If recent data changes frequently, then isolating the recent data in a smaller partition can improve update performance. The following is the definition of a materialized view for labor costs by repair date, partitioned into historical and recent data, with 2006 acting as the dividing point:

```
CREATE MATERIALIZED VIEW mv_labor_cost_by_repair_date
PARTITION BY RANGE(repair_year)
(PARTITION repair_to_2006 VALUES LESS THAN (2006)
TABLESPACE repairs_historical,
PARTITION repair_recent VALUES LESS THAN (MAXVALUE)
  TABLESPACE repairs_recent)
AS
SELECT w.repair_date_id, repair_year, sum(labor_cost)
FROM warranty_claim w, repair_date r
WHERE w.repair_date_id=r.repair_date_id
GROUP BY w.repair_date_id, repair_year;
```

If the values of a column are discrete but do not form natural ranges, the rows can be assigned to partitions according to defined lists of values. Here is a definition for a materialized view that partitions the rows into east, central, and west, based on value lists:

```
CREATE MATERIALIZED VIEW mv_labor_cost_by_location
PARTITION BY LIST(region)
(PARTITION east VALUES('Northeast','Southeast')
TABLESPACE east,
PARTITION central VALUES('Midwest','Westcentral')
TABLESPACE central,
```

```
PARTITION west VALUES('West','Southwest')
TABLESPACE west)
AS
SELECT w.loc_id, region, sum(labor_cost)
FROM warranty_claim w, location l
WHERE w.loc_id=l.loc_id
GROUP BY w.loc_id, region;
```

Often, it is desirable to divide the data evenly between partitions, facilitating the balancing of loads over multiple storage devices. Partitioning by hash values may be a good option to satisfy this purpose. Here is a materialized view definition that divides the labor cost by repair date rows into three partitions based on hashing:

```
CREATE MATERIALIZED VIEW mv_labor_cost_by_repair_date
PARTITION BY HASH(repair_date_id)
PARTITIONS 3 STORE IN (tablespace1, tablespace2, tablespace3)
AS
SELECT repair_date_id, sum(labor_cost)
FROM warranty_claim
GROUP BY repair_date_id;
```

Partition by hash may not work well in the case where the distribution of values is highly skewed. For example, if 90 percent of the rows have a given value, then at least 90 percent of them will map to the same partition, no matter how many partitions we use and no matter what hash function the system uses.

4.7.2 Microsoft's Analysis Services

Microsoft SQL Server 2005 Analysis Services supported OLAP and data mining operations. The analysis manager is used to specify a data source. Many options are supported for the data source, including Open DataBase Connectivity (ODBC) data sources. A database connection can be established to a Microsoft SQL Server database (or any other ODBC-compliant database). The dimension tables and fact tables are specified using GUI screens, and the data cube is then built. There are a series of options available including ROLAP, HOLAP, and MOLAP. There are also several options for specifying limits on the use of aggregates. The user can specify a space limit.

Figure 4.10 shows a screen from the Storage Design Wizard. The wizard selects views to materialize while displaying the progress in graph form. Note that Microsoft uses the term "aggregations" instead of materialized views in this context. OLAP systems improve performance by precalculating views and materializing the results to disk. Queries are answered from the smaller aggregations instead of reading the large fact table. Typically, there are far too many possible views to materialize them all, so the OLAP system needs to pick strategic views for materialization.

In Microsoft Analysis Services, you have several options to control the process. You may specify the maximum amount of disk space to use for the aggregates.

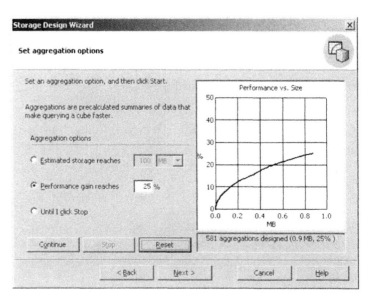

FIGURE 4.10

Print screen from Microsoft Analysis Services, Storage Design Wizard.

You also have the option of specifying the performance gain. The higher the performance gain, the more disk space is required. The Microsoft documentation recommends a setting of about 30 percent for the performance gain. Selecting a reasonable performance gain setting is problematic, because the gain is highly dependent on the data. The views are picked for materialization using a greedy algorithm, so the graph will indicate a trend toward diminishing returns. You can watch the gain on the graph and click the stop button anytime you think the gain is not worth the disk space and the associated update costs. Also, if your specified gain is reached and the curve is not leveling out, you can reset the gain higher and continue if you wish.

TIPS AND INSIGHTS FOR DATABASE PROFESSIONALS

Tip 1. The dimensional design approach is appropriate for designing a data warehouse. The resulting star schemas are much more efficient than normalized tables in the context of a data warehouse.

Tip 2. Use star schemas rather than snowflake schemas. Star schemas require fewer joins, and the schemas are more intuitive for users.

Tip 3. Conform dimensions across all business processes. Discussions between different groups of users are more fruitful if terms carry the same meaning across the entire enterprise.

Tip 4. Index dimension attributes with bitmap indexes when the attribute has a small to medium cardinality of distinct values. The bitmap indexes are efficient for star joins.

Tip 5. Use materialized views when advantageous for speeding up throughput. Note that OLAP systems automatically select views for materialization.

Tip 6. Use appropriate update strategies for refreshing materialized views. Typically this means incremental updates during a designated update window each night. However, company requirements may dictate a real-time update strategy. Occasionally, when the nature of the data leads to changes of large portions of a materialized view, it may be more efficient to run a complete refresh of that materialized view.

Tip 7. If your OLAP system offers both ROLAP and MOLAP storage options, use MOLAP only if the data is dense. ROLAP is more efficient when the data is sparse. ROLAP is good overall, but MOLAP does not scale well to large, sparse data spaces.

Tip 8. When datasets become huge, utilize partitioning and parallel processing to improve scalability. Shared nothing systems are massively parallel processing platforms that have become extremely popular for data warehousing. In general, once a data warehouse or data mart grows larger than ~500GB of raw data (size before loading into the database), shared nothing architectures will generally provide a superior architectural platform compared to scaleup solutions that simply grow the database server resources within a single box.

Tip 9. Don't go nuts with dimension tables. Additional tables in the system add complexity to the query execution plan selection process. Simply put, every table that needs to be joined can be joined in multiple ways (hash join, nested loop join, merge join, etc.). As the number of tables to join grows, the join enumeration grows, and therefore so does the compilation complexity. As a result, a large number of dimension tables can cause increased complexity (and opportunity for error) within the query compiler. Therefore, for very narrow dimension tables, 20 bytes wide or less, consider denormalizing them. This is one of the practical trade-offs between design purity and real world practicality.

4.8 SUMMARY

The decision support technologies of data warehousing and OLAP are overviewed in this chapter. Some of the physical design issues are described, and some of the solutions are illustrated with examples. The use of materialized views for faster query response in the data warehouse environment is discussed. The different general categories of OLAP storage are described, including ROLAP, MOLAP, and HOLAP, along with general guidelines for determining when one may be more appropriate than the others, based on data density. The dimensional design approach is covered briefly, with examples illustrating star and snowflake schemas. The usefulness of the data warehouse bus is demonstrated with an example, showing the relationship of conformed dimensions across multiple business processes. The data warehouse bus leads to a data warehouse constellation schema with the possibility of developing a data mart for each business process. Approaches toward efficient processing are discussed, including some hardware approaches, the appropriate use of bitmap indexes, various materialized view update strategies, and the partitioning of data.

Data warehousing offers the infrastructure critical for decision support based on large amounts of historical data. OLAP is a service that offers quick response to queries posed against the huge amounts of data residing in a data warehouse. Data warehousing and OLAP technologies allow for the exploration of data, facilitating better decisions by management.

4.9 LITERATURE SUMMARY

The books by Kimball et al. offer detailed explanations and examples for various aspects of data warehouse design. The book *The Data Warehouse Toolkit: The Complete Guide to Dimensional Modeling* is a good starting point for those interested in pursuing data warehousing. The ETL process is covered in *The Data Warehouse ETL Toolkit*.

Product-specific details and examples for Oracle can be found in *Oracle Data Warehouse Tuning for 10 g* by Powell. *SQL Server Analysis Services 2005 with MDX* by Harinath and Quinn is a good source covering Microsoft data warehousing, OLAP, and data mining.

The Patent Office Web site takes some getting used to, but the effort can be well worth it if you want to learn about emerging technology. Be prepared to sift, because not every patent is valuable. You may discover what your competition is pursuing, and you may find yourself thinking better ideas of your own.

RESOURCES

Harinath, S., and S. Quinn. *SQL Server Analysis Services 2005 with MDX,* John Wiley, 2006.

Hindshaw, F., J. Metzger, and B. Zane. Optimized Database Appliance, Patent No. U.S. 7,010,521 B2, Assignee: Netezza Corporation, Framingham, MA, issued March 7, 2006.

IBM Data Warehousing, Analysis, and Discovery: Overview. IBM Software—*www-306.ibm. com/software/data/db2bi.*

Kimball, R., L. Reeves, M. Ross, and W. Thornthwaite. *The Data Warehouse Life Cycle Toolkit*, John Wiley, 1998.

Kimball, R., and M. Ross. *The Data Warehouse Toolkit: The Complete Guide to Dimensional Modeling*, 2nd ed., John Wiley, 2002.

Kimball, R., and J. Caserta. *The Data Warehouse ETL Toolkit*, 2nd ed., John Wiley, 2004.

Microsoft SQL Server: Business Intelligence Solutions—*www.microsoft.com/sql/solutions/bi/default.mspx*.

Netezza Corporation, at *netezza.com*.

Oracle Business Intelligence Solutions—*www.oracle.com/solutions/business_intelligence/index.html*.

Patent Full-Text and Full-Page Image Databases—*www.uspto.gov/patft/index.html*.

Powell, G. *Oracle Data Warehouse Tuning for 10g*, Elsevier, 2005.

Teorey, T., S. Lightstone, and T. Nadeau. *Database Modeling and Design: Logical Design*, 4th ed., Morgan Kaufmann, 2006.

Algorithms: The Basic Methods

Now that we've seen how the inputs and outputs can be represented, it's time to look at the learning algorithms themselves. This chapter explains the basic ideas behind the techniques that are used in practical data mining. We will not delve too deeply into the trickier issues—advanced versions of the algorithms, optimizations that are possible, complications that arise in practice.

In this chapter we look at the basic ideas. One of the most instructive lessons is that simple ideas often work very well, and we strongly recommend the adoption of a "simplicity-first" methodology when analyzing practical datasets. There are many different kinds of simple structure that datasets can exhibit. In one dataset, there might be a single attribute that does all the work and the others may be irrelevant or redundant. In another dataset, the attributes might contribute independently and equally to the final outcome. A third might have a simple logical structure, involving just a few attributes that can be captured by a decision tree. In a fourth, there may be a few independent rules that govern the assignment of instances to different classes. A fifth might exhibit dependencies among different subsets of attributes. A sixth might involve linear dependence among numeric attributes, where what matters is a weighted sum of attribute values with appropriately chosen weights. In a seventh, the distances between the instances themselves might govern classifications appropriate to particular regions of instance space. And in an eighth, it might be that no class values are provided: the learning is unsupervised.

In the infinite variety of possible datasets, many different kinds of structure can occur, and a data mining tool—no matter how capable—that is looking for one class of structure may completely miss regularities of a different kind, regardless of how rudimentary those may be. The result is one kind of baroque and opaque classification structure instead of a simple, elegant, immediately comprehensible structure of another.

Each of the eight examples of different kinds of datasets sketched previously leads to a different machine learning method well suited to discovering it. The sections of this chapter look at each of these structures in turn.

5.1 INFERRING RUDIMENTARY RULES

Here's an easy way to find simple classification rules from a set of instances. Called *1R* for *1-rule*, it generates a one-level decision tree expressed in the form of a set of rules that all test one particular attribute. 1R is a simple, cheap method that often comes up with good rules for characterizing the structure in data. It turns out that simple rules frequently achieve surprisingly high accuracy. Perhaps this is because the structure underlying many real-world datasets is rudimentary, and just one attribute is sufficient to determine the class of an instance accurately. In any event, it is always a good plan to try the simplest things first.

The idea is this: We make rules that test a single attribute and branch accordingly. Each branch corresponds to a different value of the attribute. It is obvious what is the best classification to give each branch: Use the class that occurs most often in the training data. Then the error rate of the rules can easily be determined. Just count the errors that occur on the training data—that is, the number of instances that do not have the majority class.

Each attribute generates a different set of rules, one rule for every value of the attribute. Evaluate the error rate for each attribute's rule set and choose the best. It's that simple! Figure 5.1 shows the algorithm in the form of pseudocode.

To see the 1R method at work, consider the weather data presented in Table 1.2 (we will encounter it many times again when looking at how learning algorithms work). To classify on the final column, *play*, 1R considers four sets of rules, one for each attribute. These rules are shown in Table 5.1. An asterisk indicates that a random choice has been made between two equally likely outcomes. The number of errors is given for each rule, along with the total number of errors for the rule set as a whole. 1R chooses the attribute that produces rules with the smallest number of errors—that is, the first and third rule sets. Arbitrarily breaking the tie between these two rule sets gives

```
outlook: sunny    → no
         overcast → yes
         rainy    → yes
```

```
For each attribute,
   For each value of that attribute, make a rule as follows:
      count how often each class appears
      find the most frequent class
      make the rule assign that class to this attribute-value.
   Calculate the error rate of the rules.
Choose the rules with the smallest error rate.
```

FIGURE 5.1

Pseudocode for 1R.

Table 5.1 Evaluating the Attributes in the Weather Data

	Attribute	Rules		Errors	Total Errors
1	Outlook	Sunny	→ no	2/5	4/14
		Overcast	→ yes	0/4	
		Rainy	→ yes	2/5	
2	Temperature	Hot	→ no*	2/4	5/14
		Mild	→ yes	2/6	
		Cool	→ yes	1/4	
3	Humidity	High	→ no	3/7	4/14
		Normal	→ yes	1/7	
4	Windy	False	→ yes	2/8	5/14
		True	→ no*	3/6	

*A random choice was made between two equally likely outcomes.

We noted at the outset that the game for the weather data is unspecified. Oddly enough, it is apparently played when it is overcast or rainy but not when it is sunny. Perhaps it's an indoor pursuit.

5.1.1 Missing Values and Numeric Attributes

Although a rudimentary learning method, 1R does accommodate both missing values and numeric attributes. It deals with these in simple but effective ways. *Missing* is treated as just another attribute value so that, for example, if the weather data had contained missing values for the *outlook* attribute, a rule set formed on *outlook* would specify four possible class values, one each for *sunny, overcast,* and *rainy* and a fourth for *missing*.

We can convert numeric attributes into nominal ones using a simple discretization method. First, sort the training examples according to the values of the numeric attribute. This produces a sequence of class values. For example, sorting the numeric version of the weather data (Table 1.3) according to the values of *temperature* produces the sequence

64	65	68	69	70	71	72	72	75	75	80	81	83	85
Yes	no	Yes	Yes	Yes	no	no	Yes	Yes	Yes	no	Yes	Yes	no

Discretization involves partitioning this sequence by placing breakpoints in it. One possibility is to place breakpoints wherever the class changes, producing the following eight categories:

```
yes | no | yes yes yes | no no | yes yes yes | no | yes yes | no
```

Choosing breakpoints halfway between the examples on either side places them at 64.5, 66.5, 70.5, 72, 77.5, 80.5, and 84. However, the two instances with value 72 cause a problem because they have the same value of *temperature* but fall into different classes. The simplest fix is to move the breakpoint at 72 up one example, to 73.5, producing a mixed partition in which *no* is the majority class.

A more serious problem is that this procedure tends to form a large number of categories. The 1R method will naturally gravitate toward choosing an attribute that splits into many categories, because this will partition the dataset into many classes, making it more likely that instances will have the same class as the majority in their partition. In fact, the limiting case is an attribute that has a different value for each instance—that is, an *identification code* attribute that pinpoints instances uniquely—and this will yield a zero error rate on the training set because each partition contains just one instance. Of course, highly branching attributes do not usually perform well on test examples; indeed, the *identification code* attribute will never predict any examples outside the training set correctly. This phenomenon is known as *overfitting*.

For 1R, overfitting is likely to occur whenever an attribute has a large number of possible values. Consequently, when discretizing a numeric attribute, a rule is adopted that dictates a minimum number of examples of the majority class in each partition. Suppose that minimum is set at three. This eliminates all but two of the preceding partitions. Instead, the partitioning process begins

```
yes no yes yes | yes. . .
```

ensuring that there are three occurrences of *yes*, the majority class, in the first partition. However, because the next example is also *yes*, we lose nothing by including that in the first partition, too. This leads to a new division:

```
yes no yes yes yes | no no yes yes yes | no yes yes no
```

where each partition contains at least three instances of the majority class, except the last one, which will usually have less. Partition boundaries always fall between examples of different classes.

Whenever adjacent partitions have the same majority class, as do the first two partitions shown here, they can be merged together without affecting the meaning of the rule sets. Thus, the final discretization is

```
yes no yes yes yes no no yes yes yes | no yes yes no
```

which leads to the rule set

```
temperature:  ≤ 77.5 → yes
              > 77.5 → no
```

The second rule involved an arbitrary choice; as it happens, no was chosen. If we had chosen *yes* instead, there would be no need for any breakpoint at all—and as this example illustrates, it might be better to use the adjacent categories to help to break ties. In fact, this rule generates five errors on the training set and so is less effective than the preceding rule for outlook. However, the same procedure leads to this rule for humidity:

```
humidity:  ≤ 82.5 → yes
           > 82.5 and ≤ 95.5 → no
           > 95.5 → yes
```

This generates only three errors on the training set and is the best "1-rule" for the data in Table 1.3.

Finally, if a numeric attribute has missing values, an additional category is created for them, and the preceding discretization procedure is applied just to the instances for which the attribute's value is defined.

5.1.2 Discussion

In a seminal paper titled "Very Simple Classification Rules Perform Well on Most Commonly Used Datasets" (Holte 1993), a comprehensive study of the performance of the 1R procedure was reported on 16 datasets that machine learning researchers frequently use to evaluate their algorithms. Throughout, the study used *cross-validation* to ensure that the results were representative of what independent test sets would yield. After some experimentation, the minimum number of examples in each partition of a numeric attribute was set at six, not three as used for the preceding illustration.

Surprisingly, despite its simplicity 1R did astonishingly—even embarrassingly—well in comparison with state-of-the-art learning methods, and the rules it produced turned out to be just a few percentage points less accurate, on almost all of the datasets, than the decision trees produced by a state-of-the-art decision tree induction scheme. These trees were, in general, considerably larger than 1R's rules. Rules that test a single attribute are often a viable alternative to more complex structures, and this strongly encourages a simplicity-first methodology in which the baseline performance is established using rudimentary techniques before progressing to more sophisticated learning methods, which inevitably generate output that is harder for people to interpret.

The 1R procedure learns a one-level decision tree whose leaves represent the various different classes. A slightly more expressive technique is to use a different rule for each class. Each rule is a conjunction of tests, one for each attribute. For numeric attributes the test checks whether the value lies within a given interval; for nominal ones it checks whether it is in a certain subset of that attribute's values. These two types of tests—intervals and subset—are learned from the training data pertaining to each class. For a numeric attribute, the endpoints of the interval are the minimum and maximum values that occur in the training data for that class. For a nominal one, the subset contains just those values that occur for that attribute in the training data for the class. Rules representing different classes usually overlap, and at prediction time the one with the most matching tests is predicted. This simple technique often gives a useful first impression of a dataset. It is extremely fast and can be applied to large quantities of data.

5.2 STATISTICAL MODELING

The 1R method uses a single attribute as the basis for its decisions and chooses the one that works best. Another simple technique is to use all attributes and allow them to make contributions to the decision that are *equally important* and *independent* of one another, given the class. This is unrealistic, of course: What makes real-life datasets interesting is that the attributes are certainly not equally important or independent. But it leads to a simple scheme that again works surprisingly well in practice.

Table 5.2 shows a summary of the weather data obtained by counting how many times each attribute–value pair occurs with each value (*yes* and *no*) for *play*. For example, you can see from Table 1.2 that *outlook* is *sunny* for five examples, two of which have *play* = *yes* and three of which have *play* = *no*. The cells in the first row of the new table simply count these occurrences for all possible values of each attribute, and the *play* figure in the final column counts the total number of occurrences of *yes* and *no*. In the lower part of the table, we rewrote the same information in the form of fractions, or observed probabilities. For example, of the 9 days that *play* is yes, *outlook* is *sunny* for 2 days, yielding a fraction of 2/9. For *play* the fractions are different: they are the proportion of days that *play* is *yes* and *no*, respectively.

Table 5.2 The Weather Data with Counts and Probabilities

	Outlook			Temperature			Humidity			Windy			Play	
	Yes	No		Yes	No		Yes	No		Yes	No	Yes	No
Sunny	2	3	Hot	2	2	High	3	4	False	6	2	9	5
Overcast	4	0	Mild	4	2	Normal	6	1	True	3	3		
Rainy	3	2	Cool	3	1								
Sunny	2/9	3/5	Hot	2/9	2/5	High	3/9	4/5	False	6/9	2/5	9/14	5/14
Overcast	4/9	0/5	Mild	3/9	2/5	Normal	6/9	1/5	True	3/9	3/5		
Rainy	3/9	2/5	Cool	3/9	1/5								

Table 5.3 A New Day

Outlook	Temperature	Humidity	Windy	Play
Sunny	Cool	High	True	?

Now suppose we encounter a new example with the values that are shown in Table 5.3. We treat the five features in Table 5.2—*outlook, temperature, humidity,* windy, and the overall likelihood that *play* is *yes* or *no*—as equally important, independent pieces of evidence and multiply the corresponding fractions. Looking at the outcome *yes* gives

$$\text{likelihood of } yes = 2/9 \times 3/9 \times 3/9 \times 3/9 \times 9/14 = 0.0053$$

The fractions are taken from the *yes* entries in the table according to the values of the attributes for the new day, and the final 9/14 is the overall fraction representing the proportion of days on which *play* is *yes*. A similar calculation for the outcome *no* leads to

$$\text{likelihood of } no = 3/5 \times 1/5 \times 4/5 \times 3/5 \times 5/14 = 0.0206$$

This indicates that for the new day, *no* is more likely than *yes*—four times more likely. The numbers can be turned into probabilities by normalizing them so that they sum to 1:

$$\text{Probability of } yes = \frac{0.0053}{0.0053 + 0.0206} = 20.5\%$$

$$\text{Probability of } no = \frac{0.0206}{0.0053 + 0.0206} = 79.5\%$$

This simple and intuitive method is based on Bayes's rule of conditional probability. Bayes's rule says that if you have a hypothesis H and evidence E that bears on that hypothesis, then

$$\Pr[H|E] = \frac{\Pr[E|H]\Pr[H]}{\Pr[E]}$$

We use the notation that Pr[*A*] denotes the probability of an event *A* and that Pr[*A*|*B*] denotes the probability of *A* conditional on another event *B*. The hypothesis *H* is that *play* will be, say, *yes*, and Pr[*H*|*E*] is going to turn out to be 20.5 percent, just as determined previously. The evidence *E* is the particular combination of attribute values for the new day, *outlook = sunny, temperature = cool, humidity = high*, and *windy = true*. Let's call these four pieces of evidence E_1, E_2, E_3, and E_4, respectively. Assuming that these pieces of evidence are independent (given the class), their combined probability is obtained by multiplying the probabilities:

$$\Pr[yes|E] = \frac{\Pr[E_1|yes] \times \Pr[E_2|yes] \times \Pr[E_3|yes] \times \Pr[E_4|yes] \times \Pr[yes]}{\Pr[E]}$$

Don't worry about the denominator: We will ignore it and eliminate it in the final normalizing step when we make the probabilities of *yes* and *no* sum to 1, just as we did previously. The Pr[*yes*] at the end is the probability of a *yes* outcome without knowing any of the evidence *E*—that is, without knowing anything about the particular day referenced—it's called the *prior probability* of the hypothesis *H*. In this case, it's just 9/14, because 9 of the 14 training examples had a *yes* value for *play*. Substituting the fractions in Table 5.2 for the appropriate evidence probabilities leads to

$$\Pr[yes|E] = \frac{2/9 \times 3/9 \times 3/9 \times 3/9 \times 9/14}{\Pr[E]}$$

just as we calculated previously. Again, the Pr[*E*] in the denominator will disappear when we normalize.

This method goes by the name of *Naïve Bayes,* because it's based on Bayes's rule and "naïvely" assumes independence—it is only valid to multiply probabilities when the events are independent. The assumption that attributes are independent (given the class) in real life certainly is a simplistic one. But despite the disparaging name, Naïve Bayes works well when tested on actual datasets, particularly when combined with attribute selection procedures that eliminate redundant, and hence nonindependent, attributes.

One thing that can go wrong with Naïve Bayes is that if a particular attribute value does not occur in the training set in conjunction with *every* class value, things go badly awry. Suppose in the example that the training data was different and the attribute value *outlook = sunny* had always been associated with the outcome *no*. Then the probability of *outlook = sunny* given a *yes*—that is, Pr[*outlook = sunny*|yes], would be zero, and because the other probabilities are multiplied by this the final probability of *yes*, they would be zero no matter how large they were. Probabilities that are zero hold a veto over the other ones. This is not a good idea. But the bug is easily fixed by minor adjustments to the method of calculating probabilities from frequencies.

For example, the upper part of Table 5.2 shows that for *play = yes*, *outlook* is *sunny* for two examples, *overcast* for four, and *rainy* for three, and the lower part gives these events probabilities of 2/9, 4/9, and 3/9, respectively. Instead, we could add 1 to each numerator and compensate by adding 3 to the denominator, giving probabilities of 3/12, 5/12, and 4/12, respectively. This will ensure that an attribute value that occurs zero times receives a probability that is nonzero, albeit small. The strategy of adding 1 to each count is a standard technique called the *Laplace estimator* after the great eighteenth-century French mathematician Pierre Laplace. Although it works well in practice, there is no particular reason for adding to the counts: we could instead choose a small constant μ and use

$$\frac{2+\mu/3}{9+\mu}, \frac{4+\mu/3}{9+\mu}, \text{ and } \frac{3+\mu/3}{9+\mu}$$

The value of μ, which was set to 3, effectively provides a weight that determines how influential the a priori values of 1/3, 1/3, and 1/3 are for each of the three possible attribute values. A large μ says that these priors are very important compared with the new evidence coming in from the training set, whereas a small one gives them less influence. Finally, there is no particular reason for dividing μ into three *equal* parts in the numerators: we could use

$$\frac{2+\mu p_1}{9+\mu}, \frac{4+\mu p_2}{9+\mu}, \text{ and } \frac{3+\mu p_3}{9+\mu}$$

instead, where p_1, p_2, and p_3 sum to 1. Effectively, these three numbers are a priori probabilities of the values of the *outlook* attribute being *sunny*, *overcast*, and *rainy*, respectively.

This is now a fully Bayesian formulation where prior probabilities have been assigned to everything in sight. It has the advantage of being completely rigorous, but the disadvantage that it is not usually clear just how these prior probabilities should be assigned. In practice, the prior probabilities make little difference provided that there are a reasonable number of training instances, and people generally just estimate frequencies using the Laplace estimator by initializing all counts to one instead of to zero.

5.2.1 Missing Values and Numeric Attributes

One of the really nice aspects of the Bayesian formulation is that missing values are no problem at all. For example, if the value of *outlook* were missing in the example presented in Table 5.3, the calculation would simply omit this attribute, yielding

likelihood of *yes* = $3/9 \times 3/9 \times 3/9 \times 9/14 = 0.0238$

likelihood of *no* = $1/5 \times 4/5 \times 3/5 \times 5/14 = 0.0343$

These two numbers are individually a lot higher than they were before, because one of the fractions is missing. But that's not a problem because a fraction is missing in both cases, and these likelihoods are subject to a further normalization process. This yields probabilities for *yes* and *no* of 41 percent and 59 percent, respectively.

If a value is missing in a training instance, it is simply not included in the frequency counts, and the probability ratios are based on the number of values that actually occur rather than on the total number of instances.

Numeric values are usually handled by assuming that they have a "normal" or "Gaussian" probability distribution. Table 5.4 gives a summary of the weather data with numeric features from Table 1.3. As before, for nominal attributes, we

Table 5.4 The Numeric Weather Data with Summary Statistics

	Outlook			Temperature			Humidity			Windy			Play	
	Yes	No		Yes	No		Yes	No			Yes	No	Yes	No
Sunny	2	3		83	85		86	85	False	6	2		9	5
Overcast	4	0		70	80		96	90	True	3	3			
Rainy	3	2		68	65		80	70						
				64	72		65	95						
				69	71		70	91						
				75			80							
				75			70							
				72			90							
				81			75							
Sunny	2/9	3/5	*Mean*	73	74.6	*Mean*	79.1	86.2	False	6/9	2/5		9/14	5/14
Overcast	4/9	0/5	*Std. dev.*	6.2	7.9	*Std. dev.*	10.2	9.7	True	3/9	3/5			
Rainy	3/9	2/5												

calculated counts, and for numeric ones we simply listed the values that occur. Then, whereas we normalized the counts for the nominal attributes into probabilities, we calculated the mean and standard deviation for each class and each numeric attribute. Thus, the mean value of *temperature* over the *yes* instances is 73, and its standard deviation is 6.2. The mean is simply the average of the preceding values—that is, the sum divided by the number of values. The standard deviation is the square root of the sample variance, which we can calculate as follows: subtract the mean from each value, square the result, sum them together, and then divide by *one less than* the number of values.

After we have found this sample variance, find its square root to determine the standard deviation. This is the standard way of calculating mean and standard deviation of a set of numbers. (The "one less than" has to do with the number of degrees of freedom in the sample, a statistical notion that we don't want to get into in this book.)

The probability density function for a normal distribution with mean μ and standard deviation σ is given by the rather formidable expression:

$$f(x) = \frac{1}{\sqrt{2\pi}\sigma} e^{\frac{(x-\mu)^2}{2\sigma^2}}$$

But fear not! All this means is that if we are considering a *yes* outcome when *temperature* has a value, say, of 66, we just need to plug $x = 66$, $\mu = 73$, and $\sigma = 6.2$ into the formula. So the value of the probability density function is

$$f(temperature = 66 \mid yes) = \frac{1}{\sqrt{2\pi} \cdot 6.2} e^{\frac{(66-73)^2}{2 \cdot 6.2^2}} = 0.0340$$

By the same token, the probability density of a *yes* outcome when *humidity* has value, say, of 90 is calculated in the same way:

$$f(humidity = 90 \mid yes) = 0.0221$$

The probability density function for an event is closely related to its probability. However, it is not quite the same thing. If temperature is a continuous scale, the probability of the temperature being *exactly* 66—or *exactly* any other value, such as 63.14159262—is zero. The real meaning of the density function $f(x)$ is that the probability that the quantity lies within a small region around x, say, between $x - \varepsilon/2$ and $x + \varepsilon/2$, is $\varepsilon f(x)$. What we have written is correct if temperature is measured to the nearest degree and humidity is measured to the nearest percentage point. You might think we ought to factor in the accuracy figure ε when using these probabilities, but that's not necessary. The same ε would appear in both the *yes* and *no* likelihoods that follow and cancel out when the probabilities were calculated.

Using these probabilities for the new day in Table 5.5 yields

likelihood of $yes = 2/9 \times 0.0340 \times 0.0221 \times 3/9 \times 9/14 = 0.000036$

likelihood of $no = 3/5 \times 0.0221 \times 0.0381 \times 3/5 \times 5/14 = 0.000108$

which leads to probabilities

$$\text{Probability of } yes = \frac{0.000036}{0.000036 + 0.000108} = 25.0\%$$

$$\text{Probability of } no = \frac{0.000108}{0.000036 + 0.000108} = 75.0\%$$

These figures are very close to the probabilities calculated earlier for the new day in Table 5.3, because the *temperature* and *humidity* values of 66 and 90 yield similar probabilities to the *cool* and *high* values used before.

The normal-distribution assumption makes it easy to extend the Naïve Bayes classifier to deal with numeric attributes. If the values of any numeric attributes

Table 5.5 Another New Day				
Outlook	**Temperature**	**Humidity**	**Windy**	**Play**
Sunny	66	90	True	?

are missing, the mean and standard deviation calculations are based only on the ones that are present.

5.2.2 Bayesian Models for Document Classification

One important domain for machine learning is document classification, in which each instance represents a document and the instance's class is the document's topic. Documents might be news items and the classes might be domestic news, overseas news, financial news, and sport. Documents are characterized by the words that appear in them, and one way to apply machine learning to document classification is to treat the presence or absence of each word as a Boolean attribute. Naïve Bayes is a popular technique for this application because it is fast and accurate.

However, this does not take into account the number of occurrences of each word, which is potentially useful information when determining the category of a document. Instead, a document can be viewed as a *bag of words*—a set that contains all the words in the document, with multiple occurrences of a word appearing multiple times (technically, a *set* includes each of its members just once, whereas a *bag* can have repeated elements). Word frequencies can be accommodated by applying a modified form of Naïve Bayes that is sometimes described as *multinominal* Naïve Bayes.

Suppose $n_1, n_2, \ldots, n_k$ is the number of times word i occurs in the document, and $P_1, P_2, \ldots, P_k$ is the probability of obtaining word i when sampling from all the documents in category H. Assume that the probability is independent of the word's context and position in the document. These assumptions lead to a *multinomial distribution* for document probabilities. For this distribution, the probability of a document E given its class H—in other words, the formula for computing the probability $\Pr[E|H]$ in Bayes's rule—is

$$\Pr[E|H] \approx N! \times \prod_{i=1}^{k} \frac{P_i^{n_i}}{n_i!}$$

where $N = n_1 + n_2 + \ldots + n_k$ is the number of words in the document. The reason for the factorials is to account for the fact that the ordering of the occurrences of each word is immaterial according to the bag-of-words model. P_i is estimated by computing the relative frequency of word i in the text of all training documents pertaining to category H. In reality there should be a further term that gives the probability that the model for category H generates a document whose length is the same as the length of E (that is why we use the symbol $\approx$ instead of $=$), but it is common to assume that this is the same for all classes and hence can be dropped.

For example, suppose there are only the two words, *yellow* and *blue,* in the vocabulary, and a particular document class H has $\Pr[yellow|H] = 75$ percent and $\Pr[blue|H] = 25$ percent (you might call H the class of *yellowish green* documents). Suppose E is the document *blue yellow blue* with a length of $N = 3$ words.

There are four possible bags of three words. One is {*yellow yellow yellow*}, and its probability according to the preceding formula is

$$\Pr[\{\textit{yellow yellow yellow}\}|H] \approx 3! \times \frac{0.75^3}{3!} \times \frac{0.25^0}{0!} = \frac{27}{64}$$

The other three, with their probabilities, are

$$\Pr[\{\textit{blue blue blue}\}|H] = \frac{1}{64}$$

$$\Pr[\{\textit{yellow yellow blue}\}|H] = \frac{27}{64}$$

$$\Pr[\{\textit{yellow blue blue}\}|H] = \frac{9}{64}$$

Here, E corresponds to the last case (recall that in a bag of words the order is immaterial); thus, its probability of being generated by the *yellowish green* document model is 9/64, or 14 percent. Suppose another class, *very bluish green* documents (call it H'), has $\Pr[\textit{yellow}|H'] = 10$ percent, $\Pr[\textit{blue}|H'] = 90$ percent. The probability that E is generated by this model is 24 percent.

If these are the only two classes, does that mean that E is in the *very bluish green* document class? Not necessarily. Bayes's rule, given earlier, says that you have to take into account the prior probability of each hypothesis. If you know that in fact *very bluish green* documents are twice as rare as *yellowish green* ones, this would be just sufficient to outweigh the preceding 14 percent to 24 percent disparity and tip the balance in favor of the *yellowish green* class.

The factorials in the preceding probability formula don't actually need to be computed because—being the same for every class—they drop out in the normalization process anyway. However, the formula still involves multiplying together many small probabilities, which soon yields extremely small numbers that cause underflow on large documents. The problem can be avoided by using logarithms of the probabilities instead of the probabilities themselves.

In the multinomial Naïve Bayes formulation a document's class is determined, not just by the words that occur in it, but also by the number of times they occur. In general it performs better than the ordinary Naïve Bayes model for document classification, particularly for large dictionary sizes.

5.2.3 Discussion

Naïve Bayes gives a simple approach, with clear semantics, to representing, using, and learning probabilistic knowledge. Impressive results can be achieved using it. It has often been shown that Naïve Bayes rivals, and indeed outperforms, more sophisticated classifiers on many datasets. The moral is, always try the simple things first. Repeatedly in machine learning people have eventually, after an extended struggle, obtained good results using sophisticated learning methods only to discover years later that simple methods such as 1R and Naïve Bayes do just as well—or even better.

There are many datasets for which Naïve Bayes does not do so well, however, and it is easy to see why. Because attributes are treated as though they were completely independent, the addition of redundant ones skews the learning process. As an extreme example, if you were to include a new attribute with the same values as *temperature* to the weather data, the effect of the *temperature* attribute would be multiplied: all of its probabilities would be squared, giving it a great deal more influence in the decision. If you were to add 10 such attributes, then the decisions would effectively be made on *temperature* alone. Dependencies between attributes inevitably reduce the power of Naïve Bayes to discern what is going on. They can, however, be ameliorated by using a subset of the attributes in the decision procedure, making a careful selection of which ones to use.

The normal-distribution assumption for numeric attributes is another restriction on Naïve Bayes as we have formulated it here. Many features simply aren't normally distributed. However, there is nothing to prevent us from using other distributions for the numeric attributes: there is nothing magic about the normal distribution. If you know that a particular attribute is likely to follow some other distribution, standard estimation procedures for that distribution can be used instead. If you suspect it isn't normal but don't know the actual distribution, there are procedures for "kernel density estimation" that do not assume any particular distribution for the attribute values. Another possibility is simply to discretize the data first.

5.3 DIVIDE AND CONQUER: CONSTRUCTING DECISION TREES

The problem of constructing a decision tree can be expressed recursively. First, select an attribute to place at the root node and make one branch for each possible value. This splits up the example set into subsets, one for every value of the attribute. Now the process can be repeated recursively for each branch, using only those instances that actually reach the branch. If at any time all instances at a node have the same classification, stop developing that part of the tree.

The only thing left to decide is how to determine which attribute to split on, given a set of examples with different classes. Consider (again!) the weather data. There are four possibilities for each split, and at the top level they produce trees such as those in Figure 5.2. Which is the best choice? The number of *yes* and *no* classes are shown at the leaves. Any leaf with only one class—*yes* or *no*—will not have to be split further, and the recursive process down that branch will terminate. Because we seek small trees, we would like this to happen as soon as possible. If we had a measure of the purity of each node, we could choose the attribute that produces the purest daughter nodes. Take a moment to look at Figure 5.2 and ponder which attribute you think is the best choice.

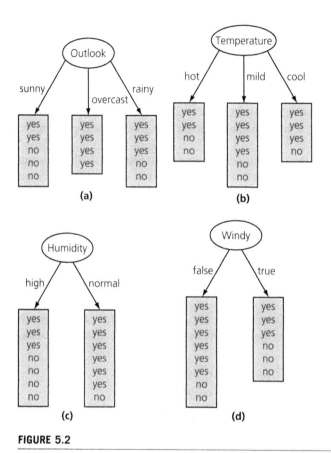

FIGURE 5.2

Tree stumps for the weather data.

The measure of purity that we will use is called the *information* and is measured in units called *bits*. Associated with a node of the tree, it represents the expected amount of information that would be needed to specify whether a new instance should be classified *yes* or *no,* given that the example reached that node. Unlike the bits in computer memory, the expected amount of information usually involves fractions of a bit—and is often less than 1! We calculate it based on the number of *yes* and *no* classes at the node; we will look at the details of the calculation shortly. But first let's see how it's used. When evaluating the first tree in Figure 5.2, the numbers of *yes* and *no* classes at the leaf nodes are [2,3], [4,0], and [3,2], respectively, and the information values of these nodes are as follows:

$$\text{info}([2,3]) = 0.971 \text{ bits}$$
$$\text{info}([4,0]) = 0.0 \text{ bits}$$
$$\text{info}([3,2]) = 0.971 \text{ bits}$$

We can calculate the average information value of these, taking into account the number of instances that go down each branch—five down the first and third and four down the second:

$$\text{info}([2,3],[4,0],[3,2]) = (5/14) \times 0.971 + (4/14) \times 0 + (5/14) \times 0.971 = 0.693 \text{ bits}$$

This average represents the amount of information that we expect would be necessary to specify the class of a new instance, given the tree structure in Figure 5.2(a).

Before we created any of the nascent tree structures in Figure 5.2, the training examples at the root constituted nine *yes* and five *no* nodes, corresponding to an information value of

$$\text{info}([9,5]) = 0.940 \text{ bits}$$

Thus, the tree in Figure 5.2(a) is responsible for an information gain of

$$\text{gain}(outlook) = \text{info}([9,5]) - \text{info}([2,3],[4,0],[3,2]) = 0.940 - 0.693 = 0.247 \text{ bits}$$

which can be interpreted as the informational value of creating a branch on the *outlook* attribute.

The way forward is clear. We calculate the information gain for each attribute and choose the one that gains the most information to split on. In the situation of Figure 5.2:

$$\text{gain}(outlook) = 0.247 \text{ bits}$$
$$\text{gain}(temperature) = 0.029 \text{ bits}$$
$$\text{gain}(humidity) = 0.152 \text{ bits}$$
$$\text{gain}(windy) = 0.048 \text{ bits}$$

so we select *outlook* as the splitting attribute at the root of the tree. Hopefully this accords with your intuition as the best one to select. It is the only choice for which one daughter node is completely pure, and this gives it a considerable advantage over the other attributes. *Humidity* is the next best choice because it produces a larger daughter node that is almost completely pure.

Then we continue, recursively. Figure 5.3 shows the possibilities for a further branch at the node reached when *outlook* is *sunny*. Clearly, a further split on *outlook* will produce nothing new, so we only consider the other three attributes. The information gain for each turns out to be

$$\text{gain}(temperature) = 0.571 \text{ bits}$$
$$\text{gain}(humidity) = 0.971 \text{ bits}$$
$$\text{gain}(windy) = 0.020 \text{ bits}$$

so we select *humidity* as the splitting attribute at this point. There is no need to split these nodes any further, so this branch is finished.

Continued application of the same idea leads to the decision tree of Figure 5.4 for the weather data. Ideally, the process terminates when all leaf nodes are

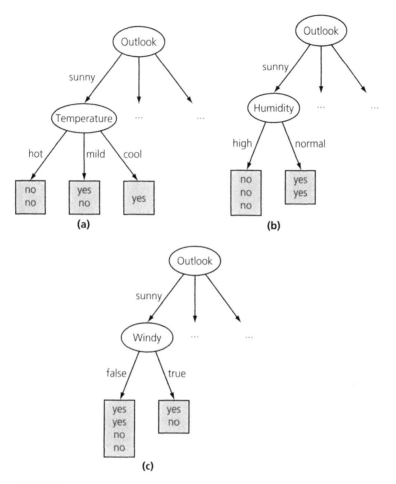

FIGURE 5.3

Expanded tree stumps for the weather data.

pure—that is, when they contain instances that all have the same classification. However, it might not be possible to reach this happy situation because there is nothing to stop the training set containing two examples with identical sets of attributes but different classes. Consequently, we stop when the data cannot be split any further.

5.3.1 Calculating Information

Now it is time to explain how to calculate the information measure that is used as a basis for evaluating different splits. We describe the basic idea in this section, then in the next we examine a correction that is usually made to counter

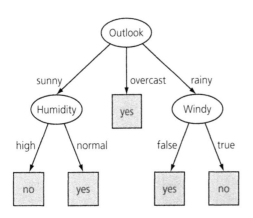

FIGURE 5.4

Decision tree for the weather data.

a bias toward selecting splits on attributes that have a large number of possible values.

Before examining the detailed formula for calculating the amount of information required to specify the class of an example given that it reaches a tree node with a certain number of *yes*'s and *no*'s, consider first the kind of properties we would expect this quantity to have:

1. When the number of either *yes*'s or *no*'s is zero, the information is zero.
2. When the number of *yes*'s and *no*'s is equal, the information reaches a maximum.

Moreover, the measure should be applicable to multiclass situations, not just to two-class ones.

The information measure relates to the amount of information obtained by making a decision, and a more subtle property of information can be derived by considering the nature of decisions. Decisions can be made in a single stage, or they can be made in several stages, and the amount of information involved is the same in both cases. For example, the decision involved in

$$\text{info}([2,3,4])$$

can be made in two stages. First decide whether it's the first case or one of the other two cases:

$$\text{info}([2,7])$$

and then decide which of the other two cases it is:

$$\text{info}([3,4])$$

In some cases the second decision will not need to be made, namely, when the decision turns out to be the first one. Taking this into account leads to the equation

$$\text{info}([2,3,4]) = \text{info}([2,7]) + (7/9) \times \text{info}([3,4])$$

Of course, there is nothing special about these particular numbers, and a similar relationship must hold regardless of the actual values. Thus, we can add a further criterion to the preceding list:

3. The information must obey the multistage property illustrated previously.

Remarkably, it turns out that there is only one function that satisfies all these properties, and it is known as the *information value* or *entropy*:

$$\text{entropy}(p_1, p_2, \ldots, p_n) = -p_1 \log p_1 - p_2 \log p_2 \ldots - p_n \log p_n$$

The reason for the minus signs is that logarithms of the fractions $p_1, p_2, \ldots, p_n$ are negative, so the entropy is actually positive. Usually the logarithms are expressed in base 2, then the entropy is in units called *bits*—just the usual kind of bits used with computers.

The arguments $p_1, p_2, \ldots$ of the entropy formula are expressed as fractions that add up to one, so that, for example,

$$\text{info}([2,3,4]) = \text{entropy}(2/9, 3/9, 4/9)$$

Thus, the multistage decision property can be written in general as

$$\text{entropy}(p, q, r) = \text{entropy}(p, q+r) + (q+r) \cdot \text{entropy}\left(\frac{q}{q+r}, \frac{r}{q+r}\right)$$

where $p + q + r = 1$.

Because of the way the log function works, you can calculate the information measure without having to work out the individual fractions:

$$\text{info}([2,3,4]) = -2/9 \times \log 2/9 - 3/9 \times \log 3/9 - 4/9 \times \log 4/9$$
$$= [-2\log 2 - 3\log 3 - 4\log 4 + 9\log 9]/9$$

This is the way that the information measure is usually calculated in practice. So the information value for the first leaf node of the first tree in Figure 5.2 is

$$\text{info}([2,3]) = -2/5 \times \log 2/5 - 3/5 \times \log 3/5 = 0.971 \text{ bits}$$

5.3.2 Highly Branching Attributes

When some attributes have a large number of possible values, giving rise to a multiway branch with many child nodes, a problem arises with the information gain calculation. The problem can best be appreciated in the extreme case when an attribute has a different value for each instance in the dataset—as, for example, an *identification code* attribute might.

Table 5.6 The Weather Data with Identification Code

ID code	Outlook	Temperature	Humidity	Windy	Play
a	Sunny	Hot	High	False	No
b	Sunny	Hot	High	True	No
c	Overcast	Hot	High	False	Yes
d	Rainy	Mild	High	False	Yes
e	Rainy	Cool	Normal	False	Yes
f	Rainy	Cool	Normal	True	No
g	Overcast	Cool	Normal	True	Yes
h	Sunny	Mild	High	False	No
i	Sunny	Cool	Normal	False	Yes
j	Rainy	Mild	Normal	False	Yes
k	Sunny	Mild	Normal	True	Yes
l	Overcast	Mild	High	True	Yes
m	Overcast	Hot	Normal	False	Yes
n	Rainy	Mild	High	True	No

Table 5.6 gives the weather data with this extra attribute. Branching on *ID code* produces the tree stump in Figure 5.5. The information required to specify the class given the value of this attribute is

$$\mathrm{info}([0,1]) + \mathrm{info}([0,1]) + \mathrm{info}([1,0]) + \ldots + \mathrm{info}([1,0]) + \mathrm{info}([0,1]),$$

which is zero because each of the 14 terms is zero. This is not surprising: the *ID code* attribute identifies the instance, which determines the class without any ambiguity—just as Table 5.6 shows. Consequently, the information gain of this attribute is just the information at the root, *info*([9,5]) = 0.940 bits. This is greater than the information gain of any other attribute, and so *ID code* will inevitably be chosen as the splitting attribute. But branching on the identification code is no good for predicting the class of unknown instances and tells nothing about the structure of the decision, which after all, are the twin goals of machine learning.

The overall effect is that the information gain measure tends to prefer attributes with large numbers of possible values. To compensate, a modification of the measure called the *gain ratio* is widely used. The gain ratio is derived by taking into account the number and size of daughter nodes into which an attribute

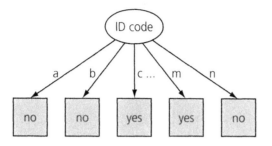

FIGURE 5.5

Tree stump for the *ID code* attribute.

splits the dataset, disregarding any information about the class. In the situation shown in Figure 5.5, all counts have a value of 1, so the information value of the split is

$$\text{info}([1,1,\ldots,1]) = -1/14 \times \log 1/14 \times 14$$

because the same fraction, 1/14, appears 14 times. This amounts to log 14, or 3.807 bits, which is a very high value. This is because the information value of a split is the number of bits needed to determine to which branch each instance is assigned, and the more branches there are, the greater this value is. The gain ratio is calculated by dividing the original information gain, 0.940 in this case, by the information value of the attribute, 3.807—yielding a gain ratio value of 0.247 for the *ID code* attribute.

Returning to the tree stumps for the weather data in Figure 5.2, *outlook* splits the dataset into three subsets of size 5, 4, and 5 and thus has an intrinsic information value of

$$\text{info}([5,4,5]) = 1.577$$

without paying any attention to the classes involved in the subsets. As we have seen, this intrinsic information value is higher for a more highly branching attribute such as the hypothesized *ID code*. Again we can correct the information gain by dividing by the intrinsic information value to get the gain ratio.

The results of these calculations for the tree stumps of Figure 5.2 are summarized in Table 5.7. *Outlook* still comes out on top, but *humidity* is now a much closer contender because it splits the data into two subsets instead of three. In this particular example, the hypothetical *ID code* attribute, with a gain ratio of 0.247, would still be preferred to any of these four. However, its advantage is greatly reduced. In practical implementations, we can use an ad hoc test to guard against splitting on such a useless attribute.

Unfortunately, in some situations the gain ratio modification overcompensates and can lead to preferring an attribute just because its intrinsic information is much lower than that for the other attributes. A standard fix is to choose the

Table 5.7 Gain Ratio Calculations for the Tree Stumps of Figure 5.2

	Outlook		Temperature		Humidity		Windy	
Info:		0.693		0.911		0.788		0.892
Gain:	0.940–	0.247	0.940–	0.029	0.940–	0.152	0.940–	0.048
	0.693		0.911		0.788		0.892	
Split info:		1.577		1.557		1		0.985
Info:	([5,4,5])		([4,6,4])		([7,7])		([8,6])	
Gain ratio:	0.247/	0.157	0.029/1.557	0.019	0.152/1	0.152	0.048/	0.049
	1.577						0.985	

attribute that maximizes the gain ratio, provided that the information gain for that attribute is at least as great as the average information gain for all the attributes examined.

5.3.3 Discussion

The divide-and-conquer approach to decision tree induction, sometimes called *top-down induction of decision trees,* was developed and refined over many years by J. Ross Quinlan of the University of Sydney, Australia. Although others have worked on similar methods, Quinlan's research has always been at the forefront of decision tree induction. The method that has been described using the information gain criterion is essentially the same as one known as ID3. The use of the gain ratio was one of many improvements that were made to ID3 over several years; Quinlan described it as robust under a wide variety of circumstances. Although a robust and practical solution, it sacrifices some of the elegance and clean theoretic motivation of the information gain criterion.

A series of improvements to ID3 culminated in a practical and influential system for decision tree induction called C4.5. These improvements include methods for dealing with numeric attributes, missing values, noisy data, and generating rules from trees.

5.4 COVERING ALGORITHMS: CONSTRUCTING RULES

As we have seen, decision tree algorithms are based on a divide-and-conquer approach to the classification problem. They work from the top down, seeking at each stage an attribute to split on that best separates the classes, then recursively processing the subproblems that result from the split. This strategy generates a decision tree, which if necessary can be converted into a set of classification rules—although if it is to produce effective rules, the conversion is not trivial.

An alternative approach is to take each class in turn and seek a way of covering all instances in it, at the same time excluding instances not in the class. This is called a *covering* approach because at each stage you identify a rule that "covers" some of the instances. By its very nature, this covering approach leads to a set of rules rather than to a decision tree.

The covering method can readily be visualized in a two-dimensional space of instances as shown in Figure 5.6(a). We first make a rule covering the *a*'s. For the first test in the rule, split the space vertically as shown in the center picture. This gives the beginnings of a rule:

```
If x > 1.2 then class = a
```

However, the rule covers many *b*'s as well as *a*'s, so a new test is added to the rule by further splitting the space horizontally as shown in the third diagram:

```
If x > 1.2 and y > 2.6 then class = a
```

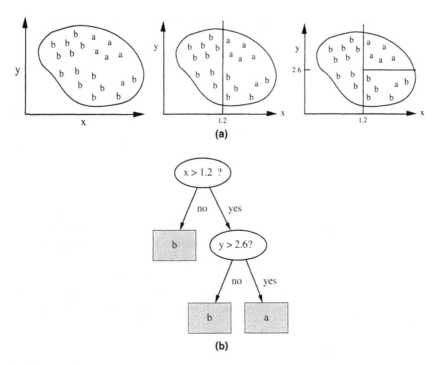

FIGURE 5.6

Covering algorithm: (a) covering the instances and (b) the decision tree for the same problem.

This gives a rule covering all but one of the *a*'s. It's probably appropriate to leave it at that, but if it were felt necessary to cover the final *a*, another rule would be necessary—perhaps

```
If x > 1.4 and y < 2.4 then class = a
```

The same procedure leads to two rules covering the *b*'s:

```
If x ≤ 1.2 then class = b
If x > 1.2 and y ≤ 2.6 then class = b
```

Again, one *a* is erroneously covered by these rules. If it were necessary to exclude it, more tests would have to be added to the second rule, and additional rules would need to be introduced to cover the *b*'s that these new tests exclude.

5.4.1 Rules versus Trees

A top-down divide-and-conquer algorithm operates on the same data in a manner that is, at least superficially, quite similar to a covering algorithm. It might first split the dataset using the *x* attribute and would probably end up splitting it at the same place, $x = 1.2$. However, whereas the covering algorithm is concerned only with covering a single class, the division would take both classes into account, because divide-and-conquer algorithms create a single concept description that applies to all classes. The second split might also be at the same place, $y = 2.6$, leading to the decision tree in Figure 5.6(b). This tree corresponds exactly to the set of rules, and in this case there is no difference in effect between the covering and the divide-and-conquer algorithms.

But in many situations there *is* a difference between rules and trees in terms of the perspicuity of the representation. For example, rules can be symmetric, whereas trees must select one attribute to split on first, and this can lead to trees that are much larger than an equivalent set of rules. Another difference is that, in the multiclass case, a decision tree split takes all classes into account, trying to maximize the purity of the split, whereas the rule-generating method concentrates on one class at a time, disregarding what happens to the other classes.

5.4.2 A Simple Covering Algorithm

Covering algorithms operate by adding tests to the rule that is under construction, always striving to create a rule with maximum accuracy. In contrast, divide-and-conquer algorithms operate by adding tests to the tree that is under construction, always striving to maximize the separation among the classes. Each of these involves finding an attribute to split on. But the criterion for the best attribute is different in each case. Whereas divide-and-conquer algorithms such as ID3 choose an attribute to maximize the information gain, the covering algorithm we will describe chooses an attribute–value pair to maximize the probability of the desired classification.

Figure 5.7 gives a picture of the situation, showing the space containing all the instances, a partially constructed rule, and the same rule after a new term has been added. The new term restricts the coverage of the rule: the idea is to include as many instances of the desired class as possible and exclude as many instances of other classes as possible. Suppose the new rule will cover a total of t instances, of which p are positive examples of the class and $t - p$ are in other classes—that

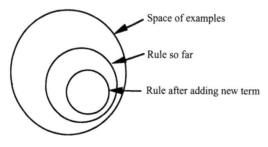

Space of examples

Rule so far

Rule after adding new term

FIGURE 5.7

The instance space during operation of a covering algorithm.

is, they are errors made by the rule. Then choose the new term to maximize the ratio *p/t*.

An example will help. For a change, we use the contact lens problem of Table 1.1. We will form rules that cover each of the three classes, *hard, soft,* and *none,* in turn. To begin, we seek a rule:

```
If ? then recommendation = hard
```

For the unknown term?, we have nine choices:

```
age = young                                 2/8
age = pre-presbyopic                        1/8
age = presbyopic                            1/8
spectacle prescription = myope              3/12
spectacle prescription = hypermetrope       1/12
astigmatism = no                            0/12
astigmatism = yes                           5/12
tear production rate = reduced              0/12
tear production rate = normal               5/12
```

The numbers on the right show the fraction of "correct" instances in the set singled out by that choice. In this case, *correct* means that the recommendation is hard. For instance, *age = young* selects eight instances, two of which recommend hard contact lenses, so the first fraction is 2/8. (To follow this, you will need to look back at the contact lens data in Table 1.1 and count up the entries in the table.) We select the largest fraction, 4/12, arbitrarily choosing between the seventh and the last choice in the preceding list, and create the rule:

```
If astigmatism = yes then recommendation = hard
```

This rule is an inaccurate one, getting only 4 instances correct out of the 12 that it covers, shown in Table 5.8. So we refine it further:

```
If astigmatism = yes and ? then recommendation = hard
```

Considering the possibilities for the unknown term ? yields the seven choices:

```
age = young                                 2/4
age = pre-presbyopic                        1/4
age = presbyopic                            1/4
spectacle prescription = myope              3/6
spectacle prescription = hypermetrope       1/6
tear production rate = reduced              0/6
tear production rate = normal               5/6
```

(Again, count the entries in Table 5.8.) The last is a clear winner, getting four instances correct out of the six that it covers, and corresponds to the rule

```
If astigmatism = yes and tear production rate = normal
    then recommendation = hard
```

Table 5.8 Part of the Contact Lens Data for Which *Astigmatism = Yes*

Age	Spectacle Prescription	Astigmatism	Tear production Rate	Recommended Lenses
Young	Myope	Yes	Reduced	None
Young	Myope	Yes	Normal	Hard
Young	Hypermetrope	Yes	Reduced	None
Young	Hypermetrope	Yes	Normal	Hard
Pre-presbyopic	Myope	Yes	Reduced	None
Pre-presbyopic	Myope	Yes	Normal	Hard
Pre-presbyopic	Hypermetrope	Yes	Reduced	None
Pre-presbyopic	Hypermetrope	Yes	Normal	None
Presbyopic	Myope	Yes	Reduced	None
Presbyopic	Myope	Yes	Normal	Hard
Presbyopic	Hypermetrope	Yes	Reduced	None
Presbyopic	Hypermetrope	Yes	Normal	None

Should we stop here? Perhaps. But let's say we are going for exact rules, no matter how complex they become. Table 5.9 shows the cases that are covered by the rule so far. The possibilities for the next term are now

```
age = young                                 2/2
age = pre-presbyopic                        1/2
age = presbyopic                            1/2
spectacle prescription = myope              3/3
spectacle prescription = hypermetrope       1/3
```

We need to choose between the first and fourth. So far we have treated the fractions numerically, but although these two are equal (both evaluate to 1), they have different coverage: one selects just two correct instances and the other selects three. In the event of a tie, we choose the rule with the greater coverage, giving the final rule:

```
If astigmatism = yes and tear production rate = normal
    and spectacle prescription = myope then recommendation = hard
```

This is indeed one of the rules given for the contact lens problem. But it only covers three of the four *hard* recommendations. So we delete these three from

Table 5.9 Part of the Contact Lens Data for Which *Astigmatism = Yes* and *Tear Production Rate = Normal*

Age	Spectacle Prescription	Astigmatism	Tear Production Rate	Recommended Lenses
Young	Myope	Yes	Normal	Hard
Young	Hypermetrope	Yes	Normal	Hard
Pre-presbyopic	Myope	Yes	Normal	Hard
Pre-presbyopic	Hypermetrope	Yes	Normal	None
Presbyopic	Myope	Yes	Normal	Hard
Presbyopic	Hypermetrope	Yes	Normal	None

the set of instances and start again, looking for another rule that is in following the form:

```
If ? then recommendation = hard
```

Using the same process, we will eventually find that *age = young* is the best choice for the first term. Its coverage is seven; the reason for the seven is that 3 instances have been removed from the original set, leaving 21 altogether. The best choice for the second term is *astigmatism = yes*, selecting 1/3 (actually, this is a tie); *tear production rate = normal* is the best for the third, selecting 1/1.

```
If age = young and astigmatism = yes and
   tear production rate = normal then recommendation = hard
```

This rule actually covers three of the original set of instances, two of which are covered by the previous rule—but that's all right because the recommendation is the same for each rule.

Now that all the hard-lens cases are covered, the next step is to proceed with the soft-lens ones in just the same way. Finally, rules are generated for the *none* case—unless we are seeking a rule set with a default rule, in which case explicit rules for the final outcome are unnecessary.

What we have just described is the PRISM method for constructing rules. It generates only correct or "perfect" rules. It measures the success of a rule by the accuracy formula p/t. Any rule with accuracy less than 100 percent is "incorrect" in that it assigns cases to the class in question that actually do not have that class. PRISM continues adding clauses to each rule until it is perfect: its accuracy is 100 percent. Figure 5.8 summarizes the algorithm. The outer loop iterates over the classes, generating rules for each class in turn. Note that we reinitialize to the full set of examples each time round. Then we create rules for that class and remove the examples from the set until there are none of that class left. Whenever we create a rule, start with an empty rule (which covers all the examples), and then

```
For each class C
  Initialize E to the instance set
  While E contains instances in class C
    Create a rule R with an empty left-hand side that predicts class C
    Until R is perfect (or there are no more attributes to use) do
      For each attribute A not mentioned in R, and each value v,
        Consider adding the condition A=v to the LHS of R
        Select A and v to maximize the accuracy p/t
          (break ties by choosing the condition with the largest p)
      Add A=v to R
    Remove the instances covered by R from E
```

FIGURE 5.8

Pseudocode for a basic rule learner.

restrict it by adding tests until it covers only examples of the desired class. At each stage choose the most promising test—that is, the one that maximizes the accuracy of the rule. Finally, break ties by selecting the test with greatest coverage.

5.4.3 Rules versus Decision Lists

Consider the rules produced for a particular class, that is, the algorithm in Figure 5.8 with the outer loop removed. It seems clear from the way that these rules are produced that they are intended to be interpreted in order—that is, as a decision list, testing the rules in turn until one applies and then using that. This is because the instances covered by a new rule are removed from the instance set as soon as the rule is completed (in the third line from the end of the code in Figure 5.8); thus, subsequent rules are designed for instances that are *not* covered by the rule. However, although it appears that we are supposed to check the rules in turn, we do not have to do so. Consider that any subsequent rules generated for this class will have the same effect—they all predict the same class. This means that it does not matter what order they are executed in: Either a rule will be found that covers this instance, in which case the class in question is predicted, or no such rule is found, in which case the class is not predicted.

Now return to the overall algorithm. Each class is considered in turn, and rules are generated that distinguish instances in that class from the others. No ordering is implied between the rules for one class and those for another. Consequently, the rules that are produced can be executed independent of order.

Order-independent rules seem to provide more modularity by each acting as an independent nugget of "knowledge," but they suffer from the disadvantage that it is not clear what to do when conflicting rules apply. With rules generated in this way, a test example may receive multiple classifications—that is, rules that apply to different classes may accept it. Other test examples may receive no classification at all. A simple strategy to force a decision in these ambiguous cases is to choose, from the classifications that are predicted, the one with the most training examples or, if no classification is predicted, to choose the category with the most training examples overall. These difficulties do not occur with decision lists because they are meant to be interpreted in order and execution stops as soon as one rule applies: the addition of a default rule at the end ensures that any test instance receives a classification. It is possible to generate good decision lists for the multiclass case using a slightly different method.

Methods such as PRISM can be described as *separate-and-conquer* algorithms: you identify a rule that covers many instances in the class (and excludes ones not in the class), separate out the covered instances because they are already taken care of by the rule, and continue the process on those that are left. This contrasts nicely with the divide-and-conquer approach of decision trees. The separate step greatly increases the efficiency of the method because the instance set continually shrinks as the operation proceeds.

5.5 MINING ASSOCIATION RULES

Association rules are like classification rules. You could find them in the same way, by executing a divide-and-conquer rule-induction procedure for each possible expression that could occur on the right side of the rule. But not only might any attribute occur on the right side with any possible value; a single association rule often predicts the value of more than one attribute. To find such rules, you would have to execute the rule-induction procedure once for every possible *combination* of attributes, with every possible combination of values, on the right side. That would result in an enormous number of association rules, which would then have to be pruned down on the basis of their *coverage* (the number of instances that they predict correctly) and their *accuracy* (the same number expressed as a proportion of the number of instances to which the rule applies). This approach is not feasible. (Note that what we are calling *coverage* is often called *support* and what we are calling *accuracy* is often called *confidence*.)

Instead, we capitalize on the fact that we are only interested in association rules with high coverage. We ignore, for the moment, the distinction between the left and right sides of a rule and seek combinations of attribute–value pairs that have a prespecified minimum coverage. These are called *item sets:* an attribute–value pair is an *item*. The terminology derives from market basket analysis, in which the items are articles in your shopping cart and the supermarket manager is looking for associations among these purchases.

5.5.1 Item Sets

The first column of Table 5.10 shows the individual items for the weather data of Table 1.2, with the number of times each item appears in the dataset given at the

Table 5.10 Item Sets for the Weather Data with Coverage 2 or Greater

	One-Item Sets	Two-Item Sets	Three-Item Sets	Four-Item Sets
1	Outlook = sunny (5)	Outlook = sunny	Outlook = sunny	Outlook = sunny
		Temperature = mild (2)	Temperature = hot	Temperature = hot
			Humidity = high (2)	Humidity = high
				Play = no (2)
2	Outlook = overcast (4)	Outlook = sunny	Outlook = sunny	Outlook = sunny
		Temperature = hot (2)	Temperature = hot	Humidity = high
			Play = no (2)	Windy = false
				Play = no (2)
3	Outlook = rainy (5)	Outlook = sunny	Outlook = sunny	Outlook = overcast
		Humidity = normal (2)	Humidity = normal	Temperature = hot
			Play = yes (2)	Windy = false
				Play = yes (2)
4	Temperature = cool (4)	Outlook = sunny	Outlook = sunny	Outlook = rainy
		Humidity = high (3)	Humidity = high	Temperature = mild
			Windy = false (2)	Windy = false
				Play = yes (2)
5	Temperature = mild (6)	Outlook = sunny	Outlook = sunny	Outlook = rainy
		Windy = true (2)	Humidity = high	Humidity = normal
			Play = no (3)	Windy = false
				Play = yes (2)
6	Temperature = hot (4)	Outlook = sunny	Outlook = sunny	Temperature = cool
		Windy = false (3)	Windy = false	Humidity = normal
			Play = no (2)	Windy = false
				Play = yes (2)
7	Humidity = normal (7)	Outlook = sunny	Outlook = overcast	
		Play = yes (2)	Temperature = hot	
			Windy = false (2)	
8	Humidity = high (7)	Outlook = sunny	Outlook = overcast	
		Play = no (3)	Temperature = hot	
			Play = yes (2)	

Table 5.10 Item Sets for the Weather Data with Coverage 2 or Greater *Continued*

	One-Item Sets	Two-Item Sets	Three-Item Sets	Four-Item Sets
9	Windy = true (6)	Outlook = overcast	Outlook = overcast	
		Temperature = hot (2)	Humidity = normal	
			Play = yes (2)	
10	Windy = false (8)	Outlook = overcast	Outlook = overcast	
		Humidity = normal (2)	Humidity = high	
			Play = yes (2)	
11	Play = yes (9)	Outlook = overcast	Outlook = overcast	
		Humidity = high (2)	Windy = true	
			Play = yes (2)	
12	Play = no (5)	Outlook = overcast	Outlook = overcast	
		Windy = true (2)	Windy = false	
			Play = yes (2)	
13		Outlook = overcast	Outlook = rainy	
		Windy = false (2)	Temperature = cool	
			Humidity = normal (2)	
. . .		. . .	. . .	
38		Humidity = normal	Humidity = normal	
		Windy = false (4)	Windy = false	
			Play = yes (4)	
39		Humidity = normal	Humidity = high	
		Play = yes (6)	Windy = false	
			Play = no (2)	
40		Humidity = high		
		Windy = true (3)		
. . .		. . .		
47		Windy = false		
		Play = no (2)		

right. These are the one-item sets. The next step is to generate the two-item sets by making pairs of one-item ones. Of course, there is no point in generating a set containing two different values of the same attribute (such as *outlook = sunny* and *outlook = overcast*), because that cannot occur in any actual instance.

Assume that we seek association rules with minimum coverage 2; thus, we discard any item sets that cover fewer than two instances. This leaves 47 two-item sets, some of which are shown in the second column along with the number of times they appear. The next step is to generate the three-item sets, of which 39 have a coverage of 2 or greater. There are 6 four-item sets, and no five-item sets—for this data, a five-item set with coverage 2 or greater could only correspond to a repeated instance. The first row of the table, for example, shows that there are five days when *outlook = sunny,* two of which have *temperature = mild,* and, in fact, on both of those days *humidity = high* and *play = no* as well.

5.5.2 **Association Rules**

Shortly we will explain how to generate these item sets efficiently. But first let us finish the story. Once all item sets with the required coverage have been generated, the next step is to turn each into a rule, or set of rules, with at least the specified minimum accuracy. Some item sets will produce more than one rule; others will produce none. For example, there is one three-item set with a coverage of 4 (row 38 of Table 5.10):

```
humidity = normal, windy = false, play = yes
```

This set leads to seven potential rules:

```
If humidity = normal and windy = false then play = yes        5/4
If humidity = normal and play = yes then windy = false        5/6
If windy = false and play = yes then humidity = normal        5/6
If humidity = normal then windy = false and play = yes        5/7
If windy = false then humidity = normal and play = yes        5/8
If play = yes then humidity = normal and windy = false        5/9
If - then humidity = normal and windy = false and play = yes  4/12
```

The figures at the right show the number of instances for which all three conditions are true—that is, the coverage—divided by the number of instances for which the conditions in the antecedent are true. Interpreted as a fraction, they represent the proportion of instances on which the rule is correct—that is, its accuracy. Assuming that the minimum specified accuracy is 100 percent, only the first of these rules will make it into the final rule set. The denominators of the fractions are readily obtained by looking up the antecedent expression in Table 5.10 (though some are not shown in the table). The final rule shown here has no conditions in the antecedent, and its denominator is the total number of instances in the dataset.

Table 5.11 shows the final rule set for the weather data, with minimum coverage 2 and minimum accuracy 100 percent, sorted by coverage. There are 58 rules,

Table 5.11 Association Rules for the Weather Data

	Association Rule			Coverage	Accuracy
1	Humidity = normal windy = false	⇒	Play = yes	5	100%
2	Temperature = cool	⇒	Humidity = normal	5	100%
3	Outlook = overcast	⇒	Play = yes	5	100%
4	Temperature = cool play = yes	⇒	Humidity = normal	3	100%
5	Outlook = rainy windy = false	⇒	Play = yes	3	100%
6	Outlook = rainy play = yes	⇒	Windy = false	3	100%
7	Outlook = sunny humidity = high	⇒	Play = no	3	100%
8	Outlook = sunny play = no	⇒	Humidity = high	3	100%
9	Temperature = cool windy = false	⇒	Humidity = normal Play = yes	2	100%
10	Temperature = cool humidity = normal windy = false	⇒	Play = yes	2	100%
11	Temperature = cool windy = false play = yes	⇒	Humidity = normal	2	100%
12	Outlook = rainy humidity = normal windy = false	⇒	Play = yes	2	100%
13	Outlook = rainy humidity = normal play = yes	⇒	Windy = false	2	100%
14	Outlook = rainy temperature = mild windy = false	⇒	Play = yes	2	100%
15	Outlook = rainy temperature = mild play = yes	⇒	Windy = false	2	100%
16	Temperature = mild windy = false play = yes	⇒	Outlook = rainy	2	100%
17	Outlook = overcast temperature = hot	⇒	Windy = false Play = yes	2	100%
18	Outlook = overcast windy = false	⇒	Temperature = hot Play = yes	2	100%
19	Temperature = hot play = yes	⇒	Outlook = overcast Windy = false	2	100%
20	Outlook = overcast temperature = hot windy = false	⇒	Play = yes	2	100%
21	Outlook = overcast temperature = hot play = yes	⇒	Windy = false	2	100%

Table 5.11 *Continued*

	Association Rule			Coverage	Accuracy
22	Outlook = overcast windy = false play = yes	$\Rightarrow$	Temperature = hot	2	100%
23	Temperature = hot windy = false play = yes	$\Rightarrow$	Outlook = overcast	2	100%
24	Windy = false play = no	$\Rightarrow$	Outlook = sunny Humidity = high	2	100%
25	Outlook = sunny humidity = high windy = false	$\Rightarrow$	Play = no	2	100%
26	Outlook = sunny windy = false play = no	$\Rightarrow$	Humidity = high	2	100%
27	Humidity = high windy = false play = no	$\Rightarrow$	Outlook = sunny	2	100%
28	Outlook = sunny temperature = hot	$\Rightarrow$	Humidity = high Play = no	2	100%
29	Temperature = hot play = no	$\Rightarrow$	Outlook = sunny Humidity = high	2	100%
30	Outlook = sunny temperature = hot humidity = high	$\Rightarrow$	Play = no	2	100%
31	Outlook = sunny temperature = hot play = no	$\Rightarrow$	Humidity = high	2	100%
…	…			…	…
58	Outlook = sunny temperature = hot	$\Rightarrow$	Humidity = high	2	100%

3 with coverage 4, 5 with coverage 3, and 50 with coverage 2. Only 7 have two conditions in the consequent, and none has more than two. The first rule comes from the item set described previously. Sometimes several rules arise from the same item set. For example, rules 9, 10, and 11 all arise from the four-item set in row 6 of Table 5.10:

```
temperature = cool, humidity = normal, windy = false, play = yes
```

which has coverage 2. Three subsets of this item set also have coverage 2:

```
temperature = cool, windy = false
temperature = cool, humidity = normal, windy = false
temperature = cool, windy = false, play = yes
```

and these lead to rules 9, 10, and 11, all of which are 100 percent accurate (on the training data).

5.5.3 Generating Rules Efficiently

We now consider in more detail an algorithm for producing association rules with specified minimum coverage and accuracy. There are two stages: generating item sets with the specified minimum coverage and from each item set determining the rules that have the specified minimum accuracy.

The first stage proceeds by generating all one-item sets with the given minimum coverage (the first column of Table 5.10) and then using this to generate the two-item sets (second column), three-item sets (third column), and so on. Each operation involves a pass through the dataset to count the items in each set, and after the pass the surviving item sets are stored in a hash table—a standard data structure that allows elements stored in it to be found quickly. From the one-item sets, candidate two-item sets are generated, and then a pass is made through the dataset, counting the coverage of each two-item set; at the end, the candidate sets with less than minimum coverage are removed from the table. The candidate two-item sets are simply all of the one-item sets taken in pairs, because a two-item set cannot have the minimum coverage unless both its constituent one-item sets have minimum coverage, too. This applies in general: a three-item set can only have the minimum coverage if all three of its two-item subsets have minimum coverage as well, and similarly for four-item sets.

An example will help to explain how candidate item sets are generated. Suppose there are five three-item sets—(A B C), (A B D), (A C D), (A C E), and (B C D)—where, for example, A is a feature such as *outlook = sunny*. The union of the first two, (A B C D), is a candidate four-item set because its other three-item subsets (A C D) and (B C D) have greater than minimum coverage. If the three-item sets are sorted into lexical order, as they are in this list, then we need only consider pairs whose first two members are the same. For example, we do not consider (A C D) and (B C D) because (A B C D) can also be generated from (A B C) and (A B D), and if these two are not candidate three-item sets, then (A B C D) cannot be a candidate four-item set. This leaves the pairs (A B C) and (A B D), which we have already explained, and (A C D) and (A C E). This second pair leads to the set (A C D E) whose three-item subsets do not all have the minimum coverage, so it is discarded. The hash table assists with this check: we simply remove each item from the set in turn and check that the remaining three-item set is indeed present in the hash table. Thus, in this example there is only one candidate four-item set, (A B C D). Whether or not it actually has minimum coverage can only be determined by checking the instances in the dataset.

The second stage of the procedure takes each item set and generates rules from it, checking that they have the specified minimum accuracy. If only rules with a single test on the right side were sought, it would be simply a matter of considering each condition in turn as the consequent of the rule, deleting it from the item set, and dividing the coverage of the entire item set by the coverage of the resulting subset—obtained from the hash table—to yield the accuracy of the corresponding rule. Given that we are also interested in association rules with multiple tests in the consequent, it looks like we have to evaluate the effect of placing each *subset* of the item set on the right side, leaving the remainder of the set as the antecedent.

This brute-force method will be excessively computation intensive unless item sets are small, because the number of possible subsets grows exponentially with the size of the item set. However, there is a better way. Note that if the double-consequent rule

```
If windy = false and play = no then outlook = sunny
                                and humidity = high
```

holds with a given minimum coverage and accuracy, then both single-consequent rules formed from the same item set must also hold:

```
If humidity = high and windy = false and play = no
    then outlook = sunny
If outlook = sunny and windy = false and play = no
    then humidity = high
```

Conversely, if one or other of the single-consequent rules does not hold, there is no point in considering the double-consequent one. This gives a way of building up from single-consequent rules to candidate double-consequent ones, from double-consequent rules to candidate triple-consequent ones, and so on. Of course, each candidate rule must be checked against the hash table to see if it really does have more than the specified minimum accuracy. But this generally involves checking far fewer rules than the brute force method. It is interesting that this way of building up candidate $(n + 1)$-consequent rules from actual n-consequent ones is really just the same as building up candidate $(n + 1)$-item sets from actual n-item sets, described earlier.

5.5.4 Discussion

Association rules are often sought for very large datasets, and efficient algorithms are highly valued. The method described previously makes one pass through the dataset for each different size of item set. Sometimes the dataset is too large to read in to main memory and must be kept on disk; then it may be worth reducing the number of passes by checking item sets of two consecutive sizes in one go. For example, once sets with two items have been generated, all sets of three items could be generated from them before going through the instance set to count the actual number of items in the sets. More three-item sets than necessary would be considered, but the number of passes through the entire dataset would be reduced.

In practice, the amount of computation needed to generate association rules depends critically on the minimum coverage specified. The accuracy has less influence because it does not affect the number of passes that we must make through the dataset. In many situations we will want to obtain a certain number of rules—say 50—with the greatest possible coverage at a prespecified minimum accuracy level. One way to do this is to begin by specifying the coverage to be rather high and to then successively reduce it, reexecuting the entire rule-finding algorithm for each coverage value and repeating this until the desired number of rules has been generated.

The tabular input format that we use throughout this book, and in particular a standard ARFF file based on it, is inefficient for many association-rule problems. Association rules are often used when attributes are binary—either present or absent—and most of the attribute values associated with a given instance are absent. This is a case for sparse data representation; the same algorithm for finding association rules applies.

5.6 LINEAR MODELS

The methods we have been looking at for decision trees and rules work most naturally with nominal attributes. They can be extended to numeric attributes either by incorporating numeric-value tests directly into the decision tree or rule induction scheme or by prediscretizing numeric attributes into nominal ones. However, there are methods that work most naturally with numeric attributes. We look at simple ones here, ones that form components of more complex learning methods, which we will examine later.

5.6.1 Numeric Prediction: Linear Regression

When the outcome, or class, is numeric, and all the attributes are numeric, linear regression is a natural technique to consider. This is a staple method in statistics. The idea is to express the class as a linear combination of the attributes, with predetermined weights:

$$x = w_0 + w_1 a_1 + w_2 a_2 + \ldots + w_k a_k$$

where x is the class; $a_1, a_2, \ldots, a_k$ are the attribute values; and $w_0, w_1, \ldots, w_k$ are weights.

The weights are calculated from the training data. Here the notation gets a little heavy, because we need a way of expressing the attribute values for each training instance. The first instance will have a class, say $x^{(1)}$, and attribute values $a_1^{(1)}, a_2^{(1)}, \ldots, a_k^{(1)}$, where the superscript denotes that it is the first example. Moreover, it is notationally convenient to assume an extra attribute a_0 whose value is always 1.

The predicted value for the first instance's class can be written as

$$w_0 a_0^{(1)} + w_1 a_1^{(1)} + w_2 a_2^{(1)} + \ldots + w_k a_k^{(1)} = \sum_{j=0}^{k} w_j a_j^{(1)}$$

This is the predicted, not the actual, value for the first instance's class. Of interest is the difference between the predicted and the actual values. The method of linear regression is to choose the coefficients w_j—there are $k + 1$ of them—to minimize the sum of the squares of these differences over all the training instances. Suppose there are n training instances; denote the ith one with a superscript (i). Then the sum of the squares of the differences is

$$\sum_{i=1}^{n} \left(x^{(i)} - \sum_{j=0}^{k} w_j a_j^{(i)} \right)^2$$

where the expression inside the parentheses is the difference between the ith instance's actual class and its predicted class. This sum of squares is what we have to minimize by choosing the coefficients appropriately.

This is all starting to look rather formidable. However, the minimization technique is straightforward if you have the appropriate math background. Suffice it to say that given enough examples—roughly speaking, more examples than attributes—choosing weights to minimize the sum of the squared differences is really not difficult. It does involve a matrix inversion operation, but this is readily available as prepackaged software.

Once the math has been accomplished, the result is a set of numeric weights, based on the training data, which we can use to predict the class of new instances. An example of this can be seen when looking at the CPU performance data. A formula can be used to predict the CPU performance of new test instances.

Linear regression is an excellent, simple method for numeric prediction, and it has been widely used in statistical applications for decades. Of course, linear models suffer from the disadvantage of, well, linearity. If the data exhibits a non-linear dependency, the best-fitting straight line will be found, where "best" is interpreted as the least mean-squared difference. This line may not fit very well. However, linear models serve well as building blocks for more complex learning methods.

5.6.3 Linear Classification: Logistic Regression

Linear regression can easily be used for classification in domains with numeric attributes. Indeed, we can use *any* regression technique, whether linear or nonlinear, for classification. The trick is to perform a regression for each class, setting the output equal to one for training instances that belong to the class and zero for those that do not. The result is a linear expression for the class. Then, given a test example of unknown class, calculate the value of each linear expression and choose the one that is largest. This method is sometimes called *multiresponse linear regression.*

One way of looking at multiresponse linear regression is to imagine that it approximates a numeric *membership function* for each class. The membership function is 1 for instances that belong to that class and 0 for other instances. Given a new instance, we calculate its membership for each class and select the biggest.

Multiresponse linear regression often yields good results in practice. However, it has two drawbacks. First, the membership values it produces are not proper probabilities because they can fall outside the range 0 to 1. Second, least-squares regression assumes that the errors are not only statistically independent but are also normally distributed with the same standard deviation, an assumption that is blatantly violated when the method is applied to classification problems because the observations only ever take on the values 0 and 1.

A related statistical technique called *logistic regression* does not suffer from these problems. Instead of approximating the 0 and 1 values directly, thereby risking illegitimate probability values when the target is overshot, logistic regression builds a linear model based on a transformed target variable.

Suppose first that there are only two classes. Logistic regression replaces the original target variable

$$Pr[1|a_1, a_2, \ldots, a_k]$$

which cannot be approximated accurately using a linear function, with

$$\log(Pr[1|a_1, a_2, \ldots, a_k])/(1 - Pr[1|a_1, a_2, \ldots, a_k])$$

The resulting values are no longer constrained to the interval from 0 to 1 but can lie anywhere between negative infinity and positive infinity. Figure 5.9(a) plots the transformation function, which is often called the *logit transformation*.

The transformed variable is approximated using a linear function just like the ones generated by linear regression. The resulting model is

$$Pr[1|a_1, a_2, \ldots, a_k] = 1/(1 + \exp(-w_0 - w_1 a_1 - \ldots - w_k a_k))$$

with weights w. Figure 5.9(b) shows an example of this function in one dimension, with two weights $w_0 = 0.5$ and $w_1 = 1$.

Just as in linear regression, weights must be found that fit the training data well. Linear regression measures the goodness of fit using the squared error. In logistic regression the *log-likelihood* of the model is used instead. This is given by

$$\sum_{i=1}^{n} (1 - x^{(i)}) \log(1 - Pr[1|a_1^{(i)}, a_2^{(i)}, \ldots, a_k^{(i)}]) + x^{(i)} \log(Pr[1|a_1^{(i)}, a_2^{(i)}, \ldots, a_k^{(i)}])$$

where the $x^{(i)}$ are either zero or one.

The weights w_i need to be chosen to maximize the log-likelihood. There are several methods for solving this maximization problem. A simple one is to iteratively solve a sequence of weighted least-squares regression problems until the log-likelihood converges to a maximum, which usually happens in a few iterations.

To generalize logistic regression to several classes, one possibility is to proceed in the way described previously for multiresponse linear regression by performing logistic regression independently for each class. Unfortunately, the resulting prob-

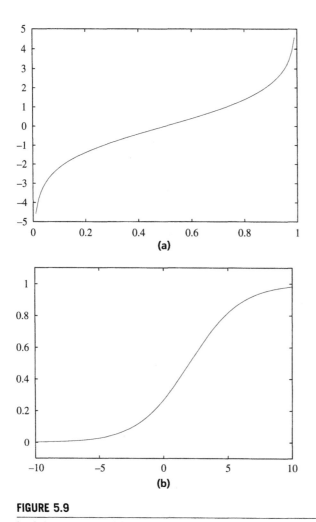

FIGURE 5.9

Logistic regression: (a) the logit transform and (b) an example logistic regression function.

ability estimates will not sum to 1. To obtain proper probabilities it is necessary to couple the individual models for each class. This yields a joint optimization problem, and there are efficient solution methods for this.

A conceptually simpler and very general way to address multiclass problems is known as *pairwise classification*. Here a classifier is built for every pair of classes, using only the instances from these two classes. The output on an unknown test example is based on which class receives the most votes. This method generally yields accurate results in terms of classification error. It can also be used to produce probability estimates by applying a method called *pairwise coupling,* which calibrates the individual probability estimates from the different classifiers.

If there are k classes, pairwise classification builds a total of $k(k-1)/2$ classifiers. Although this sounds unnecessarily computation intensive, it is not. In fact, if the classes are evenly populated pairwise classification is at least as fast as any other multiclass method. The reason is that each of the pairwise learning problem only involves instances pertaining to the two classes under consideration. If n instances are divided evenly among k classes, this amounts to $2n/k$ instances per problem. Suppose the learning algorithm for a two-class problem with n instances takes time proportional to n seconds to execute. Then the run time for pairwise classification is proportional to $k(k-1)/2 \times 2n/k$ seconds, which is $(k-1)n$. In other words, the method scales linearly with the number of classes. If the learning algorithm takes more time—say proportional to n^2—the advantage of the pairwise approach becomes even more pronounced.

The use of linear functions for classification can easily be visualized in instance space. The decision boundary for two-class logistic regression lies where the prediction probability is 0.5, that is,

$$\Pr[1|a_1,a_2,\ldots,a_k] = 1/(1 + \exp(-w_0 - w_1a_1 - \ldots - w_ka_k)) = 0.5$$

This occurs when

$$-w_0 - w_1a_1 - \ldots - w_ka_k = 0$$

Because this is a linear equality in the attribute values, the boundary is a linear plane, or *hyperplane,* in instance, space. It is easy to visualize sets of points that cannot be separated by a single hyperplane, and these cannot be discriminated correctly by logistic regression.

Multiresponse linear regression suffers from the same problem. Each class receives a weight vector calculated from the training data. Focus for the moment on a particular pair of classes. Suppose the weight vector for class 1 is

$$w_0^{(1)} + w_1^{(1)}a_1 + w_2^{(1)}a_2 + \ldots + w_k^{(1)}a_k$$

and it is the same for class 2 with appropriate superscripts. Then, an instance will be assigned to class 1 rather than class 2 if

$$w_0^{(1)} + w_1^{(1)}a_1 + \ldots + w_k^{(1)}a_k > w_0^{(2)} + w_1^{(2)}a_1 + \ldots + w_k^{(2)}a_k$$

In other words, it will be assigned to class 1 if

$$\left(w_0^{(1)} - w_0^{(2)}\right) + \left(w_1^{(1)} - w_1^{(2)}\right)a_1 + \ldots + \left(w_k^{(1)} - w_k^{(2)}\right)a_k > 0$$

This is a linear inequality in the attribute values, so the boundary between each pair of classes is a hyperplane. The same holds true when performing pairwise classification. The only difference is that the boundary between two classes is governed by the training instances in those classes and is not influenced by the other classes.

5.6.4 Linear Classification Using the Perceptron

Logistic regression attempts to produce accurate probability estimates by maximizing the probability of the training data. Of course, accurate probability estimates lead to accurate classifications. However, it is not necessary to perform probability estimation if the sole purpose of the model is to predict class labels. A different approach is to learn a hyperplane that separates the instances pertaining to the different classes—let's assume that there are only two of them. If the data can be separated perfectly into two groups using a hyperplane, it is said to be *linearly separable*. It turns out that if the data is linearly separable, there is a simple algorithm for finding a separating hyperplane.

The algorithm is called the *perceptron learning rule*. Before looking at it in detail, let's examine the equation for a hyperplane again:

$$w_0 a_0 + w_1 a_1 + w_2 a_2 + \ldots + w_k a_k = 0$$

Here, $a_1, a_2, \ldots, a_k$ are the attribute values, and $w_0, w_1, \ldots, w_k$ are the weights that define the hyperplane. We will assume that each training instance $a_1, a_2, \ldots$ is extended by an additional attribute a_0 that always has the value 1 (as we did in the case of linear regression). This extension, which is called the *bias,* just means that we don't have to include an additional constant element in the sum. If the sum is greater than zero, we will predict the first class; otherwise, we will predict the second class. We want to find values for the weights so that the training data is correctly classified by the hyperplane.

Figure 5.10(a) gives the perceptron learning rule for finding a separating hyperplane. The algorithm iterates until a perfect solution has been found, but it will only work properly if a separating hyperplane exists—that is, if the data is linearly separable. Each iteration goes through all the training instances. If a misclassified instance is encountered, the parameters of the hyperplane are changed so that the misclassified instance moves closer to the hyperplane or maybe even across the hyperplane onto the correct side. If the instance belongs to the first class, this is done by adding its attribute values to the weight vector; otherwise, they are subtracted from it.

To see why this works, consider the situation after an instance a pertaining to the first class has been added:

$$(w_0 + a_0) a_0 + (w_1 + a_1) a_1 + (w_2 + a_2) a_2 + \ldots + (w_k + a_k) a_k$$

This means the output for a has increased by

$$a_0 \times a_0 + a_1 \times a_1 + a_2 \times a_2 + \ldots + a_k \times a_k$$

This number is always positive. Thus, the hyperplane has moved in the correct direction for classifying instance a as positive. Conversely, if an instance belonging to the second class is misclassified, the output for that instance decreases after the modification, again moving the hyperplane to the correct direction.

```
Set all weights to zero

Until all instances in the training data are classified correctly

  For each instance I in the training data

    If I is classified incorrectly by the perceptron

      If I belongs to the first class add it to the weight vector

      else subtract it from the weight vector
```

(a)

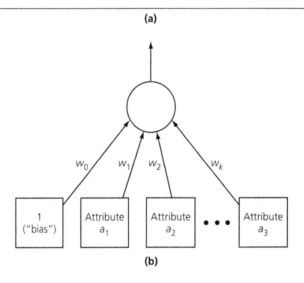

(b)

FIGURE 5.10

The perceptron: (a) learning rule and (b) representation as a neural network.

These corrections are incremental and can interfere with earlier updates. However, it can be shown that the algorithm converges in a finite number of iterations if the data is linearly separable. Of course, if the data is not linearly separable, the algorithm will not terminate, so an upper bound needs to be imposed on the number of iterations when this method is applied in practice.

The resulting hyperplane is called a *perceptron*, and it's the grandfather of neural networks. Figure 5.10(b) represents the perceptron as a graph with nodes and weighted edges, imaginatively termed a "network of neurons." There are two layers of nodes: input and output. The input layer has one node for every attribute, plus an extra node that is always set to one. The output layer consists of just one node. Every node in the input layer is connected to the output layer. The connections are weighted, and the weights are those numbers found by the perceptron learning rule.

When an instance is presented to the perceptron, its attribute values serve to "activate" the input layer. They are multiplied by the weights and summed up at the output node. If the weighted sum is greater than 0, the output signal is 1, representing the first class; otherwise, it is −1, representing the second.

5.6.5 Linear Classification Using Winnow

The perceptron algorithm is not the only method that is guaranteed to find a separating hyperplane for a linearly separable problem. For datasets with binary attributes, there is an alternative known as *Winnow,* shown in Figure 5.11(a). The structure of the two algorithms is similar. Like the perceptron, Winnow only

```
While some instances are misclassified
      for every instance a
        classify a using the current weights
        if the predicted class is incorrect
          if a belongs to the first class
            for each aᵢ that is 1, multiply wᵢ by α
            (if aᵢ is 0, leave wᵢ unchanged)
          otherwise
            for each aᵢ that is 1, divide wᵢ by α
            (if aᵢ is 0, leave wᵢ unchanged)
```

(a)

```
While some instances are misclassified
     for every instance a
       classify a using the current weights
       if the predicted class is incorrect
         if a belongs to the first class
           for each aᵢ that is 1,
             multiply wᵢ⁺ by α
             divide wᵢ⁻ by α
           (if aᵢ is 0, leave wᵢ⁺ and wᵢ⁻ unchanged)
         otherwise for
           for each aᵢ that is 1,
             multiply wᵢ⁻ by α
             divide wᵢ⁺ by α
           (if aᵢ is 0, leave wᵢ⁺ and wᵢ⁻ unchanged)
```

(b)

FIGURE 5.11

The Winnow algorithm: (a) the unbalanced version and (b) the balanced version.

updates the weight vector when a misclassified instance is encountered—it is *mistake driven*.

The two methods differ in how the weights are updated. The perceptron rule employs an additive mechanism that alters the weight vector by adding (or subtracting) the instance's attribute vector. Winnow employs multiplicative updates and alters weights individually by multiplying them by the user-specified parameter α (or its inverse). The attribute values a_i are either 0 or 1 because we are working with binary data. Weights are unchanged if the attribute value is 0, because then they do not participate in the decision. Otherwise, the multiplier is α if that attribute helps to make a correct decision and $1/\alpha$ if it does not.

Another difference is that the threshold in the linear function is also a user-specified parameter. We call this threshold θ and classify an instance as belonging to class 1 if and only if

$$w_0 a_0 + w_1 a_1 + w_2 a_2 + \ldots + w_k a_k > \theta$$

The multiplier α needs to be greater than 1. The w_i are set to a constant at the start.

The algorithm we have described doesn't allow negative weights, which—depending on the domain—can be a drawback. However, there is a version, called *Balanced Winnow*, which does allow them. This version maintains two weight vectors, one for each class. An instance is classified as belonging to class 1 if

$$\left(w_0^+ - w_0^-\right)a_0 + \left(w_1^+ - w_1^-\right)a_1 + \ldots + \left(w_k^+ - w_k^-\right)a_k > \theta$$

Figure 5.11(b) shows the balanced algorithm.

Winnow effectively homes in on the relevant features in a dataset—therefore it is called an *attribute-efficient* learner. That means that it may be a good candidate algorithm if a dataset has many (binary) features and most of them are irrelevant. Both Winnow and the perceptron algorithm can be used in an online setting in which new instances arrive continuously, because they can incrementally update their hypotheses as new instances arrive.

5.7 INSTANCE-BASED LEARNING

In instance-based learning the training examples are stored verbatim, and a distance function is used to determine which member of the training set is closest to an unknown test instance. Once the nearest training instance has been located, its class is predicted for the test instance. The only remaining problem is defining the distance function, and that is not difficult to do, particularly if the attributes are numeric.

5.7.1 The Distance Function

Although there are other possible choices, most instance-based learners use Euclidean distance. The distance between an instance with attribute values $a_1^{(1)}, a_2^{(1)}, \ldots,$

$a_k^{(1)}$ (where k is the number of attributes) and one with values $a_1^{(2)}, a_2^{(2)}, \ldots, a_k^{(2)}$ is defined as

$$\sqrt{\left(a_1^{(1)} - a_1^{(2)}\right)^2 + \left(a_2^{(1)} - a_2^{(2)}\right)^2 + \ldots + \left(a_k^{(1)} - a_k^{(2)}\right)^2}$$

When comparing distances, it is not necessary to perform the square root operation; the sums of squares can be compared directly.

One alternative to the Euclidean distance is the Manhattan or city-block metric, where the difference between attribute values is not squared but just added up (after taking the absolute value). Others are obtained by taking powers higher than the square. Higher powers increase the influence of large differences at the expense of small differences. Generally, the Euclidean distance represents a good compromise. Other distance metrics may be more appropriate in special circumstances. The key is to think of actual instances and what it means for them to be separated by a certain distance—what would twice that distance mean, for example?

Different attributes are measured on different scales, so if the Euclidean distance formula were used directly, the effects of some attributes might be completely dwarfed by others that had larger scales of measurement. Consequently, it is usual to normalize all attribute values to lie between 0 and 1, by calculating

$$a_i = \frac{v_i - \min v_i}{\max v_i - \min v_i}$$

where v_i is the actual value of attribute i, and the maximum and minimum are taken over all instances in the training set.

These formulae implicitly assume numeric attributes. Here, the difference between two values is just the numeric difference between them, and it is this difference that is squared and added to yield the distance function. For nominal attributes that take on values that are symbolic rather than numeric, the difference between two values that are not the same is often taken to be one, whereas if the values are the same the difference is zero. No scaling is required in this case because only the values 0 and 1 are used.

A common policy for handling missing values is as follows. For nominal attributes, assume that a missing feature is maximally different from any other feature value. Thus, if either or both values are missing, or if the values are different, the difference between them is taken as one; the difference is zero only if they are not missing and both are the same. For numeric attributes, the difference between two missing values is also taken as one. However, if just one value is missing, the difference is often taken as either the (normalized) size of the other value or one minus that size, whichever is larger. This means that if values are missing, the difference is as large as it can possibly be.

5.7.2 Finding Nearest Neighbors Efficiently

Although instance-based learning is simple and effective, it is often slow. The obvious way to find which member of the training set is closest to an unknown test instance is to calculate the distance from every member of the training set and select the smallest. This procedure is linear in the number of training instances: in other words, the time it takes to make a single prediction is proportional to the number of training instances. Processing an entire test set takes time proportional to the product of the number of instances in the training and test sets.

Nearest neighbors can be found more efficiently by representing the training set as a tree, although it is not obvious how. One suitable structure is a *kD-tree*. This is a binary tree that divides the input space with a hyperplane and then splits each partition again, recursively. All splits are made parallel to one of the axes, either vertically or horizontally, in the two-dimensional case. The data structure is called a *kD-tree* because it stores a set of points in *k*- dimensional space, *k* being the number of attributes.

Figure 5.12(a) gives a small example with $k = 2$, and Figure 5.12(b) shows the four training instances it represents, along with the hyperplanes that constitute the tree. Note that these hyperplanes are *not* decision boundaries: decisions are made on a nearest-neighbor basis as explained later. The first split is horizontal (*h*), through the point (7,4)—this is the tree's root. The left branch is not split further: it contains the single point (2,2), which is a leaf of the tree. The right branch is split vertically (*v*) at the point (6,7). Its left child is empty, and its right child contains the point (3,8). As this example illustrates, each region contains just one point—or, perhaps, no points. Sibling branches of the tree—for example, the two daughters of the root in Figure 5.12(a)—are not necessarily developed to the same depth. Every point in the training set corresponds to a single node, and up to half are leaf nodes.

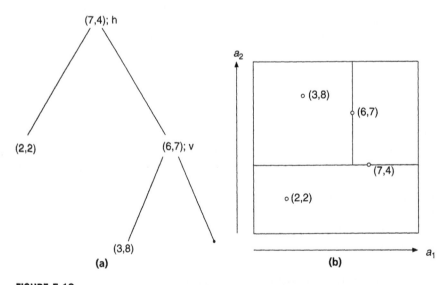

(a) (b)

FIGURE 5.12

A *kD*-tree for four training instances: (a) the tree and (b) instances and splits.

How do you build a *k*D-tree from a dataset? Can it be updated efficiently as new training examples are added? And how does it speed up nearest-neighbor calculations? We tackle the last question first.

To locate the nearest neighbor of a given target point, follow the tree down from its root to locate the region containing the target. Figure 5.13 shows a space like that of Figure 5.12(b) but with a few more instances and an extra boundary. The target, which is not one of the instances in the tree, is marked by a star. The leaf node of the region containing the target is colored black. This is not necessarily the target's closest neighbor, as this example illustrates, but it is a good first approximation. In particular, any nearer neighbor must lie closer—within the dashed circle in Figure 5.13.

To determine whether one exists, first check whether it is possible for a closer neighbor to lie within the node's sibling. The black node's sibling is shaded in Figure 5.13, and the circle does not intersect it, so the sibling cannot contain a closer neighbor. Then back up to the parent node and check *its* sibling—which here covers everything above the horizontal line. In this case it *must* be explored, because the area it covers intersects with the best circle so far. To explore it, find its daughters (the original point's two aunts), check whether they intersect the

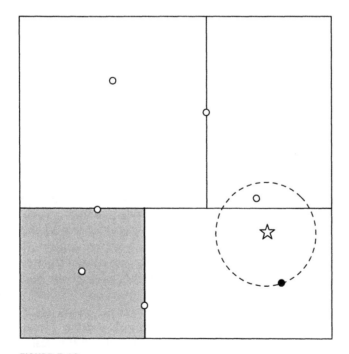

FIGURE 5.13

Using a *k*D-tree to find the nearest neighbor of the star.

circle (the left one does not, but the right one does), and descend to see whether it contains a closer point (it does).

In a typical case, this algorithm is far faster than examining all points to find the nearest neighbor. The work involved in finding the initial approximate nearest neighbor—the black point in Figure 5.13—depends on the depth of the tree, given by the logarithm of the number of nodes, $\log_2 n$. The amount of work involved in backtracking to check whether this really is the nearest neighbor depends a bit on the tree and on how good the initial approximation is. But for a well-constructed tree whose nodes are approximately square, rather than long skinny rectangles, it can also be shown to be logarithmic in the number of nodes.

How do you build a good tree for a set of training examples? The problem boils down to selecting the first training instance to split at and the direction of the split. Once you can do that, apply the same method recursively to each child of the initial split to construct the entire tree.

To find a good direction for the split, calculate the variance of the data points along each axis individually, select the axis with the greatest variance, and create a splitting hyperplane perpendicular to it. To find a good place for the hyperplane, locate the median value along that axis and select the corresponding point. This makes the split perpendicular to the direction of greatest spread, with half the points lying on either side. This produces a well-balanced tree. To avoid long skinny regions, it is best for successive splits to be along different axes, which is likely because the dimension of greatest variance is chosen at each stage. However, if the distribution of points is badly skewed, choosing the median value may generate several successive splits in the same direction, yielding long, skinny hyperrectangles. A better strategy is to calculate the mean rather than the median and use the point closest to that. The tree will not be perfectly balanced, but its regions will tend to be squarish because there is a greater chance that different directions will be chosen for successive splits.

An advantage of instance-based learning over most other machine learning methods is that new examples can be added to the training set at any time. To retain this advantage when using a kD-tree, we need to be able to update it incrementally with new data points. To do this, determine which leaf node contains the new point and find its hyperrectangle. If it is empty, simply place the new point there. Otherwise split the hyperrectangle, splitting it along its longest dimension to preserve squareness. This simple heuristic does not guarantee that adding a series of points will preserve the tree's balance nor that the hyperrectangles will be well shaped for nearest-neighbor search. It is a good idea to rebuild the tree from scratch occasionally—for example, when its depth grows to twice the best possible depth.

As we have seen, kD-trees are good data structures for finding nearest neighbors efficiently. However, they are not perfect. Skewed datasets present a basic conflict between the desire for the tree to be perfectly balanced and the desire for regions to be squarish. More important, rectangles—even squares—are not the best shape to use anyway, because of their corners. If the dashed circle in Figure

5.13 were any bigger, which it would be if the black instance were a little farther from the target, it would intersect the lower right corner of the rectangle at the top left and then that rectangle would have to be investigated, too—despite the fact that the training instances that define it are a long way from the corner in question. The corners of rectangular regions are awkward.

The solution? Use hyperspheres, not hyperrectangles. Neighboring spheres may overlap, whereas rectangles can abut, but this is not a problem because the nearest-neighbor algorithm for kD-trees described previously does not depend on the regions being disjoint. A data structure called a *ball tree* defines k-dimensional hyperspheres ("balls") that cover the data points, and arranges them into a tree.

Figure 5.14(a) shows 16 training instances in two-dimensional space, overlaid by a pattern of overlapping circles, and Figure 5.14(b) shows a tree formed from these circles. Circles at different levels of the tree are indicated by different styles of dash, and the smaller circles are drawn in shades of gray. Each node of the tree represents a ball, and the node is dashed or shaded according to the same convention so that you can identify which level the balls are at. To help you understand the tree, numbers are placed on the nodes to show how many data points are deemed to be inside that ball. But be careful; this is not necessarily the same as the number of points falling within the spatial region that the ball represents. The regions at each level sometimes overlap, but points that fall into the overlap area are assigned to only one of the overlapping balls (the diagram does not show which one). Instead of the occupancy counts in Figure 5.14(b), the nodes of actual ball trees store the center and radius of their ball; leaf nodes record the points they contain as well.

To use a ball tree to find the nearest neighbor to a given target, start by traversing the tree from the top down to locate the leaf that contains the target and find the closest point to the target in that ball. This gives an upper bound for the target's distance from its nearest neighbor. Then, just as for the kD-tree, examine the sibling node. If the distance from the target to the sibling's center exceeds its radius plus the current upper bound, it cannot possibly contain a closer point; otherwise the sibling must be examined by descending the tree further. In Figure 5.15 the target is marked with a star and the black dot is its closest currently known neighbor. The entire contents of the gray ball can be ruled out: it cannot contain a closer point because its center is too far away. Proceed recursively back up the tree to its root, examining any ball that may possibly contain a point nearer than the current upper bound.

Ball trees are built from the top down, and as with kD-trees the basic problem is to find a good way of splitting a ball containing a set of data points into two. In practice you do not have to continue until the leaf balls contain just two points: you can stop earlier, once a predetermined minimum number is reached—and the same goes for kD-trees. Here is one possible splitting method. Choose the point in the ball that is farthest from its center, and then a second point that is farthest from the first one. Assign all data points in the ball to the closest one of these two cluster centers, then compute the centroid of each cluster and the

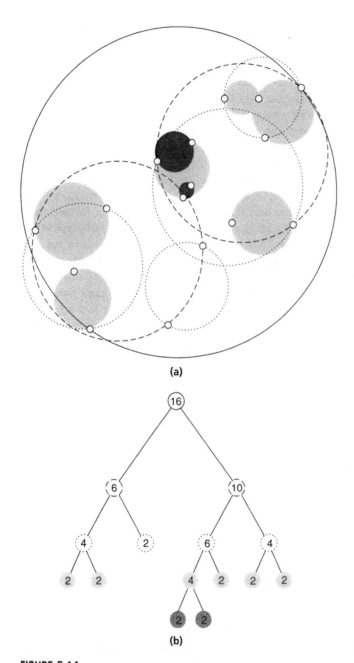

(a)

(b)

FIGURE 5.14

Ball tree for 16 training instances: (a) instances and balls and (b) the tree.

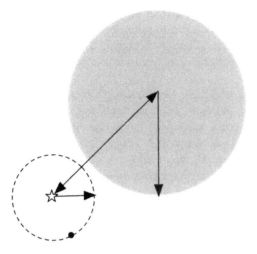

FIGURE 5.15

Ruling out an entire ball (gray) based on a target point (star) and its current nearest neighbor.

minimum radius required for it to enclose all the data points it represents. This method has the merit that the cost of splitting a ball containing n points is only linear in n. There are more elaborate algorithms that produce tighter balls, but they require more computation. We will not describe sophisticated algorithms for constructing ball trees or updating them incrementally as new training instances are encountered.

5.7.3 Discussion

Nearest-neighbor instance-based learning is simple and often works very well. In the method described previously, each attribute has exactly the same influence on the decision, just as it does in the Naïve Bayes method. Another problem is that the database can easily become corrupted by noisy exemplars. One solution is to adopt the k-nearest-neighbor strategy, where some fixed, small, number k of nearest neighbors—say five—are located and used together to determine the class of the test instance through a simple majority vote. (Note that we used k to denote the number of attributes earlier; this is a different, independent usage.) Another way of proofing the database against noise is to choose the exemplars that are added to it selectively and judiciously; improved procedures address these shortcomings.

The nearest-neighbor method originated many decades ago, and statisticians analyzed k-nearest-neighbor schemes in the early 1950s. If the number of training instances is large, it makes intuitive sense to use more than one nearest neighbor, but clearly this is dangerous if there are few instances. It can be shown that when

k and the number n of instances both become infinite in such a way that $k/n \rightarrow$ 0, the probability of error approaches the theoretic minimum for the dataset. The nearest-neighbor method was adopted as a classification method in the early 1960s and has been widely used in the field of pattern recognition for more than three decades.

Nearest-neighbor classification was notoriously slow until kD-trees began to be applied in the early 1990s, although the data structure itself was developed much earlier. In practice, these trees become inefficient when the dimension of the space increases and are only worthwhile when the number of attributes is small—up to 10. Ball trees were developed much more recently and are an instance of a more general structure sometimes called a *metric tree.* Sophisticated algorithms can create metric trees that deal successfully with thousands of dimensions.

Instead of storing all training instances, you can compress them into regions. A simple technique, mentioned at the end of Section 5.1, is to just record the range of values observed in the training data for each attribute and category. Given a test instance, you work out which ranges the attribute values fall into and choose the category with the greatest number of correct ranges for that instance. A slightly more elaborate technique is to construct intervals for each attribute and use the training set to count the number of times each class occurs for each interval on each attribute. Numeric attributes can be discretized into intervals, and "intervals" consisting of a single point can be used for nominal ones. Then, given a test instance, you can determine which intervals it resides in and classify it by voting, a method called *voting feature intervals.* These methods are approximate, but fast, and can be useful for initial analysis of large datasets.

5.8 CLUSTERING

Clustering techniques apply when there is no class to be predicted but rather when the instances are to be divided into natural groups. These clusters presumably reflect some mechanism at work in the domain from which instances are drawn, a mechanism that causes some instances to bear a stronger resemblance to each other than they do to the remaining instances. Clustering naturally requires different techniques to the classification and association learning methods we have considered so far.

The result of clustering can be expressed in different ways. The groups that are identified may be exclusive so that any instance belongs in only one group. Or they may be overlapping so that an instance may fall into several groups. Or they may be probabilistic, whereby an instance belongs to each group with a certain probability. Or they may be hierarchical, such that there is a crude division of instances into groups at the top level, and each of these groups is refined further—perhaps all the way down to individual instances. Really, the choice among these possibilities should be dictated by the nature of the mechanisms that are thought to underlie the particular clustering phenomenon. However, because these mechanisms are rarely known—the very existence of clusters is, after all, something that we're trying to discover—and for pragmatic reasons too, the choice is usually dictated by the clustering tools that are available.

We will examine an algorithm that forms clusters in numeric domains, partitioning instances into disjoint clusters. Like the basic nearest-neighbor method of instance-based learning, it is a simple and straightforward technique that has been used for several decades.

5.8.1 Iterative Distance-Based Clustering

The classic clustering technique is called *k-means*. First, you specify in advance how many clusters are being sought: this is the parameter k. Then k points are chosen at random as cluster centers. All instances are assigned to their closest cluster center according to the ordinary Euclidean distance metric. Next the centroid, or mean, of the instances in each cluster is calculated—this is the "means" part. These centroids are taken to be new center values for their respective clusters. Finally, the whole process is repeated with the new cluster centers. Iteration continues until the same points are assigned to each cluster in consecutive rounds, at which stage the cluster centers have stabilized and will remain the same forever.

This clustering method is simple and effective. It is easy to prove that choosing the cluster center to be the centroid minimizes the total squared distance from each of the cluster's points to its center. Once the iteration has stabilized, each point is assigned to its nearest cluster center, so the overall effect is to minimize the total squared distance from all points to their cluster centers. But the minimum is a local one; there is no guarantee that it is the global minimum. The final clusters are sensitive to the initial cluster centers. Completely different arrangements can arise from small changes in the initial random choice. In fact, this is true of all practical clustering techniques: it is almost always infeasible to find globally optimal clusters. To increase the chance of finding a global minimum, people often run the algorithm several times with different initial choices and choose the best final result—the one with the smallest total squared distance.

It is easy to imagine situations in which *k*-means fails to find a good clustering. Consider four instances arranged at the vertices of a rectangle in two-dimensional space. There are two natural clusters, formed by grouping together the two vertices at either end of a short side. But suppose that the two initial cluster centers happen to fall at the midpoints of the *long* sides. This forms a stable configuration. The two clusters each contain the two instances at either end of a long side—no matter how great the difference between the long and the short sides.

5.8.2 Faster Distance Calculations

The *k*-means clustering algorithm usually requires several iterations, each involving finding the distance of k cluster centers from every instance to determine its cluster. There are simple approximations that speed this up considerably. For example, you can project the dataset and make cuts along selected axes, instead of using the arbitrary hyperplane divisions that are implied by choosing the nearest cluster center. But this inevitably compromises the quality of the resulting clusters.

Here's a better way of speeding things up. Finding the closest cluster center is not so different from finding nearest neighbors in instance-based learning. Can the same efficient solutions—kD-trees and ball trees—be used? Yes! Indeed they can be applied in an even more efficient way, because in each iteration of k-means all the data points are processed together, whereas in instance-based learning test instances are processed individually.

First, construct a kD-tree or ball tree for all the data points, which will remain static throughout the clustering procedure. Each iteration of k-means produces a set of cluster centers, and all data points must be examined and assigned to the nearest center. One way of processing the points is to descend the tree from the root until reaching a leaf and check each individual point in the leaf to find its closest cluster center. But it may be that the region represented by a higher interior node falls entirely within the domain of a single cluster center. In that case all the data points under that node can be processed in one blow!

The aim of the exercise, after all, is to find new positions for the cluster centers by calculating the centroid of the points they contain. The centroid can be calculated by keeping a running vector sum of the points in the cluster, and a count of how many there are so far. At the end, just divide one by the other to find the centroid. Suppose that with each node of the tree we store the vector sum of the points within that node and a count of the number of points. If the whole node falls within the ambit of a single cluster, the running totals for that cluster can be updated immediately. If not, look inside the node by proceeding recursively down the tree.

Figure 5.16 shows the same instances and ball tree as Figure 5.14, but with two cluster centers marked as black stars. Because all instances are assigned to the closest center, the space is divided in two by the thick line shown in Figure 5.16(a). Begin at the root of the tree in Figure 5.16(b), with initial values for the vector sum and counts for each cluster; all initial values are zero. Proceed recursively down the tree. When node A is reached, all points within it lie in cluster 1, so cluster 1's sum and count can be updated with the sum and count for node A, and we need descend no further. Recursing back to node B, its ball straddles the boundary between the clusters, so its points must be examined individually. When node C is reached, it falls entirely within cluster 2; again, we can update cluster 2 immediately and need descend no further. The tree is only examined down to the frontier marked by the dashed line in Figure 5.16(b), and the advantage is that the nodes below need not be opened—at least, not on this particular iteration of k-means. Next time, the cluster centers will have changed and things may be different.

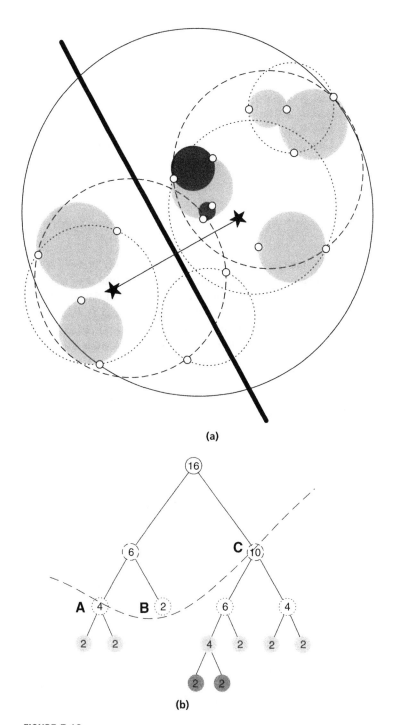

(a)

(b)

FIGURE 5.16

A ball tree: (a) two cluster centers and their dividing line and (b) the corresponding tree.

5.8.3 Discussion

Many variants of the basic k-means procedure have been developed. Some produce a hierarchical clustering by applying the algorithm with $k = 2$ to the overall dataset and then repeating, recursively, within each cluster.

How do you choose k? Often nothing is known about the likely number of clusters, and the whole point of clustering is to find out. One way is to try different values and choose the best. To do this you need to learn how to evaluate the success of machine learning.

5.9 RESOURCES

The 1R scheme was proposed and thoroughly investigated by Holte (1993). It was never really intended as a machine learning "method": the point was more to demonstrate that simple structures underlie most of the practical datasets being used to evaluate machine learning methods at the time and that putting high-powered inductive inference methods to work on simple datasets was like using a sledgehammer to crack a nut. Why grapple with a complex decision tree when a simple rule will do? The method that generates one simple rule per class is the result of work by Lucio de Souza Coelho of Brazil and Len Trigg of New Zealand, and it has been dubbed *hyperpipes*. A simple algorithm, it has the advantage of being extremely fast and is feasible even with an enormous number of attributes.

Bayes was an eighteenth-century English philosopher who set out his theory of probability in "An Essay towards Solving a Problem in the Doctrine of Chances," published in the *Philosophical Transactions of the Royal Society of London* (Bayes 1763); the rule that bears his name has been a cornerstone of probability theory ever since. The difficulty with the application of Bayes's rule in practice is the assignment of prior probabilities. Some statisticians, dubbed Bayesians, take the rule as gospel and insist that people make serious attempts to estimate prior probabilities accurately—although such estimates are often subjective. Others, non-Bayesians, prefer the kind of prior-free analysis that typically generates statistical confidence intervals. With a particular dataset, prior probabilities are usually reasonably easy to estimate, which encourages a Bayesian approach to learning. The independence assumption made by the Naïve Bayes method is a great stumbling block, however, and some attempts are being made to apply Bayesian analysis without assuming independence. The resulting models are called *Bayesian networks* (Heckerman et al., 1995).

Bayesian techniques had been used in the field of pattern recognition (Duda & Hart, 1973) for 20 years before they were adopted by machine learning researchers (e.g., see Langley et al., 1992) and made to work on datasets with redundant attributes (Langley & Sage, 1994) and numeric attributes (John & Langley, 1995). The label *Naïve Bayes* is unfortunate because it is hard to use this method without feeling simpleminded. However, there is nothing naïve about its use in appropriate circumstances. The multinomial Naïve Bayes model, which is particularly appropriate for text classification, was investigated by McCallum and Nigam (1998).

The classic paper on decision tree induction is by Quinlan (1986), who described the basic ID3 procedure developed in this chapter. A comprehensive description of the method, including the improvements that are embodied in C4.5, appears in a classic book by Quinlan (1993), which gives a listing of the complete C4.5 system, written in the C programming language. PRISM was developed by Cendrowska (1987), who also introduced the contact lens dataset.

Association rules are introduced and described in the database literature rather than in the machine learning literature. Here the emphasis is very much on dealing with huge amounts of data rather than on sensitive ways of testing and evaluating algorithms on limited datasets. The algorithm introduced in this chapter is the a priori method developed by Agrawal and his associates (Agrawal et al., 1993a, 1993b; Agrawal & Srikant, 1994). A survey of association-rule mining appears in an article by Chen et al. (1996).

Linear regression is described in most standard statistical texts, and a particularly comprehensive treatment can be found in a book by Lawson and Hanson (1995). The use of linear models for classification enjoyed a great deal of popularity in the 1960s; Nilsson (1965) provided an excellent reference. He defined a *linear threshold unit* as a binary test of whether a linear function is greater or less than zero and a *linear machine* as a set of linear functions, one for each class, whose value for an unknown example is compared and the largest chosen as its predicted class. In the distant past, perceptrons fell out of favor on publication of an influential book that showed they had fundamental limitations (Minsky & Papert, 1969); however, more complex systems of linear functions have enjoyed a resurgence in recent years in the form of neural networks. Nick Littlestone introduced the Winnow algorithms in his PhD thesis in 1989 (Littlestone, 1988, 1989). Multiresponse linear classifiers have found a new application recently for an operation called *stacking* that combines the output of other learning algorithms (see Wolpert, 1992). Friedman (1996) described the technique of pairwise classification, Fürnkranz (2002) further analyzed it, and Hastie and Tibshirani (1998) extended it to estimate probabilities using pairwise coupling.

Fix and Hodges (1951) performed the first analysis of the nearest-neighbor method, and Johns (1961) pioneered its use in classification problems. Cover and Hart (1967) obtained the classic theoretic result that, for large enough datasets, its probability of error never exceeds twice the theoretic minimum; Devroye et al. (1996) showed that k-nearest neighbor is asymptotically optimal for large k and n with $k/n \rightarrow 0$. Nearest-neighbor methods gained popularity in machine learning through the work of Aha (1992), who showed that instance-based learning can be combined with noisy exemplar pruning and attribute weighting and that the resulting methods perform well in comparison with other learning methods.

The kD-tree data structure was developed by Friedman et al. (1977). Our description closely follows an explanation given by Andrew Moore in his PhD thesis (Moore, 1991); Moore, along with Omohundro (1987), pioneered its use in machine learning. Moore (2000) described sophisticated ways of constructing ball trees that perform well even with thousands of attributes. We took our ball tree example from lecture notes by Alexander Gray of Carnegie-Mellon University. The voting feature intervals method mentioned in the *Discussion* subsection at the end of Section 5.7 is described by Demiroz and Guvenir (1997).

The k-means algorithm is a classic technique, and many descriptions and variations are available (e.g., see Hartigan, 1975). The clever use of kD-trees to speed up k-means clustering, which we chose to illustrate using ball trees instead, was pioneered by Moore and Pelleg (2000) in their X-means clustering algorithm. That algorithm also contains some other innovations.

Further Techniques in Decision Analysis

This chapter presents techniques in the use of decision analysis. Most individuals would not make a monetary decision by simply maximizing expected values if the amounts of money involved were large compared to their total wealth. That is, most individuals are risk averse. So, in general, we need to model an individual's attitude toward risk when using decision analysis to recommend a decision. Section 6.1 shows how to do this using a personal utility function. Rather than assess a utility function, a decision maker may prefer to analyze the risk directly. In Section 6.2, we discuss risk profiles, which enable the decision maker to do this. Some decisions do not require the use of utility functions or risk profiles because one decision alternative dominates the other for all decision makers. In Section 6.3, we present examples of such decisions. Both influence diagrams and decision trees require that we assess probabilities and outcomes. Sometimes assessing these values precisely can be a difficult and laborious task.

For example, it would be difficult and time consuming to determine whether the probability that the S&P 500 will be above 1500 in January is 0.3 or 0.35. Sometimes further refinement of these values would not affect our decision anyway. Section 6.4 shows how to measure the sensitivity of our decisions to the values of outcomes and probabilities. Often, before making a decision we have access to information, but at a cost. For example, before deciding to buy a stock, we may be able to purchase the advice of an investment analyst. In Section 6.5, we illustrate how to compute the value of information, which enables us to determine whether the information is worth the cost.

6.1 MODELING RISK PREFERENCES

In some cases, we may choose the alternative with the largest expected value. However, many people maximize expected value when the amount of money is small relative to their total wealth. The idea is that in the long run they will end

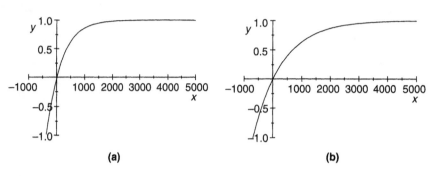

(a)   **(b)**

FIGURE 6.1

The function $U_{500}(x) = 1 - e^{-x/500}$ function is (a), whereas the $U_{1000}(x) = 1 - e^{-x/1000}$ function is in (b).

up better off by so doing. When an individual maximizes expected value to reach a decision, the individual is called an **expected value maximizer.** On the other hand, most people would not invest $100,000 in NASDIP because that is too much money relative to their total wealth. In the case of decisions in which an individual would not maximize expected value, we need to model the individual's attitude toward risk in order to use decision analysis to recommend a decision. One way to do this is to use a **utility function,** which is a function that maps dollar amounts to utilities. We discuss such functions next.

6.1.1 The Exponential Utility Function

The exponential utility function is given by

$$U_r(x) = 1 - e^{-x/r}$$

In this function the parameter r, called the **risk tolerance,** determines the degree of risk-aversion modeled by the function. As r becomes smaller, the function models more risk-averse behavior. Figure 6.1(a) shows $U_{500}(x)$, whereas Figure 6.1(b) shows $U_{1000}(x)$. Notice that both functions are concave (opening downward), and the one in Figure 6.1(b) is closer to being a straight line. The more concave the function is, the more risk-averse is the behavior modeled by the function. To model risk-neutrality (i.e., simply being an expected value maximizer), we would use a straight line instead of the exponential utility function, and to model risk-seeking behavior, we would use a convex (opening upward) function. Here we concentrate on modeling risk-averse behavior.

EXAMPLE 6.1

Suppose Sam decides his risk tolerance r is equal to 500. Then for Sam

EU(Buy NASDIP)

$= EU(NASDIP)$

$= 0.25U_{500}(\$500) + 0.25U_{500}(\$1000) + 0.5U_{500}(\$2000)$

$= 0.25(1 - e^{-500/500}) + 0.25(1 - e^{-1000/500}) + 0.5(1 - e^{-2000/500})$

$= 0.86504.$

$EU(Leave\ \$1000\ in\ bank) = U_{500}(\$1005) = 1 - e^{-1005/500} = 0.86601$

So Sam decides to leave the money in the bank.

EXAMPLE 6.2

Suppose Sue is less risk averse than Sam, and she decides that her risk tolerance r equals 1000. For Sue,

EU (Buy NASDIP)

$= EU(NASDIP)$

$= 0.25U_{1000}(\$500) + 0.25U_{1000}(\$1000) + 0.5U_{1000}(\$2000)$

$= 0.25(1 - e^{-500/1000}) + 0.25(1 - e^{-1000/1000}) + 0.5(1 - e^{-2000/1000})$

$= 0.68873.$

$EU(Leave\ \$1000\ in\ bank) = U_{1000}(\$1005) = 1 - e^{-1005/1000} = 0.63396$

So Sue decides to buy NASDIP.

Assessing r

In the preceding examples, we simply assigned risk tolerances to Sam and Sue. You should be wondering how an individual arrives at her or his personal risk tolerance. Next, we show a method for assessing it.

One way to determine the personal value of r in the exponential utility function is to consider a gamble in which you will win $\$x$ with probability 0.5 and lose $-\$x/2$ with probability 0.5. Your value of r is the largest value of x for which you would choose the lottery over obtaining nothing. This is illustrated in Figure 6.2.

EXAMPLE 6.3

Suppose we are about to toss a fair coin. I would certainly like the gamble in which I win $10 if a heads occurs and lose $5 if a tails occurs. If we increased the amounts to $100 and $50, or even to $1000 and $500, I would still like the gamble. However, if we increased the amounts to $1,000,000 and $500,000, I would no longer like the gamble because I cannot afford a 50 percent chance of losing $500,000. By going back and forth like this (similar to a binary cut), I can assess my personal value of r. For me, r is about equal to 20,000. (Professors do not make all that much money.)

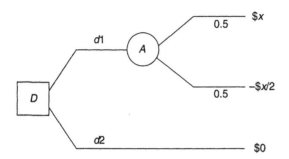

FIGURE 6.2

You can assess the risk tolerance r by determining the largest value of x for which you would be indifferent between $d1$ and $d2$.

You may inquire as to the justification for using this gamble to assess r. In the following notice that for any r

$$0.5(1-e^{-r/-r})+.5(1-e^{-(-r/2)/r}) = 0.0083$$

and

$$1-e^{-0/r} = 0$$

We see that for a given value of risk tolerance r, the gamble in which one wins $\$r$ with probability 0.5 and loses $-\$r/2$ with probability 0.5 has about the same utility as receiving $\$0$ for certain. We can use this fact and then work in reverse to assess r. That is, we determine the value of r for which we are indifferent between this gamble and obtaining nothing.

Constant Risk Aversion

Another way to model a decision problem involving money is to consider one's total wealth after the decision is made and the outcomes occur. The next example illustrates this condition.

EXAMPLE 6.4

Suppose Joe has an investment opportunity that entails a 0.4 probability of gaining $4000 and a 0.6 probability of losing $2500. If we let $d1$ be the decision alternative to take the investment opportunity and $d2$ be the decision alternative to reject it (i.e., he receives $0 for certain), then

$$E(d1) = 0.4(\$4000)+0.6(-\$2500) = \$100$$
$$E(d2) = \$0$$

So if Joe were an expected value maximizer, clearly he would choose the investment opportunity.

Suppose next that Joe carefully analyzes his risk tolerance, and he decides that for him $r = \$5000$. Then

$$EU(d1) = 0.4(1 - e^{-4000/5000}) + 0.6(1 - e^{-(-2500)/5000}) = -0.1690$$
$$E(d2) = 1 - e^{-0/5000} = 0$$

The solved decision tree is shown in Figure 6.3(a). So given Joe's risk tolerance, he would not choose this risky investment.

EXAMPLE 6.5

Suppose Joe's current wealth is $10,000, and he has the same investment opportunity as in the previous example. Joe might reason that what really matters is his current wealth after he makes his decision and the outcome is realized. Therefore, he models the problem instance in terms of his final wealth rather than simply the gain or loss from the investment opportunity. Doing this, we have

$$EU(d1) = 0.4(1 - e^{-(10,000+4000)/5000}) + 0.6(1 - e^{-(10,000-2500)/5000}) = 0.8418$$
$$E(d2) = 1 - e^{-10,000/5000} = 0.8647$$

The solved decision tree is shown in Figure 6.3(b). The fact that his current wealth is $10,000 does not affect his decision. The decision alternative to do nothing still has greater utility than choosing the investment opportunity.

EXAMPLE 6.6

Suppose next that Joe rejects the investment opportunity. However, he does well in other investments during the following year, and his total wealth becomes $100,000. Further suppose that he has the exact same investment opportunity he had a year ago. That is, Joe has an investment opportunity that entails a 0.4 probability of gaining $4000 and a 0.6 probability of losing $2500. He again models the problem in terms of his final wealth. We then have

$$EU(d1) = 0.4(1 - e^{-(100,000+4000)/5000}) + 0.6(1 - e^{-(100,000-2500)/5000})$$
$$= 0.9999999976$$

$$E(d2) = 1 - e^{-100,000/5000} = 0.9999999980$$

The solved decision tree is shown in Figure 6.3(c). Although the utility of the investment opportunity is now close to that of doing nothing, it is still smaller, and he still should choose to do nothing.

It is a property of the exponential utility function that an individual's total wealth cannot affect the decision obtained using the function. A function such as this is called a **constant risk-averse utility function.** If one uses such a function to model one's risk preferences, one must reevaluate the parameters in the function when one's wealth changes significantly. For example, Joe should reevaluate his risk tolerance r when his total wealth changes from $10,000 to $100,000.

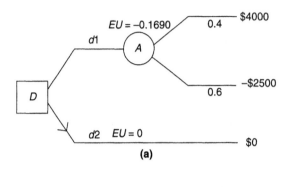

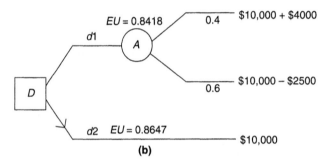

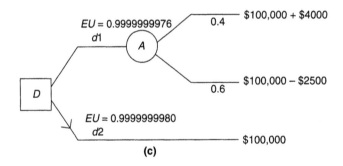

FIGURE 6.3

The solved decision tree for Example 6.4 is shown in (a). Solved decision trees for that same example when we model in terms of total wealth are shown in (b) and (c). The total wealth in (b) is $10,000, whereas in (c) it is $100,000.

The reason the exponential utility function displays constant risk aversion is that the term for total wealth cancels out of an inequality comparing two utilities. For example, consider again Joe's investment opportunity that entails a 0.4 probability of gaining $4000 and a 0.6 probability of losing $2500. Let w be Joe's total wealth. The first inequality in the following sequence of inequalities compares the utility of choosing the investment opportunity to doing nothing when we consider the total wealth w, whereas the last inequality compares the utility of choosing the investment opportunity to doing nothing when we do not consider total wealth. If you follow the inequalities in sequence, you will see that they are all equivalent to each other. Therefore, consideration of total wealth cannot affect the decision:

$$0.4\left(1-e^{-(w+4000)/5000}\right)+0.6\left(1-e^{-(w-2500)/5000}\right)<\left(1-e^{-w/5000}\right)$$

$$0.4\left(1-e^{-w/5000}e^{-4000/5000}\right)+0.6\left(1-e^{-w/5000}e^{-(-2500)/5000}\right)<1-e^{-w/5000}$$

$$1-0.4\left(e^{-w/5000}e^{-4000/5000}\right)-0.6\left(-e^{-w/5000}e^{-(-2500)/5000}\right)<1-e^{-w/5000}$$

$$-0.4\left(e^{-w/5000}e^{-4000/5000}\right)-0.6\left(-e^{-w/5000}e^{-(-2500)/5000}\right)<-e^{-w/5000}$$

$$-4\left(e^{-4000/5000}\right)-0.6\left(e^{-(-2500)/5000}\right)<-1$$

$$0.4\left(1-e^{-4000/5000}\right)+0.6\left(1-e^{-(-2500)/5000}\right)<1-1$$

$$0.4\left(1-e^{-4000/5000}\right)+0.6\left(1-e^{-(-2500)/5000}\right)<1-e^{-0/5000}$$

6.1.2 A Decreasing Risk-Averse Utility Function

If a change in total wealth can change the decision obtained using a risk-averse utility function, then the function is called a **decreasing risk-averse utility function.** An example of such a function is the logarithm function. We show this by using this function to model Joe's risk preferences.

EXAMPLE 6.7

As in Example 6.4, suppose Joe has an investment opportunity that entails a 0.6 probability of gaining $4000 and a 0.4 probability of losing $2500. Again let $d1$ be the decision alternative to take the investment opportunity and $d2$ be the decision alternative to reject it. Suppose Joe's risk preferences can be modeled using $\ln(x)$. First, let's model the problem instance when Joe has a total wealth of $10,000. We then have that

$$EU(d1) = 0.4\ln(10{,}000+4000)+0.6\ln(10{,}000-2500) = 9.1723$$
$$EU(d2) = \ln 10{,}000 = 9.2103$$

So the decision is to reject the investment opportunity and do nothing.

Next let's model the problem instance when Joe has a total wealth of $100,000. We then have that

$$EU(d1) = 0.4\ln(100{,}000+4000)+0.6\ln(100{,}000-2500) = 11.5134$$
$$EU(d2) = \ln 100{,}000 = 11.5129$$

So now the decision is to take the investment opportunity.

Modeling risk attitudes is discussed much more in (Clemen, 1996).

6.2 ANALYZING RISK DIRECTLY

Some decision makers may not be comfortable assessing personal utility functions and making decisions based on such functions. Rather, they may want to directly analyze the risk inherent in a decision alternative. One way to do this is to use the variance as a measure of spread from the expected value. Another way is to develop risk profiles. We discuss each technique in turn.

6.2.1 Using the Variance to Measure Risk

We start with an example.

EXAMPLE 6.8

Suppose Patricia is going to make the decision modeled by the decision tree in Figure 6.4. If Patricia simply maximizes expected value, it is left as an exercise to show

$$E(d1) = \$1220$$
$$E(d2) = \$1200$$

So $d1$ is the decision alternative that maximizes expected value. However, the expected values by themselves tell us nothing of the risk involved in the alternatives. Let's also compute the variance of each decision alternative. If we choose alternative $d1$, then

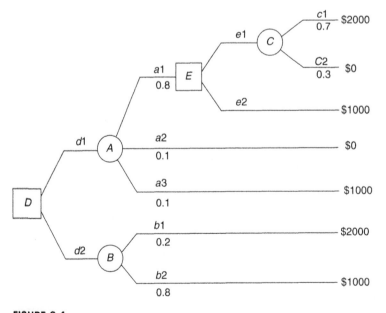

FIGURE 6.4

The decision tree discussed in Example 6.8.

$$P(2000) = 0.8 \times 0.7 = 0.56$$
$$P(1000) = 0.1$$
$$P(0) = 0.8 \times 0.3 + 0.1 = 0.34$$

Notice that there are two ways $0 could be obtained. That is, outcomes $a1$ and $c1$ could occur with probability 0.8×0.3, and outcome $a2$ could occur with probability 0.1. We then have that

$$\text{Var}(d1) = (2000 - 1220)^2 P(2000) + (1000 - 1220)^2 P(1000) + (0 - 1220)^2 P(0)$$
$$= (2000 - 1220)^2 \times 0.56 + (1000 - 1220)^2 \times 0.1 + (0 - 1220)^2 \times 0.34$$
$$= 851{,}600$$
$$\sigma_{d1} = \sqrt{851{,}600} = 922.82$$

It is left as an exercise to show that

$$\text{Var}(d2) = 160{,}000$$
$$\sigma_{d2} = 400$$

So if we use the variance as our measure of risk, we deem $d1$ somewhat more risky, which means if Patricia is somewhat risk averse she might choose $d2$.

Using the variance alone as the measure of risk can sometimes be misleading, as the next example illustrates.

EXAMPLE 6.9

Now suppose Patricia is going to make the decision modeled by the decision tree in Figure 6.5. It is left as an exercise to show that

$$E(d1) = \$2900$$
$$\text{Var}(d1) = 32{,}490{,}000$$
$$\sigma_{d1} = 5700$$

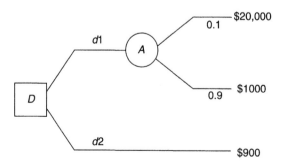

FIGURE 6.5

The decision tree discussed in Example 6.9.

and

$$E(d2) = \$900$$
$$Var(d2) = 0$$
$$\sigma_{d2} = 0$$

If Patricia uses only the variance as her measure of risk, she might choose alternative $d2$ because $d1$ has such a large variance. Yet alternative $d1$ is sure to yield more return that alternative $d2$.

We see that the use of the variance alone as our measure of risk can be very misleading. This is a mistake some investors make. That is, they notice that one mutual fund has had a much higher expected return over the past 10 years than a second mutual fund, but they reject the first one because it also has had a much higher variance. Yet if they looked at each year, they would see that the first one always dominates the second one.

6.2.2 Risk Profiles

The expected value and variance are summary statistics, and therefore information is lost if all we report are these values. Alternatively, for each decision alternative, we could report the probability of all possible outcomes if the alternative is chosen. A graph that shows these probabilities is called a **risk profile.**

EXAMPLE 6.10

Consider again Patricia's decision—discussed in Example 6.8. There, we computed the probability of all possible outcomes for each decision. We used those results to create the risk profiles in Figure 6.6. From these risk profiles, Patricia can see that there is a good chance she could end up with nothing if she chooses alternative $d1$, but she also has a good chance of obtaining $2000. On the other hand, the least she could end up with is $1000 if she chooses alternative $d2$, but probably this is all she will obtain.

A **cumulative risk profile** shows for each amount x the probability that the payoff will be less than or equal to x if the decision alternative is chosen. A cumulative risk profile is a cumulative distribution function. Figure 6.7 shows the cumulative risk profiles for the decision in Example 6.8.

6.3 DOMINANCE

Some decisions do not require the use of utility functions or risk profiles because one decision alternative dominates the other for all decision makers. We discuss dominance next.

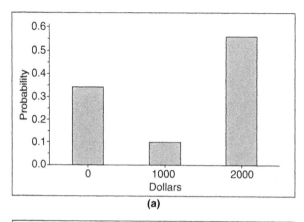

(a)

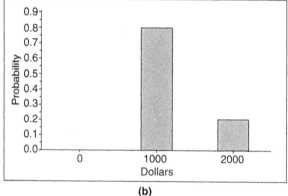

(b)

FIGURE 6.6

Risk profiles for the decision in Example 6.8: (a) Risk profile for decision alternative $d1$; (b) risk profile for decision alternative $d2$.

6.3.1 Deterministic Dominance

Suppose we have a decision that can be modeled using the decision tree in Figure 6.8. If we choose alternative $d1$, the least amount of money we will realize is $4, whereas if we choose alternative $d2$, the most amount of money we will realize is $3. Assuming that maximizing wealth is the only consideration in this decision, there is then no reasonable argument one can offer for choosing $d2$ over $d1$, and we say $d1$ deterministically dominates $d2$. In general, decision alternative $d1$ **deterministically dominates** decision alternative $d2$ if the utility obtained from choosing $d1$ is greater than the utility obtained from choosing $d2$ regardless of the outcomes of chance nodes. When we observe deterministic dominance, there is no need to compute expected utility or develop a risk profile.

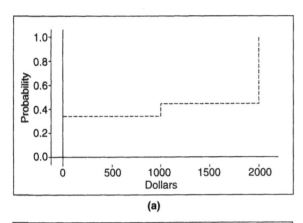

(a)

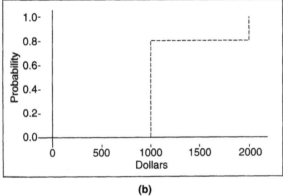

(b)

FIGURE 6.7

Cumulative risk profiles for the decision in Example 6.8: (a) Cumulative risk profile for decision alternative $d1$; (b) comulative risk profile for decision alternative $d2$.

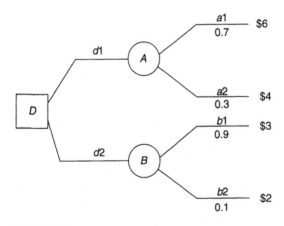

FIGURE 6.8

Decision alternative $d1$ deterministically dominates decision alternative $d2$.

6.3.2 **Stochastic Dominance**

Suppose we have a decision that can be modeled using the decision tree in Figure 6.9. If the outcomes are $a1$ and $b2$, we will realize more money if we choose $d1$, whereas if the outcomes are $a2$ and $b1$, we will realize more money if we choose $d2$. So there is no deterministic dominance. However, the outcomes are the same for both decisions, namely $6 and $4, and, if we choose $d2$, the probability is higher that we will receive $6. So again, assuming that maximizing wealth is the only consideration in this decision, there is no reasonable argument for choosing $d1$ over $d2$, and we say alternative $d2$ stochastically dominates alternative $d1$.

A different case of stochastic dominance is illustrated by the decision tree in Figure 6.10. In that tree, the probabilities are the same for both chance nodes,

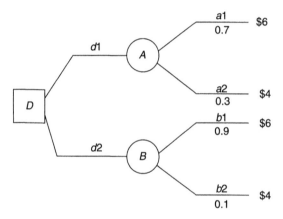

FIGURE 6.9

Decision alternative $d2$ stochastically dominates decision alternative $d1$.

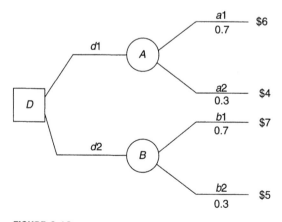

FIGURE 6.10

Decision alternative $d2$ stochastically dominates decision alternative $d1$.

but the utilities for the outcomes of B are higher. That is, if $b1$ occurs we realize $7, whereas if $a1$ occurs we realize only $6, and if $b2$ occurs we realize $5, whereas if $a2$ occurs we realize only $4. So again, assuming that maximizing wealth is the only consideration in this decision, there is no reasonable argument for choosing $d1$ over $d2$, and we say alternative $d2$ stochastically dominates alternative $d1$.

Although it often is not hard to recognize stochastic dominance, it is a bit tricky to define the concept. We do so next in terms of cumulative risk profiles. We say that alternative $d2$ **stochastically dominates** alternative $d1$ if the cumulative risk profile $F_2(x)$ for $d2$ lies under the cumulative risk profile $F_1(x)$ for $d1$ for at least one value of x and does not lie over it for any values of x. That is, for at least one value of x

$$F_2(x) < F_1(x)$$

and for all values of x

$$F_2(x) \le F_1(x)$$

This is illustrated in Figure 6.11.

Why should this be the definition of stochastic dominance? Look again at Figure 6.11. There is no value of x such that the probability of realizing x or less is smaller if we choose $d1$ than if we choose $d2$. So there is no amount of money that we may want or require that would make $d1$ the better choice.

Figure 6.12 shows two cumulative risk profiles that cross, which means we do not have stochastic dominance. Now the decision alternative chosen can depend on an individual's preference. For example, if the amounts are in units of $100, and Mary needs at least $400 to pay her rent or else be evicted, she may choose alternative $d1$. On the other hand, if Sam needs at least $800 to pay his rent or else be evicted, he may choose alternative $d2$.

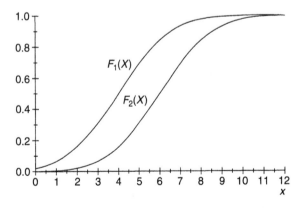

FIGURE 6.11

If $F_1(x)$ is the cumulative risk profile for $d1$ and $F_2(x)$ is the cumulative risk profile for $d2$, then $d2$ stochastically dominates $d1$.

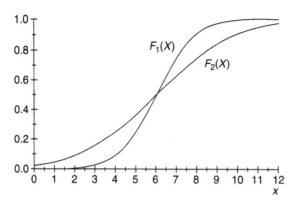

FIGURE 6.12

There is no stochastic dominance.

6.3.3 Good Decision versus Good Outcome

Suppose Scott and Sue are each about to make the decision modeled by the decision tree in Figure 6.10, Scott chooses alternative $d1$, and Sue chooses alternative $d2$. Suppose further that outcomes $a1$ and $b2$ occur. So Scott ends up with $6, and Sue ends up with $5. Did Scott make a better decision than Sue? We just claimed that there is no reasonable argument for choosing $d1$ over $d2$. If we accept that claim, we cannot now conclude that Scott made the better decision. Rather, Scott made a **bad decision with a good outcome**, whereas Sue made a **good decision with a bad outcome.** The quality of a decision must be judged based on the information available when the decision is made, not on outcomes realized after the decision is made.

One of the authors (Rich Neapolitan) amusingly remembers the following story from his youth. When his uncle Hershell got out of the army, he used his savings to buy a farm in Texas next to his parents' farm. The ostensible reason was that he wanted to live near his parents and resume his life as a farmer. Somewhat later, oil was discovered on his farm, and Hershell became wealthy as a result. After that Rich's dad used to say, "Everyone thought Hershell was not too bright when he wasted money on a farm with such poor soil, but it turns out he was shrewd like a fox."

6.4 SENSITIVITY ANALYSIS

Both influence diagrams and decision trees require that we assess probabilities and outcomes. Sometimes assessing these values precisely can be a difficult and laborious task. As noted earlier, it would be difficult and time consuming to determine whether the probability that the S&P 500 will be above 1500 in January is 0.3 or 0.35. Further refinement of these values may not affect a decision. Next, we discuss **sensitivity analysis,** which is an analysis of how the values of outcomes and probabilities can affect our decision. After introducing the concept with simple models, we show a more detailed model.

6.4.1 Simple Models

We show a sequence of examples.

EXAMPLE 6.11

Suppose that currently IBM is at $10 a share, and you feel there is a 0.5 probability it will be go down to $5 by the end of the month and a 0.5 probability it will go up to $20. You have $1000 to invest, and you will either buy 100 shares of IBM or put the money in the bank and earn a monthly interest rate of 0.005. Although you are fairly confident of your assessment of the outcomes, you are not very confident of your assessment of the probabilities. In this case, you can represent your decision using the decision tree in Figure 6.13. Notice in that tree that we represented the probability of IBM going up by a variable p. We then have

$$E(Buy\ IBM) = p(2000) + (1-p)(500)$$
$$E(Bank) = \$1005$$

We will buy IBM if $E(Buy\ IBM) > E(Bank)$, which is the case if

$$p(2000) + (1-p)(500) > 1005$$

Solving this inequality for p, we have

$$p > 0.337$$

We have determined how sensitive our decision is to the value of p. As long as we feel that the probability of IBM going up is at least equal to 0.337, we will buy IBM. We need not refine our probabilistic assessment further.

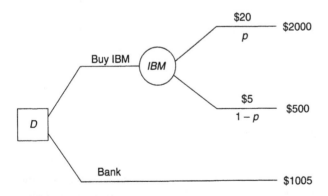

FIGURE 6.13

As long as p is greater than 0.337, buying IBM maximizes expected value.

EXAMPLE 6.12

Suppose you are in the same situation as in the previous example, except that you feel that the value of IBM will be affected by the overall value of the Dow Jones Industrial Average in 1 month. Currently, the Dow is at 10,500 and you assess that it will either be at 10,000 or 11,000 at the end of the month. You feel confident assessing the probabilities of your stock going up dependent on whether the Dow goes up or down, but you are not confident assessing the probability of the Dow going up or down. Specifically, you model your decision using the decision tree in Figure 6.14. We then have

$$E(Buy\ IBM) = p(0.6 \times 2000 + 0.4 \times 500) + (1-p)(0.3 \times 2000 + 0.7 \times 500)$$
$$E(Bank) = 1005$$

We will buy IBM if $E(Buy\ IBM) > E(Bank)$, which is the case if

$$p(0.6 \times 2000 + 0.4 \times 500) + (1-p)(0.3 \times 2000 + 0.7 \times 500) > 1005$$

Solving this inequality for p, we have

$$p > 0.122$$

As long as we feel that the probability of the Dow going up is at least equal to 0.122, we will buy IBM.

In **a two-way sensitivity analysis** we simultaneously analyze the sensitivity of our decision to two quantities. The next example shows such an analysis.

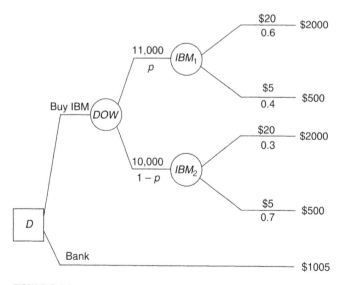

FIGURE 6.14

As long as p is greater than 0.122, buying IBM maximizes expected value.

EXAMPLE 6.13

Suppose you are in the same situation as in the previous example, except you are confident in your assessment of the probability of the Dow going up, but you are not confident in your assessment of the probabilities of your stock going up dependent on whether the Dow goes up or down. Specifically, you model your decision using the decision tree in Figure 6.15. We then have

$$E(Buy\ IBM) = 0.4(q \times 2000 + (1-q) \times 500) + 0.6(r \times 2000 + (1-r) \times 500)$$
$$E(Bank) = 1005$$

We will buy IBM if $E(Buy\ IBM) > E(Bank)$, which is the case if

$$0.4(q \times 2000 + (1-q) \times 500) + 0.6(r \times 2000 + (1-r) \times 500) > 1005$$

Simplifying this inequality, we obtain

$$q > \frac{101}{120} - \frac{3r}{2}$$

The line $q = 101/120 - 3r/2$ is plotted in Figure 6.16.

Owing to the previous inequality, the decision that maximizes expected value is to buy IBM as long as the point (r,q) lies above that line. For example, if $r = 0.6$ and $q = 0.1$ or $r = 0.3$ and $q = 0.8$, this would be our decision. However, if $r = 0.3$ and $q = 0.1$, it would not be the decision.

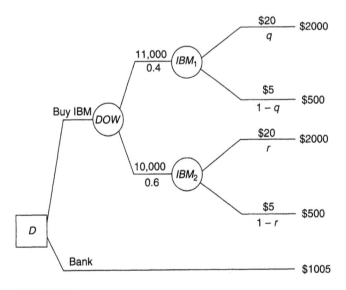

FIGURE 6.15

For this decision we need to do a two-way sensitivity analysis.

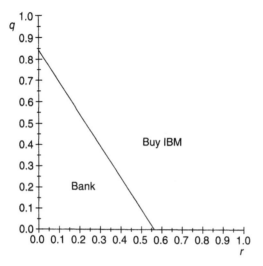

FIGURE 6.16

The line $q = 101/120 - 3r/2$. As long as (r,q) is above this line, the decision that maximizes expected value in Example 6.13 is to buy IBM.

EXAMPLE 6.14

Suppose you are in the same situation as in the previous example, except you are not comfortable assessing any probabilities in the model. However, you do feel that the probability of IBM going up if the Dow goes up is twice the probability of IBM going up if the Dow goes down. Specifically, you model your decision using the decision tree in Figure 6.17. We then have

$$E(Buy \ IBM) = p(q \times 2000 + (1-q) \times 500 + (1-p)[(q/2) \times 2000 + (1-q/2) \times 500)$$
$$E(Bank) = 1005$$

We will buy IBM if $E(Buy \ IBM) > E(Bank)$, which is the case if

$$p(q \times 2000 + (1-q) \times 500) + (1-p)((q/2) \times 2000$$
$$+ (1-q/2) \times 500) > 1005$$

Simplifying this inequality yields

$$q > \frac{101}{150 + 150p}.$$

Figure 6.18 plots the curve $q = 101/(150 + 150p)$. The decision that maximizes expected value is to buy IBM as long as the point (p,q) lies above that curve.

We can also investigate how sensitive our decision is to the values of the outcomes. The next example illustrates this sensitivity.

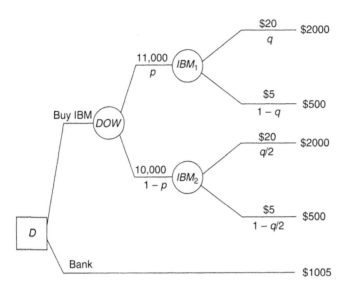

FIGURE 6.17

For this decision, we need to do a two-way sensitivity analysis.

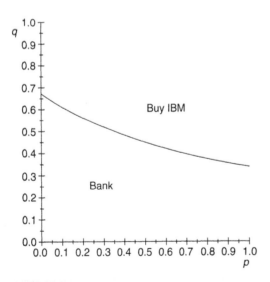

FIGURE 6.18

The curve $q = 101/(150 + 150p)$. As long as (p,q) is above this curve, the decision that maximizes expected value in Example 6.14 is to buy IBM.

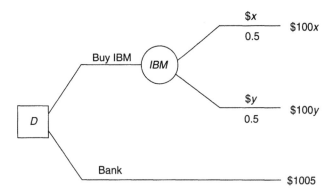

FIGURE 6.19
This decision requires a two-way sensitivity analysis of the outcomes.

EXAMPLE 6.15

Suppose you are in the situation discussed in Example 6.11. However, you are not confident as to your assessment of how high or low IBM will go. That is, currently IBM is at $10 a share, and you feel there is a 0.5 probability it will go up by the end of the month and a 0.5 probability it will go down, but you do not assess how high or low it will be.

As before, you have $1000 to invest, and you will either buy 100 shares of IBM or put the money in the bank and earn a monthly interest rate of 0.005. In this case, you can represent your decision using the decision tree in Figure 6.19. We then have

$$E(Buy\ IBM) = 0.5(100x) + 0.5(100y)$$
$$E(Bank) = \$1005$$

We will buy IBM if $E(Buy\ IBM) > E(Bank)$, which is the case if

$$0.5(100x) + 0.5(100y) > 1005$$

Simplifying this inequality yields

$$y > \frac{201}{10} - x$$

Figure 6.20 plots the curve $y = 201/10 - x$. The decision that maximizes expected value is to buy IBM as long as the point (x,y) lies above that curve.

6.4.2 A More Detailed Model

The examples given so far have been oversimplified and therefore do not represent decision models one would ordinarily use in practice. We did this to illustrate the concepts without burdening you with too many details. Next, we show an example of a more detailed model, which an investor might actually use to model a decision.

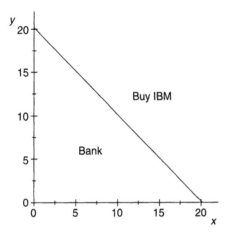

FIGURE 6.20

The line $y = 201/10 - x$. As long as (x,y) is above this line, the decision that maximizes expected value in Example 6.15 is to buy IBM.

EXAMPLE 6.16

Some financial analysts argue that the small investor is best served by investing in mutual funds rather than in individual stocks. The investor has a choice of many different types of mutual funds. Here we consider two that are quite different. "Aggressive" or "growth" mutual funds invest in companies that have high growth potential and ordinarily do quite well when the market in general performs well, but they do quite poorly when the market does poorly. "Allocation" funds distribute their investments among cash, bonds, and stocks. Furthermore, the stocks are often in companies that are considered "value" investments because for some reason they are considered currently undervalued. Such funds are ordinarily more stable. That is, they do not do as well when the market does well or as poorly when the market performs poorly.

Assume that Christina plans to invest $1000 for the coming year, and she decides she will either invest the money in a growth fund or in an allocation fund or will put it in a 1-year CD which pays 5 percent. To make her decision, she must model how these funds will do based on what the market does in the coming year, and she must assess the probability of the market performance in the coming year. Based on how these funds have done during market performances in previous years, she is comfortable assessing how the funds will do based on market performance. She feels that the market probably will not do well in the coming year because economists are predicting a recession, but she is not comfortable assessing precise probabilities. So she develops the decision tree in Figure 6.21. Given that tree, the growth fund should be preferred to the bank if

$$1600p + 1000q + 300(1 - p - q) > 1050$$

Simplifying this expression yields

$$q > (15 - 26p)/14$$

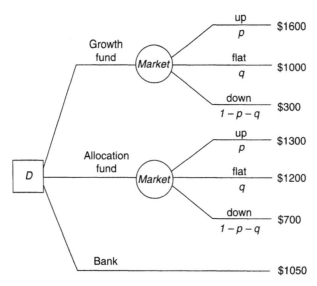

FIGURE 6.21

A decision tree modeling the decision whose alternatives are a growth mutual fund, an allocation mutual fund, and the bank.

Based on this inequality, Figure 6.22(a) shows the region in which she should choose the growth fund and the region in which she should choose the bank if these were her only choices. Notice that the regions are bounded above by the line $q = 1 - p$. The reason is that we must have $q + p \le 1$.

The allocation fund should be preferred to the bank if

$$1300p + 1200q + 900(1 - p - q) > 1050$$

Simplifying this expression yields

$$q > (3 - 8p)/6$$

Based on this inequality, Figure 6.22(b) shows the region in which she should choose the allocation fund and the region in which she should choose the bank if these were her only choices.

The growth fund should be preferred to the allocation fund if

$$1600p + 1000q + 300(1 - p - q) > 1300p + 1200q + 900(1 - p - q)$$

Simplifying this expression yields

$$q > (6 - 9p)/4$$

Based on this inequality, Figure 6.22(c) shows the region in which she should choose the growth fund and the region in which she should choose the allocation fund if these were her only choices.

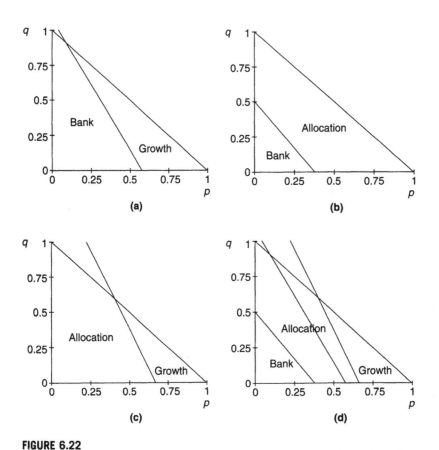

FIGURE 6.22

If the only choice is between the growth fund and the bank, Christina should use (a); if it is between the allocation fund and the bank, she should use (b); if it is between the growth fund and the allocation fund, she should use (c); and if she is choosing from all three alternatives, she should use (d).

Finally, the lines for all of the previous three comparisons are plotted in Figure 6.22(d). This diagram shows the regions in which she should make each of the three choices when all three are being considered.

The values in the previous examples were exaggerated from what we (the authors) actually believe. For example, we do not believe growth funds will go up about 60 percent in good market conditions. We exaggerated the values so that it would be easy to see the regions in the diagram in Figure 6.22(d). Other than that, this example illustrates how one of us makes personal investment decisions. It is left as an exercise for you to assess your own values and determine the resultant region corresponding to each investment choice.

6.5 VALUE OF INFORMATION

Figure 6.23 shows the decision tree in Figure 6.21, but with values assigned to the probabilities. It is left as an exercise to show that, given these values, the decision that maximizes expected value is to buy the allocation fund, and

$$E(D) = E(\text{allocation fund}) = \$1190$$

This is shown in Figure 6.23. Before making a decision, we often have the chance to consult with an expert in the domain that the decision concerns.

Suppose in the current decision we can consult with an expert financial analyst who is perfect at predicting the market. That is, if the market is going up, the analyst will say it is going up; if it will be flat, the analyst will say it will be flat; and if it is going down, the analyst will say it is going down. We should be willing to pay for this information, but not more than the information is worth. Next, we show how to compute the expected value (worth) of this information, which is called the expected value of perfect information.

6.5.1 Expected Value of Perfect Information

To compute the expected value of perfect information we add another decision alternative, which is to consult the perfect expert. Figure 6.24 shows the decision

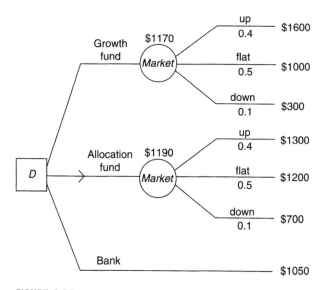

FIGURE 6.23

Buying the allocation fund maximizes expected value.

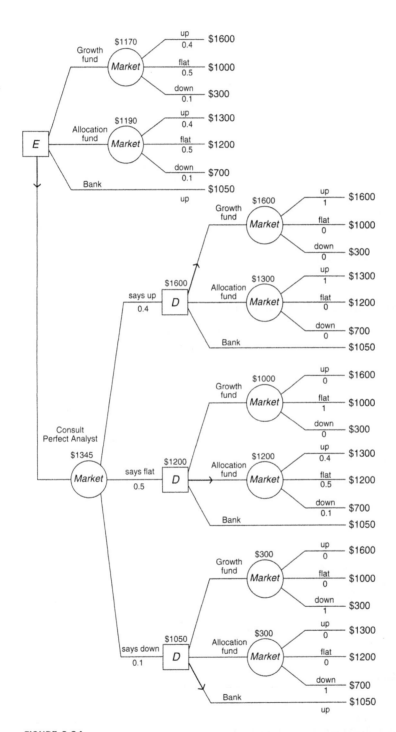

FIGURE 6.24

The maximum expected value without consulting the perfect expert is $1190, whereas the expected value of consulting that expert is $1345.

tree in Figure 6.23 with that alternative added. Next, we show how the probabilities for that tree were obtained. Because the expert is perfect, we have

$$P(\text{Expert} = \text{says up} \mid \text{Market} = \text{up}) = 1$$
$$P(\text{Expert} = \text{says flat} \mid \text{Market} = \text{flat}) = 1$$
$$P(\text{Expert} = \text{says down} \mid \text{Market} = \text{down}) = 1$$

We therefore have

$P(\text{up} \mid \text{says up})$

$$= \frac{P(\text{says up} \mid \text{up})P(\text{up})}{P(\text{says up} \mid \text{up})P(\text{up}) + P(\text{says flat} \mid \text{up})P(\text{flat}) + P(\text{says down} \mid \text{down})P(\text{down})}$$

$$= \frac{1 \times .4}{1 \times 0.4 + 0 \times 0.5 + 0 \times 0.1} = 1$$

It is not surprising that this value is 1, because the expert is perfect. This value is the far right and uppermost probability in the decision tree in Figure 6.24. It is left as an exercise to compute the other probabilities and solve the tree. We see that

$$E(\text{Consult Perfect Analyst}) = \$1345$$

Recall that without consulting this analyst, the decision alternative that maximizes expected utility is to buy the allocation fund, and

$$E(D) = E(\text{allocation fund}) = \$1190$$

The difference between these two expected values is the **expected value of perfect information** (EVPI). That is,

$$EVPI = E(\text{Consult Perfect Analyst}) - E(D)$$
$$= \$1345 - \$1190 = \$155$$

This is the most we should be willing to pay for the information. If we pay less than this amount, we will have increased our expected value by consulting the expert, whereas if we pay more, we will have decreased our expected value.

We showed decision trees in Figures 6.23 and 6.24 so that you could see how the expected value of perfect information is computed. However, as is usually the case, it is much easier to represent the decisions using influence diagrams. Figure 6.25 shows the decision tree in Figure 6.23 represented as an influence diagram and solved using Netica. Figure 6.26 shows the decision tree in Figure 6.24 represented as an influence diagram and solved using Netica. We have added the conditional probabilities of the Expert node to that diagram. (Recall that Netica does not show conditional probabilities.) Notice that we can obtain the EVPI

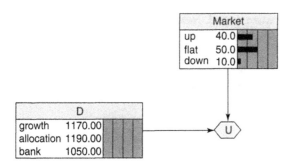

FIGURE 6.25

The decision tree in Figure 6.23 is represented as an influence diagram and solved using Netica.

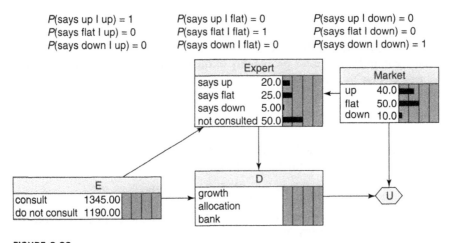

FIGURE 6.26

The decision tree in Figure 6.24 is represented as an influence diagram and solved using Netica.

directly from the values listed at decision node E in the influence diagram in Figure 6.26. That is,

$$EVPI = E(\text{consult}) - E(\text{do not consult})$$
$$= \$1345 - \$1190 = \$155$$

6.5.2 Expected Value of Imperfect Information

Real experts and tests ordinarily are not perfect. Rather, they are only able to give estimates, which are often correct. Let's say we have a financial analyst who has been predicting market activity for 30 years and has had the following results:

1. When the market went up, the analyst said it would go up 80 percent of the time, would be flat 10 percent of the time, and would go down 10 percent of the time.
2. When the market was flat, the analyst said it would go up 20 percent of the time, would be flat 70 percent of the time, and would go down 10 percent of the time.
3. When the market went down, the analyst said it would go up 20 percent of the time, would be flat 20 percent of the time, and would go down 60 percent of the time.

We therefore estimate the following conditional probabilities for this expert:

$$P(\text{Expert} = \text{says up} \mid \text{Market} = \text{up}) = 0.8$$

$$P(\text{Expert} = \text{says flat} \mid \text{Market} = \text{up}) = 0.1$$

$$P(\text{Expert} = \text{says down} \mid \text{Market} = \text{up}) = 0.1$$

$$P(\text{Expert} = \text{says up} \mid \text{Market} = \text{flat}) = 0.2$$

$$P(\text{Expert} = \text{says flat} \mid \text{Market} = \text{flat}) = 0.7$$

$$P(\text{Expert} = \text{says down} \mid \text{Market} = \text{flat}) = 0.1$$

$$P(\text{Expert} = \text{says up} \mid \text{Market} = \text{down}) = 0.2$$

$$P(\text{Expert} = \text{says flat} \mid \text{Market} = \text{down}) = 0.2$$

$$P(\text{Expert} = \text{says down} \mid \text{Market} = \text{down}) = 0.6$$

Figure 6.27 shows the influence diagram in Figure 6.25 with the additional decision alternative that we can consult this imperfect expert. We also show the

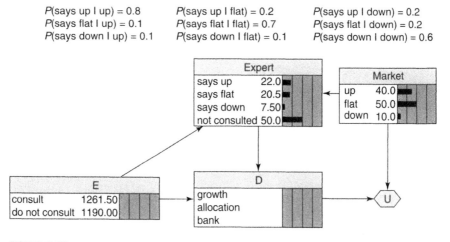

FIGURE 6.27

An influence diagram that enables us to compute the expected value of imperfect information.

conditional probabilities of the Expert node in that diagram. The increased expected value we realize by consulting such an expert is called the **expected value of imperfect information** (EVII). It is given by

$$EVII = E(\text{consult}) - E(\text{do not consult})$$
$$= \$1261.50 - \$1190 = \$71.50.$$

This is the most we should pay for this expert's information.

6.6 NORMATIVE DECISION ANALYSIS

The analysis methodology presented in this and the previous chapter for recommending decisions is called **normative decision analysis** because the methodology prescribes how people should make decisions rather than describes how people do make decisions. In 1954, L. Jimmie Savage developed axioms concerning an individual's preferences and beliefs. If an individual accepts these axioms, Savage showed that the individual must prefer the decisions obtained using decision analysis. Tversky and Kahneman (1981) conducted a number of studies showing that individuals do not make decisions consistent with the methodology of decision analysis. That is, their studies indicate that decision analysis is not a descriptive theory. Kahneman and Tversky (1979) developed prospect theory to describe how people actually make decisions when they are not guided by decision analysis. In 2002, Dan Kahneman won the Nobel Prize in economics for this effort. An alternative descriptive theory of decision making is regret theory (Bell, 1982).

Fundamental Concepts of Genetic Algorithms

Evolutionary strategies address highly complex optimization and search problems through an emulation of natural selection. They also incorporate a form of parallel processing to effectively evaluate a large population of possible solutions. Their ability to solve high-dimensional, highly complex problems that are often intractable, slow, brittle, or difficult to formulate with conventional analytical techniques has made genetic algorithms and evolutionary programming a critical component in intelligent systems that require adaptive behavior, systematic exploration of alternatives, and multiobjective and multiconstraint optimization. This chapter introduces the concepts underlying genetic algorithms and evolutionary programming. They are necessary in order to understand the nature of genetic algorithms and evolutionary programming in the context of fuzzy model tuning and in the context of advanced predictive and classification models.

Although not the first to explore the idea of combining the mechanics of evolution and computer programming, the field of genetic and evolutionary algorithms can be traced back to John H. Holland's 1975 book *Adaptation in Natural and Artificial Systems: An Introductory Analysis with Applications to Biology, Control, and Artificial Intelligence* (see Resources). John Holland formalized the concepts underlying the genetic algorithm and provided the mathematic foundations for incrementally and formally improving their search techniques. Holland was primarily interested in the nature of adaptive systems. The adaptive nature of his genetic models provided the foundation for this broad and robust field of computer science. As we will see in this chapter, evolutionary strategies allow model designers and data mining engineers to optimize their models, generate new and robust predictive models, and explore highly complex decision spaces.

7.1 THE VOCABULARY OF GENETIC ALGORITHMS

Much of the literature in evolutionary strategies adopts its nomenclature from biologic models. Thus, we speak of chromosomes, alleles, mutations, breeding, goodness of fit, and survival of the fittest. Before moving on with a complete and detailed analysis of the algorithm and how it works, we need to understand the principal nomenclatures and how they relate to the components of the algorithm. A preview of the vocabulary will make reading and understanding the material in this chapter much easier. It is not always possible, while maintaining an uncluttered and coherent discussion of the genetic process, to ensure that every term is introduced before it is used.

7.1.1 Allele

The value at a particular locus in the genome is called the *allele*. In a binary representation, this will be a one or a zero. In a real number representation, the allele will be an integer or floating-point number.

7.1.2 Annealing

Annealing (often called simulated annealing) is a process for disrupting the current state of a genetic algorithm to avoid premature convergence to a solution. In a genetic algorithm, this is accomplished through mutation, the random introduction of new individuals into a population, the retention of a few poor-performing individuals, and changes in the size and compactness of future populations.

7.1.3 Breeding

A new population of possible solutions to the current problem is primarily (but not completely) created through a process that resembles biologic *breeding*. High-performance individuals (those with very good fitness values) are mated to produce offspring in a process somewhat analogous to sexual reproduction; that is, their genetic material is distributed to one or more offspring. Figure 7.1 illustrates how a crossover at a single point on the chromosome produces a new offspring from two parents.

In this breeding example, a left part of one parent's genome and a right part of another parent's genome are exchanged to create a new individual with the combined genetic material from both parents.

7.1.4 Chromosome (Individual)

A collection of genomes representing a potential solution to the problem is called a *chromosome*. This is the genetic material of the genetic algorithm. A chromosome may consist of multiple genomes, each expressing a feature of the target system that must be considered a constraint or an objective function. For example,

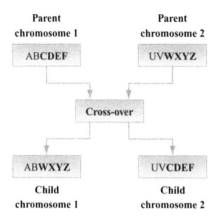

FIGURE 7.1

Breeding through a single-point crossover.

FIGURE 7.2

One possible solution to a TSP.

a genetic algorithm that solves the traveling salesman problem (TSP)[1] would encode the order of cities in its chromosome. Figure 7.2 shows a collection of cities and one possible route between these cities.

There are a large number of possible routes for even a small number of cities (in that the number of routes grows with the factorial of the number of cities).

---

[1]The objective of the traveling salesman problem (TSP) is to find the shortest route in time, capital, or distance between all cities without visiting any city twice. The general TSP problem has applicability in a wide range of configuration and design problems (such as the design and manufacture of microprocessor chips).

Table 7.1 The City Index Numbers

City	Index
Atlanta	1
Baltimore	2
Chicago	3
Dallas	4
Los Angeles	5
Las Vegas	6
Memphis	7
New York	8
San Francisco	9
Seattle	10

For eight cities, for example, the combinatorial complexity is 8! or more than 40,000 possible routes. We can simplify the encoding of the chromosome by assigning each city an index number. Table 7.1 shows the index values for each table.

Using this encoding, the TSP is encoded in a chromosome by specifying a possible path. The path is the set of edges in the route graph. In this problem, we are always starting in Seattle. This becomes the start and end of the directed graph. Figure 7.5 shows the chromosome for the route shown in Figure 7.3.

The chromosome defines a directed graph with the edges *(10,9)*, *(9,5)*, *(5,6)*, and so forth. If the TSP problem can start at any city, the starting city can be encoded as part of the genome as a separate parameter. A potential solution can be created for a path by generating a set of unique random numbers in the first nine positions within the range *[1,9]*, in that the last genome locus must return the path to the origin (in this case, Seattle).

	TSP Chromosome								
9	5	6	4	7	1	2	8	3	10

FIGURE 7.3

A chromosome expressing a TSP solution.

7.1.5 **Constraints**

Constraints define the feasibility of a schedule. Objectives define the optimality of a schedule. Although objectives *should* be satisfied, constraints *must* be satisfied. In a crew-scheduling system, for example, the schedule might have three constraints: the precedence relationship between jobs, the availability of the crew at the time it is needed, and a match between the type of crew and the skills required for the job. These constraints must be obeyed and define the properties of a feasible and workable solution. (See Section 7.1.8 for additional details.)

7.1.6 **Convergence**

The process of breeding a genetic algorithm's population over a series of generations to arrive at the chromosome with the best fitness value is known as *convergence*. That is, the population converges on a solution. Convergence is controlled by the fitness function: Fitter chromosomes survive to the next generation and breed new chromosomes that (hopefully) improve the average fitness of the population. This continues until the fitness does not improve; thus, it converges on a final value.

7.1.7 **Crossover (Recombination)**

The process of creating a new chromosome by combining or "mating" two or more high-performance chromosomes is known as *crossover*. In a crossover, the genetic material of one chromosome is swapped in some manner with the genetic material of another chromosome to produce one or more offspring. There are several techniques for combining the genetic material (genomes), such as one-point, two-point, and uniform crossover. These techniques are discussed in the detailed analysis of the algorithm.

7.1.8 **Feasible Solution**

A genetic algorithm must start with and always generate *feasible solutions*. Otherwise, the solution, even if its goodness of fit is the best, is useless. Feasible solutions must consider the nature of the objective function and constraints placed on the system. For example, consider the TSP. If a business constraint on the route plan specifies that the salesperson must visit all west coast cities before any other cities, a schedule that creates an initial route from Seattle to Chicago violates this constraint and is not a feasible solution. In a crew schedule, a solution that schedules a task when a critical and necessary piece of equipment is unavailable or that assigns a task to a crew that does not have the necessary skill set or cannot work in the task's geographic area is not a feasible solution.

7.1.9 Fitness Function

The *fitness function* is a measure associated with the collective objective functions that indicates the fitness of a particular chromosome (or the phenotype) in terms of a desired solution. A genetic algorithm is a directed search. This search is controlled by the fitness function. For minimization problems, the fitness function usually approaches zero as the optimal value. For maximization problems, the fitness function usually approaches some upper boundary threshold as its optimal value. For multiobjective functions, the fitness function often approaches some saddle point in the overall solution space. In the TSP, we want to minimize the distance, and thus we need a fitness function that approaches zero. One possible fitness function, shown in Equation 7.1, is fairly straightforward (it is 1 minus the inverse of the sum of the distances):

$$f = 1 - \frac{1}{\sum_{i=1}^{N-1} d(c_i, c_{i+1})} \tag{7.1}$$

For N cities, this function sums the distance between each successive city in the graph stored in the current chromosome. This fraction is subtracted from 1. Smaller distances will yield relatively larger fractions, thus driving the fitness function toward zero. When the entire population of potential paths has been evaluated, those with the smallest fitness will be the best solution found during that generation.

7.1.10 Generation

A genetic algorithm creates a new population of candidate solutions until a termination condition is reached. Each new population is known as a *generation*. A maximum number of generations is one of the termination conditions for a genetic algorithm.

7.1.11 Genome

A particular feature in the chromosome is represented by a *genome*. In many cases, a chromosome may consist of a single genome, but for multiobjective and multiconstraint problems, a chromosome can consist of several genomes. The nature of a genome depends on the underlying data representation. For bit (or binary) representations, the genome is a series of bits. For a real number representation, the genome is an integer or floating-point number.

7.1.12 Genotype

The complete structure of a chromosome is often called the *genotype*. It is simply a handy way of referring to all genomes. The actual instance of a chromosome (the actual values of the genotype) is called the phenotype.

7.1.13 Goodness of Fit

The *goodness of fit* is a measure of how close the fitness function value is to the optimum value. A fitness function returns a goodness-of-fit value for each chromosome.

7.1.14 Locus

A *locus* in a chromosome is simply a position in the genome. In the TSP chromosome (see Figure 7.3), there are ten node positions in the genome. Each of these values is a locus in the underlying chromosome.

7.1.15 Mutation

One of the ways in which a genetic algorithm attempts to improve the overall fitness of a population as it moves toward a final, optimal solution is by randomly changing the value of an allele. This process is called *mutation*. Mutation enriches the pool of phenotypes in the population, combats local minimum and maximum regions (and as such is a form of annealing), and ensures that new potential solutions, independent of the current set of chromosomes, will emerge in the population at large.

7.1.16 Objective Function

An *objective function* defines the purpose of the genetic algorithm and is the value that will be either minimized or maximized. Each genetic algorithm must have one or more objective functions. It is the objective function value that is measured by the fitness function and evaluated for its goodness of fit.

7.1.17 Performance

A general way of looking at the fitness of a chromosome is its *performance* in the population. Chromosomes with high goodness-of-fit values are considered high-performance segments of the population. Those chromosomes below some goodness-of-fit threshold are considered low-performance chromosomes.

7.1.18 Phenotype

The actual values of a genome (its position in the solution space) are called the *phenotype*. Whereas the genotype expresses the overall properties of the genetic algorithm by defining the nature of the chromosome, the phenotype represents an individual expression of the genome (or genotype). This is somewhat similar to the relationship between classes and objects in an object-oriented programming language: A class represents the definition of an object, whereas an object represents a concrete instantiation of a class.

7.1.19 **Population**

A collection of chromosomes with their values is a *population*. A genetic algorithm starts by creating a large population of potential solutions represented as chromosomes. As the algorithm continues, new populations of old and new chromosomes are created and processed. In some genetic algorithm implementations the total population size is fixed, whereas in others the population size can increase or decrease depending on the nature of the problem space.

7.1.20 **Schema**

Many of the mathematic foundations of genetic algorithms are built on the evaluation of emerging and transient bit patterns in the population. A pattern of bits that repeats through the high-performance region of the population provides a method of explaining how a genetic algorithm converges on a solution. In general practice, however, an understanding of *schema* patterns provides little, if any, benefit in the management of a genetic algorithm.

7.1.21 **Selection**

How individual chromosomes are chosen for crossover and mutation is based on the process of *selection*. Selection is used to pick the high-performance segment of the population for crossover breeding, to pick a few chromosomes for mutation, and in some problems to pick a few low-performance chromosomes for inclusion in the next generation (simply to ensure a mix of genetic material).

7.1.22 **Survival of the Fittest**

In a fashion similar to natural evolution, individuals in a genetic algorithm survive from one generation to the next based on their goodness-of-fit values. The fittest individuals are preserved and reproduce (see Section 7.1.3), which is referred to as *survival of the fittest*. In this way, the average goodness of fit of the entire population begins to converge on the best possible set of solutions.

7.1.23 **System**

A genetic algorithm is connected to an underlying *system*. The current phenotype values in the chromosome are the parameters used to run the system and evaluate the system's outcome in terms of goodness of fit. For example, a genetic algorithm that solves the TSP has chromosomes containing possible paths between all cities. The system it calls is the graph analyzer that computes the total travel time for each chromosome. The graph analyzer generally contains an N × N table of the distances between each city. Table 7.2 shows part of this table of intercity distances.

Table 7.2 Intercity Distances for TSP Route Analysis

From		1	2	3	4	5	6	7	8	9	10
							To				
Atlanta	1	0	600	900	1200	2900	1800	400	800	2800	2500
Baltimore	2	600	0	450	1150	2890	1940	510	200	2820	2470
Chicago	3	900	450	0	640	2100	1100	480	700	1950	2200
Dallas	4	1200	1150	640	0	1100	570	630	1020	1500	2050
Los Angeles	5	2900	2890	2100	1100	. . .					
Las Vegas	6	1800	1940	1100	570		. . .				
Memphis	7	400	510	480	630			. . .			
New York	8	800	200	700	1020				. . .		
San Francisco	9	2800	2820	1950	1500					. . .	
Seattle	10	2500	2470	2200	2050						. . .

In this route table (routes *[10][10]*), any chromosome phenotype can be decoded though the following distance function.

```
Function real d(integer fromCity, integer toCity){
   return(routes[fromCity][toCity]);
}
```

(See the fitness function definition in Section 7.1.9 for the actual system fitness function that uses this route intercity distance function.) Thus, the genetic algorithm sets up the population of candidate routes. Each chromosome is then made part of the parameters of the route analysis system, which computes and returns the fitness.

7.1.24 Termination Conditions

A genetic algorithm must be told when to stop searching for a solution. The criteria for stopping are called *termination conditions*. The criteria include the maximum number of generations having been reached, the amount of computer time having been exceeded, one or more individuals having fitness values that satisfy the objective function, or the best fitness function in successive generations having reached a plateau. A genetic algorithm can use one or more of these terminating conditions.

7.2 OVERVIEW

One of the principal uses of a genetic algorithm is optimization: The process of finding the best solution to a problem under a set of objectives and constraints. Finding the best solution usually, but not necessarily, means finding the maximum or minimum value for the variable representing the objective function. Because genetic algorithms can search large, highly nonlinear, and often noisy landscapes, they are ideal as solution engines for optimization problems involving a large number of constraints and many different (sometimes conflicting) objective functions. Some everyday examples include the following:

- Project, crew, and class scheduling; delivery and distribution routing (the TSP); container packing (the classical "knapsack" problem); timetabling; assembly line balancing; configuration management; and retail shelf-location planning.

- Regression and trend curve fitting, automatic cluster detection, and route identification.

- Process control, engineering structural design, integrated circuit design, urban planning, and highway capacity analysis.

- Evolution of neural networks, optimization of fuzzy models, general function optimization, exploration of game theory scenarios, protein folding and related modeling of molecular systems, and high-throughput screening and drug discovery and design.

- Capital budgeting, portfolio suitability, balancing, and mix analysis; sales, inventory, and consumption forecasting; new product pricing; and economic models.

- Network topology configuration, server capacity planning, fault detection, application scheduling, web design, and database design.

Genetic algorithms are also used in a wide spectrum of evolutionary programming systems. Evolutionary programs breed and mutate mathematic, logical, and fuzzy expressions to produce an optimal model. Not only are evolutionary programs another form of knowledge discovery (data mining), but they form an important class of solutions for rule-based and mathematics-based models.

7.2.1 Generate and Test

A genetic algorithm is an enhancement to one of the earliest approaches in machine problem solving. The approach is known as generate and test. Using this strategy, a new solution to the current problem state (which, of course, may be a partition of the final problem state) is generated and tested. If it satisfies the criteria for a solution, it is accepted;[2] otherwise, a new potential solution is

---

[2]In some cases, a set of candidate solutions is collected from the generate-and-test process. These candidates are then ranked by additional evaluation criteria and the best of the potential solutions is selected.

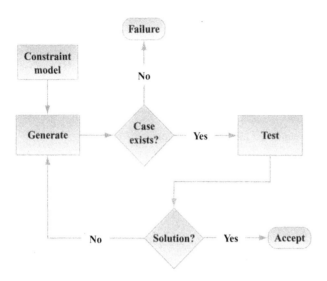

FIGURE 7.4

The generate-and-test process.

generated and tested. Because the generate-and-test method is always guided by an allowable outcome, it is called a directed search. Figure 7.4 illustrates this process.

A generator, using a model of constraints, creates a possible solution case to the current problem. The testing program evaluates the solution according to the current problem state. If the solution solves the current problem state, it is accepted; otherwise, another potential solution is produced (or, if no other solutions are available, the process terminates with a failure).

The core of the generate-and-test method is the ability of the generator to produce a set of well-formed, nonredundant candidate solutions. The test process incorporates two capabilities: The ability to run the candidate solution against the target system and the ability to compare the results to a valid solution. It is the comparison between a potential solution and an acceptable solution that drives the generate-and-test methodology. Where the criteria for a successful solution can be specified, the generate-and-test approach has proved to be a powerful tool and has been used in variety of difficult and computationally intensive problems in such areas as configuration, design, and graph generation.

7.2.2 The Genetic Algorithm

A genetic algorithm (GA) is a form of the generate-and-test paradigm. Like the generate-and-test method, it is a directed search and works by generating a large number of possible solutions and testing each of these against an allowable outcome. The genetic algorithm, as the name implies, breeds a solution to complex

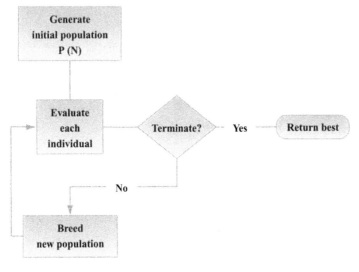

FIGURE 7.5

Organization of a genetic algorithm.

optimization and search problems using techniques that simulate the processes of natural evolution. The genetic algorithm starts with a large population of potential (or feasible) solutions and through the application of recombination (also called crossover) and mutation evolves a solution that is better than any previous solution over the lifetime of the genetic analysis. Figure 7.5 shows the organization of a genetic algorithm.

7.2.3 How a Genetic Algorithm Works

The genetic algorithm works by creating an initial population of N possible solutions in the form of candidate chromosomes (or simply, individuals). Each of these individuals represents the target system. The encoding of the target system's parameters in the individual is used to run the system and measure the outcome against an objective function. The objective function measures the goodness of fit of the individual. The better this goodness of fit, the closer the individual is to representing a solution. After all individuals in the population have been evaluated for their goodness of fit, we decide whether to continue or to stop. If the terminating condition is not met, a new population is created by saving the top K best individuals, removing the bottom M poorly performing individuals, and replacing these with new individuals created by merging the parameters of the top best-performing individuals. New chromosomes are also created by randomly mutating the parameters in a few of the existing individuals.

As the genetic algorithm creates and tests each population of chromosomes, it is searching for better and better solutions to the underlying problem. This

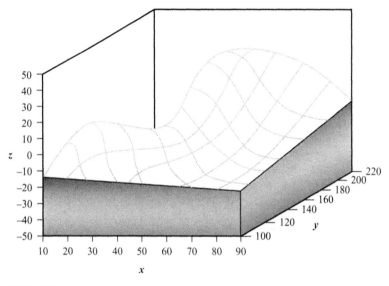

FIGURE 7.6

The solution space terrain for $z = f(x, y)$.

search takes the form of a walkover of the underlying surface of the solution space. For example, consider Equation 7.2 and a genetic algorithm that seeks to maximize the variable z as a solution to the function in continuous variables x and y:

$$z = f(x, y) \tag{7.2}$$

If we plot z over the possible values of x and y, we develop a terrain map of the solution surface for this function. Figure 7.6 shows a portion of the terrain map that we will use in the discussion of how the genetic algorithm works.

The genetic algorithm searches through this terrain to find the values of x and y that maximize z. This is essentially a process known as hill climbing. In hill climbing, the search mechanism explores the terrain around its current position looking for values in the independent variables that will increase the value of the target (or dependent) variable. It then moves in this direction (hence the analogy with climbing a hill). A major problem with hill climbing is its tendency to become stuck in a local maximum (or minimum, depending on the objective function). For example, Figure 7.7 shows a hill-climbing mechanism selecting a random position on the terrain.

Examining the surrounding terrain, the hill-climbing mechanism moves to the left and up. Through a series of proximity tests, it works its way, as illustrated in Figure 7.8, to the top of the hill.

By generating a series of values for x and y, the search mechanism can work its way up the slope, always moving in the direction that gives a larger value of z.

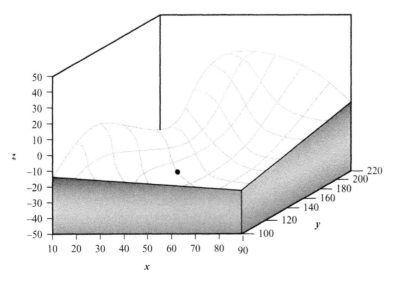

FIGURE 7.7

A random search point on the terrain.

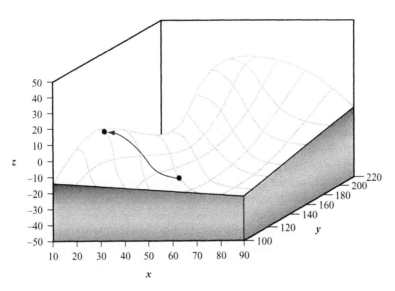

FIGURE 7.8

Hill climbing moving up a hill.

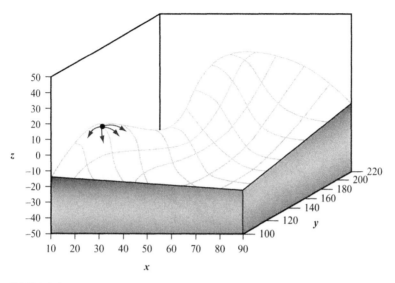

FIGURE 7.9

Arriving at the top of the hill.

Eventually, as we can see in Figure 7.9, the search mechanism arrives at the top of the hill. There is no way to go except back down.

This hill-climbing example illustrates not only the way the search mechanism works but a significant weakness in the search methodology. Although we have arrived at the top of a hill, it is not the hill that maximizes the value of z (this hill lies off to the right). Once the hill-climbing mechanism starts up a slope, it has no way of going back down to find another, perhaps better, hill. Thus, hill climbing is always subject to finding local maximums (or minimums). We can compensate for this tendency to find local maximum or minimum regions through a process called simulated annealing. This approach saves the current maximum and then in effect "shakes" the surface to start the search point rolling around the terrain. It then starts the hill climbing from this new point. However, for any realistically large, complex, and often noncontiguous surface, this approach is very inefficient. In real-world systems, the underlying terrain is often very hilly, with gaps, steep ravines, and long gullies.

Not only does a hill-climbing mechanism have little chance of finding a global maximum in such a surface, but there is no way for the search mechanism to ensure that any maximum is in fact the global maximum (or minimum).

A genetic algorithm significantly improves the hill-climbing methodology of generate-and-test by selecting many possible maximums throughout the surface and then using the fitness function to breed better and better solutions as each of the randomly placed points moves up (or down) adjacent slopes. Figure 7.10 illustrates a population of potential solutions that would form the initial set of chromosomes for a genetic algorithm.

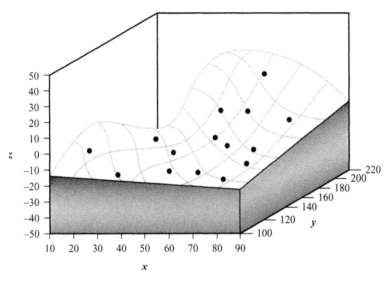

FIGURE 7.10

An initial population of possible solutions.

Table 7.3 Crossover Example

	Parent	**Child**
Genome N	(50,120)	(84,120)
Genome $N + 1$	(84,173)	(50,173)

In Figure 7.10 we can see that the candidate solutions are scattered widely over the underlying terrain. Each point with an x, y coordinate value yields a value for z. Our fitness function is simply the value of z. The higher the value, the better the goodness of fit. In the genetic algorithm, the initial population of solutions and each subsequent population are subjected to a set of transformations, as follows:

- A collection of the best chromosomes (solutions) is retained.

- The bottommost poor solutions are removed.

- The members of a random set of the best solutions are "mated" to produce a set of children that shares the genetic material of their parents. This is the process called crossover. For example, Table 7.3 shows a crossover for two genomes. In this case, the first locus (the x value) is swapped to generate two new children. The purpose of crossover is to increase variety and robustness in the population while preserving the genetic values of the best solutions.

■ Another random (but sparse) set of the population is subjected to mutation. This involves randomly changing the value of a chromosome locus to a random but permissible value. Mutation is a form of annealing, which introduces new genetic material into the population.

■ Every so often a completely new chromosome is created and inserted into the population. This is also a form of annealing and, like mutation, introduces completely new genetic material into the population.

This process of breeding new solutions (creating a new population) by selecting the chromosomes with the largest fitness value and applying crossover and mutation continues for generation after generation. Figure 7.11 illustrates the population after a few generations.

Although there are still a few poor-performance chromosomes (because of the unpredictable random effects of individual crossovers and mutations), the average performance of all chromosomes has improved. Most of the solution points are beginning to move toward the global maximum. We also note that the points that have climbed the local maximum slopes are also being removed because their fitness function values are consistently less than the points that are moving toward the global maximum.

As we continue this process over a large number of generations, the ranking of chromosomes by their goodness of fit guides the search toward the global maximum. Figure 7.12 shows the result: the fitness function eventually finds the maximum (optimal) value of z.

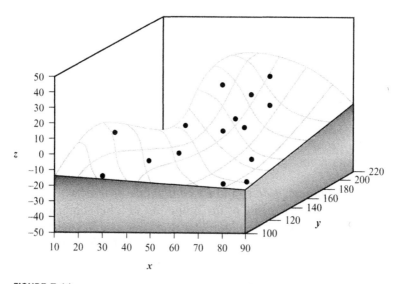

FIGURE 7.11

The solution population after several generations.

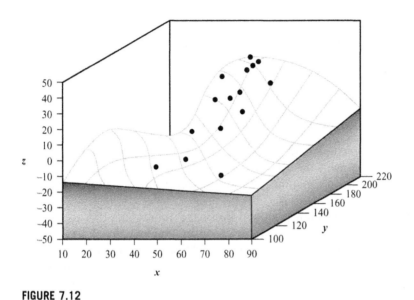

FIGURE 7.12

The maximum (optimal) value of *z*.

In summary, genetic algorithms are a form of directed search. They work through the repetitive application of genetic operators and a fitness function to a population of potential solutions. The genetic operators breed new solutions. The fitness function selects the best of these new solutions. The genetic algorithm ranks the best solutions, applies the genetic operators to breed new solutions, and evaluates these against the fitness function. This process usually continues until no more improvement in a potential solution is found (or until another termination condition is reached).

7.2.4 Strengths and Limitations of Genetic Algorithms

Although genetic algorithms are powerful tools for search and optimization, they are not without their problems and limitations. In this section, we review a few of their principal strong points and weak points.

The Ability to Solve Nonlinear, Noisy, and Discontinuous Problems

Although a genetic algorithm has many of the properties of a hill-climbing algorithm, it is actually a more sophisticated form of a stochastic search engine. The general capabilities of a stochastic search are more robust and broader than simple hill climbing. In particular, genetic algorithms are capable of solving highly nonlinear problems that involve discontinuous surfaces, noise, and internal dependencies (such as lead and lag relationships). Nonlinearity is a common property of most real-world problems, occurring in manufacturing, inventory management,

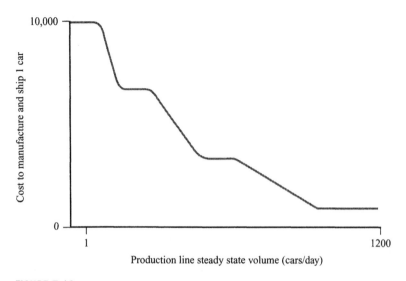

FIGURE 7.13

A nonlinear production cost curve.

portfolio mix optimization, construction, retailing, and a wide spectrum of other industries.

For example, in the normal course of running a production line the cost to assemble, paint, and ship 100 cars for the ABC Motor Company is N. If $N = 20,000$, the cost per car is $200. What is the cost to assemble, paint, and ship a single car? What is the individual cost to assemble, paint, and ship 1 million cars? Both of these questions involve a nonlinear system. The cost of setup, labor, electricity, and other factors means that producing a single car (or any small number of cars) is far more expensive than a large number of cars in a production system. Figure 7.13 illustrates this nonlinear relationship between cost and production line volume.

The plateau regions in the function are generally related to the cost of energy and materials that often have quantity-based cost thresholds. On the other hand, the wear and tear on equipment alone means that the cost per car on a run of 1 million cars will steadily increase. The growth and decay curves in these examples are typical examples of nonlinear functions.

The Ability to Solve Complex Optimization Problems

The genetic algorithm's ability to rapidly and thoroughly search a large, complex, and high-dimensional space allows it to solve multiobjective and multiconstraint optimization problems. In a multiple objective function schedule, the optimal solution often represents a saddle (or compromise) point in the solution space. Optimization in the presence of multiobjective functions usually means finding a way to rank the utility or importance of each objective and then finding a way to judge the optimality of a feasible solution based on the goodness of fit or rank of their optimality measures.

As a rather simple example using a crew scheduler, if each objective function (f) returns a value between 0 and 100, indicating how close the schedule is to the optimal (0 = best, 100 = worst), we can find an optimality ranking for a multi-objective function schedule by evaluating Equation 7.3:

$$franked = \frac{\sum_{i=1}^{N} f_i \times w_i}{\sum_{i=1}^{N} w_i} \qquad (7.3)$$

where N is the number of objective functions and w_i is the weight (or utility) value of that objective function. By selecting schedules with the smallest weighted average objective function, the feasible schedules with the closest optimality fit will continually percolate to the top. This form of evaluating a collection of objective functions makes it easy to combine both minimizing and maximizing objective functions in the same analysis (maximizing functions simply return the inverse of the fitness value).

A Complete Dependence on the Fitness Function

As a directed search technique, the fitness function evaluates each solution and ranks it according to a goodness of fit. If a fitness function cannot be defined, a genetic algorithm cannot be used to solve the problem. If a fitness function does not correctly define a separable universe of good and bad solutions (or if the fitness function is coded incorrectly), the genetic algorithm will behave according to the clarity and focus of the faulty fitness function and will fail to find the correct solution. And because a genetic algorithm is highly sensitive to the underlying gradient of the solution space, a fitness function must provide a way of guiding the search. The algorithm must be able to tell when it is moving in the right direction—that is, when in fact it is getting close to a solution.

Genetic algorithms are also sensitive to intelligent proximity and search capabilities built into the search methodology. This is both a strength and a weakness. The ability to encode intelligence into the fitness function so that degrees of fitness can be evaluated allows the genetic algorithm to rank chromosomes that are "close to" the main goodness-of-fit criteria. This process can help guide the search through a rough or chaotic solution space. At the same time, a lack of focus in the fitness function can spread the search over a larger segment of the population, slowing and often obscuring the optimization process. Finding a balance between the flexibility and brittleness of the fitness function is often a difficult task.

A Sensitivity to Genetic Algorithm Parameters

Genetic algorithms are intrinsically sensitive to the way in which new populations are generated; that is, they are sensitive to the way in which future populations inherit high-performance properties and the way in which new potential solutions emerge in future populations. Essentially, this means that the stability, coherence, and convergence of genetic algorithms depend on the rate of mutation and the crossover frequency. The higher the rate of the crossover and mutation properties, the more variation appears in the population. This may initially provide a rich pool of possible solutions. However, as the frequency rates increase, the continuity of high-performance individuals is lost among the resulting randomness. At some point, the algorithm becomes less and less stable and the genome itself becomes more and more random.

Two significant problems are associated with a lack of robustness in a genetic algorithm: premature convergence and delayed convergence. When the population size is too small or the genetic diversity is too small, a genetic algorithm can converge too quickly on a local optimum. On the other hand, if the population size is too large or the genetic diversity is too large, an optimal solution may not emerge (because of the continual emergence of randomness in the genomes) or the convergence to a solution may take a long time.

A Sensitivity to Genome Encoding

Genetic algorithms are also responsive, but perhaps to a lesser degree, to the underlying coding scheme used to represent the genome. Traditional genome coding has been done through a bit string so that mutations can work in a way similar to random genetic miscoding in biologic systems. Production genetic algorithms—those that have been deployed into regular use and are solving real-world problems, especially those used in complex, multiobjective business applications—commonly use real numbers as genomes. The use of numbers rather than bit strings provides not only higher evaluation performance but the ability to more easily control the underlying distribution (statistical) properties of the genome.

Summary of Genetic Algorithm Strengths and Limitations

To summarize, genetic algorithms belong to a class of directed search methods that are be used for both solving optimization problems and modeling the core of evolutionary systems. They use a heuristic rather than analytical approach, and thus their solutions are not always exact and their ability to find a solution often depends on a proper and sometimes fragile specification of the problem representation and the parameters that drive the genetic algorithm.

7.3 THE ARCHITECTURE OF A GENETIC ALGORITHM

In the previous section, we discussed the underlying concepts of the genetic algorithm and how the stochastic search and fitness functions work together to find a value for an objective function. We also reviewed some of the principal strengths and weaknesses of genetic algorithms. Now we turn to the actual mechanics of the genetic algorithm; how a genetic algorithm is designed, structured, and organized for a particular problem; the meaning and application of the algorithm parameters; and the specification of constraints, objectives, and fitness functions.

To illustrate the mechanics of a genetic algorithm and how the various algorithm parameters affect the search methods, we will use a small, five-city TSP. In this problem, shown in Figure 7.14, we want to find the shortest complete path (or tour) between cities Able, Baker, Charlie, Delta, and Echo. To simplify the example, we are not attempting to find a circuit (that is, we need not return to the starting city).

To compute the path between the cities, we need to store the intercity distances in a way that allows for a rapid evaluation of the path. The mileage between these cities, shown in Table 7.4, is maintained in a distance matrix ($D[\ ][\ ]$),

An alternative way of storing city-to-city distances, of course, is through a grid coordinate system. In this approach, each city is associated with an *x-y* coordinate in an $N \times M$ map. Table 7.5 shows a coordinate table for the five cities.

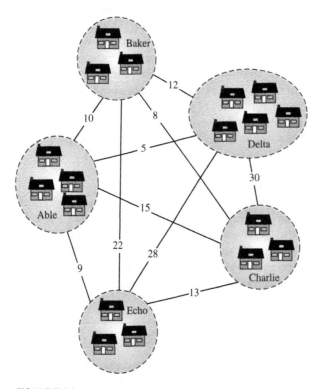

FIGURE 7.14

The five-city TSP.

Table 7.4 The Intercity Distance Matrix

	Able	Baker	Charlie	Delta	Echo
Able	0	10	15	5	9
Baker	10	0	8	12	22
Charlie	15	8	0	30	13
Delta	5	12	30	0	28
Echo	9	22	13	28	0

Table 7.5 The City Coordinate Map

	Grid Coordinates	
	x	y
Able	3	3
Baker	5	1
Charlie	7	4
Delta	8	2
Echo	4	6

With a coordinate table, the distance between any two cities (C_n, C_m) is the Euclidean distance from the coordinates of C_n and C_m. Equation 7.4 is the distance metric:

$$d(C_n, C_m) = \sqrt{(x_m - x_n)^2 + (y_m - y_m)^2} \qquad (7.4)$$

The choice of representation depends to a large degree on how the distance metric is actually used. If the distance must be associated with road, rail, water, and other physical transportation systems, the intercity distance map is the preferred representation method because it can capture the actual mileage between two cities based on actual driving or commuter rail distances (for example). Also, when the distances between cities are not symmetric—that is, traveling from city C_1 to city C_2 is not the same as traveling from city C_2 to city C_1—the intercity matrix should be used. The Euclidean distance, on the other hand, is the straight-line mileage between two cities. In some problems, where the approximate distance is sufficient, the grid coordinate method can be used.

With five cities, there are 120 possible paths (because there are 5! possible combinations of cities). Our genetic algorithm will explore this space. Its objective is to minimize the transit length among the cities.

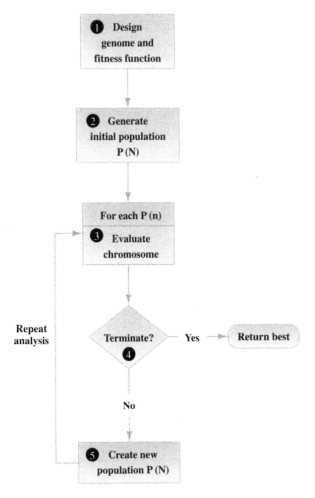

FIGURE 7.15

The control and analysis flow in a genetic algorithm.

Keeping the previous paragraph in mind, we can turn to the internal workings of the genetic algorithm. Figure 7.15 shows the schematic flow of control and analysis in the genetic algorithm.

7.3.1 One: Design a Genome Representation and Fitness Function

The efficiency and processing power of a genetic algorithm depend on the way the problem is expressed in a chromosome and the fitness function that evaluates the chromosome. This is the first step in using a genetic algorithm (see ❶). The design of a chromosome or genome set to properly represent a problem is one of the crucial architectural decisions in the use of a genetic algorithm.

Genome Structural Design

A population consists of a collection of chromosomes. Each chromosome consists of one or more genomes. Every chromosome represents a possible solution. The way in which the chromosome is designed can, therefore, have a significant effect on processing speed, convergence, and the overall ease of crossover and mutation. It is important to understand that the values of a chromosome are the parameters of a solution and must always be associated with an evaluation system that can use the parameters to produce a state or outcome of the system. The degree to which this outcome is a better or worse solution, given the chromosome's parameter values, is measured by the fitness function (which is discussed in the next section).

In the TSP, an obvious chromosome representation is a genome with five loci, representing the order in which the cities are visited. The number in the locus is the city at the row location in the distance matrix ($D[\ ][\ ]$). Figure 7.16 shows a possible chromosome (a phenotype) for a route through five cities.

This chromosome describes a tour: start at Able, travel to Charlie, travel to Echo, travel to Delta, and then travel to Baker. A new chromosome can easily be developed using this presentation by generating five unique random numbers between 1 and 5. For a simple route through five cities, a chromosome that is a permutation of the cities is most likely the simplest and the best.

Chromosome design is, however, highly dependent on the problem. Consider a circuit through the same five cities. A circuit has the constraint that we must return to the starting city.

We can either modify the fitness function to consider the implicit loop or design a slightly different chromosome to make the circuit explicit and speed up fitness computation. An extra locus is added to the end of the chromosome. This site contains the city index of the first locus. Figure 7.17 shows a possible chromosome (a phenotype) for a circuit through the five cities.

Locus (allele) positions				
1	2	3	4	5
1	3	5	4	2

FIGURE 7.16

A route chromosome in the TSP.

Locus (allele) position					
1	2	3	4	5	6
1	3	5	4	2	1

FIGURE 7.17

A circuit chromosome in the TSP.

In the circuit representation, however, the genetic algorithm is not free to perform crossover and mutate operations over the complete chromosome. Locus 5 completes the circuit and must always have the same value as the first locus. Thus, ease of representation increases complexity in the control strategies of the genetic algorithm.

Chromosomes can consist of more than single values. A chromosome locus can be a vector, a matrix, or a tree structure. The representation depends on the problem. As a simple example, suppose we change the objective of the five-city TSP to find the shortest route through the city considering traffic patterns during the day. Heavy traffic in city C_i effectively extends the distance between cities (C_i, C_j). We can represent this by a length multiplier associated with the *from* (or starting) city. Table 7.6 lists the effective lengths between cities—with the travel time between each city pair extended by the traffic multiplier.

For example, for the route segment Able to Baker (or to any other city) at 1615 (4:15 p.m.), the multiplier is 1.4, indicating, perhaps, moderately heavy rush-hour traffic. The distance from Able to Baker is 10 miles. The multiplier converts this to an effective distance of 14 miles (10 times 1.4). The chromosome representation now must consider two values: the city and the time of day of arrival at the city. Figure 7.18 shows the organization of the city and time-of-day genome.

Table 7.6 The City Traffic Multipliers

		Time of Day					
	From To	0000 0530	0531 0730	0731 0930	0931 1600	1601 1900	1901 2400
Able		1.0	1.2	1.4	1.1	1.4	1.2
Baker		1.0	1.2	1.3	1.3	1.2	1.1
Charlie		1.0	1.5	1.7	1.4	1.3	1.2
Delta		1.0	1.3	1.5	1.4	1.1	1.0
Echo		1.3	1.4	1.2	1.0	1.0	1.0

FIGURE 7.18

The city route and time-of-day genome.

Each genome locus in this representation consists of a 1×2 vector containing the city and the time of day. An initial population is generated by selecting a random permutation of cities and, for each city, a random arrival time.[3] The search process proceeds by breeding routes that minimize path length subject to the best time of day of city arrival times. More complex route scheduling problems can be solved in this manner.

For example, city C_i may have N possible routes though the city. Baltimore, Maryland, for instance, has I-695 (the beltway), the harbor tunnel, the I-95 tunnel, and the Francis Scott Key Bridge, each connecting cities south of Baltimore (such as Washington, DC) to cities north of Baltimore (such as Wilmington and Philadelphia). Each route has its own length, or a traffic multiplier. A TSP algorithm could consider the order of the cities, the route through the city, and the time of arrival. Because every city has a different number of possible routes, the routing locus would be drawn from a different population of random highways associated with the city in the city locus of the genome.

The TSP illustrates one of the structural difficulties in designing a chromosome representation that is easy to use and amendable to genetic operators such as crossover and mutation. As we will see in the discussion of breeding techniques (see Conventional Crossover (Breeding) Techniques section), a genome with a simple linear sequence of cities almost always produces an incorrect genome when subjected to conventional "cut-and-splice" crossover operations, as well as an incorrect genome when subjected to conventional locus (site) mutation. Following the conventional crossover and mutation operations, we will take up more advanced issues in designing genomes for permutation and precedence-based (time-sequenced) problems.[4]

Genome Representations

In addition to the most effective and efficient way to encode parameters into chromosomes, the underlying form of the representation is also important. Historically, chromosomes have been encoded as bit strings. Figure 7.19 illustrates the bit (or binary) organization of the five-city TSP search.

Unlike the use of actual numbers, which employ arrays or matrices for the genome, a binary representation uses a continuous string of 1 and 0 values. The

---

[3]Nothing in the genetic search process requires a uniform distribution of random times. For business trip schedules or crew scheduling, we might limit the random time to business hours, say 0630 to 1700 (or 1430 hours to allow end-of-day tear down and travel time). Naturally, as we will see in the discussion of fitness functions, we could also assign very large multipliers to nonwork times to force the search mechanism to only schedule trips during a specific range of work hours.

[4]Separating the discussion of genome design into two sections makes it easier for readers unfamiliar with either genetic algorithm breeding operators or with scheduling, routing, covering, and TSPs to understand the fundamentals and then appreciate the difficulties in genomes that involve locus dependencies.

Locus (allele) positions				
1	2	3	4	5
0001	0011	0101	0100	0010

FIGURE 7.19

The binary route chromosome in the TSP.

chromosomes in Table 7.5 would be represented as *0001001100100100*. Bit strings provide several general benefits in genetic search:

- As a string of 1s and 0s, they are a compact representation.

- Crossover operations are simplified. The mating process simply slices the bit string at some random point and appends the string fragments without regard to the actual values.

- Mutation is a simple matter of flipping a random bit in the string.

- They provide a pattern analysis space for the evaluation of schemata (patterns of high-performance genomes that move through the population). Whether or not schemata analysis contributes any significant control improvement to genetic algorithms is a matter of some debate. Most business genetic algorithms in scheduling, production management, logistics, data exploration, pricing, and similar areas evaluate the fitness function and the average fitness of the population without regard to the propagation of schemata patterns.

Binary representations, however, all have some significant problems:

- They must be converted to a real number for use as a parameter to the underlying system. This involves traversing the bit string from right to left, and for each nonzero position, computing the value (2^n, where n is the bit position) and adding it to the total of the under-generation value.

- They make feasibility and unique chromosome constraint checking difficult (the requirements for feasibility and uniqueness are discussed in Section 7.3.2).

- They make generating random values in a specific range a more tedious process.

- They are often a source of deep representation problems in genetic algorithms. Because we are (as a general rule) unaccustomed to working in base 2 arithmetic, debugging and tracing the operations of a genetic algorithm are often difficult and are flawed by mistakes in either binary encoding or interpreting the output of the algorithm.

- They are (generally) unnecessary. Nearly all problems can be expressed with integer or floating-point numbers as the parameters. Using a variety of random number generators (uniform, Gaussian, binomial, and so forth), these parameters can be used in crossover and mutation operations in ways that are easy to understand, easy to implement, easy to constrain, and less prone to errors of encoding or interpretation.

All genetic and evolutionary programming problems discussed in the Cox's book, *Fuzzy Modeling and Genetic Algorithms for Data Mining and Exploration* (2005), use real numbers as loci in their chromosomes. This has proved, in the problems designed and deployed by the author, to be an effective and robust means of genome representation. Although there are some debates in the literature about the performance of real numbers versus bit strings, in actual applications (many involving large problem spaces and complex genomes) the difference in genome representation has been far outweighed by the efficiencies associated with ranking (sorting), selecting, and the evaluation of the fitness function in the target system.

Fitness Functions

In the TSP, we have a single objective function and a small set of constraints. Because we want to find the shortest route through the cities, the fitness function (shown in Equation 7.5) is the sum of the paths between the cities in the chromosome:

$$f = \sum_{i=1}^{N-1} d\left(c_i, c_{i+1}\right) \qquad (7.5)$$

Here,

> f is the fitness of the chromosome.
> N is the number of cities in the chromosome (in this case, five cities).
> c_i is the ith city in the chromosome. This is the ith locus in the genome and indexes the corresponding row in the distance matrix.
> $d(\ )$ is a function that returns the distance between two cities using their index values in the distance matrix.

Genetic algorithms can be used to solve multiobjective and multiconstraint problems. As a general practice, objective functions are encoded as a set of genomes, whereas hard constraints are part of the underlying system evaluation and affect the fitness function in terms of the feasibility of a solution. Soft constraints, on the other hand, are often encoded as penalty functions in the fitness evaluation.

For example, suppose the TSP had two objectives: Find the shortest and find the least expensive route through the cites. The cost to travel from city c_i to city c_j can be encoded, as illustrated in Table 7.7, by adding a table of highway tolls to the problem.

Note that unlike distances, the toll costs are sometimes different depending on whether the path is c_i, c_j or c_j, c_i, in that many toll roads charge for traffic moving in one direction but not in another. With the city distance and the toll costs matrices in hand, we can formulate a fitness function that looks for the minimum path

Table 7.7 The Intercity Toll Matrix

	Able	Baker	Charlie	Delta	Echo
Able	0	2	0	3	0
Baker	2	0	4	0	2
Charlie	2	4	0	0	2
Delta	3	0	0	0	0
Echo	0	2	2	0	0

length and the minimum cost. One simple way to design a fitness function, as illustrated in Equation 7.6, is to take the sum of the path length and the toll costs:

$$f = \sum_{i=1}^{N-1} d(c_i, c_{i+1}) + t(c_i, c_{i+1}) \tag{7.6}$$

Here,

  f is the fitness of the chromosome.
  N is the number of cities in the chromosome (in this case, five cities).
  c_i is the ith city in the chromosome. This is the ith locus in the genome and indexes the corresponding row in the distance matrix.
  $d(\ )$ is a function that returns the distance between two cities using their index values in the distance matrix.
  $t(\ )$ is a function that returns the toll costs between two cities using their index values in the toll matrix.

Thus, for equal path lengths, paths with no tolls (or very small tolls) will have a better minimization fitness value than paths with larger tolls. We can also design a fitness function to seek for the shortest path *only* on toll roads. In this case, we want to penalize any solution that does not use a toll road. Equation 7.7 shows one possible way to encode a penalty into the fitness function:

$$f = \sum_{i=1}^{N-1} d(c_i, c_{i+1}) + \frac{1}{t(c_i, c_{i+1}) + 1} \tag{7.7}$$

In this case, when $t(\ ) = 0$ or near zero, the fraction is close to 1 and will increase the value of the fitness function. For all values of $t(\ ) \gg 0$, the fraction becomes very small and contributes to the minimization of the solution. The fitness function minimizes route distance and maximizes toll costs. Thus, this fitness function will seek the shortest and most expensive route through the cities.

The idea of multiobjective and multiconstraint genetic searches can encompass a large number of possible objective functions. The fitness function determines the optimum balance between individual fitness and a composite solution. For problems that involve many objective functions, it is not generally possible to find a solution that is optimal for each objective function. In the previous example, there are two objective functions:

1. Minimize the total route distance between N cities.
2. Minimize (or maximize) the toll costs.

We cannot simultaneously find the shortest route and the route with the least costs unless they just happen to coincide. In the real world, the solution with the minimum spanning route and the route that minimizes the toll costs will lie in a space somewhere between the two objectives. As the number of objective functions and penalty constraints increases, these saddle points become more and more difficult to define. For example, consider a slightly more complex genetic search system that incorporates, as shown in Table 7.8, a table of speed limits between cities.

The genetic algorithm now has three objective functions:

1. Minimize the total route distance between N cities.
2. Minimize the toll costs.
3. Minimize the time to travel the route.

Finding the optimal saddle point in the solution space that simultaneously satisfies all three constraints involves designing a fitness function that penalizes long routes, penalizes routes that involve toll roads, and penalizes route segments that have slow speed limits. Equation 7.8 shows one possible fitness function for this problem:

$$f = \sum_{t=1}^{N-1} d(c_i, c_{i+1}) + t(c_i, c_{i+1}) + (70 - s(c_i, c_{i+1})) \qquad (7.8)$$

Table 7.8 The Intercity Speed Limit Matrix

	Able	Baker	Charlie	Delta	Echo
Able	0	55	65	70	65
Baker	55	0	70	60	65
Charlie	65	70	0	70	70
Delta	70	60	70	0	65
Echo	65	65	70	65	0

Here,

f is the fitness of the chromosome.

N is the number of cities in the chromosome (in this case, five cities).

c_i is the ith city in the chromosome. This is the ith locus in the genome and indexes the corresponding row in the distance matrix.

$d(\ )$ is a function that returns the distance between two cities using their index values in the distance matrix.

$t(\ )$ is a function that returns the toll costs between two cities using their index values in the toll matrix.

$s(\ )$ is a function that returns the speed limit between two cities using their index values in the speed limit matrix.

Knowing that the speed limit on interstate highways (which connect most of the cities) is between 65 and 70 mph, we subtract the intercity speed limit from 70 (the maximum speed) to give a penalty weight to this part of the fitness function. The closer the city-to-city speed limit is to 70 mph the smaller the difference, and hence the smaller the contribution to the size of the fitness function (and thus, it contributes to minimizing the overall function). Naturally, other possible encoding forms that require no knowledge of the maximum speed limit exist, such as the inverse relationship we used to maximize the use of tolls (in that we are, in effect, maximizing the speed over the route). See Equation 7.5 for this use of the inverse (or fractional) weighting.

Multigenome Fitness Functions

In the previous discussion, the fitness function was associated with a single route through the cities. Each chromosome represented a possible route and had its own fitness function. Every chromosome was also independent of every other chromosome in the population (i.e., in terms of fitness, although chromosomes are related to other individuals through parent–child relationships generated by the crossover process). We now consider a slightly more complex TSP version—one associated with crew scheduling, project management, assembly line balancing, and similar operations. Instead of a single five-city path, the genetic algorithm is asked to schedule a set of N crews who must visit all five cities during the day. We have an electrical, a road repair, and a vehicle maintenance crew, thus $N = 3$. Figure 7.20 shows the organization of the crew trip-scheduling chromosome.

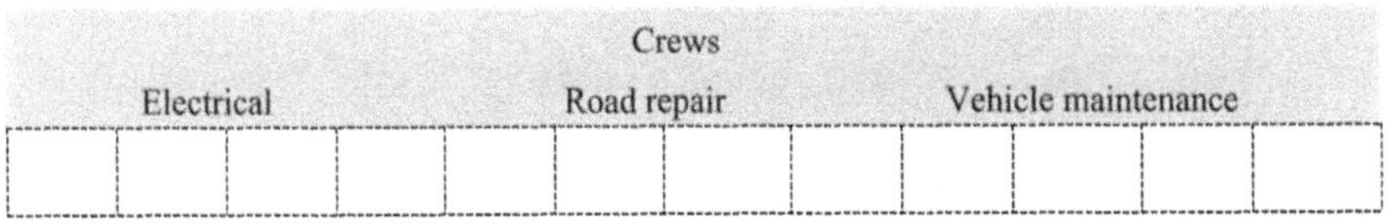

FIGURE 7.20

The crew trip-scheduling chromosome.

The objective of the genetic search is to find the crew trip schedule that minimizes the distance traveled by the three crews. One way to do this, as shown in Equation 7.9, is through a direct minimization fitness function that simply sums the path length for the three crews:

$$f = f_e(\ ) + f_r(\ ) + f_v(\ ) \tag{7.9}$$

Here,

f is the fitness of the chromosome.
$f_e(\ )$ is the fitness of the electrical path.
$f_r(\ )$ is the fitness of the road repair crew path.
$f_v(\ )$ is the fitness of the vehicle maintenance crew.

Another way to formulate a fitness function is to measure the fitness of a solution relative to the total distance traveled by any set of crews in a schedule. Thus, the best solution will be the smallest relative to the crews that took the longest path through the five cities. Equation 7.10 illustrates this type of fitness function:

$$f = 1 + \frac{d_t}{d_{max}} \tag{7.10}$$

Here,

f is the fitness of the chromosome.
d_t is the total distance traveled by the three crews.
d_{max} is the maximum distance traveled by any set of crews. This is discovered by iterating through the population and finding the crew schedule with the longest path length.

Basing a fitness function on factors spread over, or intrinsic to the population, is often used when the individual solutions have a high degree of variability. For example, consider a crew-scheduling system with the following characteristics:

- Crews are assigned pending jobs for the day.
- Depending on the distance to the jobs, crews may work on a variable number of jobs (that is, because a crew can only work 8 hours, the mix of jobs and the distance to each job—from the main office or from a previous job—determines the number of jobs that can be done).
- The company wants as many jobs as possible completed each day.

In this case, we want to maximize jobs but minimize the travel time between jobs (in that long travel times incur elevated fuel costs, can lead to excessive wear and tear on equipment, and increase the probability that the previous job will start late or remain incomplete for that day). A fitness function that only evaluates the schedule of a single chromosome independent of all other schedules cannot take into account the variability in the number of actual jobs scheduled coupled to the distance traveled to satisfy those jobs. Hence, a population-based fitness function is more appropriate. Equation 7.11 shows one possible fitness function:

$$f = (N - J_i) + \frac{d_i}{d_{max}} \qquad (7.11)$$

Here,

    f is the fitness of the chromosome.

    N is the total number of jobs being assigned to the crews on this day.

    J_i is the number of jobs scheduled for the three crews.

    d_i is the total distance traveled by the three crews.

    d_{max} is the maximum distance traveled by any set of crews. This is discovered by iterating through the population and finding the crew schedule with the longest path length.

This is a minimization fitness function: the smaller the value, the better the fitness. Thus, for two candidate schedules, s_1 and s_2, the one that schedules the most jobs is the best (as J_i approaches N, the value becomes smaller and smaller). If both schedules have the same number of planned jobs, the one with the smallest overall distance traveled is the best.

Designing the genome representation of the problem parameters and selecting a fitness function to measure each chromosome's goodness of fit is the first phase in using a genetic algorithm. We now turn to the actual mechanics of the algorithm, exploring the iterative process of breeding a solution.

7.3.2 Two: Generate Initial Population—P(N)

A genetic algorithm begins with a population of potential solutions. These solutions are encoded in the chromosomes. An initial population of potential routes consists of randomly generated combinations of cities (see Figure 7.15, ❷). Each genome site (locus) is the next city in the route. Thus, a genome of (*3,2,4,1*) would be a path from Charlie to Baker to Delta to Able. Table 7.9 is part of this population of N potential solutions.

There are two general performance objectives on the generation of all populations in a genetic algorithm (and they apply to initial populations as well as future populations that are bred from the initial population):

1. First, each potential solution must be a feasible solution. Feasibility means that the solution obeys all hard constraints on the solution. If the TSP problem, for example, specifies a particular city as the starting point, randomly generated solutions that do not start with this city are not feasible solutions. It is often difficult in real-world problems to ensure that each solution is feasible, and this constraint often means that the mechanics of the genetic algorithm are intricately connected to the mechanics of the application.

Table 7.9 A Population of TSP Solutions

Genome	Locus Values				
1	1	3	2	5	4
2	3	5	4	1	2
3	2	1	4	3	5
4	3	1	4	5	2
5	5	2	4	3	1
6	1	5	2	4	3
:					
:					
N	1	4	5	3	2

2. Second, each potential solution must be a unique solution. This is a constraint on the population that is often overlooked in the literature on genetic algorithms, generally because most of the problems in the academic literature involve solving simple problems (such as this small TSP problem in which duplicate paths would not appreciably slow down the search process). Finding duplicate or nonunique solutions is often a difficult task because a duplicate genome is not always obvious. For example, if the direction of the path is immaterial, the genome *(1,2,3,4)* is the same as *(4,3,2,1)* because both represent the same path.

In some applications, of course, one or both of these objectives cannot be met, either because knowing what is a feasible solution is impossible outside the internals of the application or because recognizing duplicates is either topologically impossible or would cost more in evaluation time than actually reevaluating a duplicate chromosome. The inability to recognize duplicate chromosomes is more often true in evolutionary programming models than in genetic algorithms.

Population Diversity

A critical factor that bears on the performance of a genetic algorithm is population diversity. Diversity is a measure of the robustness of chromosome representations—that is, how well they are distributed over the possible solution space. Early diversity is essential in the genetic algorithm, whereas later diversity indicates a problem with convergence. Diversity can be assessed in several ways; the following are two common methods.

By computing the variation in the fitness values over a population. This is essentially, as shown in Equation 7.12, the standard error of the fitness function (the degree of variation from the average fitness):

$$f^v = \frac{1}{N} \sum_{i=1}^{N} \sqrt{(f_a - f_i)^2} \qquad (7.12)$$

Here,

> f^v is the average variance of the population chromosomes as measured by the variance of their fitness values.
> N is the total number of chromosomes in the population.
> f_a is the average population fitness.
> f_i is fitness of the ith chromosome.

A large variance indicates a robust degree of variation in the fitness functions, whereas a small variance indicates a more compact and less varied population of fitness functions.

By computing the average change in fitness between successive generations. The idea behind a genetic algorithm is convergence, through selective breeding, on an optimal set of solutions. One way of examining diversity in the population is by computing the change in average fitness from one generation to the next. Equation 7.13 shows a simple method of tracking this change:

$$f_\Delta = \frac{1}{k} \sum_{n=2}^{K} \overline{f}_n - \overline{f}_{n-1} \qquad (7.13)$$

Here,

> f_Δ is the average change in the fitness from one generation to the next.
> K is the total number of generations elapsed in the genetic search.
> $\overline{f}_n - \overline{f}_{n-1}$ is the average fitness of the nth generation.

Plotting the change in the average population fitness from one generation to the next is a key indicator of convergence. As new and better solutions are created, the difference between the average fitness in each successive generation should move toward zero.

Diversity measures the richness of the gene pool and plays an important part in the early stages of a genetic search. Creating an initial population with high diversity depends on a deep understanding of the problem space and the ability to create chromosomes that are scattered throughout the possible solution terrain. Maintaining genetic diversity through the search process rests on both the nature of the crossover operations as well as the rate of mutations and spontaneous birth in the overall population.

Population Size

Determining the size of the initial population is a difficult but crucial step in using a genetic algorithm. Each chromosome in the population represents a point somewhere in the solution terrain. When the population is too small, as illustrated in Figure 7.21, the genetic algorithm can only search a small region of the possible solution space.

When the population is very small in relation to the possible search space, a genetic algorithm will either take a long time to find a reasonable solution or will wander around the terrain, often locking on a local minimum or maximum. On the other hand, a population that is too large, as shown in Figure 7.22, relative to the solution space covers too much of the underlying search space.

Such a large population often lacks genetic diversity (because it covers so much terrain) and can require a very high number of generations to percolate high-performing chromosomes out of the large number of lower- or moderate-performing chromosomes.

An analysis of the optimal population size for many combinatorial and permutation problems in which the potential solution space becomes very large for even a small number of variables (such as the TSP) rests on the use of probability theory to judge the probability that an optimal solution lies within a population N chromosomes. These studies indicate that the performance of even large TSPs is not critically dependent on the population size if the population is reasonably large (144 chromosomes for a 30-city problem, and 409 chromosomes for a 75-city problem).

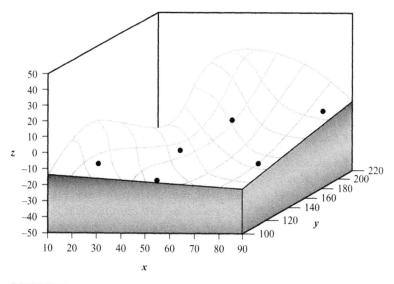

FIGURE 7.21

A small population spread over the solution space.

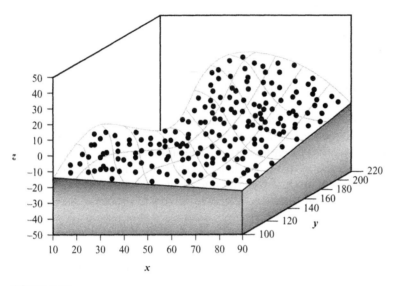

FIGURE 7.22

A large population spread over the solution space.

A good rule of thumb connects the initial population size to the number of variables in the algorithm (the number of loci in the chromosome) and the number of possible states in the solution space. An initial population, as shown in Equation 7.14, should be at least as large as five times the number of variables or about half the maximum number of possible states, whichever is smaller:

$$p = \min\left((5 \times v), \left(\frac{1}{2} \times s\right)\right) \qquad (7.14)$$

Here,

p is the population estimate.

v is the total number of variables or chromosome loci.

s is the number of possible states in the solution space.

In a TSP, the maximum number of routes is n! ($1 \times 2 \times 3 \times 4 \dots \times n$), meaning that the solution space has grown very large very fast. The five-city TSP, however, has only 120 possible routes. With this rule of thumb, the population size estimate is 25 individuals: the minimum of 25 (five times the five chromosome loci) and 60 (one-half the possible 120 states). Although the maximum number of states is small enough to include all possible solutions in the initial population, this would actually impede the genetic search. The genetic process of breeding and mutating new solutions in a population that as an initial condition already contains all possible solutions can easily result in a protracted search through the population, as the crossover process will simply produce duplicates that must be discarded.

7.3.3 **Three: Evaluate the Chromosome**

This is the core functional component of the genetic algorithm: evaluating a chromosome associates a goodness-of-fit or performance measure to each chromosome in the population (see Figure 7.15, ❸). But assigning this goodness of fit is not necessarily a part of the genetic algorithm itself. In many large-scale business applications (e.g., inventory optimization, manufacturing assembly line balancing, and crew and project scheduling), the solution represents a configuration or a set of parameters that must be processed by the connected system. As illustrated schematically in Figure 7.23, the system generates an actual outcome whose degree of performance (or "goodness") is measured by the fitness function.

Figure 7.23 outlines the basics of the genetic algorithm's evaluation process. The iterative analysis of each chromosome creates a population of solutions ranked by their "goodness" as measured by the fitness function. The process is fairly straightforward:

1. The evaluation process is applied to each chromosome (potential solution) in the current population. Much of the mechanism in a genetic algorithm is concerned with the production of this population of chromosomes.

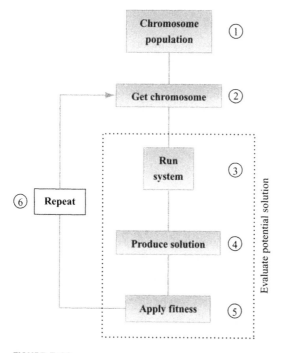

FIGURE 7.23

Evaluating a chromosome.

2. The next chromosome is selected from the population.

3. The solution configuration in the chromosome is used to execute the underlying system. In some cases, the system itself is embedded in the fitness function (as is the case with the TSP). In many other cases, the chromosome's values are passed to a larger system. For example, consider a genetic algorithm that performs trend fitting. The chromosome might contain the coefficients and powers of the equation terms. These values are passed to a regression engine that forms the equation, reads a file of data points, and computes the standard error from the differences between actuals and estimates. The regression engine is the "system" connected to the genetic algorithm.

4. From the chromosome configuration, a solution is produced by the underlying system. In some cases, of course, the chromosome and the system are the same (as in the TSP model). In other cases, such as the trend-fitting model, the solution is the standard error of estimate produced from the equation described by the chromosome's coefficients and exponent values.

5. Apply a fitness function to the solution in order to assign a performance rank to the current chromosome. The fitness analysis actually changes the content of the chromosome by storing a goodness-of-fit measure.

6. Go back and get the next chromosome in the population. The evaluation process is repeated for each chromosome (unless some special application-specific control strategy interrupts this cycle).

Thus, in summary, a chromosome is a potential solution. The "system" is the process that creates an outcome state (a solution) based on the content of a chromosome. It is this outcome space that is evaluated by the genetic algorithm based on the fitness function. Because the evaluation process is the core of the genetic algorithm and because it is dependent completely on the fitness function, the genetic algorithm as a whole is critically dependent on a proper formulation of its fitness function.

7.3.4 Four: Terminate

Like biologic evolution that goes on and on, a genetic algorithm continues to run, evolving solutions until explicitly terminated. After each population is evaluated, the algorithm checks a set of termination conditions (see Figure 7.15, ❹). The following are several common termination conditions used in genetic algorithms:

- The maximum number of generations has been reached.
- A maximum elapse (wall clock) time has been reached.
- A maximum amount of computer resources has been used.
- A chromosome with a particular fitness value emerges.
- The average (or best) fitness function value reaches a steady state over successive generations. Normally this is a tolerance comparison (for example, stop when the change in the fitness function is less than 0.001 over 100 generations).

- The average (or best) fitness function value oscillates over the generations.
- The average fitness reaches an early steady state or begins to decay. A sudden or gradual lack of average fitness indicates a problem in the way high-performing chromosomes are bred and their offspring propagated into the next generation. This is sometimes caused by mutation rates that are too high.

These termination conditions are often used in combination. A genetic algorithm can be terminated after a certain number of generations, when a particular average fitness has been achieved, or when the fitness function does not change after a specific number of generations.

A genetic algorithm's termination conditions can also include a set of policy rules associated with the underlying application. These *if-then-else* rules are often invoked to check the way the search behavior is evolving, as well as to apply additional postevaluation logic to the population.

7.3.5 **Five: Create a New Population—P(N)**

Next to the evaluation of each chromosome's fitness, the techniques for breeding each succeeding generation of chromosomes are the most crucial components of a genetic algorithm. It is this phase that is intended to balance the dual and often conflicting objectives of increasing the average population fitness and increasing genetic diversity (see Figure 7.15, ❺). Figure 7.24 outlines the step-by-step process of breeding a new generation from an old generation; descriptions of the steps follow.

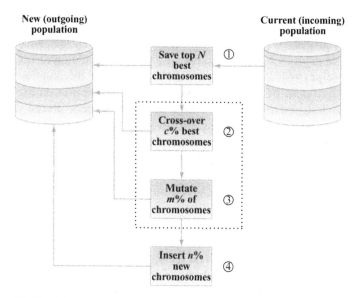

FIGURE 7.24

Breeding a new population of chromosomes.

1. The top N best (high-performance) chromosomes are retained. Some percentage of the chromosomes with the best fitness values is retained and moved to the next generation. These chromosomes will also form the core (but not complete) collection of chromosomes for the breeding (crossover) process that generates new child chromosomes.

2. Of the fittest chromosomes, a percentage ($c\%$) of these will become parents and generate one or more children in the new population. There are several stochastic-based techniques for selecting which pair of chromosomes will be mated, the most common being a form of roulette wheel that assigns a chromosome a chance of being selected based on its degree of fitness. These techniques are discussed in more detail later in this chapter.

3. After selecting the top-performing individuals and breeding new child chromosomes from the randomly chosen parents, a small number of chromosomes ($m\%$) in the new population are subjected to mutation. Mutation increases genetic diversity by a process of selecting a random locus in the chromosome and changing its value to a random (but allowable) value.

4. Not a usual part of traditional genetic algorithms, inserting a small number ($n\%$) of new chromosomes with randomly valued genomes can, along with mutation, increase genetic diversity in the population. Inserting new chromosomes often provides an effective form of simulated annealing when the mutation rate alone appears to be insufficient.

The idea behind breeding a new population is analogous to the evolution of fitter organisms in a biologic population. Crossover (the equivalent of sexual reproduction) exchanges the genetic material of two parents and produces one or more offspring. If the genetics of the parents have a high degree of fitness, the crossover (or breeding) process is designed to produce children that also have genetics with an elevated degree of fitness, but because of the scrambling of the genomes their chromosomes will lie in a slightly different area of the solution terrain. Mutation, the equivalent of a fault in chromosome transcription during biologic reproduction, is designed to introduce a small amount of genetic diversity in the population. Like biologic mutation, some are advantageous and others are fatal (in terms of improving the fitness of the population). Although there is no direct biologic counterpart to the insertion of new individuals into the population (aside from some ancient beliefs in spontaneous generation), one way of looking at the creation of new chromosomes is a localized form of complete genome mutation.

Strategies for Chromosome Selection

Which chromosomes in the current population do we select to become members of the next generation, to breed with another chromosome, or to have their existing genome changed through mutation? This is the process of selection. In many cases, a different process is used for selecting the set of fittest individuals, for selecting parents for crossover, or for selecting chromosomes for mutation. Different selection techniques have differing access probabilities depending on how they are used in the genetic algorithm. We now discuss several common techniques.

The Elitist Strategy

Using an elitist strategy, a percentage of the chromosomes with the best fitness function values are selected. Elitism is not only used to pick chromosomes for breeding but to directly copy chromosomes into the next generation. In many cases, an elitist technique is used in combination with other selection methods to ensure that some of the strongest chromosomes always make it into successive generations. The elitist selection technique is implicit in the first step of the genetic algorithm mechanism shown in Figure 7.13.

Proportional Fitness

Using a proportional (or roulette wheel) fitness strategy, a wide spectrum of chromosomes with varying degrees of fitness is selected. The selection is biased toward chromosomes with best fitness values. Proportional fitness works in two steps: it first creates a conceptual roulette wheel weighted according to the best fitness function values, and then it essentially spins the wheel and finds the chromosome that fits in the currently weighted slot. In a conventional approach to proportional selection, the ratio of each unique fitness value and the sum of the total fitness values in the population is used to create the roulette wheel. For populations that contain repeating fitness functions, using a weighted frequency count of the fitness function provides a way of maintaining the same type of roulette wheel approach.

Equation 7.15 shows how the wheel slice is calculated:

$$w = \frac{f_i}{\sum\limits_{k=1}^{N} f_k} \tag{7.15}$$

Here,

> f_i is the fitness of the ith chromosome.
> f_k is the fitness of the kth chromosome.
> N is the number of chromosomes in the population.

This equation works well for maximization functions because the larger the individual fitness value, the larger its fraction of the sum of all fitness values and the larger its proportion of the wheel. For minimization functions, the magnitude of the numbers must be reversed. Equations 7.16 and 7.17 show one way of reversing the magnitude of the fitness functions:

$$f^R = (f_{\max} - f_i) + 1 \tag{7.16}$$

$$w = \frac{f^R}{\sum_{k=1}^{N} f_k^R} \tag{7.17}$$

Here,

> f^R is the reversed magnitude fitness function.
> f_i is the fitness of the ith chromosome.
> f_{max} is the maximum fitness among all chromosomes in the population.
> f_k is the fitness of the kth chromosome.
> N is the number of chromosomes in the population.

Examining a small portion of the TSP population illustrates how the weighted roulette wheel is created from the fitness value. Because we are attempting to minimize the route through the five cities, the wedge expression from Equation 7.17 is used. Table 7.10 shows the fitness (path length) values for a set of city routes, their adjusted fitness values, and their proportion of the fitness roulette.

The ratio (w) derived from the total sum of adjusted fitness values in the population specifies the weighted slot in the underlying roulette wheel. Figure 7.25 shows this roulette wheel (not exactly to scale) proportioned according to the magnitude of the adjusted fitness values.

The actual proportional fitness algorithm is easy to understand and implement. Listing 7.1 shows the basic logic. This code computes a random fitness level (max_fitness) from the sum of the population's individual fitness values. The algorithm then loops through the population, summing each chromosome's fitness (into cumm_ fitness). When the algorithm encounters a chromosome with a fitness greater than or equal to the max_ fitness value, that chromosome is selected. Note that it is important that the population not be sorted by fitness. Otherwise, the selection process is significantly biased (and will simply function as a slightly more complicated form of elitism).

Table 7.10 The TSP Fitness and Fitness Ratios

	Tour	Raw Fitness	Magnitude Adjusted	w
1	Able, Baker, Echo, Delta, Charlie	90	1	0.007
2	Able, Echo, Charlie, Baker, Delta	34	57	0.387
3	Able, Echo, Delta, Baker, Charlie	57	34	0.232
4	Able, Baker, Charlie, Echo, Delta	59	32	0.217
5	Able, Charlie, Echo, Delta, Baker	68	23	0.156
	Sum	308	147	1.000

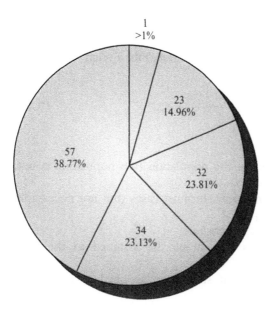

FIGURE 7.25

The proportional fitness roulette wheel.

Listing 7.1   The proportional fitness approach.

```
Proportional Selection:
  For each chromosome (i)
     total_fitness = total_fitness + chromosome(i).fitness
  End for each

  max_fitness = total_fitness * random()
  cumm_fitness=0
  for each chromosome(i)
     cumm_fitness = cum_fitness + chromosome(i).fitness
     If chromosome(i).fitness > max_fitness
       Then select(chromosome(i))
  end for each
```

Proportional fitness selection suffers from two general problems. This first has already been directly encountered: It is difficult to use on minimization problems. Often, the fitness function for minimization must be converted to a maximization function. Although to some degree this solves the selection problem, it introduces semantic confusion into the problem (the best chromosome in the TSP problem, for instance, will continually be assigned a fitness value that is the maximum of all other fitness functions, and thus we are seeking the minimum tour but the fitness maximizes the fitness value). The second problem is directly related to how the roulette wheel is constructed. The proportional fitness selection will fail (it will drive the population to early convergence) if some of the chromosomes have fitness values that are much larger than all other fitness values.

Ranking Using a linear ranking strategy, an ordered population of chromosomes is assigned fitness values based on their position or rank within the population. There are many mathematic means of converting a rank into a relative or subjective fitness:

$$f_i = \frac{(N-r) \times (f_{max}^u - f_{min}^u)}{N-1} + f_{min}^u \qquad (7.18)$$

Here,

N is the number of chromosomes in the population (the population count, obviously, must be greater than 1).

r is the current rank of the chromosome. In most cases (but not necessarily all) for the ith chromosome $r = i$.

f_i is the fitness assigned to the ith chromosome.

f_{max}^u is the maximum user fitness that should be assigned to the best-performing individual.

f_{min}^u is the minimum user fitness that should be assigned to the worst-performing individual.

The ranking strategy prevents extremely fit individuals from dominating the population during the early generations of the search process. Thus, the ranking technique can effectively maintain diversity and inhibit convergence. The outcome of ranking can be used with an elitist selection or with other selection approaches (such as proportional fitness). One constraint on the use of ranking is the requirement that the population be reordered and reranked for each generation.

Tournament Generally used for large diverse populations, this approach is somewhat akin to the divide-and-conquer strategy in search and sorting. In a tournament selection, a set of k chromosomes is selected randomly from the population (where $k = 2$ is the usual size). From the set of k chromosomes, the individual with the best fitness is selected. For example, using the TSP chromosomes in Table 7.10, the tournament strategy could select genomes 2 (Able, Echo, Charlie, Baker, Delta) and 4 (Able, Baker, Charlie, Echo, Delta). Chromosome 2 would be selected over 4 because 2 has a better raw fitness function (34 miles instead of 59 miles). This process of selecting a group and picking the best (fittest) chromosome is continued as long as a selection process is needed.

Tournament differs from proportional fitness because it is indifferent to the relative frequency or range of fitness values. It is only sensitive to the fitness ranking within the population. Because it is essentially probing the population in blocks of k chromosomes (with replacement, so that chromosomes may participate in multiple tournaments), the tournament approach can select a wider spectrum of chromosomes with varying degrees of fitness.

Random Using a random strategy, a random chromosome in the population is selected. Random selection is used to pick chromosomes for breeding and to directly copy chromosomes into the next generation. In hybrid algorithms, a random strategy is used in combination with other selection methods to ensure that a mix of chromosomes with a wide spectrum of fitness values always makes it into successive generations.

Selection strategies are malleable; that is, a genetic algorithm can switch from one strategy to the next during the search. An example is using an elitist strategy for a few generations to quickly increase the average fitness and then switching to proportional fitness to ensure some continued measure of fitness diversity in the population. In the next section, we will discuss the actual process of breeding new chromosomes. The breeding mechanism is tightly coupled to the selection strategy.

Conventional Crossover (Breeding) Techniques

A genetic algorithm derives its name from the way in which potential solutions are developed. They are bred from existing solutions using a process with analogies to sexual reproduction in biologic organisms. The process of mating and reproduction in a genetic algorithm is called crossover. This name follows from the way in which genetic material is exchanged. Pieces of the genetic material from two parents are exchanged by extracting a set of loci from one parent and a set of loci from another parent and appending or inserting them in the corresponding position in each other's genome. Thus, they move in an X pattern as the genome segments cross over each other. Figure 7.26 illustrates the way two chromosomes mate and breed two offspring.

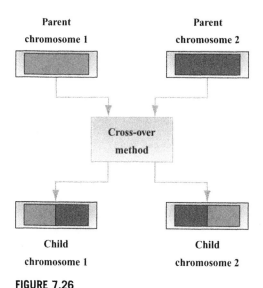

FIGURE 7.26

Mating and breeding of chromosomes.

Like biologic reproduction, reproduction in genetic algorithms is intended to create better chromosomes from already highly performing parents while at the same time adding genetic diversity to the gene pool (the population of chromosomes in the current generation). Philosophically, a genetic algorithm is a directed eugenics program designed to breed better and better individuals. This section examines the principal methods of crossover and explains how they work in the search algorithm's breeding program. As discussed in the section on genome design (see Genome Structural Design section), conventional crossover cannot be used for the TSP. Breeding and mutation techniques for the TSP and similar connectionist problems are discussed in the section titled Advanced Crossover and Mutation Techniques.

A Crew Scheduling Cost Model

To illustrate crossover (and mutation, in the next section), we will explore a small and quite simple cost modeling system for crew-to-job assignment. The model contains two tables: an $N \times M$ matrix of jobs and their duration times and an $N \times M$ matrix of crews and their daily charge rates. Table 7.11 shows the job and crew schedules.

This is a cost minimization problem. We want to assign the crews to the jobs in order to find the minimum cost schedule. There are fewer crews than jobs, and thus some crews will be assigned to multiple jobs. The total cost for a schedule is shown in Equation 7.19 (which is also the fitness function):

$$f = \sum_{i=1}^{K} d(i) \times r(c(i)) \tag{7.19}$$

Here,

K is the number of jobs. In this case, there are five jobs.

f is the total cost of the job assignments and is the fitness assigned to the
    ith job-to-*crew* chromosome.

Table 7.11 Job ID and Duration and Crew ID and Rate

Job ID	Duration	Crew ID	Rate
J1	6	C1	10
J2	5	C2	15
J3	9	C3	20
J4	8		
J5	3		

$d(\ )$ is duration of the ith job (chromosome locus).

$r(\ )$ is the rate of the crew assigned to the ith job.

$c(\ )$ is the crew found in the ith genome locus.

Because the number of jobs is static, the genome representation can be straightforward: five locus sites. Each locus contains the crew assigned to the job (that is, it contains the index to Table 7.11, the crew table). Figure 7.27 is a schematic of the job-to-crew costing chromosome.

The genetic search mechanism generates a population of candidate cost plans by assigning crews randomly to the five jobs. Our only constraint is that every crew must be used at least once. Table 7.12 shows a small part of the initial population.

This small job-cost planning model now provides the background needed to explore the various types of conventional crossover techniques. These techniques are used to breed new cost models based on the genetic material in parents (ultimately chosen through one of the selection strategies). The next section explores the single-point crossover in some detail. The remaining crossover patterns are extensions of this basic concept.

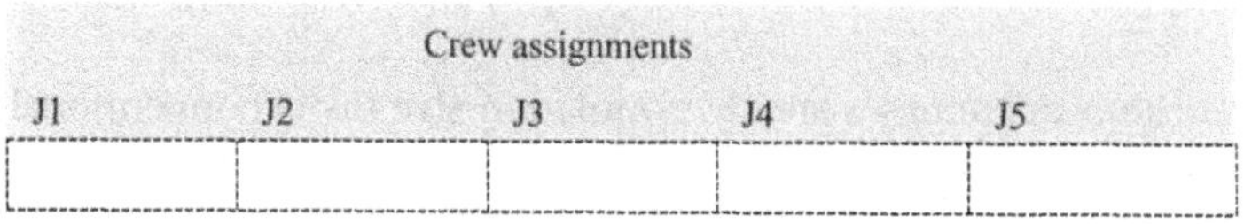

FIGURE 7.27

The job-to-crew assignment genome.

Table 7.12 Initial Population of Job Cost Genomes

	Jobs with Crew Assignment				
	J1	**J2**	**J3**	**J4**	**J5**
1	C1	C3	C3	C2	C3
2	C2	C3	C1	C1	C1
3	C2	C1	C2	C3	C3
4	C3	C1	C2	C2	C1
5	C2	C2	C2	C1	C3
6	C3	C2	C2	C1	C3

Single-Point Crossover

In single-point crossover, a single point along the genome is selected. Two parent chromosomes are selected from the population. A crossover point is chosen at random. The genome segments to the right (or left) of the point are swapped, creating two new chromosomes (the children). Figure 7.28 schematically illustrates the crossover process that produces new children from the genetic material of the parents. The single-point crossover is immediately after the second locus in the chromosome.

In this example, the children inherit the first two loci from the parents. Child 1 inherits the right-hand genetic material from parent 2, whereas child 2 inherits the right-hand genetic material from parent 1. The children are usually inserted into the new population, displacing either the parents or two chromosomes whose fitness values are less than the parents' fitness value. Table 7.13 shows the small job assignment population with each chromosome's fitness (cost) and the average population fitness.

Through some selection process, individuals 2 and 4 are chosen as parents. The single-point crossover is at the second locus (at job $J2$). As Table 7.14 shows, the crossover generates two new chromosomes (c_1 and c_2). Both have fitness values less than the maximum fitness of the two parents. Even without removing two lower-performing chromosomes, this average population is improved (a change of 16.91).

If the genetic algorithm maintains a steady population size (as is conventional in most but not all situations), the two new children replace poorer-performing genomes. In this case, chromosomes 1 and 4 are removed and the new children

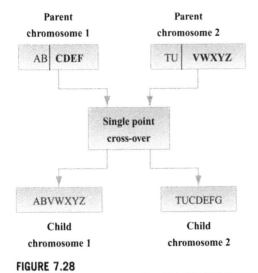

FIGURE 7.28

The single-point crossover process.

Table 7.13 Job Cost Genomes with Fitness Values (Costs)

	Jobs with Crew Assignments					
	J1	J2	J3	J4	J5	Cost
1	C1	C3	C3	C2	C3	520.00
2	C2	C3	C1	C1	C1	318.00
3	C2	C1	C2	C3	C3	495.00
4	C3	C1	C2	C2	C1	455.00
5	C2	C2	C2	C1	C3	440.00
6	C3	C2	C2	C1	C3	470.00
					Average Fitness	449.66

Table 7.14 Job Cost Genomes with Fitness Values (Costs)

	Jobs with Crew Assignments					
	J1	J2	J3	J4	J5	Cost
1	C1	C3	C3	C2	C3	520.00
2	C2	C3	C1	C1	C1	318.00
3	C2	C1	C2	C3	C3	495.00
4	C3	C1	C2	C2	C1	455.00
c_1	C2	C3	C2	C2	C1	370.00
c_2	C3	C1	C1	C1	C1	394.00
5	C2	C2	C2	C1	C3	440.00
6	C3	C2	C2	C1	C3	470.00
					Average Fitness	432.75

take their place. Table 7.15 shows both the new population with the children of 2 and 4 and the significant increase in the average population fitness.

Not every crossover will improve the fitness of the population. In fact, in addition to the goal of finding better and better chromosomes, breeding has the goal of increasing genetic diversity in the population. Only through genetic diversity can a genetic algorithm economically and effectively explore a sufficient portion

Table 7.15 Job Cost Genomes with Fitness Values (Costs)

	Jobs with Crew Assignments					
	J1	J2	J3	J4	J5	Cost
1	C2	C3	C2	C2	C1	370.00
2	C2	C3	C1	C1	C1	318.00
3	C3	C1	C1	C1	C1	394.00
4	C3	C1	C2	C2	C1	455.00
5	C2	C2	C2	C1	C3	440.00
6	C3	C2	C2	C1	C3	470.00
					Average Fitness	407.83

of the solution terrain. The other forms of crossover provide different approaches to breeding new offspring. Each technique has its own place in attempts to gain better (fitter) individuals.

Double-Point Crossover

In double-point crossover, two points along the genome are selected at random. The genome segment to the left of the rightmost point is swapped with the genome to the right of the leftmost point, creating two new children. Figure 7.29 schematically illustrates the crossover process that produces new children from the genetic material of the parents. The crossover points are immediately after the second locus and immediately before the last locus in the chromosome.

In terms of exchanging genetic material and how it is used, the double-point process is almost exactly like the single-point process: the children inherit the loci to the right of the rightmost point and to the left of the leftmost point. The genetic material to be swapped is bounded by the two random point values. Child 1 inherits bounded genetic material from parent 2, whereas child 2 inherits the bounded genetic material from parent 1. The advantage of the double-point crossover is its inherent ability to introduce a higher degree of variability (randomness) into the selection of genetic material.

Uniform Crossover

Uniform crossover works at the individual locus level rather than with segments of the genome. Loci positions are picked at random from the genomes and exchanged. Figure 7.30 schematically illustrates the crossover process that produces new children from the genetic material of parents.

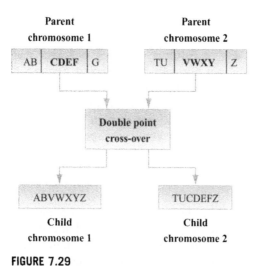

FIGURE 7.29

The double-point crossover process.

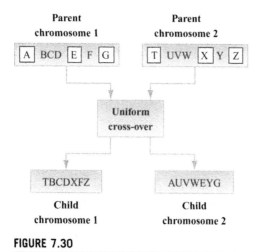

FIGURE 7.30

The uniform crossover process.

The probability of selecting a locus for exchange, called the *mixing rate*, can be very low or very high. A mixing rate of 0.5, for example, means that any locus in the genome has a 50 percent chance of being selected for exchange. The mixing rate acts like a variable rheostat, increasing or decreasing the probability that the nth locus on the genome in parent 1 will exchange its value with the nth locus on the genome in parent 2. Although uniform crossover has the advantage of precisely controlling the amount of genetic variability in the population, it also has two significant disadvantages. First, because the crossover is done at the individual gene (locus) level rather with sets or patterns of genes, behavior that evolves as patterns in the population will not normally be preserved. Second, if the mix rate is too high, too much genetic diversity (that is, noise) emerges in each successive population and the search mechanism cannot find an accurate solution. On the other hand, if the mix rate is too low, not enough genetic diversity will emerge and the search mechanism cannot efficiently spread over the solution terrain.

Weighted (Arithmetic) Crossover

Weighted (or arithmetic) crossover is unlike the other crossover operations. Weighted crossover modifies rather than exchanges genetic material and works at the complete genome level rather than with segments of the genome. The crossover appears in the way a weighting factor is used. A weighting factor (w) in the range $[0,1]$ is selected before each crossover. Loci are picked at random from the genomes and exchanged. Equation 7.20 is the crossover process that produces new children from the genetic material of the parents:

$$c_1 = (w \times p_1) + ((1-w) \times p_2)$$
$$c_2 = ((1-w) \times p_1) + (w \times p_2)$$

(7.20)

Here,

    c_1 is child 1 from the crossover operation.
    c_2 is child 2 from the crossover operation.
    p_1 is the first selected parent.
    p_2 is the second selected parent.
    w is the weighing factor in the range $[0,1]$.

The weight values act like scaling factors over the range of the chromosome. The values are rescaled (from 0 n, where n is the value of the genome at that locus). Table 7.16 illustrates the creation of child c_1 from two parents when the scaling weight is 0.4 (see Table 7.13 for the underlying chromosomes).

Arithmetic scaling mathematically distorts the genome values in a predictable manner, but it does not rely on the mixing of genetic materials. From the author's experience in production models, weighted crossover (unless the weight is carefully adjusted) tends to produce lower average population fitness than the single- or double-point crossover. Table 7.17 (based on the data in Table 7.13) shows the result of applying weighted crossover to individuals *(2,4)*.

In this instance, the crossover reduces the average fitness of the population. Naturally, the same decrease in fitness can result from any of the other crossover techniques. This example simply illustrates that different crossover methods yield

Table 7.16 Creating Child c_1 from Parents $(2,4)$, where $w = (0.4)$

	J1	J2	J3	J4	J5
P_1	90.00	100.00	90.00	80.00	30.00
P_2	120.00	50.00	135.00	120.00	30.00
P_1* w	36.00	40.00	36.00	48.00	12.00
P_2* (1–w)	72.00	30.00	81.00	72.00	18.00
Total	**108.00**	**70.00**	**117.00**	**120.00**	**30.00**

Table 7.17 Job Cost Genomes with Fitness Values (Costs)

	Jobs with Crew Assignments					
	J1	J2	J3	J4	J5	Cost
1	C1	C3	C3	C2	C3	520.00
2	90.00	100.00	90.00	80.00	30.00	318.00
3	C2	C1	C2	C3	C3	495.00
4	120.00	50.00	135.00	120.00	30.00	455.00
c_1	108.00	70.00	117.00	120.00	30.00	445.00
c_2	173.60	80.00	75.60	76.60	30.00	435.80
5	C2	C2	C2	C1	C3	440.00
6	C3	C2	C2	C1	C3	470.00
				Average Fitness		**596.46**

different fitness values (as you would expect), and, in this case, the single-point crossover for these two parents results in a better set of offspring.

Analytical Crossover

The analytical crossover method is a final crossover technique that, like the weighted approach, works at the complete chromosome level. This technique is somewhat iterative and, like tournament selection, considers the best and worst fitness of two selected parents:

$$c_1 = p_b + s \times (p_b - p_w)$$
$$c_2 = p_b$$

(7.21)

Here,

c_1 is child 1 from the crossover operation.
c_2 is child 2 from the crossover operation.
p_b is the parent with the best fitness.
p_w is the parent with the worst fitness.
s is a scaling factor in the range [0,1].

The scaling factor is a random number that changes the range of the difference between each of the parent genome sites. This can sometimes lead to infeasible solutions because the scaled value is unallowable. As a consequence, analytical crossover generally has a search parameter, k, that attempts to find a new value of s that will produce a feasible solution. After the number of searches exceeds k, $s = 0$, so that the best-fit parent is also returned as the first child. Other modifications to this technique are also implemented, such as searching through the population for acceptable parents instead of changing the scaling factor.

Breeding techniques create new chromosomes in the population. By breeding individuals with a high fitness ranking, the genetic search process hopes to introduce new individuals that are slightly superior to some other chromosomes in the population. These fitter chromosomes, over generations, place selective pressure on the population and slowly replace less fit individuals. Breeding alone, however, is insufficient in many cases. Genetic algorithms can become locked in a local region of the solution space because of a general lack of diversity in the current gene pool. The next section takes up issues and techniques related to one of the conventional methods for recovering genetic diversity.

Conventional Mutation (Diversity) Techniques

Genetic algorithms are sensitive to genetic diversity. In some cases, the diversity introduced by crossover breeding is insufficient to explore the underlying solution space. The population becomes confined to a small region of the solution space. Breeding simply moves the search around and around this region. Figure 7.31 illustrates this problem. Each point represents the average fitness of the entire population.

In this figure, the genetic algorithm is wandering around a small region of the potential solution space. Any combination of the current genetic material is insufficient to produce individuals that move outside this region. To solve this problem, genetic algorithms use the concept of mutation. Mutation, as the name implies, randomly changes the value of a genome locus. Through mutation, genetic diversity can be maintained or reintroduced into the population. Figure 7.32 illustrates the locked population in Figure 7.31 with a few mutations in one of the generations.

Mutation operators must be applied carefully and sparingly to the population. Too much mutation and the genome loses its ability to retain any pattern, and although the population may be scattered over a wide region of the solution terrain, the search mechanism has no way of improving its performance. Only a

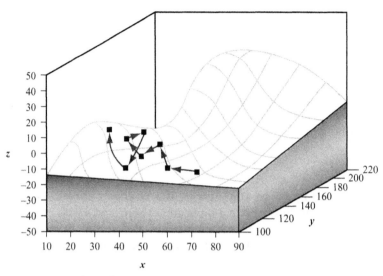

■ = Average population fitness

FIGURE 7.31

A population without sufficient genetic diversity.

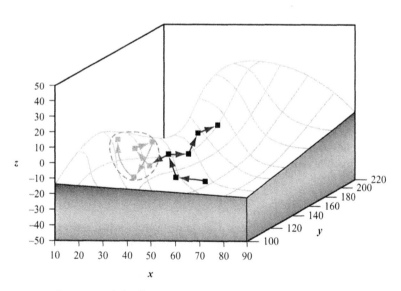

■ = Average population fitness

 = Average population fitness (without mutation)

FIGURE 7.32

Genetic diversity through mutation.

small number of individuals should be subject to mutation during a generation. In many genetic algorithms, a parameter of the search system itself determines whether or not a mutation is applied to any chromosomes during the current generation. This section discusses the various types of conventional mutation operators. With the exception of the binary inversion technique, these mutation operators are designed to work on integer and real-number genomes. A knowledge of the loci allowed range of values is necessary for each operator that works on numbers instead of bit strings.

Binary (Bit) Inversion

For genomes represented by binary (bit) strings, the inversion operator simply flips the value of a randomly chosen bit. A 1-bit becomes zero, and a 0-bit becomes one. Because of the nature of binary chromosomes, this is the primary and often principal mutation operator used in classical (binary-represented) genetic algorithms.

Uniform Replacement

Uniform mutation replaces a randomly selected gene (locus) with a value chosen from a uniform random distribution between the upper and lower domain bounds for the gene. This is the most frequently used mutation operator because it requires only the range of allowed values for the gene.

Distribution-Based Replacement

Instead of a value uniformly drawn from the domain of the gene, this operator updates the gene position with a statistical value drawn from some probability distribution. Normally, a Gaussian distribution is used (and the value is truncated or regenerated if it lies outside the allowable range for the gene). However, a binomial (Poisson or other type) of distribution can also be used.

Central-and-Limits Replacement

The central-and-limits mutation replaces the gene value with one of three randomly chosen values: the upper boundary value from the gene's domain, the lower boundary value from the gene's domain, or the value from the center of the domain *(upper-lower)/2)*. Generally, the mutation operator has differing probabilities for each assignment: a high probability for boundary values and a smaller probability for the center of distribution value. The central-and-limits mutation operator often provides a way of introducing a significant amount of genetic diversity into the population and is useful in the early stages of evolution. The sharp three-step process of assigning the minimum, maximum, or middle domain values "shakes" the genome in a way similar to simulated annealing.

Nonuniform Decay

The nonuniform decay operator is designed to slowly reduce genetic diversity caused by mutation as the number of generations increases. The operation begins to drive the probability of a mutation toward zero as the number of generations increases. Equation 7.22 shows one possible representation for the decay mutation operator:

$$p_m = p_m \times \min\left(\frac{l}{g^c}, 1\right) \tag{7.22}$$

Here,

   p_m is the current probability that a gene will mutate.

   t is the switchover limit. When $l = 1$, the decay begins right after the first generation. When $l > 1$, the mutation probability stays at its initial value until $g^c = l$, after which time it begins to fall.

   g^c is the current generation count $(1,2,3, \ldots , n)$.

The nonuniform decay operator keeps genetic diversity relatively high during the early generations of the search but slowly eliminates mutation as the search mechanism begins to evolve toward the target solution. In many cases, a form of decay mutation is switched on by the search mechanism if it determines that convergence is being inhibited (possibly by too much mutation).

Advanced Crossover and Mutation Techniques

Breeding approaches that use the conventional crossover and mutation methods discussed in the previous section will not work for a large family of problems involving structural, time, and flow dependencies between genes. Typical examples include the following:

- Resource-constrained project, crew, and machine (job shop) scheduling.
- Packing and containerization problems in logistics.
- Transportation route scheduling (such as the TSP family of problems).
- Configuration planning.

These problems are encountered frequently in the real worlds of business, industry, and government. They all share a common property: The sequence of genome values represents a collection of discrete objects that are being arranged in a particular order. It is the attributes of the objects that determine the goodness of fit, not the value of the object itself. For example, returning to the TSP, consider the single-point crossover operation (at the second locus) shown in Table 7.18.

The crossover operators generate tours with duplicate cities (Charlie in child 1 and Able in child 2). Conventional mutation operators also generate duplicate tours (because a tour includes all cities, mutating any of the five cities to another city will automatically create a duplicate city in the tour). To address these problems, a large number of alternate crossover and mutation techniques have been

Table 7.18 Invalid Conventional Crossover for the TSP

			City Tour		
p_1	Charlie	Baker	Charlie	Able	Echo
p_2	Baker	Able	Echo	Delta	Charlie
c_1	Charlie	Baker	Echo	Delta	Charlie
c_2	Baker	Able	Charlie	Able	Echo

developed. This section discusses a few of the more common and easy-to-implement methods, addressing crossover issues first and then mutation techniques.

Greedy Crossover

The greedy crossover approach (also called the nearest-neighbor crossover) was first formalized by Grefenstette in 1985 (see Resources). The algorithm assembles offspring tours in a small but effective number of steps, as shown in Listing 7.2.

Listing 7.2   Algorithm for offspring tours.

```
Let t be the current tour
Let c₁ be the current city

Select one parent as the base
The first city in the parent is chosen as the starting node.
  This is the current city (c₁ )
  t = c₁
Repeat:
  Examine the connecting edges leaving c₁ in both parents.
  Make a list of all cities on the connecting edges
  Remove any cities already in the tour
  If the list is empty exit repeat
  The edge with the shorter duration is used as the next city in
  the tour.
  Set this next city as c₁
  t = append(c₁ )
End repeat
For each unused city (cᵤ )
  t = append(cᵤ )
End for each
child = t
```

The idea of crossover occurs as the algorithm searches for the next segment in a tour by comparing the length of the next edge in the tour. The algorithm is repeated for each parent to produce two children. In this section we examine,

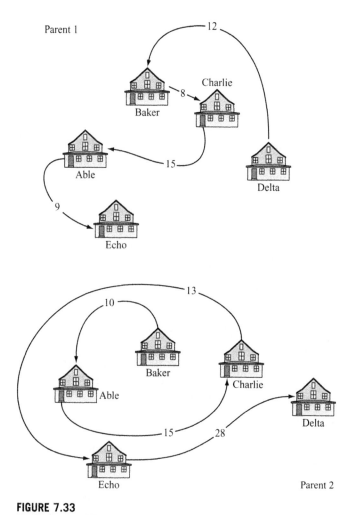

FIGURE 7.33

Two five-city tours.

for compactness, the generation of one child from the two candidate parents. Figure 7.33 shows the two tours defined by the distance measurements in Table 7.4. The numbers on the edges are the distances between the connected cities.

Using these two tours, the greedy crossover works in the following steps to produce one of two possible children:

1. Select a parent as the base. In this example, we choose the second parent. This starts the template for constructing a child. The template now appears as follows:

Baker	?	?	?	?

2. Find the edges in both parents from Baker to the next city. These are *(Baker,Able)* in parent 2 and *(Baker,Charlie)* in parent 1. Choose the edge that has the shortest distance. This edge becomes the next segment in the tour. The shortest edge is *(Baker,Charlie)* in parent 2, with a length of 8 miles. The template now appears as follows:

Baker	Charlie	?	?	?

3. Find the edges in both parents from Charlie to the next city. These are *(Charlie,Echo)* in parent 2 and *(Charlie,Able)* in parent 1. The shortest edge is *(Charlie,Echo)* in parent 2, with a length of 13 miles. This becomes the next edge and the template now appears as follows:

Baker	Charlie	Echo	?	?

4. Find the edges in both parents from Echo out to the next city. These are *(Echo,Delta)* and *(Echo,<terminate>)*. Thus, *Delta* is selected as the next city node, as follows:

Baker	Charlie	Echo	Delta	?

5. Find the edges in both parents from *Delta* out to the next city. These are *(Delta,Baker)* in parent 1 and *(Delta,<terminate>)* in parent 2. *Baker* has already been used in the tour and is removed from the candidate list. *Delta* is a terminal city in the parent 2 tour and is removed. We now complete the tour by adding *Able*, the only unused city, as follows:

Baker	Charlie	Echo	Delta	Able

Figure 7.34 shows the tour created by the greedy crossover, using parent 2 as the starting point (the template basis).

The greedy algorithm has created a valid tour with a length of 54 miles (8 + 13 + 28 + 5). This is about midway between the lengths of the incoming parents, which have tour length of 44 and 66, respectively. A second child is created by selecting the remaining parent (parent 1) as the base and reapplying the algorithm.

The greedy (or nearest-neighbor) crossover approach produces feasible offspring tours with a minimum of exception processing. This is a by-product of its reliance on graph theory to drive the generation of a tour based on edges. To complete this section on advanced crossover techniques, we examine two methods that are modeled after the conventional single-point crossover. Both of these generate infeasible solutions and must employ exception handling to compensate for duplicate and missing cities.

City Pivot Crossover

The city pivot approach selects a city in the tour at random. This city becomes the crossover point in the same manner as conventional single-point crossover

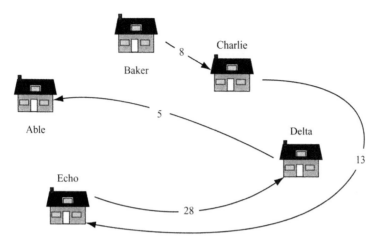

FIGURE 7.34

The child tour from greedy crossover.

			City Tour		
Table 7.19 City Pivot Crossover on Baker					
p_1	Delta	Baker	Charlie	Echo	Able
p_2	Able	Echo	Delta	Baker	Charlie
c_1	Delta	Baker	Able	Echo	Charlie

except that (1) the crossover position is not the same for both chromosomes but is relative to the location of the city in each tour and (2) a compression technique must be used to ensure that duplicate cities do not appear in the offspring chromosomes. Table 7.19 illustrates how a child chromosome is produced from the city pivot crossover when *Baker* is selected as the crossover city.

In the crossover at *Baker*, we have two tour segments sliced by *Baker*: *(Delta, Baker)* in parent 1 and *(Able,Echo,Delta)* in parent 2. *Delta* is a duplicate and is removed from the second segment. When they are spliced together, the offspring *(Delta,Baker, Able,Echo,Charlie)* form a valid tour.

Position Pivot Crossover

The position pivot crossover approach, shown in Table 7.20, is similar to the conventional single-point crossover discussed previously. In this method, a crossover position is selected at random along the length of the tour. The child chromosome consists of the tour in parent 1 on the left and parent 2 on the right.

Table 7.20 Position Pivot Crossover on Locus 2

			City Tour		
p_1	Delta	Baker	Charlie	Echo	Able
p_2	Able	Echo	Delta	Baker	Charlie
c_1	Delta	Baker	Able	Baker	Charlie

Table 7.21 The Random Swap Mutation

			City Tour		
p_1 (before)	Delta	Baker	Charlie	Echo	Able
p_1 (after)	Delta	Able	Charlie	Echo	Baker

However, this crossover approach must also ensure that (1) any duplicate cities (those that appear, for instance, to the left of the crossover point) are not included in the final tour and (2) any missing cities (those that for example appear to the left of the crossover but are not included in the left-hand chromosome) are included in the final chromosome.

In the crossover at locus 2, we have two tour segments: *(Charlie,Echo,Able)* in parent 1 and *(Delta,Baker,Charlie)* in parent 2. *Delta* is a duplicate and is removed from the second segment. *Able* is missing from the offspring when the left set of p_1 *(Delta,Baker)* is crossed with the right side of p_2 *(Delta,Baker,Charlie)*. We now delete *Delta* and push *Able* onto the tour. When they are spliced together, the offspring *(Delta,Baker, Able,Baker,Charlie)* form a valid tour.

The next section discusses the various types of genome mutations. For chromosomes in which relationships are defined as connected edges, these mutation operators change the chromosome structure instead of changing the value of a single gene.

Random Swap Mutation

In random swap, two loci (chosen at random) have their values swapped. As illustrated in Table 7.21, this results in a valid tour.

Move-and-Insert Gene Mutation

Using move-and-insert, a genome locus (chosen at random) is moved before or after another randomly chosen locus in the genome. Table 7.22 shows the offspring when *Baker* is selected as an insert before a point and *Echo* is selected as the city node to move.

Table 7.22 The Move-and-Insert Gene Mutation

			City Tour		
p_1 (before)	Delta	**Baker**	Charlie	**Echo**	Able
p_1 (after)	Delta	Echo	Baker	Charlie	Able

Table 7.23 The Move-and-insert Gene Mutation

			City Tour		
p_1 (before)	Delta	Baker	Charlie	Echo	Able
p_1 (after)	Delta	Charlie	Echo	Able	Baker

Table 7.24 The Order Reversal Mutation

			City Tour		
$p_1^{(before)}$	Delta	Baker	Charlie	Echo	Able
$p_1^{(after)}$	Delta	Echo	Charlie	Baker	Able

Move-and-Insert Sequence Mutation

Sequence mutation is similar to the gene move-and-insert, but instead of a single locus a sequence of loci are moved and inserted. Table 7.23 shows the offspring when *Baker* is selected as an insert before a point and the gene sequence *(Charlie,Echo,Able)* is selected as the set of nodes to move.

Order Reversal Mutation

With order reversal, a series of the genome loci (chosen at random) have their values reversed. As illustrated in Table 7.24, this results in a valid tour. Although treated here as important mechanisms for modifying the organization of a schedule, configuration, or route, they can also be used with conventional genetic algorithms (with varying degrees of effect on the population diversity).

7.4 PRACTICAL ISSUES IN USING A GENETIC ALGORITHM

To use a genetic algorithm, generally you must have the ability to perform the following functions:

- Generate possible solutions to a problem.
- Set the properties of the genetic algorithm so that it can converge on a solution.
- Measure the goodness of those solutions in terms of the outcome from the underlying model.
- Change the system if the solutions are not very good.

The practical issues confronted with analysts in using a genetic algorithm usually fall within two areas: properly setting the population, breeding, and mutation properties of the genetic algorithm; and finding ways to model large, highly complex systems without executing the real-world model itself. The next section addresses the last two of these issues.

7.4.1 Execution Times for Real-World Systems

In many cases, the execution time is fairly straightforward; that is, the fitness function and the system that processes the potential solution are essentially the same. Finding the maximum value for a function, the shortest circuit through a set of cities, the least cost to assemble a piece of equipment, or the maximum carrying capacity of a road system are straightforward applications of mathematic models. That is, a genetic algorithm does not need to depend on dispatching a fleet of vehicles to follow a potential tour and then actually clocking their time between cities spread over several states to find the shortest route. A road atlas and a table of intercity distances from the atlas are sufficient to build a credible and accurate TSP model. On the other hand, this disconnect between physical reality and the genetic model does not always exist. In such cases, a genetic algorithm may be difficult or impossible to use. This brings us to a set of issues associated with applying genetic algorithms to complex, large-scale, real-world models.

This disconnect is not universal. Some genetic algorithms are attached to complex business, industrial, and government policy models. In these cases, running one generation of 50 chromosomes could take anywhere from several hours to several days. For example, suppose we want a genetic algorithm to optimize (that is, minimize) point-of-sales transaction throughput time in a commercial relational database. Unless we have a reliable mathematic model of how the database performs under specific loads with a specific set of configuration parameters, the genetic algorithm must run its evaluation against a working relational database. Our genetic algorithm can generate configuration parameters for the relational database, feed in a large collection of transactions, and measure the throughput time. The same set of transactions is used over and over to measure the change in processing and total throughput times.

Some combination of virtual-memory-swap area size, disk space, table page size, transaction (or job) queue length, number of page buffers, and column indexing will produce the best database configuration. However, the time to reconfigure a dedicated relational database with a new page size, buffer count, and different column indexing could take anywhere from 4 to 5 minutes. Processing all transactions (say a mix of 150,000 query and update transactions, with a reasonable amount of noise such as bad SKU numbers, invalid quantities, out of stock responses, and so on) might take an additional 3 minutes. Thus, Equation 7.23 is the time per chromosome:

$$c_t = t_t + t_r + t_p \qquad (7.23)$$

Here,

c_t is the current chromosome evaluation elapse time.
t_t is the tear-down and setup time for each evaluation.
t_r is the runtime to evaluate the chromosome.
t_p is the intergeneration processing time.

As a result, the total time to optimize the database, shown in Equation 7.24, is the sum of the individual chromosome evaluation times the number of chromosomes in the population times the total number of generations used to evolve the solution:

$$E_t \approx N \times \sum_{i=1}^{P} (ct)i \qquad (7.24)$$

Here,

E_t is the total evolution elapse time.
N is the total number of generations.
P is the number of chromosomes in the population.
g_t is generation elapse time (see the previous equation).
t_r is the runtime.
t_p is the intergeneration processing time.

When ct is 8 minutes, then for 50 chromosomes a database-tuning generation will take 400 minutes or 6.6 hours (a bit less than a full workday of processing). For 20 generations, the total optimization time is 132 hours (or 5.5 full days). This time frame is not the norm, but it can be typical for many real-world applications that involve large-scale complex systems.

7.4.2 Setting Process Parameters

Translating the concepts of a genetic algorithm into a working engine involves not only designing ways to represent the basic data structures but ways of setting the principal properties or parameters of the genetic algorithm. Most commercial or off-the-shelf genetic algorithms provide default values for these parameters, but a brief review of the typical values for each major parameter also provides a checklist for the control properties necessary in a genetic algorithm.

Population Size

The initial number of chromosomes in the population depends on the number of variables in the search. For a "typical" problem of moderate complexity, a population of 50 chromosomes is often a good starting point. In many genetic algorithms, the population size remains the same from generation to generation. In others, the population size can expand or contract depending on the degree of genetic diversity, the rate of convergence, or other factors in the search process.

Population Generation

There are generally two types of population management techniques in a genetic algorithm. In the steady-state model, a single population is constantly updated. In the dynamic-state model, a new population is created form the old population of each generation. As a general guideline, dynamic populations are often easier to maintain and usually provide a higher intrinsic degree of diversity.

Maximum Number of Generations

One of the primary termination conditions is a limitation on the maximum number of generations. The default value for this parameter is difficult to set independently of the number of variables and the number of objective functions. However, a default of 2.5 times the population size is often a good maximum generation count estimate.

Type of Crossover

The type of crossover used in breeding depends on the nature of the chromosome—that is, whether it is a binary or real number representation, the length of the chromosome, the possible number of states that can exist, and the amount of genetic diversity needed in the search model. A relatively good choice is double-point crossover during the early generations of the model, converting to single-point crossover in later generations. For scheduling, configuration, and other dependency problems, the greedy (or nearest-neighbor) algorithm is almost always the best choice.

Type of Mutation

The type of permissible mutation depends on the genome representation. The bit inversion technique is used for binary chromosomes, whereas a wider range of mutation options is available for real-number representations. For real numbers, the uniform replacement is an excellent default mutation type (and for scheduling and network or dependency problems, random swap is a good default mutation technique).

Retention Rate

The retention rate is a percentage of the population and determines how many of the top-performing chromosomes in a ranked (sorted) population will be selected and copied into the next generation (or for steady-state modes that will remain in the existing population). A default value of 10 to 15 percent is a good estimate.

Breeding Rate

Whether or not a chromosome is selected for breeding (crossover) is often determined by a probability tied to its fitness relative to all other fit chromosomes in the population (this is the case with proportional fitness). In many cases, however, the algorithm selects the first $2n + 1$ chromosomes in the population and breeds these (subject to the crossover rate) in order to create the next generation of offspring. The quantity n is tied to the breeding rate, which is expressed as a percentage of the population.

Crossover Rate

The crossover rate is a probability that a chromosome will be selected for breeding. This is used when the search algorithm uses a breeding rate to pick chromosomes for crossover. A default value between [0.5] and [0.9] (say 0.66) is a good default estimate for the crossover rate. In some genetic searches, the crossover rate can begin low and increase if the average fitness of the population does not significantly improve over a specified number of generations.

Mutation Rate

The mutation rate determines the probability that a chromosome will have one of its genes changed through a mutation technique. In general, mutation rates should be very low to sustain genetic diversity but not overwhelm the population with too much noise. Equation 7.25 shows a good default mutation probability rate:

$$m_r = \max\left(0.01, \frac{1}{N}\right)$$

(7.25)

Here,

m_r is the current probability of mutation.
N is the population size.

The mutation rate is inversely proportional to the population size, but not less than 0.001 is a good default value. For a population of 125 chromosomes, this is max(0.01,0.008), or [0.01].

New Individual Rate

In some genetic algorithms, new individuals are introduced into the next generation. These individuals have randomly valued genes (created in the same way as the genetic algorithm's initial population). New individuals can significantly increase genetic diversity but can also have an adverse effect on convergence if overused. As a rule of thumb, if new individuals are introduced into the population, the probability should be half the mutation rate ($0.5 * m_r$).

7.5 REVIEW

Genetic algorithms form a family of directed optimization and search techniques that can solve highly complex and often highly nonlinear problems. They can be used to explore very large problem spaces and find the best solution based on multiobjective functions under a collection of multiple constraints. In this chapter we examined the fundamental nature of genetic algorithms, how they work, and how they evolve or breed solutions to problems. You should now understand the principal nature of the genetic algorithm and be familiar with such concepts and ideas as the following:

- The types of problems solved by genetic algorithms.
- The organization and flow of control in a genetic algorithm.
- How a problem solution is encoded in a chromosome
- The design and use of a fitness function.
- How to introduce and limit diversity in a population.
- How to measure and control convergence in a population.
- How to select the correct crossover and mutation types and rates.
- How to set the process parameters for a genetic algorithm.
- The strengths and weaknesses of genetic algorithms.

Genetic algorithms play an important role in tuning, optimizing, and measuring the performance of adaptive models. They can be instrumental in evolving parameters that keep models responsive to many external stresses.

7.6 RESOURCES

Cox, E. "Fundamental Concepts of Genetic Algorithms," *Fuzzy Modeling and Genetic Algorithms for Data Mining and Exploration*, Morgan Kaufmann, 2005.

Goldberg, D. E. "A Note on Boltzmann Tournament Selection for Genetic Algorithms and Population-Oriented Simulated Annealing," in *Complex Systems*, Volume 4, pp. 445–460, 1990.

Goldberg, D. E. *Genetic Algorithms in Search, Optimization, and Machine Learning*, Addison-Wesley, 1989.

Goldberg, D. E. "Real-Coded Genetic Algorithms, Virtual Alphabets, and Blocking," *Complex Systems*, Volume 5, pp. 139–167, 1991.

Goldberg, D. E., and K. Deb. "A Comparative Analysis of Selection Schemes Used in Genetic Algorithms," *Foundations of Genetic Algorithms*, G. J. E. Rawlins (ed.), pp. 69–93, Morgan Kaufmann, 1991.

Goldberg, D. E., and J. Richardson. "Genetic Algorithms with Sharing for Multimodal Function Optimization," *Genetic Algorithms and Their Applications: Proceedings of the Second International Conference on Genetic Algorithms*, pp. 41-49, 1987.

Goldberg, D. E., K. Deb, and J. H. Clark. "Genetic Algorithms, Noise, and the Sizing of Populations," *Complex Systems*, Volume 6, pp. 333-362, 1992.

Grefenstette, J., R. Gopal, R. Rosmaita, and D. Gucht. "Genetic Algorithms for the Traveling Salesman Problem," *Proceedings of the Second International Conference on Genetic Algorithms*, Erlbaum, 1985.

Holland, J. H. *Adaptation in Natural and Artificial Systems: An Introductory Analysis with Applications to Biology, Control, and Artificial Intelligence*, University of Michigan Press, 1975.

Krishnakumar, K. "Micro-Genetic Algorithms for Stationary and Non-Stationary Function Optimization," *SPIE: Intelligent Control and Adaptive Systems*, Volume 1196, 1989.

Syswerda, G. "Uniform Crossover in Genetic Algorithms," *Proceedings of the Third International Conference on Genetic Algorithms*, J. Schaffer (ed.), pp. 2-9, Morgan Kaufmann, 1989.

Data Structures and Algorithms for Moving Objects Types

8

In this chapter, based on the discrete model described in Section 8.3, we develop data structures for its data types as well as algorithms for a selected collection of its operations. In the design of operations in the abstract model (Section 8.2), all operations have been defined to be applicable to all combinations of argument types for which they could make any sense for the user (i.e., they are overloaded). This leads to a large set of functionalities for operations. At the implementation level, the number of algorithms for the operations increases, because it is not always the case that different argument types for one overloaded operation can be handled by the same algorithm. Hence, we reduce the scope of our study; the kind of reduction will be described in Section 8.2.1.

Section 8.1 describes the employed data structures in detail. This is the basis for describing and analyzing algorithms. Section 8.2 introduces algorithms for operations on temporal data types, and Section 8.3 investigates algorithms for lifted operations.

8.1 DATA STRUCTURES

Data structures designed for use as attribute data types in a database environment must satisfy some requirements.

8.1.1 General Requirements and Strategy

Values are placed into memory under the control of the database management system (DBMS), which in turn, implies that one should not use pointers, and representations should consist of a small number of memory blocks that can be moved efficiently between secondary and main memory.

One way to satisfy these requirements is described in the following text. Data types are generally represented by a record (called the *root record*), which contains some fixed-size components and possibly one or more references to arrays. Arrays are used to represent the varying size components of a data type value and are allocated to the required size. All pointers are expressed as array indexes.

Another aspect is that many of the data types are set valued. Sets will be represented in arrays. We always define a unique order on the set domains and store elements in the array in that order. In this way, we can enforce that two set values are equal if, and only if, their array representations are equal; this makes efficient comparisons possible. Further, all implemented algorithms must run on these block-based data structures.

A final aspect is that different algorithms processing the same kind of objects usually prefer different internal object representations. In contrast to traditional work on algorithms, the focus here is not on finding the most efficient algorithm for one single problem (operation), together with a sophisticated data structure, but rather on considering our algebra as a whole and on reconciling the various requirements posed by different algorithms within a single data structure for each data type. In addition, it is our goal to identify algorithmic schemes that can be applied to a large number of operations.

8.1.2 Nontemporal Data Types

The base types int, real, string, bool, and instant are represented by a record, which consists of a corresponding programming language value together with a Boolean flag indicating whether the value is defined. For string, the value is a character array of fixed length. For instant, the value is of an auxiliary data type coordinate, which is a rational number of a certain precision. Two predefined constants, *mininstant* and *maxinstant,* describe the first and last representable instants in the past and the future, respectively. This means we assume a bounded and not an infinite time domain at the discrete level.

Next, we look at the spatial data types, which all use the type *coordinate* for representing coordinates. A point value is represented by a record with two values x and y of the *coordinate* type and a *defined* flag. A points value is a finite set of points in the plane. It is represented by a (root) record containing a reference to an array. Each element of the array represents one point by its two coordinates. Points are in (x, y)-lexicographic order.

A line value at the discrete level is a finite set of line segments that are intersection free.[1] It is represented as a root record with one array of *halfsegments*. The idea of halfsegments is to store each segment twice: once for the left (i.e., smaller) endpoint and once for the right endpoint. These are called the *left* and *right halfsegments*, respectively, and the relevant point in the halfsegment is

---

[1] The reason is that we can then reuse the so-called *ROSE algebra* implementation, which has this requirement. Of course, it is also possible to allow intersections of segments that lead to different algorithms if lines are involved.

called the *dominating* point. The purpose of this is to support *plane-sweep* algorithms, which traverse a set of segments from left to right and have to perform an action (e.g., insertion into a sweep status structure) on encountering the left and another action on meeting the right endpoint of a segment. Each halfsegment is represented as a pair of `point` values for the endpoints plus a flag to indicate the dominating endpoint. Halfsegments are ordered in the array following a lexicographic order extended by an angle criterion to treat halfsegments with the same dominating point.

A `region` value is given by the set of line segments forming its boundary. At a higher structural level, it is a finite set of edge-disjoint faces. A `region` value is represented by a root record with three arrays. The first array (segments) contains a sequence of records, where each record contains a halfsegment plus an additional field *next-in-cycle*, which links the segments belonging to a cycle (in clockwise order for outer cycles, counterclockwise for hole cycles, so the area of the face is always to the right). Therefore, one can traverse cycles efficiently. The second and third arrays (cycles and faces arrays) represent the list of cycles and faces, respectively, belonging to the `region` value. They are also suitably linked together so that one can traverse the list of cycles belonging to a face, for example.

Exercise 8.1 Let us have a closer look at the halfsegment representation of the types *line* and *region*.

1. Let $N \in \{\mathbb{I}, \mathbb{Q}, \mathbb{R}\}$ (i.e., N is either the set of integer numbers, rational numbers, or real numbers). Let $P = N \times N$ be the set of points based on N. Define the lexicographical order relation $<_P$ on P.
2. Let H be the set of halfsegments defined over P. Define an order relation $<_H$ on H. Take into account the possible topological configurations of two halfsegments. Assume the ROSE algebra case in which two halfsegments are intersection free (i.e., either disjoint or share exactly one common end point).
3. Draw a region consisting of two triangles, one inside the other; name the segments $s_1, \ldots, s_6$. Determine the region's halfsegment sequence. To each halfsegment attach a flag indicating on which side the interior of the region is located. ■

For the three data types `points`, `line`, and `region` we also introduce several *summary fields* stored in the respective root records. Their goal is to provide certain data about the object in constant time instead of executing an expensive algorithm for their computation. Values for these fields can be easily calculated during the construction of a spatial object. The minimum bounding box of an object, which is an axis-parallel rectangle, is given by the field *object_mbb*. The field *no_components* keeps the number of points for a `points` value, the number of connected components for a `line` value, and the number of faces for a `region` value. For `line` values, the field *length* returns the total length of line segments as a real number. The fields *perimeter* and *area* store corresponding real numbers for a *region* value. In addition, for all the arrays used in the representation there is a field giving their actual length. Hence, one can determine the number of segments or faces for a region value, for example.

The range data types rint, rreal, rstring, rbool, and periods are represented by a root record containing an array whose entries are interval records ordered by value (all intervals must be disjoint and nonadjacent—hence, there is a total order). An interval record contains four components (*s, e, lc, rc*), where *s* and *e* are the start and end value of the interval, respectively (therefore of type int, real, etc.), and *lc* and *rc* are Booleans indicating whether the interval is left closed or right closed, respectively. Summary fields are also defined for range types. The number of intervals is stored in the field *no_components* as an integer. The minimal and maximal values assumed in a set of intervals are given in the fields *min* and *max*, respectively, of the corresponding data types. For periods values, the sum of the lengths of all intervals is kept in the field *duration*.

An intime value of type iint, ireal, istring, ibool, ipoint, or iregion is represented by a corresponding record (*instant, value*), where *value* is of the corresponding data type.

8.1.3 Temporal Data Types

All temporal data types are represented by the so-called *sliced representation* (Section 8.3.1). It describes a value of a temporal (moving) data type as a set of units. A unit is represented by a record containing a pair of values (interval, unit function). The *interval* defines the time interval for which the unit is valid; it has the same form (*s, e, lc, rc*) as intervals in the range types. The *unit function* represents a "simple" function from time to the corresponding nontemporal type α, which returns a valid α value for each time instant in *interval*. For each temporal type there will be a corresponding *unit function* data structure. The time intervals of any two distinct units are disjoint; hence, units can be totally ordered by time.

Units for the discretely changing types const(int), const(string), and const(bool) use as a unit function a value of the corresponding nontemporal type. Hence, for a unit (*i, v*), the function is $f(t) = v$.

The ureal unit function is represented by a record (*a, b, c, r*), where *a, b, c* are real numbers and *r* is a Boolean value. The function represented by this four-tuple is

$$f(t) = at^2 + bt + c \quad \text{if } r \text{ false}$$

and

$$f(t) = \sqrt{at^2 + bt + c} \quad \text{if } r \text{ is } true$$

Hence, we can represent (piecewise) quadratic polynomials and square roots.

A upoint unit function is represented by a record (x_0, x_1, y_0, y_1), representing the function $f(t) = (x_0 + x_1 t, y_0 + y_1 t)$. Such functions describe a linearly moving point. We also call the tuple (x_0, x_1, y_0, y_1) an *mpoint* ("moving point").

A uregion unit function is represented by a record containing three arrays: an *msegments* array, a *cycles* array, and a *faces* array. The *msegments* ("moving segments") array stores the "msegments" of the unit, using lexicographic order on the tuples defining the msegment. As for region, each msegment record has an additional field *next-in-cycle*, and msegments of a cycle are linked in cyclic order, always having the interior of the face at their right. The *cycles* and *faces* arrays are managed the same as region. The *cycles* array keeps a record for each cycle in the uregion unit, containing a pointer (represented by an array index) to the *first-mseg-in-cycle* and a pointer to the *next-cycle-in-face*. The *faces* array stores one record per face, with a pointer to the *first-cycle-in-face*.

A value of a temporal data type incorporates a collection of units and is represented as a root record containing an array of units ordered by their time interval.

Summary fields, which are later used in various algorithms, are added to the root record of the moving object or to the record representing the unit, respectively. At the object level, for all temporal types, the field *no_units* keeps the number of units as an integer, and the field *deftime* stores a periods value representing the set of time intervals for which the moving object is defined. The value for *deftime* is obtained from merging the definition time intervals of the units. We also call this the *deftime index*. The information in the root record of the periods value is integrated into the root record of the moving object, which now contains a *deftime* array as well as its *units* array. For the nonspatial temporal types mint, mreal, mstring, and mbool, the fields *min* and *max* contain the minimum and maximum values of the respective data type that the object takes in all its definition time. For the spatiotemporal types mpoint and mregion, the field *object_pbb* constitutes the *projection bounding box*, which represents the minimum rectangle of all points in the 2D space that at some time instant belong to the spatiotemporal object.

At the unit level, for the ureal type, the fields *unit_min* and *unit_max* hold real numbers for the minimum and maximum values, respectively, assumed by the unit function. For the types upoint and uregion, the field *unit_pbb* contains the *unit projection bounding box* for the spatial projection of the unit. For the uregion type, the field *unit_no_components* contains the number of moving faces of the unit as an integer; the fields *unit_perimeter* and *unit_area* represent ureal unit functions describing the development of the perimeter and the area during the unit interval; and the field *unit_ibb* includes the *unit interpolation bounding box*, which is a "moving rectangle" and a more precise filter than the unit projection bounding box. It connects the bounding box of the uregion projection at the start time of the unit with the bounding box of the projection at the end time. It is stored as a record (a_{xmin}, b_{xmin}, a_{xmax}, b_{xmax}, a_{ymin}, b_{ymin}, a_{ymax}, b_{ymax}), representing one linear function f_i for each bounding box coordinate (x_{min}, x_{max}, y_{min}, and y_{max}), with the value $f_i = a_i t + b_i$. The various projection bounding boxes are later used for a sequence of filter steps.

8.2 ALGORITHMS FOR OPERATIONS ON TEMPORAL DATA TYPES

This section gives algorithmic descriptions of operations on temporal data types for projection into domain and range (Section 8.2.2), for interaction with values from domain and range (Section 8.2.3), and for rate of change (Section 8.2.4).

8.2.1 Common Considerations

Selecting a Subset of Algorithms

The abstract model described in Section 8.2 puts the emphasis on consistency, closure, and genericity; in particular, all operations have been defined to be applicable to all combinations of argument types for which they could make any sense. The result is a large set of functionalities for operations. This set is even enlarged by the fact that it is not always the case that the same algorithm can handle different argument types for one operation. To make it manageable, we reduce the scope of our algorithm descriptions as follows. First, we do not study algorithms for operations on nontemporal types as such; this type of algorithm on static objects has been studied before in the computational geometry and spatial database literature.

An example would be an algorithm for testing whether a point value is located in a region value. However, we will study the lifted versions of these operations that involve moving objects. Second, we do not consider the types mpoints and mline or any signature of an operation involving these types. These types have been added to the abstract model mainly for reasons of closure and consistency; they are by far not as important as the types mpoint and mregion, which are in the focus of interest. Third, we do not consider predicates based on topology; these are the predicates touches, attached, overlaps, on_border, and in_interior. They are, of course, useful, but we limit the scope of our considerations here. Fourth, we do not deal with the mregion × mregion case, because its treatment follows a rather complex algorithmic scheme. You are referred to the original literature (see Section 8.4).

Together with the restrictions just mentioned, it is not so easy to figure out which functionalities remain. Therefore, in the following sections, we list explicitly which signatures remain to be considered for each operation.

Notations

From now on, we denote the first and second operand of a binary operation by a and b, respectively. We denote the argument of unary operations by a. In complexity analysis, m and n are the numbers of units (or intervals) of, respectively, a and b, whereas r is the number of units in the result. If a is a type having a variable size, we denote by M the number of "components" of a. That is, for example, if a is of type points, then M is the number of points contained in a; but if a is of type mregion, then M is the number of moving segments comprising

Table 8.1 Notations

Symbol	Meaning
a, b	First and second argument
m, n, r	Numbers of units of first and second arguments and of the result
M, N, R	Sizes of arguments and of result
u, v, w	Sizes of two argument units and of a result unit
$u_{max}, v_{max}, w_{max}$	Maximal sizes of units for the two arguments and for the result
d	Size of a *deftime* index

a. In any case, the size of *a* is $O(M)$. For the second argument *b* and for the result of an operation, we use the same meaning N and R, respectively. If *a* (respectively, *b*, or the result) is of type `mregion`, we denote by *u* (respectively, *v, w*) the number of moving segments comprising one of its units and by u_{max} (respectively, v_{max}, w_{max}) the maximum number of moving segments contained in a unit. Finally, let *d* denote the size of the *deftime* index of a moving object. For easy lookup, these notations are summarized in Table 8.1.

All complexity analyses done in this chapter consider CPU time only. So this assumes that the arguments are already in main memory and does not address the problem of whether they need to be loaded entirely or if this can be avoided.

Most of the operations are polymorphic (i.e., allow for several combinations of argument and result types). To avoid long listings of signatures but still to be precise about which signatures are admitted, we use the following abbreviation scheme, illustrated here for the `rangevalues` operator: For $\alpha \in \{$`int, bool, string, real`$\}$:

```
rangevalues    mα  → rα
```

Here, α is a type variable ranging over the types mentioned; each binding of α results in a valid signature. Hence, this specification expands into the list:

```
rangevalues    mint    → rint
               mbool   → rbool
               mstring → rstring
               mreal   → rreal
```

Refinement Partitions

We now describe an algorithmic scheme that is common to many operations. In the following text, we call an argument of a temporal type a *moving argument*. Every binary operation whose arguments are moving ones requires a preliminary step, where a *refinement partition* of the units of the two arguments is computed. A refinement partition is obtained by breaking units into other units (Figure 8.1)

FIGURE 8.1

Two sets of time intervals are on the left; their refinement partition is on the right.

that have the same value but are defined on smaller time intervals, so that a resulting unit of the first argument and one of the second argument are defined either on the same time interval or on two disjoint time intervals. We denote the number of units in the refinement partition of both arguments by p. Note that $p = O(n + m)$. We use M' (respectively, N') with the same meaning as M (respectively, N), referring to the size of the refined partition of the units of a (respectively, b). We compute the refinement partition by a parallel scan of the two lists of units with a complexity of $O(p)$.

This complexity is obvious for all types that have units of a fixed size—hence, for all types but `mregion`. Even for the latter type, this complexity can be achieved if region units are not copied, but pointers to the original units are passed to the subalgorithm processing a pair of units for a given interval of the refinement partition. If the refinement partition for two `mregion` arguments is computed explicitly (copying units), the complexity is $O(M' + N')$.

For many operations, whose result is one of the temporal types, a postprocessing step is needed to merge adjacent units having the same value. This requires time $O(r)$.

Filtering Approach

Even if not stated, each algorithm *filters* its arguments using the auxiliary information (i.e., the summary fields) provided by them, which varies according to argument types (see Section 8.1). The term *filter* is widely used in geometric query processing to describe a prechecking on approximations. For example, a spatial join on two sets of regions may be implemented by first finding pairs of overlapping bounding boxes (also called MBRs, minimal bounding rectangles) and then performing a precise check of the qualifying pairs' geometries. The first is then called the *filter step* and the latter the *refinement step*. In this book and elsewhere, the term is also used to describe prechecking on approximations of two single spatial data type values, before running a more expensive precise algorithm.

For filtering, minimum and maximum values (stored in the *min* and *max* fields of the root record) for moving nonspatial types as well as bounding boxes for nontemporal spatial types are used. For `mpoint` and `mregion`, filtering is performed using projection bounding boxes. Moreover, for `mregion`, two more filtering steps, with increased selectivity, are performed using first projection bounding boxes and then interpolation bounding boxes of individual units.

8.2.2 Projection to Domain and Range

The operations described in this section get a *moving* or *intime* value as operand and compute different kinds of projections either with respect to the temporal component (i.e., the domain) or the function component (i.e., the range) of a moving value.

deftime. This operation returns all times for which a moving object is defined. The signatures for all $\alpha \in$ {int, bool, string, real, point, region} are as follows:

deftime   mα → periods

The algorithmic scheme for all operations is to read the intervals from the *deftime* index incorporated into each argument object. The time complexity is $O(r) = O(d)$.

rangevalues. This operation is defined for one-dimensional argument types only and returns all unit values assumed over time as a set of intervals. We obtain the following signatures for $\alpha \in$ {int, bool, string, real}:

rangevalues   mα → rα

For the type mbool, in $O(1)$ time we look up the minimal range value *min* and the maximal range value *max* of the moving Boolean. The result is one of the interval sets {[*false, false*]}, {[*true, true*]}, or {[*false, true*]}. For the types mint and mstring, we scan the mapping (i.e., the unit function values), insert the range values into a binary search tree, and finally traverse the tree and report the ordered sequence of disjoint intervals. This takes $O(m + m \log k)$ time if k is the number of different values in the range. For the type mreal, we use the summary fields *unit_min* and *unit_max* of each real unit. As each unit function is continuous, it is guaranteed that all values in the range [*unit_min, unit_max*] are assumed so that we obtain an interval of values. The task is to compute the union of all these intervals as a set of disjoint intervals. This can be done by sorting the endpoints of intervals and then sweeping along this one-dimensional space, maintaining a counter to keep track of whether the current position is covered or not, in O ($m \log m$) time.

The projection of a moving point into the plane may consist of points and of lines; these can be obtained separately by the operations locations and trajectory.

locations. This operation returns the isolated points in the projection of an *mpoint* as a *points* value. This kind of projection is especially useful when a moving point never changes its position or does it in discrete steps only. Thus, its signature is as follows:

```
locations   mpoint → points
```

In the first step, we scan all units of the `mpoint` value and compute for each unit the projection of its three-dimensional segment into the plane. As a result, we obtain a collection of line segments and points (the latter given as degenerate line segments with equal endpoints). This computation takes $O(m)$ time. From this result, only the points have to be returned, and only those points that do not lie on one of the line segments. Therefore, in the second step, we perform a segment intersection algorithm with plane sweep, where we traverse the collection from left to right and only insert line segments into the sweep status structure. For each point, we test whether there is a segment in the current sweep status structure containing the point. If this is the case, we ignore the point; otherwise, the point belongs to the result and is stored (automatically in lexicographic order) in a `points` value. This step and also the total time takes $O((m + k) \log m)$, if k is the number of intersections of the projected segments.

`trajectory`. This operation computes the more natural projection of a continuously moving point as a *line* value. Its signature is as follows:

```
trajectory   mpoint → line
```

In the first step, we *scan* all units of the `mpoint` value, ignore those units with three-dimensional segments vertical to the *xy*-plane, and compute for each remaining unit the projection of its three-dimensional segment into the plane. This takes $O(m)$ time. In the second step, we perform a plane sweep algorithm to find all pairs of intersecting, collinear, or touching line segments, and we return a list of intersection-free segments. This needs $O(m' \log m)$ where $m' = m + k$ and k is the number of intersections in the projection. Note that $k = O(m^2)$. In the third step, we insert the resulting segments into a *line* value. Because sorting is needed for this, $O(m' \log m')$ time is required; this is also the total time needed for this algorithm, which can be as bad as $O(m^2 \log m^2)$ in terms of parameter m.

`traversed`. This operation computes the projection of a moving region into the plane:

```
traversed   mregion → region
```

Let us first consider how to compute the projection of a single region unit into the plane. We use the observation that each point of the projection in the plane either lies within the region unit at its start time or is traversed by a boundary segment during the movement. Consequently, the projection is the geometric

Algorithm *traversed*(*mr*)

Input: a moving region *mr*

Output: a region representing the trajectory of *mr*

Method:

Step 1: Let *L* be a list of line segments, initially empty;

    for each region unit **do**
        compute the region value *r* at start time;
        put each line segment of *r* together with a flag indicating whether it is
            a *left* or *right* segment into *L* (it is a left segment if the interior of
            the region is to its right);
        project each moving segment of the unit into the plane and put these
            also with a left/right flag into *L*
    endfor

Step 2: Sort the (half)segments of *L* in *x, y*-lexicographical order;

Step 3: Perform a plane sweep algorithm over the segments in *L*, keep track in
the sweep status structure of how often each part of the plane is covered by projection areas, and write segments belonging to the boundary (i.e., segments that
separate 0-areas from *c*-areas with *c* > 0) into a list *L'*

Step 4: Sort the segments of *L'* in lexicographical order, and insert them into a
`region` value

end.

FIGURE 8.2

Algorithm *traversed.*

union of the start value of the region unit and all projections of moving segments
of the region unit into the plane.

The algorithm has four steps. In the first step, all region units are projected
into the plane. In the second step, the resulting set of segments is sorted, to
prepare a plane sweep. In the third step, a plane sweep is performed on the
projections in order to compute the segments forming the contour of the
covered area of the plane. In the fourth step, a `region` value has to be constructed
from these segments. In a bit more detail, the algorithm is as shown in
Figure 8.2.

The time complexity of the first step is $O(M)$. The second step needs $O(M \log M)$; the third step needs $O(M' \log M)$, where $M' = M + K$ and K is the number
of intersections of segments in the projection. The final step takes $O(R \log R)$,
where R is the number of segments in the contour of the covered area. In
the worst case, we may have $R = \Theta(M')$. Hence, the total time complexity is
$O(M' \log M')$.

inst, val. For values of *intime* types, these two trivial projection operations yield their first and second component, respectively, in $O(1)$. For $\alpha \in \{$int, bool, string, real, point, region$\}$ we obtain the signatures:

```
inst   iα → instant
val    iα → α
```

8.2.3 Interaction with Domain/Range

atinstant. This operation restricts the moving entity given as an argument to a specified time instant. For $\alpha \in \{$int, bool, string, real, point, region$\}$ we obtain the following signatures:

```
atinstant   mα × instant → iα
```

The algorithmic scheme, which is the same for all types, first performs a binary search on the array containing the units to determine the unit containing the argument time instant t and then to evaluate the moving entity at time t. For types mint, mbool, and mstring, this is trivial. For types mpoint and mreal, it is simply the evaluation of low-degree polynomial(s) at t. For all these types the time needed is $O(\log m)$. For type mregion, each moving segment in the appropriate region unit is evaluated at time t to get a line segment. A proper region data structure is then constructed, after a lexicographic sort of halfsegments, in time $O(R \log R)$. The total complexity is $O(\log m + R \log R)$.

atperiods. This operation restricts the moving entity given as an argument to a specified set of time intervals. For $\alpha \in \{$*int, bool, string, real, point, region*$\}$ we obtain the following:

```
atperiods   mα × periods → mα
```

For all types, it is essentially required to form an intersection of two ordered lists of intervals, where in each list binary search is possible. There are three kinds of strategies. The first strategy is to perform a parallel scan on both lists returning those units of a (or parts thereof) whose time interval is contained in time intervals of b. The complexity is $O(m + n)$. The second strategy performs for each unit in a a binary search on b for its start time. Then it scans along b to determine intersection time intervals and produce corresponding copies of this unit. The complexity is $O(m \log n + r)$. A variant is to switch the role of the two lists and hence obtain complexity $O(n \log m + r)$. The third strategy is more sophisticated. For the first interval in b, we perform a binary search for the unit s in a containing (or otherwise following) its start time. For the last interval in b, we perform a binary search for the unit e in a containing (or otherwise preceding) its end time. Compute q as the number of units between s and e (using the indexes of s and e). This has taken $O(\log m)$ time so far. Now, if $q < n \log m$, then do a parallel scan of b and the range of a between s and e computing result units. Otherwise, first for each interval in b, perform a binary search on a for its start time, and afterward scan along a to determine intersection time intervals and produce corresponding copies of this unit. The time required is either $O(\log m + n + q)$, if $q < n \log m$, or $O(n \log m + r)$, if $q \geq n \log m$. The total time required is $O(\log m + n + \min(q, n \log m) + r)$, because if $q < n \log m$, then $q = \min(q, n \log m)$; otherwise, $n \log m = \min(q, n \log m)$.

We expect that often m will be relatively large and n and r be small. For example, let $n = 1$ and $r = 0$. In this case, the complexity reduces to $O(\log m)$. On the other hand, if $n \log m$ is large, then the complexity is still bounded by $O(\log m + n + q)$ (note that $r \leq q$), which is in turn bounded by $O(m + n)$ (because $q \leq m$). Hence, this strategy gracefully adapts to various situations, is output sensitive, and never more expensive than the simple parallel scan of both lists of intervals.

For type `mregion` copying into result units is more expensive and requires a complexity of $O(\log m + n + \min(q, n \log m) + R)$, where R is the total number of *msegments* in the result.

`initial, final`. These operations provide the value of the operand at the first and last instant of its definition time, respectively, together with the value of the time itself. For $\alpha \in \{$`int, bool, string, real, point, region`$\}$ we obtain the following signatures:

`initial, final    m`$\alpha \rightarrow$ `i`α

For all types the first (last) unit is accessed and the argument is evaluated at the start (end) time instant of the unit. The complexity is $O(1)$, but for type `mregion` it is $O(R \log R)$ required to build the `region` value.

`present`. This operation allows us to check whether the moving value exists at a specified instant or is ever present during a specified set of time intervals. For $\alpha \in \{$`int, bool, string, real, point, region`$\}$, we obtain the following signatures:

`present    m`α `× instant →` `bool`
`           m`α `× periods →` `bool`

When the second parameter is an instant, for all types the approach is to perform a binary search on the *deftime* array for the time interval containing the specified instant. Time complexity is $O(\log d)$. When the second parameter is a period, for all types the approach is similar to the one used for `atperiods`. Differences are as follows: Instead of using the list of units of the first parameter, its *deftime* array is used; as soon as the result becomes *true*, the computation can be stopped (*early stop*); and no result units need to be reported. Time complexity is, depending on the strategy followed, $O(d + n)$, $O(d \log n)$ or $O(n \log d)$, $O(\log d + n + \min(q, n \log d))$. An overall strategy could be to determine q in $O(\log d)$ time and then—because all parameters are known—to select the cheapest among these strategies.

at. The purpose of this operation is the restriction of the moving entity to a specified value or range of values. For $\alpha \in \{$int, bool, string, real$\}$ and $\beta \in \{$point, points, line, region$\}$ we obtain the following signatures:

at   m$\alpha \times \alpha$ $\rightarrow$ mα
     m$\alpha \times$ rα $\rightarrow$ mα
     mpoint $\times \beta$ $\rightarrow$ mpoint
     mregion $\times$ point $\rightarrow$ mpoint
     mregion $\times$ region $\rightarrow$ mregion

The general approach for the restriction to a specified value is based on a scan of each unit of the first argument, which is checked for equality with the second argument. For mbool, mint, and mstring, the equality check for units is trivial, whereas for mreal and mpoint we need to solve equations, produce a corresponding number of units in the output, and possibly merge adjacent result units with the same value. In any of the previous cases complexity is $O(m)$.

For mregion $\times$ point, we use the algorithm for the more general case of the operation inside(mpoint $\times$ mregion) (see Section 8.3). The kernel of this algorithm is the intersection between a line in 3D, which corresponds to a (moving) point, and a set of trapeziums in 3D, which corresponds to a set of (moving) segments. In the increasing order of time, with each intersection the (moving) point alternates between entering and leaving the (moving) region represented by trapeziums, and the list of resulting units is correspondingly produced. In this particular case, point b corresponds to a vertical line in 3D (assuming an (x, y, t)-coordinate system, and the complexity is $O(M + K \log k_{max})$, where K is the overall number of intersections between moving segments of a and (the line of) point b, and k_{max} is the maximum number of intersections between b and the moving segments of a unit of a.

For the restriction to a specified range of values, different approaches are used. For mbool, it is simply a scan of a's units, with $O(m)$ complexity. For mint and mstring, a binary search on b's range is performed for each unit of a, with an $O(m \log n)$ complexity.

For mreal, the problem is illustrated in Figure 8.3. For each unit of a, we have to find parts of the unit function intersecting b by means of a binary search on the intervals of b (using the lowest value of a given by the *min* field in the current unit) plus a scan along b. For each intersection of the unit function of a with an interval of b, we return a unit with the same unit function and an appropriately restricted time interval. The complexity is $O(m \log n + r)$.

For mpoint $\times$ points, for each unit of a, we do a binary search on b with the x interval of the *unit_pbb* to find the first point of b that is inside that x interval. Starting from the found point, we scan the points of b checking each of them first to see if they are in the *unit_pbb* and then whether they intersect the moving point. Then, we sort the resulting units. The complexity is $O(m \log N + K' + r \log r)$, where K' is the sum, over all units, of the number of points of b that are inside the x interval of the respective *unit_pbb*. An alternative approach is to

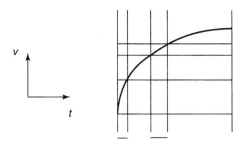

FIGURE 8.3

The at operation on a real unit and a set of real intervals. Two units with the same unit function and the time intervals shown at the bottom are returned.

compute for each unit of *a* the intersection of the *unit_pbb* and of the *object_pbb* of *b* as a filter. If the bounding boxes intersect, we compute the intersection of the moving point with each point of *b* and then sort the resulting units. The complexity is $O(mN + r \log r)$.

For mpoint × line, for each unit of *a*, we prefilter by intersecting its *unit_pbb* with *b*'s *object_mbb* and process intersecting pairs by computing the intersection between the mpoint value of *a*'s current unit (a line segment in 3D) and each line segment of *b* (which is a vertical rectangle in 3D), producing result units corresponding to intersections. Afterward, we sort the result units. The complexity is $O(mN + r \log r)$.

For mpoint × region, we use the algorithm for the more general case of operation inside(mpoint × mregion). This means, that initially we convert the region value into a uregion unit, replacing segments by corresponding (vertical) msegments. The complexity is $O(mN + K \log k_{max})$, where *K* is the total number of intersections of mpoints (3D segments) in *a* with msegments in *b*, and k_{max} is the maximal number of msegments of *b* intersected by a single mpoint value.

For mregion × region, we use the algorithm for intersection in the more general case, mregion × mregion (see Section 8.3).

atmin, atmax. These operations restrict the moving value to the time when it is minimal or maximal. For $\alpha \in \{int, bool, string, real\}$, we obtain the following signatures:

atmin, atmax mα → mα

For all types we scan the units to see if their value is the minimum (respectively, maximum) as given by the *min* (respectively, *max*) field of the moving object. For mreal the comparison is done with the *unit_min* or *unit_max* summary field. If the unit qualifies, its time interval is reduced to the corresponding instant or interval. The complexity is $O(m)$.

passes. This allows us to check whether the moving value ever assumed (one of) the value(s) given as a second argument. For $\alpha \in$ {int, bool, string, real} and $\beta \in$ {point, points, line, region}, we obtain the following signatures:

```
passes  mα      × α      → bool
        mpoint  × β      → bool
        mregion × β      → bool
```

For mbool, compare b with index *min* or *max*, with a complexity of $O(1)$. For mint, mstring, and mreal, we scan each unit (in the latter case use *unit_min* and *unit_max* values as a filter) and stop when a matching value is found. The complexity is $O(m)$.

For mpoint × β and mregion × β, we proceed as for the at operation, but stop and return *true* as soon as an intersection is discovered. In the worst case, complexities are the same as for the at operation.

8.2.4 **Rate of Change**

The following operations deal with an important property of any time-dependent value—namely, its rate of change:

```
derivative    mreal  → mreal
derivable     mreal  → mbool
speed         mpoint → mreal
velocity      mpoint → mpoint
mdirection    mpoint → mreal
```

They all have the same global algorithmic scheme and scan the mapping of the units of the argument moving object a, computing in constant time for each unit of a a corresponding result unit, possibly merging adjacent result units with the same value. The total time needed is $O(m)$. In the following text, we briefly discuss the meaning of an operation and how the result unit is computed from the argument unit.

derivative. This operation has the obvious meaning (i.e., it returns the derivative of a moving real as a moving real). Unfortunately, in this discrete model it cannot be implemented completely. Recall that a real unit is represented as $u = (i, (a, b, c, r))$, which, in turn, represents the real function

$$at^2 + bt + c$$

if $r = false$, and the function

$$\sqrt{at^2 + bt + c}$$

if $r = $ true, both defined over the interval i. Only in the first case is it possible to represent the derivative again as a real unit—namely, the derivative is

$2at + b$—which can be represented as a unit $u' = (i, (0, 2a, b, false))$. In the second case, $r = true$, we assume that the result unit function is undefined. Because for any moving object units exist only for time intervals with a defined value, we return no result unit at all.

This partial definition is problematic, but it seems to be better than not offering the operation at all. On the other hand, the user must be careful when applying this function. To alleviate the problem, we introduce next an additional operation: `derivable` (not present and not needed in the abstract model).

`derivable`. This new operation checks for each unit of a moving real whether or not it describes a quadratic polynomial whose derivative is representable by a real unit. It returns a corresponding Boolean unit.

`speed`. This operation computes the speed of a moving point as a real function. Because each `upoint` unit describes a linear movement, the resulting *ureal* unit contains just a real constant, whose computation is trivial.

`velocity`. This operation computes the velocity of a moving point as a vector function. Again, because of the linear movement within a *upoint* unit, the velocity is constant at all times of the unit's interval $[t_0, t_1]$. Hence, each result unit contains a constant moving point representing the vector function:

$$\textbf{velocity}\ (u, t) = \left(\frac{x(t_1) - x(t_0)}{t_1 - t_0}, \frac{y(t_1) - y(t_0)}{t_1 - t_0} \right)$$

`mdirection`. For all times of a moving point's life span, it returns the angle between the x-axis and the tangent (i.e., the direction) of a moving point at time t. Because of linear movement within a `upoint` unit, the direction is also constant within the unit's interval. A special case arises if, for two temporally consecutive units u and v, two endpoints coincide—that is, if, $x_u(t_1) = x_v(t_0)$ and $y_u(t_1) = y_v(t_0)$. Then, `mdirection`(v, t) is assigned to this common endpoint, in agreement with the formal definition of semantics from the abstract model.

Exercise 8.2 Let v be a `upoint` unit and t be a time instant. Give the precise formula for **mdirection**(v, t).   ∎

`turn`. This operation computes the change of direction of a moving point at all times of its life span. Within a `upoint` unit u, there is no change of the direction, because the unit function is linear. Hence (also in the endpoints), `turn`$(u, t) = 0$ holds for all times of the unit's interval and for all `upoint` units. This is not an interesting result; hence, this operation need not be implemented within this particular discrete model.

8.3 ALGORITHMS FOR LIFTED OPERATIONS

This section gives algorithmic descriptions of *lifted operations*. Recall that these are operations originally defined for nontemporal objects are now applied to "moving" variants of the arguments. We consider predicates (Section 8.3.1), set operations (Section 8.3.2), aggregation (Section 8.3.3), numeric properties (Section 8.3.4), distance and direction (Section 8.3.5), and Boolean operations (Section 8.3.6).

8.3.1 Predicates

`isempty`. This predicate checks, for each time instant, whether the argument is defined. For $\alpha \in$ {`int, bool, string, real, point, region`}, we obtain the signatures:

`isempty    m`α `→ mbool`

The result is defined from *mininstant* to *maxinstant* (the "bounds" of time introduced in Section 8.1.2). We scan the *deftime* index returning units with value *true* for intervals where a is defined and units with value *false* in the other case. The complexity is $O(d)$.

`=, ≠`. These predicates check for equality of the arguments over time. For $\alpha \in$ {`int, bool, string, real, point, region`}, we obtain the signatures:

1. `m`α `× `α ` → mbool`
2. `m`α `× m`α ` → mbool`

The general approach for operations of group 1 is based on a scan of each unit of the first argument, which is checked for equality with the second argument. The equality check for all cases but `mregion` is done as in the corresponding cases for the `at` operation (see Section 8.2.3), except that a Boolean unit is returned, and so complexities are the same. For `mregion` the equality check for units is done as follows. First, check whether u and N are equal numbers. If not, we report a single unit $(i, false)$, where i is the time interval of the argument unit. Otherwise, we proceed as follows: We consecutively take each moving segment s of the current unit of a. If s is *static* (i.e., does not change in time), we search for a matching segment in b (*). If this search fails, we return $(i, false)$. Otherwise, we continue this procedure, until s is not static or s is the last segment. If s is the last segment and static, we return $(i, true)$ (i.e., the projection of the unit is equal to b). Otherwise, s is not static, and we compare s with all segments of b, finding k intersections at the instants $t_1, \ldots, t_k$ such that s is equal to a segment in b. If $k = 0$, we return $(i, false)$. Otherwise, for each intersection at time t_i, we do the following: For each moving segment s of the current unit, we evaluate s at time

t_i and take this segment to search for a matching segment in b (*). If the search succeeds for all s, we have found a matching region and return (i, *true*). Otherwise, we continue with t_{i+1}. If for all t_i no matching regions have been found, we return (i, *false*).

This algorithm is based on the observation that if the `uregion` unit has only a single moving segment, then it can be equal to a static region only in a single instant of time. Steps labeled (*) take time $O(\log N)$, because halfsegments in the `region` representation are ordered lexicographically. The worst-case complexity per unit is $O(kN \log N)$. In the worst case, $k = O(N)$, but in most practical cases, k is a small constant. Assuming the latter, the total complexity is $O(mN \log N)$. In fact, in practice, in almost all cases during the evaluation of a unit an early stop will occur so that most units will be evaluated in $O(1)$ time, and if the moving region is never equal to the static region, this can be determined in $O(m)$ time.

The general approach for the operations of group 2 is based on a parallel scan of units of the refinement partition. Each pair of units is checked for equality. For `mbool`, `mint`, and `mstring`, such a check is trivial. For `mreal` and `mpoint` we first check whether coefficients are the same: if so, we produce the output unit; otherwise, we intersect the curves and produce the output units (at most a small constant number). In any of the previous cases, the complexity is $O(p)$.

For `mregion`, we process each pair of units with time interval i of the refinement partition as follows: If u and v are different, then we return (i, *false*). Otherwise, we perform a parallel scan of the lists of moving segments to find a pair (s_1, s_2) of different segments. If no pair of different segments is discovered, we return (i, *true*). Otherwise, let s' be the smaller segment among s_1 and s_2 (this segment is guaranteed not to appear in the other list) and compare s' with the remaining segments of the other list, finding k intersections at times $t_1, \ldots, t_k$ such that s' finds an equal counterpart. If $k = 0$, we return (i, *false*). Otherwise, for each time t_i we evaluate both units, sort the obtained segments, and perform a parallel scan to check for equality. We can stop early if a non-matching pair of segments is found. Otherwise, we return an appropriate result unit (*).

Noting that a step labeled (*) requires time $O(u \log u)$, the per-unit time complexity is $O(ku \log u)$. In the worst case $k = O(u)$, but in most practical cases, k is a small constant. Assuming the latter, the total complexity is $O(p\, u_{max} \log u_{max})$. Again, if the two moving regions are never equal, then a pair of units will almost always be handled in $O(1)$ time, and the total time will be $O(p)$.

`intersects`. This predicate checks whether the arguments intersect. Signatures considered are as follows:

```
intersects    points  × mregion  → mbool
              region  × mregion  → mbool
              line    × mregion  → mbool
              mregion × mregion  → mbool
```

For `points × mregion`, we use the corresponding algorithm for the `inside` predicate (see the following text). The `mregion × mregion` case for a number of operations is rather complex and not described here (see Section 8.4). This scheme can be specialized to the cases `region × mregion` and `line × mregion`.

`inside`. This predicate checks if *a* is contained in *b*. Signatures considered are as follows:

```
inside  mregion × points  → mbool
        mregion × line    → mbool
        mpoint  × region   → mbool
        point   × mregion  → mbool
        mpoint  × mregion  → mbool
        points  × mregion  → mbool
        mpoint  × points   → mbool
        mpoint  × line     → mbool
        line    × mregion  → mbool
        region  × mregion  → mbool
        mregion × region   → mbool
        mregion × mregion  → mbool
```

In the first two cases, the result of the operation is always *false*. For `mpoint × region` and `point × mregion` we use the more general algorithm for case `mpoint × mregion` (briefly described in Section 8.2.3). For each unit, the `upoint` value is a line segment in 3D that may stab some of the moving segments of the `uregion` value, which are trapeziums in 3D. In the order of time, with each intersection the `upoint` value alternates between entering and leaving the `uregion` value. Hence, a list of Boolean units is produced that alternates between *true* and *false*. In case no intersections are found, we need to check whether, at the start time of the unit interval, the point was inside the region. This can be implemented by a well-known technique in computational geometry—the "plumbline" algorithm—which counts how many segments in 2D are above the point in 2D. The complexity is $O(N' + K \log k_{max})$.

Exercise 8.3 Assume a `upoint` unit *up* and a `uregion` unit *ur* with the same unit interval $i = (s, e, lc, rc)$ after the refinement partition. According to this description, formulate an algorithm `upoint_inside_uregion(up, ur)` that computes a mapping (sequence) of constant Boolean units expressing when *up* was and was not inside *ur* during *i*. For simplicity, assume that *i* is closed. It is straightforward but a bit lengthy to treat the other cases. ■

In case of `points × mregion`, for each of the points of *a* use the algorithm for the case `point × mregion`. The complexity is $O(M(N + K \log k_{max}))$. For `mpoint × points`, consider each unit of *a*, and for each point of *b* check whether the moving point passes through the considered point. If so, we produce a unit with a *true* value at the right time instant. Afterward sort all produced units by time, then add remaining units with a *false* value. The complexity is $O(mN + r \log r)$. The case `mpoint` × `line` is similar to the previous one, but also consider that, if the projection of a moving segment overlaps with a segment of b, the corresponding result unit is defined on a time interval rather than a single instant. For `line` × `mregion`, `region` × `mregion`, and `mregion` × `region` proceed as in the more general case `mregion mregion`.

<, ≤, ≥, >. These predicates check the order of the two arguments. For $\alpha \in \{$`int, bool, string, real`$\}$, we obtain the signatures:

$$
\begin{array}{rcl}
\langle, \leq, \geq, \rangle & \alpha \times m\alpha & \to \text{mbool} \\
& m\alpha \times \alpha & \to \text{mbool} \\
& m\alpha \times m\alpha & \to \text{mbool}
\end{array}
$$

Algorithms are analogous to those for operation =.

8.3.2 Set Operations

We recall that for set operations regularized set semantics are adopted. For example, forming the union of a `region` and a `points` value yields the same `region` value, because a region cannot contain isolated points.

`intersection`. This predicate computes the intersection of the arguments. For $\alpha \in \{$`int, bool, string, real, point`$\}$ and $\beta \in \{$`points, line, region`$\}$, we obtain the following signatures:

1. $m\alpha$ × α → $m\alpha$
   `Mpoint` × β → `mpoint`
   `mregion` × `point` → `mpoint`
   `mregion` × `region` → `mregion`
2. $m\alpha$ × $m\alpha$ → $m\alpha$
   `mpoint` × `mregion` → `mpoint`
   `mregion` × `mregion` → `mregion`

For all signatures of group 1, we use the corresponding algorithms for operation `at` (see Section 8.2.3).

For the signatures of group 2 (both arguments are moving ones and belong to the same point type), we do a parallel scan of the refinement partition units; for time intervals where the values of the argument are the same, we produce a result unit with such a value. For the cases `mpoint` and `mreal`, this requires solving equation(s). In any case, the complexity is $O(p)$.

The algorithm for case `mpoint` × `mregion` is analogous to the corresponding one for the `inside` operation (see Section 8.3.1), but it reports `upoint` units with the same value as a instead of Boolean units with a *true* value and no unit instead of Boolean units with a *false* value. The `mregion` × `mregion` case is not treated here (see Section 8.4).

union. This operation computes the union of the arguments. Signatures considered are as follows:

```
union  mpoint  × region   → mregion
       mpoint  × mregion  → mregion
       point   × mregion  → mregion
       mregion × region   → mregion
       mregion × mregion  → mregion
```

For mpoin × region, the result is region b for all times for which a is defined (because of the regularized set semantics). Hence, d corresponding uregion units have to be constructed, getting time intervals from scanning the *deftime* index of a. Because sorting is required once to put msegments in the uregion units into the right order, the complexity is $O(dN + N \log N)$. For mpoint × mregion and point × mregion, we simply return b as the result. For mregion × region, we use the more general algorithm for the case mregion × mregion (see Section 8.4).

minus. This operation computes the difference of a and b. For $\alpha \in \{$int, bool, string, real, point$\}$ and $\beta \in \{$points, line, region$\}$, we obtain the following signatures:

```
1. mα       × α        → mα
   α        × mα       → mα
   mα       × mα       → mα
   mpoint   × β        → mpoint
   point    × mregion  → mpoint
   mpoint   × mregion  → mpoint
2. region   × mpoint   → mregion
   mregion  × point    → mregion
   mregion  × mpoint   → mregion
   mregion  × points   → mregion
   mregion  × line     → mregion
3. mregion  × region   → mregion
   region   × mregion  → mregion
   mregion  × mregion  → mregion
```

For all cases where the type of a is a point type (group 1), algorithms are similar to those for intersection, except for the production of result units. The complexities are the same as for the corresponding algorithms for intersection. Algorithms for the cases in group 2 are trivial because of the regularized set semantics. For region × mpoint, we simply transform a into a moving region defined on the same definition time as b, with a complexity $O(dM + M \log M)$ (as discussed previously for union(mpoint × region)), whereas for other type combinations of group 2, we simply return a as the result. For mregion × region and region × mregion, we use the algorithm for the more general case mregion × mregion (see Section 8.4).

8.3.3 **Aggregation**

Aggregation in the unlifted mode reduces sets of points to points. In the lifted mode, it does this for all times of the life span of a moving object. In our reduced type system, we only have to consider moving regions.

center. This operation computes the center of gravity of a moving region over its whole life span as a moving point. The signature is as follows:

center   mregion × mpoint

The algorithm scans the mapping of uregion units. Because a uregion unit develops linearly during the unit interval $i = [t_0, t_1]$, the center of gravity also evolves linearly and can be described as a upoint unit. It is, therefore, sufficient to compute the centers of the regions at times t_0 and t_1 and to determine the pertaining linear function afterward. For computing the center of a region, we first triangulate all faces of the region. This can be done in time $O(u \log u)$ and results in $O(u)$ triangles (see Section 8.4). For each triangle in constant time, we compute its center viewed as a vector and multiply this vector by the area of the triangle. For all triangles, we sum up these weighted products and divide this sum by the sum of all weights (i.e., the areas of all triangles). The resulting vector is the center of the region. Please note that the center of gravity can lie outside of all faces of the region. Altogether, the time complexity for computing the center is $O(u \log u)$. For a uregion unit, by interpolation between the centers at its start and end times, a corresponding upoint unit is determined. The total time for the center operation on a moving region is $O(M \log umax)$.

Exercise 8.4 Let *ur* be a uregion unit and *t* be a time instant. Give the precise formula for **center**(*ur*, *t*).   ∎

8.3.4 **Numeric Properties**

These operations compute some lifted numeric properties for moving regions:

no_components   mregion → mint
perimeter   mregion → mreal
area   mregion → mreal

Here, no_components returns the time-dependent number of components (i.e., faces) of a moving region as a moving integer, and perimeter and area yield the respective quantities as moving reals. The algorithmic scheme is the same for all three operations and very simple. We scan the sequence of units and return the value stored in the respective summary field *unit_no_components*, *unit_perimeter*, or *unit_area*, possibly merging adjacent units with the same unit function. This requires $O(m)$ time for *m* units.

The values for the summary fields are computed when their uregion unit is constructed. The *unit_no_components* is determined as a by-product when the structure of faces within the unit is set up (see Section 8.1). For the *unit_perimeter* function, we have to consider that the boundary of a `uregion` unit consists of moving segments; for each of them, the length evolves by a linear function. Hence, the perimeter, being the sum of these lengths, also evolves by a linear function. The perimeter function can be computed either by summing up the coefficients of all moving segments' length functions or by a linear interpolation between the start and end time perimeter of the unit.

For the *unit_area* function the computation is slightly more complex. The area of a simple static polygon (a cycle) c consisting of the segments $s_0, \ldots, s_{n-1}$ with $s_i = ((x_i, y_i), (x_{(i+1) \bmod n}, y_{(i+1) \bmod n}))$ may be determined by calculating the areas of the trapeziums under each segment s_i down to the x axis[2] and subtracting the areas of the trapeziums under the segments at the bottom of the cycle from the areas of the trapeziums under the segments at the top of the cycle. We can express this by the following formula:

$$area(c) = \sum_{i=0}^{n-1} (x_{(i+1) \bmod n} - x_i) \cdot \frac{y_{(i+1) \bmod n} + y_i}{2}$$

Note that if cycles are connected clockwise, then in this formula top segments will yield positive area contributions and bottom segments negative ones, as desired. Hence, the formula computes correctly a positive area value for outer cycles (see Section 8.1.2). Indeed, for hole cycles (represented in counterclockwise order), it computes a negative value, which is also correct, because the areas of hole cycles need to be subtracted from the region area. This means that we can simply compute for all cycles of a region their area according to the previous formula and form the sum of these area contributions to determine the area of the region.

In a `uregion` unit, where we have moving segments, we can replace each x_i and each y_i by a linear function. For a moving unit cycle c we therefore have

$$area(c, t) = \sum_{i=0}^{n-1} (x_{(i+1) \bmod n}(t) - x_i(t)) \cdot \frac{y_{(i+1) \bmod n}(t) + y_i(t)}{2}$$

Each factor in the sum is the difference, respectively, sum of two linear functions. Hence, it is a linear function again, and therefore the product is a quadratic polynomial. The sum of all quadratic polynomials is a quadratic polynomial as well. Again, we can sum up the area function contributions over all moving cycles of a `uregion` unit to get the area function for the unit. The cost of computing the *unit_perimeter* and *unit_area* fields is clearly linear in the size of the unit—that is, $O(u)$ time. In all cases, it is dominated by the remaining cost for constructing the `uregion` unit.

---

[2]This assumes that y values are positive. If they are not, we can instead form trapeziums by subtracting a sufficiently negative y value.

8.3.5 Distance and Direction

In this section, we discuss lifted distance and direction operations.

distance. The distance function determines the minimum distance between its
two argument objects for each instant of their common life span. The pertaining
signatures are for $\alpha, \beta \in \{\text{point}, \text{region}\}$:

distance	mreal	× real	→ mreal
	mreal	× mreal	→ mreal
	mα	× β	→ mreal
	mα	× mβ	→ mreal

For all function instances, the algorithm scans the mapping of the units of the
moving object(s) and returns one or more ureal units for each argument unit.
The computation of the distance between an mreal value and a real value s
leads to several cases. If $ur = (i, (a, b, c, r)) \in$ ureal with $i = [t_0, t_1]$, $t_0 < t_1$, and
$r = false$, the unit function of ur describes the quadratic polynomial $at^2 + bt + c$.
The distance between ur and s is then given by the function $f(t) = at^2 + bt +
c - s$, which is a quadratic polynomial too. Unfortunately, this function usually
does not always yield a positive value for all $t \in i$, as required in the definition of
distance. Therefore, it is necessary to determine the instants of time when $f(t) =
0$ and to invert the value of the function in those time intervals when it is
negative.

To program this, we need to distinguish various cases, which is a bit tedious.
In any case, we obtain as a result either one, two, or three new ureal units. If
$r = true$, the function of ur describes the square root polynomial:

$$\sqrt{at^2 + bt + c}$$

The distance between ur and s is then given by the following function:

$$\sqrt{at^2 + bt + c} - s$$

Unfortunately, this term is not expressible by a square root polynomial and thus
not by an ureal unit. Hence, this operation is not implementable within this
discrete model.

Similarly as discussed previously for the derivative operation, we believe it
is better to offer a partial implementation than none. Hence, for square root polynomial units, we consider the result as undefined and return no unit at all (again,
as for derivative). The derivative operation can also be used here to check for
which part of the argument the result could be computed. In both cases, the time
complexity is $O(1)$ per unit and $O(m)$ for a moving real.

The algorithm for computing the distance between two mreal values is similar
to the previous one, because a real value in the previous context can be regarded
as a "static" moving real. The difference is that first a refinement partition of both
moving reals has to be computed, which takes $O(m + n)$. If $ur = (i, (a, b, c, r))$

and $vr = (i, (d, e, f, s))$ are corresponding `ureal` units of both refined moving reals with $r = s = false$, their distance is given by the quadratic polynomial $(a - d)t_2 + (b - e)t + (c - f)$, which has to be processed as in the previous algorithm. If $r = true$ or $s = true$, no unit is returned. The time complexity of this algorithm is $O(m + n)$.

We now consider the case of an `mpoint` value and a `point` value $p = (x', y')$ with $x', y' \in$ `real`. If $up = (i, (x_0, x_1, y_0, y_1)) \in$ `upoint` with $x_0, x_1, y_0, y_1 \in$ `real`, the evaluation of the linearly moving point at time t is given by $(x(t), y(t)) = (x_1t + x_0, y_1t + y_0)$. Then, the distance is

$$\text{distance}((up, p), t) = \sqrt{(x(t) - x')^2 + (y(t) - y')^2}$$
$$= \sqrt{(x_1t + x_0 - x')^2 + (y_1t + y_0 - y')^2}$$

Further evaluation of this term leads to a square root of a quadratic polynomial in t, which is returned as a `ureal` unit. The time complexity for a moving point and a point is $O(m)$. The distance calculation between two `mpoint` values requires first the computation of the refinement partition in $O(m + n)$ time. The distance of two corresponding `upoint` units up and vp is then determined similarly to the previous case and results again in a square root of a quadratic polynomial in t, which is returned as a `ureal` unit. This algorithm requires $O(m + n)$ time.

The remaining operation instances can be grouped according to two algorithmic schemes. The first algorithmic scheme relates to the distance computation between a moving point and a region, between a moving point and a moving region, and between a moving region and a point. The second algorithmic scheme refers to the distance computation between a moving region and a region as well as between two moving regions. The grouping is possible because the spatial argument objects can be regarded as "static" spatiotemporal objects. Therefore, the first algorithmic scheme deals with the distance between a moving point and a moving region, and the second algorithmic scheme deals with the distance between two moving regions. Both algorithmic schemes are rather complex and are not dealt with here (see Section 8.4).

`direction`. This operation returns the angle of the line from the first to the second point at each instant of the common life span of the argument objects:

```
direction   mpoint × point  → mreal
            point  × point  → mreal
            mpoint × mpoint → mreal
```

Unfortunately, the results of these operation instances cannot be represented as a moving real because their computation requires the use of the arc tangent function. This can be shown as follows: Given two points $p = (x_1, y_1)$ and $q = (x_2, y_2)$, the slope between the horizontal axis and the line through p and q can be determined by the following:

$$\tan \alpha = \frac{y_2 - y_1}{x_2 - x_1}. \text{ Thus, } \alpha = \arctan \frac{y_2 - y_1}{x_2 - x_1} \text{ holds}$$

We can continue this to the temporal case. For two upoint units (after the calculation of the refinement partition), as well as for a upoint unit and a point value, this leads to

$$\alpha(t) = \arctan \frac{y_2(t) - y_1(t)}{x_2(t) - x_1(t)} \text{ and } \alpha(t) = \arctan \frac{y_2(t) - y_1}{x_2(t) - x_1}, \text{ respectively}$$

Consequently, this operation is not implementable in this discrete model.

8.3.6 Boolean Operations

Boolean operations are included in the scope of operations to be temporally lifted.

and, or. These operators represent the lifted logical conjunction disjunction connectives, respectively. Their signatures are as follows:

```
and, or   mbool × bool  → mbool
          mbool × bool  → mbool
```

For the first operator instance, we scan all Boolean units in a and evaluate for each unit the unlifted logical connective applied to its Boolean value and to b, returning a corresponding unit. Time complexity is $O(m)$. For the second operator instance, we compute the refinement partition and then proceed in the same way for pairs of units. Time complexity is $O(p)$.

not. This operation is the lifted logical negation operator. Its signature is as follows:

```
not       mbool → mbool
```

Here, we just scan the units, negating their values, in $O(m)$ time.

8.4 RESOURCES

The presentation in this chapter is based on the article by Cotelo Lema et al. (2003), which gives a detailed study of algorithms for the operations using the representations of the discrete model in Forlizzi et al. (2000). The article by Cotelo Lema et al. (2003) especially deals with the mregion × mregion case for the set operations intersection, union, and difference and for the predicates intersects and inside, as well as with distance operations between two moving spatial objects. The more complicated algorithms have been omitted here. That article also considers data structures for spatial data types, which are similar to those in Güting et al. (1995) for the *ROSE* algebra.

Other resources about spatial data structures and algorithms can be found in computational geometry literature (de Berg et al., 2000; Preparata & Shamos, 1991) and in spatial database literature (Rigaux et al., 2002; Shekhar & Chawla, 2003). The plane sweep paradigm is explained in Bentley and Ottmann (1979). Triangulation of a region, needed for the center operation, is described in Garey et al. (1978).

Improving the Model

This chapter looks at improving a model, which presupposes that at least a model exists. However, just because a model exists doesn't mean that it has no problems, or that it is the best or most appropriate model that the data permits. This chapter looks at the process of turning the initially created model into one that better fits the data and the business problem. Although most of the processes apply as much to improving an explanatory model as to improving a classificatory model, most of the issues here are addressed as if the model to be improved is classificatory—except, of course, where the issues discussed are specific to one type of model or the other.

The process of improving a model can, for discussion purposes, be broken into two broad categories: discovering where the model has problems and fixing the discovered problems.

This chapter is divided into two major, but very connected, sections that align with these two categories and their associated activities:

1. The first major section discusses how to determine model performance by performing a number of checks.
2. The second major section covers what to do about the results of the checks, or, essentially, how to fix the model.

These two activities—diagnosing model problems and applying remedies—are both applied in order to refine the initial model. This chapter presents the second step in the mining/refining process.

Regardless of where it occurs, the ultimate purpose underlying all of the issues and processes discussed in this chapter is to deliver a model that represents the business-relevant, meaningful relationships in the dataset as perfectly as the data permits and to do so as simply as possible. (In fact, this can serve as a good definition of business data mining!)

It is in this stage of refining the initial mined model that a data miner must expect to start revisiting earlier parts at least of the mining process and perhaps of the whole modeling process. None of the processes is carried out in isolation from any other part. Mining is an interactive whole, and all of the processes

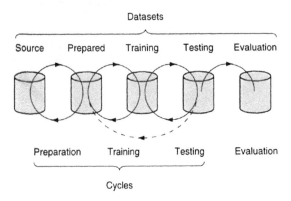

FIGURE 9.1

Interaction between mining activities and datasets.

interact—hopefully to improve the model. It is here, too, that the main use of training and test datasets comes into its own. As Figure 9.1 shows, mining involves many loops through an iterative cycle in order to create the best possible model in the training dataset that performs as well as possible in the test dataset. That bears repeating—models are created on the data in the training dataset, but all of the checking for problems and improvements happens in the test dataset.

During the following discussion, it is very important to remain aware of which dataset is being used for which purpose. In every case in this chapter, whenever there's a change to the data—to the variables included in a model, to the individual variables, or to any other feature or parameter of the model, or if there is any adjustment to the data—the cycle works as follows: rebuild the model in the *training* dataset, and look for any change in results when applying the new model in the *test* dataset.

If the data needs adjusting, remember to make the necessary adjustments in all three datasets, but don't change the instances (records) that are included in the datasets. That is to say, for any individual model or integrated group of models, it's important that the same records stay in each dataset throughout. If the datasets were rebuilt from scratch on each modification, as modeling progressed the model would be tested on data that in earlier iterations had been used for training. This mixing of training and test data would pretty much invalidate the purpose of the separate datasets and wholly undermine the purpose of the evaluation dataset altogether.

Throughout this chapter, the terms *predict* and *predictive* are used with their usual colloquial meaning. In some cases, an exception is made so that a clear distinction can be drawn between classification and prediction. This is because, at the present state of the art, a miner builds predictive models only by combining particular system modeling skills and techniques with classificatory and explanatory modeling. However, it is normal usage to speak of a classificatory model "predicting" an output value when it is actually making a class assignment, which is why in this chapter it is the colloquial use of *prediction* that is intended. Where predictive is used other than in its meaning of "most likely class assignment," the context will make that clear.

9.1 LEARNING FROM ERRORS

We are all encouraged to learn from our mistakes, and it's no different when mined models make the mistakes. There is a lot to be learned from closely examining the errors made by a classification model. These errors represent the difference between what the model predicts and what the actual outcome turns out to be in the real world. Whenever a model turns out to be worth considering for application, the next step is to look at the errors that it makes in the test dataset—and often, actually looking is a useful thing to do, not merely looking in a metaphoric sense. However, suppose a model showed a binary outcome, BUYER, taking values of either 1 or 0. The initial classification model made (with WizWhy) would likely predict either 1 or 0. Graphical error plots aren't very helpful in this case. The absolute value of the error can only be either 0 or 1, and the best way to look at binary outcome model performance is to use the confusion matrix. For a binary classification model predicting a binary outcome, the confusion matrix reveals the most about the model's performance.

Suppose a model produced a continuous score that was turned into a binary classification. The *residual value,* or simply the *residual,* is the name given to the difference between the predicted and the actual values. In this case, actually looking at the residuals from the continuous score as well as looking at the confusion matrix begins to be helpful. Residual values are determined by subtracting the predicted value from the actual value. Symbolically, this might be represented as $r = a - p,$ where r represents the residual value, a represents the actual value, and p represents the predicted value. In the case of the continuous score classification model, the actual values are all between 0 and 1, so the predictions should also be (and actually are in this example) between 0 and 1—thus, all predicted values are positive numbers. Obviously, in the case when the actual value is 0, all of the residual values have to be negative, because 0 minus any positive number has to give a negative result, and the predictions are all positive numbers. Similarly, when the actual value is 1, all the residuals will be positive because 1 (the actual value) minus any positive number between 0 and 1 (the prediction) has to return a positive result.

It's worth remarking that many tools do not limit the range of their predictions to the range found in the training dataset, and using such a tool in this example could result in predicted values that lie outside the range of 0-1. This would make a difference in the appearance of the plotted graph, but it would make no material difference to the interpretation of the plots.

9.1.1 **Looking at Errors**

The first graphical display (see Figure 9.2) shows the predicted values versus the residual value. This is the place to start because at runtime—that is, when the model is applied in the real world to real-world data—nothing is known about the actual value except for the prediction made by the model. The prediction is intended to be the best possible estimate of the actual value given the data available. (Usually, if the real-world, runtime data includes the value to be predicted, there isn't any need to make the prediction.) It is important to get a feel for (and later to quantify) the differences between the model's predictions of the values and the actual values. In the training (and test and evaluation) datasets, the actual value is known, because that is what is being used to train (test or evaluate) the model. So it is quite possible to check the residuals made by the model. It is always possible to characterize the pattern made by the residuals across the range of the prediction. Very often, the pattern has nothing to offer toward improving the model. However, sometimes the pattern of the residuals can be used to improve the model, and it is this sort of pattern that a miner must seek.

Predicted versus Residual Diagnostic Plot

The points shown in Figure 9.2 form what is known as an *XY plot.* Each point is plotted in a position on the graph to represent its values on two measurements, the predicted value and the residual value. For example, the extreme left point shown is at a value of about 0.75 on the prediction scale and about −0.75 on the residual scale. The coincidence of these two values isn't accidental. The residual

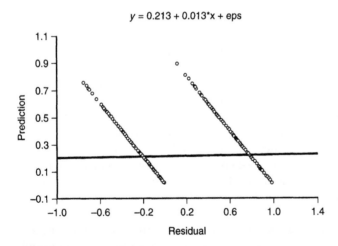

$$y = 0.213 + 0.013\text{*}x + eps$$

FIGURE 9.2

Prediction versus residual XY scatterplot in CREDIT estimating BUYER with continuous prediction and binary actual values.

value indicates, being negative, that the actual value was 0 and, as shown, the predicted value was 0.75. With an actual value of 0, using $r = a - p$ to create the residual, this has to produce a residual value equal in magnitude, but opposite in sign, to the predicted value. Thus, with an actual value of 0 and a predicted value of 0.75, the residual has to be $r = 0 - 0.75 = -0.75$. Because this is the case for all the residuals when the actual value is 0, they have to line up in a 45-degree slope because in every case, the magnitude of the residual is identical to the magnitude of the prediction. When the actual value is 1, the magnitude of the residual is not identical to the predicted value, but an analogous situation arises, and these residuals too arrange themselves in a 45-degree sloping line. The two lines are displaced only by whether the actual value was 0 or 1. (Because the graph is not reproduced exactly square, the appearance of the angle of slope may not seem to be 45 degrees. A simple algebraic calculation of line slope, however, will indicate the slope as 45 degrees, and it is this algebraic sense of slope that is intended in this discussion.)

Pay close attention to the almost horizontal line that crosses the plot at a value of approximately 0.2 on the prediction (*y*) axis. This is a linear regression line fitted to the residual values. Linear regression is often thought of as producing a prediction and, although there is no interest in its predictive role here, if it were to be used predictively, it would be estimating the predicted values using only the information in the residuals. Clearly, if the model has done a good job, the residuals won't be useful for predicting the model's predictions; if the residuals did carry any information about how to make a better prediction, the prediction could be improved—and that is precisely the point that the plot in Figure 9.2 is used to check.

The almost horizontal regression line shown in Figure 9.2 indicates that in this case, the residuals do, in fact, carry almost no additional information. In the regression equation shown above the illustration, the number "0.013" shows the amount of slope. A slope of 0 is absolutely horizontal, and in this plot, it is very close to horizontal. A slope of 0 would mean that regardless of the predicted value, the best value to predict for the residual would be approximately 0.2, which is the average value of all the residuals. But why is the regression line tilted even a little bit? Doesn't this indicate that there is some minute improvement possible?

Recall that the model was created on the training dataset. This plot and all of the others examined here are built in the test dataset. In the training dataset, the plot does produce an absolutely flat line. The test dataset, however, isn't identical with the training dataset; thus, the model isn't quite a perfect fit. However, by eyeball, this line is near enough flat to indicate that the model in practice fits both datasets (training and test) about equally well, or equally badly. The average residual error is about 0.2 regardless of the predicted value or the actual value.

For the more technically inclined reader, it is possible to determine if this slope is statistically significantly different from one that is absolutely horizontal. However, beware of such measures. With the very high numbers of instances prevalent in data mining, every difference can become statistically significant, but statistical significance, although important in context, isn't a good measure in this case. For a miner, by far the best practice is to eyeball the residuals and to become familiar with the look and feel of these plots.

Predicted versus Actual Diagnostic Plot

The other useful XY plot that a miner needs to become familiar with shows predicted versus actual values. Figure 9.3 shows a predicted/actual plot for the same model as in Figure 9.2. This is similar to the previous plot except that the values form vertical columns. Because BUYER takes only two values, the predictions are constrained to line up at one of those two values on this graph. The fitted regression line shown here crosses the column at BUYER = 0 with a prediction value of about 0.19. At BUYER = 1, the prediction value is about 0.29. These two values represent the mean of the predicted values in each column and therefore the mean of the prediction values for each class. In other words, when the actual value of BUYER is 0, the average value of all of the predicted values is about 0.19; when the actual value of BUYER is 1, the average value of all of the predicted values is about 0.29. The slope of the line, in some sense, represents the quality of the model, but a considerable improvement over chance.

9.1.2 Predicting Errors

Looking at the errors in the form of residuals provides a fair amount of information. However, if the original dataset could somehow be used to predict what the

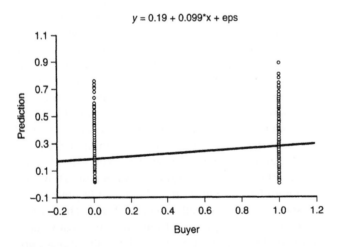

FIGURE 9.3

Prediction versus actual XY scatterplot in CREDIT estimating BUYER with continuous prediction and binary actual BUYER values.

errors were going to be, that prediction of the errors could be used to improve the prediction. In a sense, that is what the linear regression tried to do with the results shown in Figure 9.2.

Data mining tools are, or should be, very good at characterizing relationships, whether linear or nonlinear. The resulting relationship between the actual and predicted values, however rough and imprecise, should at least be linear, so a linear comparison is quite a reasonable way to check on the actual relationship. However, as a sort of "sanity check," it's worth building a model that attempts to predict the value of the residual. Again, this model will be built using the training dataset input battery and predicting the residual value in the training dataset as the output battery. This process of creating the residual test model is illustrated in Figures 9.4, 9.5, and 9.6.

To make the initial model and residual model:

1. Build an initial model (Figure 9.4).

2. Apply the initial model to the training dataset, creating a set of predictions (Figure 9.4).

3. Calculate the residuals using the predicted values in the training dataset (Figure 9.4).

4. Add a variable to the training dataset input battery containing the value of the residual (Figure 9.5).

5. Build a second model to predict residuals using all of the training data *except* the original output variable and the predicted values (Figure 9.5).

Thus, the residual test model must not include any actual values or predicted values from the original model. If using a multiple-algorithm mining tool, it's worth building the second model with a different algorithm than the original model.

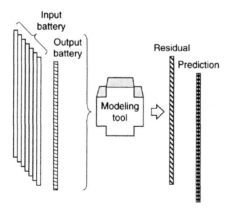

FIGURE 9.4

Initial model predicts the output battery.

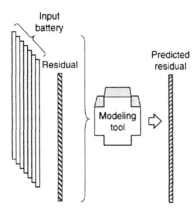

FIGURE 9.5

Residual model uses original input battery and residual as output battery.

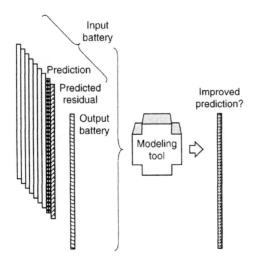

FIGURE 9.6

Residual test model adds prediction and predicted residual to original input battery to model the original output battery.

Next, build the residual test model (Figure 9.6):

1. Include the prediction and predicted residuals in the input battery.
2. Build a model to predict the original output battery.

In doing this for the binary classification of BUYER, it turns out that the residual model isn't all that good. The original model shows a correlation

Table 9.1a Original Model

Model	Is 1	Is 0	Tot	Efficiency
Class 1	313	420	733	42.70%
Class 0	334	1732	2066	83.83%
Tot	647	2152	2799	73.06%

Table 9.1b Residuals Test Model Result in Test Dataset

Model	Is 1	Is 0	Tot	Efficiency
Class 1	357	491	848	42.10%
Class 0	290	1661	1951	85.14%
Tot	647	2152	2799	72.10%

coefficient (one way of estimating how well a model makes its predictions) of about 0.06. The model predicting the residuals has a correlation with the residuals of about 0.02. However, the test is what happens if the output from the two models—the original prediction and the residual models—are combined to predict BUYER, as shown in Figure 9.5. Is there any improvement?

Actually, applying the combined model to the training dataset does, in this case, produce an apparent improvement—in the training dataset. However, when the combined model is applied to the test dataset, the situation changes. Tables 9.1a and 9.1b show the story. Table 9.1a duplicates the confusion matrix for the original model. This is the confusion matrix for the best classification model for classifying BUYER. If the residual test model does in fact improve performance, then the confusion matrix will show it. However, as Table 9.1b shows, although model performance in the training dataset may have been improved, it certainly hasn't happened in the test dataset.

What has happened here is that the combined model has learned some of the noise—relationships that exist in the training data but not in the test data. However, do notice that whereas overall performance is down and performance classifying BUYER = 1 is also down (both marginally), performance on classifying BUYER = 0 seems somewhat improved. In truth, these small changes are almost certainly due to nothing more than noise and instability in the model and, to all intents and purposes, information from the residuals in this case makes no meaningful difference. That is to say that minute fluctuations in performance of this magnitude (or larger) should be expected simply by applying the model to different, fully representative datasets. The conclusion? In this case, the residuals contain no additional usable relationship in predicting the actual value.

9.1.3 Continuous Classifier Residuals

With only two classes, the residual plot and predicted/actual plot can produce only limited additional insight over that offered by the confusion matrix. In fact, for a two-class output classification, the confusion matrix pretty much offers the best insight into the workings of the model. When the output variable is to all intents and purposes a continuous variable, confusion matrices become totally impractical, and the only way to understand model performance is by using these plots.

As in the previous example, start with an XY plot of the residual values versus the predicted values. When the output variable is continuous, it is necessary to order the residuals by the prediction value. It doesn't really matter whether the order is from least to greatest or greatest to least, just so long as the miner knows which end represents which values.

Figure 9.7 shows the residuals plot for a real-world dataset. A couple of features jump out from this image, even at a quick glance. One feature is that the mean value of the errors is about 0. In fact, with the exception of a couple of distortions (to be mentioned in a moment), the mean of the residual values is specifically set by the model to be 0, and this point is significant enough to be worth additional discussion.

Most algorithms that fit functions, curves, and other characterizations to data use one of a relatively few methods to determine how good the fit is, and the algorithms adjust their parameters until the fit, according to the criterion chosen,

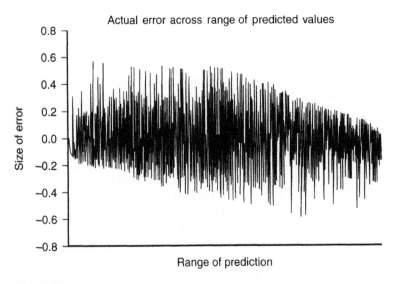

FIGURE 9.7

Ordered residuals from a model predicting a continuous predictor variable.

is as good as possible. There are, in fact, relatively few metrics for determining the level of fitness, but the most popular for continuous variables is mean least squares (MLS). This involves minimizing the sum of the weighted squares of the residuals. It is a feature of MLS, and of most of the other goodness of fit metrics, that the mean of the residuals is 0—at least in the training dataset. There are other metrics that do not require the best fit to produce residuals with a mean of 0, but their popularity, at least in general purpose mining tools, is vanishingly small compared to MLS. In fact, at this writing, all of the commercial tools known to the author use goodness-of-fit tests that should produce mean-of-zero residuals.

The point here is that when the miner looks at the residuals in the test dataset, they may not have a mean of 0. Generally speaking, the divergence from 0 represents a problem of some sort—insufficient data, poor model, problems with the data, inappropriate modeling tool, or some other problem. However, if the divergence from 0 in the test dataset is large, it may be worth checking the mean of the residuals in the training dataset. If it isn't 0 there, either the tool or algorithm is somehow "broken" or the tool is using some other best-fit metric. As noted, at this writing, all of the commercially available tools should produce residuals averaging 0 and will likely continue to do so. But there are alternatives. Just because the residuals do not have a mean of 0, it does not *necessarily* follow that there is a problem, but it does bear investigation.

In general then (and as of this writing), the mean of residuals in the test dataset should be 0. In addition, a straight line fitted across the range of the prediction with linear regression should fit through the center of the residual distribution and should be flat along the zero point. Thus, ideally, not only should the mean of the residuals be 0, but across the range of the prediction the residuals also should fit around the zero line. The mean of the residual distribution in Figure 9.7 does fall along the zero point, but it doesn't fit the zero line. At the left end of the plot, the mean seems to be above the zero point, and at the right end below it. Is this a problem?

The "shoulders" are illustrated in Figure 9.8 along with a zero line. In fact, this is a fairly common appearance of residuals, and in this case, it doesn't represent any problem with the model at all. This is a case where the actual values of the output range vary between 0 and 1. What is happening here is that the model is limiting its predicted output to remain within the range of the actual values seen when training. The residuals appear to be fairly random in size except where the limiting clips them.

The underlying model in this case may attempt to make predictions that vary outside the limits of 0 and 1. However, the limit on the output says, in effect, "If the prediction attempted is less than 0, make it 0. If the prediction attempted is greater than 1, make it 1. If it's between 0 and 1, use the value as it is." Thus, as the range of the prediction approaches 0 (at the left end) and 1 (at the right end), the possible range of the error is clipped, resulting in the regular "shoulders" shown.

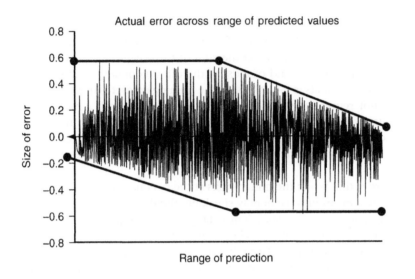

FIGURE 9.8

Ordered residuals highlighting features of the distribution.

Even with these clipped shoulders, the distribution of the residuals is fairly close to a normal distribution, as Figure 9.9 shows. This is a histogram of the residuals, along with a normal curve for comparison. This is another diagnostic test that the model has fit the data well. Recall that whatever the distribution of the input data, and however nonlinear the relationships between input battery and output battery, a mining tool should, if effective, characterize the fit between input and output to include any peculiarities of distribution and to accommodate any nonlinearity present. What remains should pretty much be random noise, which is typically (although not always) characterized by being normally distributed. Almost all—from the author's experience, more than 99 percent—of all business mining situations produce residuals that are at least approximately normal or distorted from normal. However, dealing with other types of residual distribution when modeling with continuous input and output battery variables is an advanced modeling topic not covered here. In effect, if the residuals' distribution is far from normal, it almost certainly indicates a potential problem with the model.

If the histogram of residuals in the test dataset is far from normal, compare it with the histogram of residuals in the training dataset. If the distributions are dissimilar between training and test datasets, the problem is most likely with the data. If the distributions are similar and both are far from normal, the culprit may well be the modeling tool. If possible, try a different algorithm and check again. However, it's possible that the input battery, while being generally representative, isn't representative over particular ranges. In other words, the input data may be

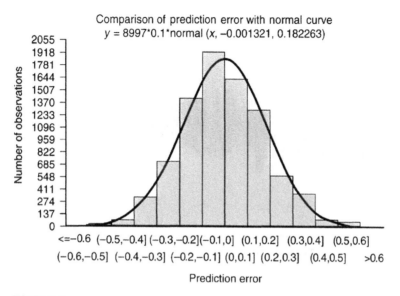

FIGURE 9.9

Histogram of residual distribution.

clustered so that some parts of the range are relatively sparsely described by the data available. The answer, of course, may be more, or better, or more balanced data.

9.1.4 Continuous Classifier Residuals versus Actual Values Plot

Figures 9.7 and 9.8 showed the residual values plotted against the predicted values in an XY plot. Recall that at runtime, the best available estimate of the actual value is the prediction produced by the model. We know for sure that there will be errors, and using training and test datasets (which have actual values for the output variable available to train the model), it's possible to know the actual residual error. Looking at plots of residuals versus predicted values graphically shows what can be expected when the model is actually deployed. Figures 9.7 and 9.8 show that the model constructed in this data produces unbiased errors. This doesn't mean that the model is as good as it can be—it might be possible, for instance, to reduce the variance of the residuals, which will result in a model that produces more accurate predictions. However, what these figures do show is that there is no systematic error in the model at runtime. If, for instance, all of the predictions were high when the predict value was near the top of its range and low when the predict value was near the bottom of its range, that would be a type of systematic error, and it could be corrected. However, no such systematic error appears.

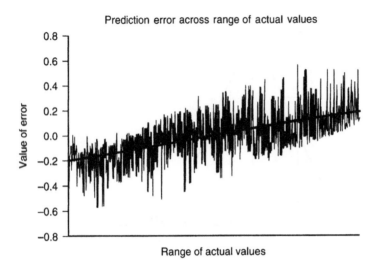

FIGURE 9.10

Actual versus residual plot.

Figure 9.10, on the other hand, seems to show exactly such a systematic error. This shows the residuals, in the same dataset, and uses the same model as in Figure 9.8. This time, however, the residuals are plotted against the ordered actual value rather than the ordered predicted value. The mean of these residuals is also 0, but the linear regression line fitted shows a clear rise from left to right. Does this represent a systematic error?

No, actually it doesn't, at least not a systematic error in the model or in the raw prediction. There is a systematic bias here, but with the data available, there isn't anything that can be done about it as far as the predictions produced by the model are concerned. So what does it represent?

Actually, it's no more than the result of the limit function. Consider the effect of the limit function on the left end of the range. The raw model would make errors by predicting values that are outside the output variable's actual range. These values are "trimmed" off by the limit function. On the left side where the actual value is approaching 0 (as a result of trimming), all of the positive errors that the unlimited model would have made have been truncated, leaving only the negative errors, thus pulling down the average values. On the right side, the reverse is true—the negative errors have been removed, leaving only the positive errors. Thus, the limit function has produced this bias. So there is indeed a bias in the estimates or predictions of the output value, but this bias has been deliberately and knowingly introduced to ensure that the predictions stay in the original range of the output.

Beware when evaluating residual plots because, although bias is evident here, it isn't unanticipated and shouldn't be unexpected. The algorithm embedded in the tool that produced these models is of a type that doesn't inherently limit itself to making predictions that remain in the original range of the output. The algorithm in the tool, then, is occasionally trying to predict values of more than 1 and less than 0. Some algorithms do indeed behave this way, whereas others inherently will not make predictions that are outside the range present in the training data. The tools that implement algorithms that can make out-of-range predictions often do indeed "adjust" the predictions to maintain them inside the actual range in the output battery. (One of the better-known statistical techniques that makes similar adjustments is logistic regression, so this is not a "data mining algorithm problem." It's simply one way of dealing with prediction range difficulties in any quantitative model.)

So although there is bias here, there is nothing "wrong" in this particular case. However, the miner needs to take careful note whenever this type of pattern occurs and to make quite sure that the source of any bias like this is fully understood and is not, in fact, a problem with the data, the modeling tool, or the model.

9.1.5 Continuous Classifier Actual versus Predicted Values Plot

Another plot that a miner should routinely examine is an XY plot of actual values versus predicted values, as is shown in Figure 9.11. In addition to the data points, shown by small circles, the line running from lower left to upper right is a linear

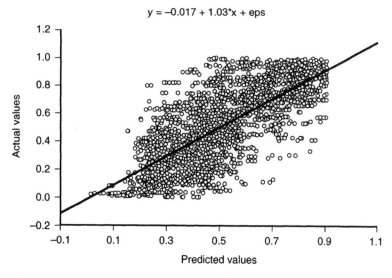

FIGURE 9.11

Actual versus predicted values scatterplot.

regression line fitted to the points. The equation for the line is shown below the title of the plot.

A glance at this figure shows clearly that the actual values range from 0 to 1 and that the predicted values range only from 0 to 0.9. At first glance, this seems to be strange, and it's worth investigating why the tool produced predictions with this pattern. Perhaps there is some error in the settings for the tool, or perhaps the training data was somehow missing any values above 0.9. Whatever the reason, this needs to be checked because it is an unexpected finding. (In this case, it turned out to be a bug in the limit code.)

The problem here is that the distributions of predicted values and actual values differ. Different distributions mean that the predictions are biased because, in an ideal model, the distributions of predicted and actual values will be identical. A quite reasonable way to check would be to compare histograms of the two distributions. However, the model checking techniques later in this section reveal distribution problems as well as other useful information.

It's also well worth the time to try to fit a curve to this type of plot, as shown in Figure 9.12. The relationship should be linear, however much the points vary about the diagonal. The curve fitted should be very close to a straight line, although it almost certainly won't be perfect. Data mining tools should model nonlinearity very well, so the predicted/actual values relationship should be pretty much linear, with all of the nonlinearity accounted for in the model. If there is an evident curve that clearly fits the data better than the diagonal, it is an indication that the model is *underspecified*, which means not complex enough to capture

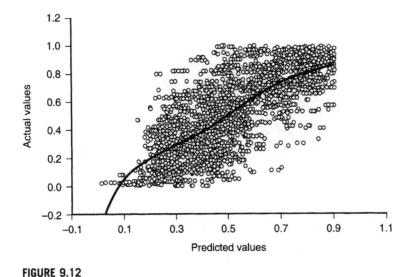

FIGURE 9.12

Actual versus predicted values scatterplot with nonlinear fitted curve.

the nonlinearity present. (An *overspecified* model captures too much complexity, so it characterizes noise.)

Remember that the fit may not be a perfect straight line not only because of random variation, but also because the model was fitted to the training data and all of these evaluations have to be made in the test dataset. In Figure 9.12, the curve shown potentially had a great deal of flexibility and could have been very curved indeed—if the data warranted it. Except for the lower left portion, which is essentially out of the range of the plot, the curve appears to be close to a straight line; this shows that the model has done a good job of modeling any nonlinearity present in the input battery to output battery relationship. (As it turns out, in the dataset used for this illustration, there happened to be a highly nonlinear relationship between the batteries, so the model has, in fact, done a good job of characterizing it.)

Returning now to Figure 9.11, regardless of why the prediction range is truncated, the diagonal regression line shows that this model has characterized the relationships well. The ideal result would show that all of the predicted values were identical to the actual values. If that were the case, the XY plotted points would all fall exactly on the diagonal running from (predicted value, actual value) 0,0 to 1,1. The points themselves by no means fit this ideal, but the regression fitted to this predicted/actual plot line does fall almost exactly on this ideal. On the left of the plot, it passes almost exactly through the 0,0 point, and on the right, it passes almost equally exactly through the 1,1 point. In addition, the slope of the linear regression line is close to perfect, which would be a slope of 1:1. The number "1.03" in the regression equation below the plot title in Figure 9.11 indicates that for every change of 1 unit in Y, this line changes by 1.03 in X, which is indeed very close to 1:1.

Thus, on average, the model has pretty well captured the relationship between the input dataset, as expressed in the Figure 9.12 scatterplot, of predicted value versus actual output value. But pretty well on average isn't perfect. Although there are 10,000 points in this test dataset, some of them are poor as predicted values because they lie far from the line. The final basic question that a miner needs to be able to answer is, how good a model can be expected? Part of the answer to that question can be determined from a variance plot, which is addressed in the next section.

9.1.6 Continuous Classifier Variance Plot

Figure 9.13 shows the variance plot associated with this dataset. This shows the variance of the error, or residual, across the range of the prediction. A prediction of 0 is shown on the left increasing across the plot until, at the right side, there is a prediction of maximum value (which should be 1, although we now know that it's actually 0.9 as a result of the bug in the limit function).

Variance is a straightforward measurement. It simply expresses how much the value of a group of values varies from the mean value of the group. In this case,

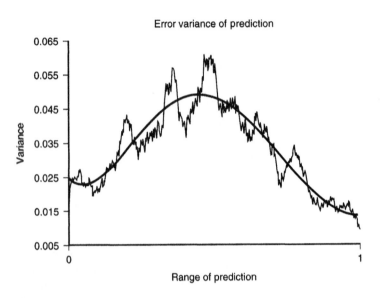

Error variance of prediction

FIGURE 9.13

Actual and smoothed variance in residual across the range of the prediction.

the measurement is of how much the residual, or error, varies from the predicted value. In this case, it indicates the limits of confidence for any particular value of the prediction. (Showing confidence bands above and below the predicted value is another way of showing the same information, but it is more difficult for a miner to generate. A spreadsheet program such as Excel can be easily used to create a variance plot—or almost any of the plots shown if they aren't available elsewhere—and can therefore be used as a basic mining technique.)

The curve shown fairly much speaks for itself. The variance is highest around the middle values of the prediction and is lowest when the prediction is nearest to 1. Variance can be extremely useful in understanding the model's performance. However, Figure 9.14 shows what, on a cursory glance, may seem to be an almost identical plot. However, although the differences are small, for explaining model performance this plot may serve better than the previous one. This figure shows the standard deviation of the error over the range of the prediction.

Because we know (from Figure 9.9) that the distribution of the error term is nearly normal, it is relatively easy to explain the "reliability" of the prediction from the properties of the standard deviation. For instance (and these figures can easily be found in a table describing the area under the standard normal curve in any basic statistical text), because approximately 68 percent of the instances fall within ± one standard deviation of the mean, then in the worst case prediction (which seems to be a prediction of about 0.5), we know that 68 percent of the actual values will fall between about 30.22 from the prediction value, so between $0.5 - 0.22 = 0.28$ and $0.5 + 0.22 - 0.72$. (The value of 0.22 is derived from the

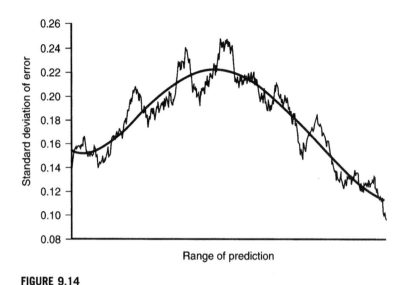

FIGURE 9.14

Actual and smoothed standard deviation of error in residual across the range of the prediction.

maximum height of the fitted curve in Figure 9.14.) Thus, it's fairly easy to determine that about 70 percent of the time, when this model predicts the value to be 0.5, the true value will lie between 0.28 and 0.72.

Similarly, for any point on the curve, the reliability of the prediction can be easily described in terms of how many of the actual values (as a percentage) can be expected to be within what distance of the predicted value.

9.1.7 Perfect Models

Perfect models rarely, if ever, occur. Even very good models that are close to perfect are highly suspicious. Genuinely, justifiably perfect models are only likely when either the problem is utterly trivial and the relationship and predictions are obvious, or when leakage from anachronistic variables feeds information back from future to past. If any suspiciously good model turns up (that is, one that is far better than expected), it is worth checking very, very carefully to discover the nature and source of the error.

9.1.8 Summary of Classification Model Residual Checking

Looking at residuals and comparing them with actual and predicted values in the structured way described here are important. This is a diagnostic technique used to determine if there are problems with the data and with the modeling tool, the model, or both. Although working through the explanations here may be time

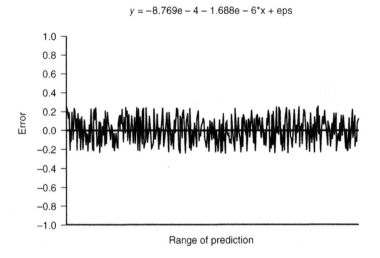

$y = -8.769e - 4 - 1.688e - 6*x + eps$

Range of prediction

FIGURE 9.15

Example of ideal residual distribution.

consuming and obtaining experience from many models may take time, with practice and experience, performing the diagnostic checks shown here is a quick and easy way to discover potential problems.

The miner uses residual error versus prediction plots to look for possible problems with the data, the model, or the modeling tool. Figure 9.15 illustrates an ideal distribution of residuals. The fitted regression line is nearly flat and fits at the zero point as well as possible. The residuals are uniform in amplitude and density across the whole plot. Figure 9.16 shows one result from an underspecified model. In this case, the model hasn't captured all of the nonlinearity present in the dataset. Figure 9.17 shows a different underspecification problem. In this case, the amplitude of the residual increases as the prediction value increases. (It could also have decreased as the prediction value increased, or it could have had some other identifiable pattern.) In this case, it is most likely that the model has insufficient flexibility to transform the nonlinearity in one or more of the input variables.

In the example discussed in this section (an example which is taken from an actual engagement), it was quick and easy to discover a problem with the modeling tool used (Figure 9.11). It was also quick and easy to discover that an apparent bias between actual and predicted values was in fact introduced by the modeling tool and not, as had been suspected by the client, the result of a problem with the model itself (Figure 9.10). In addition, using Figures 9.13 or 9.14, the modeler is in a good position to begin to build an explanation of the performance of the model. Figures 9.7, 9.8 (which expands the explanation of 9.7), and 9.9 quickly demonstrated that the tool had built a robust model once the "shoulders" in Figure 9.7 had been explained.

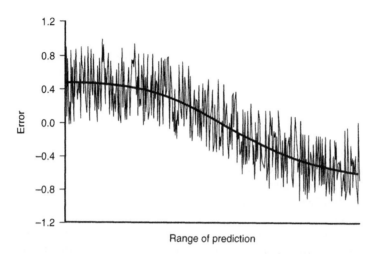

FIGURE 9.16

Residuals from an underspecified model showing nonlinearity.

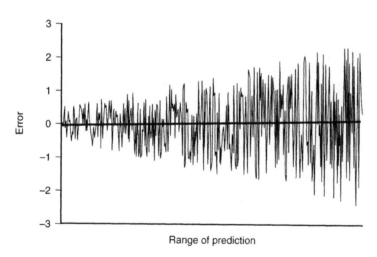

FIGURE 9.17

Residuals from an underspecified model showing residual error scatterplot dependent on prediction values.

In brief, looking at plots of residual values across the range of the predictions can be illuminating to a miner and will help the miner get the model right.

9.1.9 Improving Explanatory Models

Diagnosing problems with an explanatory model is, in a sense, much easier and less technically exact than doing so with classification models. Essentially, either an explanatory model does provide a convincing, relevant, applicable explanation that serves to address the business problem, or it doesn't! If it does, no further diagnosis is needed—the model works. If it doesn't, that in itself is pretty much the diagnosis.

Given a diagnosis that the model performance needs improving and that it is because the model is at fault and not the miner's ability to explain, several actions may well improve the model's quality.

One major problem arises when the data doesn't seem to represent relationships of interest. Perhaps it actually doesn't. That's not a problem with the model, of course, but an indication that better data is needed. However, it often turns out that reformatting the data will reveal relationships that seemed hidden. (See Section 9.2.3.) Tools that display relationships, such as the self-organizing map (SOM), are quite sensitive to distributional changes. (See the section titled Problem: Reformatting Data.) Other tools, such as Single-Variable Chi-squared Automatic Interaction Detection (SVCHAID), improve their explanatory power when business-relevant features are extracted from the dataset.

Sometimes the model seems to reveal nothing of interest. The possible conclusions derived from a model may be nothing but broad generalities that are hard to practically apply to the problem. On other occasions, a model might seem to deliver a host of trivial detail, but that very detail seems to obscure the interesting relationships as if in a froth of trivia. Either of these circumstances may be caused by having the model complexity, and its power to extract detail from the data, set either too low (in the case of overly general models) or too high (in the case of extremely detailed models). This ability of a model to capture detail is called its *specificity,* and when the model does not capture enough detail, it is called *underspecified.* When it captures only the froth of detail, the model is *overspecified.* Setting an appropriate level of specification is as important in an explanatory model as it is in a classificatory model. (See Section 9.2.4)

For explanatory models, it is essential that any important relationships be presented as clearly as possible. All that has to be done to completely obfuscate an explanation based on ordinal or categorical variable relationships is to assign inappropriate numbers to those categories. Inappropriate numeration of categorical values is a real problem when using explanatory tools that can only model numeric variables, like a SOM. However, the appropriate numeration of categories can retain clear explanations—an important consideration when explaining categorical variable relationships. (See the section titled Reformatting Data: Normalizing Ranges.)

Sometimes it is convenient, or easier to understand, if categories are used to explain a relationship, even when the underlying variable is a continuous number.

A process called *binning* turns continuous variables into categories. The important trick for explanatory models is to use meaningful categories rather than arbitrary ones that may hide meaningful structure. Sometimes the implicit structure of the data reveals meaningful bin structures in a numeric variable, although it is always preferable to use expert knowledge, if it's available, to create and label the bins. When relevant labels are applied to the bins, they can help clarify a relationship more than trying to describe the relationship numerically. (See the section Reformatting Data: Binning)

9.2 IMPROVING MODEL QUALITY, SOLVING PROBLEMS

Most of the rest of this chapter looks at how to address the problems that became apparent from the diagnostic tests described in Section 9.1. This section focuses on what changes might be made to improve the quality of the model given one or more problems revealed by the model diagnostics. Unless the model is justifiably perfect, one or more of the diagnostic checks will point to areas where the initial model can be improved. Even if no particularly egregious problems were revealed when the initial model was diagnosed, the model can probably still be improved by applying the techniques in this section. In fact, although these are presented as "solutions" to particular discovered problems, this section really introduces techniques for improving a model's quality. Thus, the techniques described in this section shouldn't be viewed as only a set of solutions to problems; these techniques should be employed in the pursuit of general good practices in basic data mining.

Improving the quality of a model means understanding what "quality" means in terms of a model. There are lots of ways to characterize the quality of a model. Partly, of course, it depends on the type of model. As far as evaluating the quality of explanatory models goes, it's the quality of the explanation that counts. Based on the needs of the business problem, of course, judging the quality of an explanatory model is pretty much a subjective exercise. There are some useful guidelines for delivering the results of explanatory models to their greatest advantage, which allow a miner to make the most of what any explanatory model has to offer. But the actual performance of the explanatory model is a qualitative, rather than a quantitative, assessment. If it works, it works. If not, it doesn't work.

However, the ability of classificatory models to address the business problem, which is still pretty much a qualitative issue, can be judged against each other on technical criteria. In addition to the diagnostic tests described in the previous section, it's useful to become familiar with understanding and interpreting any other quality measures provided by a mining tool. The fundamental diagnostic tests of a model's quality were discussed in Section 9.1—interpreting confusion matrices, XY plots of residuals, predicted values, actual values, and residual histograms. These are the fundamental and crucial determinants of model quality.

If the quality measures provided by a mining tool leave any doubt about the nature of the problem, the real answer is to return to the diagnostic tests described in this chapter. These are powerful and useful precisely because they not only reveal problems but also can be easily interpreted to reveal what needs to be done to improve the model. Many model quality measures provided by mining tools are useful, but only indicate model quality on some selected scale, giving no indication of what might be done to improve the model. The key to successful modeling is to use measures that both indicate quality and direct attention to what needs to be adjusted.

The remainder of this section expands on and explains the catalyst methodology MIII for improving model quality. It is intended to stand on its own, but its full richness and power can be appreciated only when it is used to supplement the methodology.

9.2.1 Problem: The Data Doesn't Support the Model

A miner might find that the input battery doesn't relate to the output battery—in other words, the data doesn't support the model needed. This might be indicated when the following occurs:

- There is no significant difference in naïve and mined model performance.
- There is an almost flat regression line in the predicted versus actual XY plot.
- There are significant clusters present in the input battery with a high degree of separation between them.

This is a perennial data mining problem. The data available to fill the input battery simply doesn't have any useful relationship to the output battery. Given the input and output batteries, no data miner is going to get a useful model if this is genuinely the situation. However, all is certainly not lost!

For one important point, no is often a good answer. For some reason, we have been trained to think of no as a bad answer. However, justified knowledge of the limits of a dataset—to answer a question, to enable a decision, or to guide an action—is useful, not useless, to know. Discovering that a dataset does not allow an answer, at least as presently posed, is useful information that can be used constructively to guide action, decisions, insight, and future activities. This mining-justified discovery of the limits to knowledge available in a dataset is every bit as useful, in context, as would have been the justified representations of relevant relationships in data expressed as a mined model, had one been possible. It's useful in a different way, of course. The actions, decisions, insights, or activities are different than if a useful model had been generated. At the very least, such an answer may save the use of resources committed to a project on the basis of faulty or unfounded decisions not supported by the data. At best, it may provoke, or justify, collecting data that relates to the business problem of interest.

The best approach is to find more or different data—that is, data that hopefully holds the relationships of interest. However, discovering that a dataset does not contain any useful relationships to the object of interest is a useful contribution of knowledge to the search for appropriate data. Part of the process of discovering data to mine requires creating a pool of candidate measurements. Discovering that a dataset doesn't support the model of interest can contribute a great deal to the search for appropriate candidate measurements because it clearly shows measurements that need not be further considered. It may indeed show whole related areas that need not be pursued.

The "useless" dataset may also provide clues as to what other dataset may be worth investigating. The presence of such clues depends on the source of the supplied dataset. The question is, was the mining dataset generated from original source data or from some secondary source? If from a secondary source, and the original data is available, it's not at all unlikely that going back to the original data and beginning again will turn up different, possibly better results. The problem is that secondary data, such as that from a data warehouse or from a standardized database, may well have had many of the interesting relationships removed inadvertently.

This happens because data for, say, warehousing is cleaned, summarized, and prepared to suit the needs of the warehouse. As far as the warehouse is concerned, this is a necessary and useful contribution. However, preparing the data for the warehouse imposes business and other rules, normalizes data, and performs other adjustments needed from the viewpoint of what the warehouse is intended to support. Cleaned and prepared in this way, the data may no longer have its original relationships to the mining output battery intact. Although it may well be a lot of work, it is always possible that the original data may be of more value than the secondary source data.

As a final consideration, although by technical measures a model may seem of little use, "it ain't necessarily so!" The truth is that the credit card solicitation model is, by most technical criteria, useless. The dataset hardly supports a predictive model of any technical merit whatever. Nonetheless, for solving a business problem, it is a very good model. Even in its raw form, it seems to hold the promise of doubling the response rate, and it is no shabby model that can double a response rate! So however little improvement there seems to be and however poor a model seems to be, technical criteria are not the only—and may not even be the most important—criteria by which to judge a model.

9.2.2 Problem: The Data Partially Doesn't Support the Model

Another possible problem is that the input battery doesn't sufficiently define the relationship to the output battery over all or part of the output range—in other words, the data doesn't support the model needed. This might be indicated when the value of the smoothed residual variance estimate is so great over some or all of the plot as to make the predictions unsatisfactory.

The issue here is that over some part of the output battery's range, the prediction is simply not accurate enough to provide the necessary level of confidence to use the model—at least, not when it makes predictions in the problematic part of the range. Depending on how much of the range is problematic, it is possible that some of the suggested remedies in Section 9.2.1 might help. However, and more to the point, because most of the output range of the model is working sufficiently well, what is really needed is to improve the accuracy over the problematic part of the range.

Rather than rebuild the entire dataset from scratch, it is worthwhile to work to discover additional data that better defines the relationship over the problematic part of its range. First, look in the existing dataset itself. Careful explanatory modeling may reveal features in the input battery that, when introduced into the dataset as dummy variables, do elucidate the relationship more clearly.

Whether extracting features helps depends to some degree on which underlying algorithm the modeling tool uses. Different algorithms are sensitive to different types of patterns. Because this is the case, it's often helpful to combine the outputs of two different models, each generated by a different underlying algorithm. The way to do this is straightforward. Build the best model with one tool supporting, say, a decision tree. Build the best model with identical input and output batteries with another tool supporting, say, a neural network. Take the two separate predictions, form them into a new input battery, and, using the original output battery as the new output battery, build a third model that combines the predictions of the two original models. This method, illustrated in Figure 9.18, often results in a model with less variance than either of the original models.

Another variant of the same technique may also help, even when using the same underlying algorithm in this case. Good practice may have excluded a large number of the variables in the input battery as redundant. (See, for example, Section 9.2.16.) If this is the case, try constructing a separate model on the original output battery, but form the input battery entirely from the discarded variables from the original model's input battery. With the second model in hand, combine the two models as just described. These two models, even if constructed with the same tool, may show less variance than a single model constructed with all of the variables now in use.

9.2.3 Problem: Reformatting Data

A miner might find that the tool (algorithm) selected to make the model cannot deal with the data in the format provided. This might be indicated when the following occurs:

- There is no significant difference in naïve and mined model performance.
- There is an almost flat regression line in predicted versus actual XY plot.
- The "tails" (outer edges) of the distribution are smaller than the comparison normal curve shows should be expected.

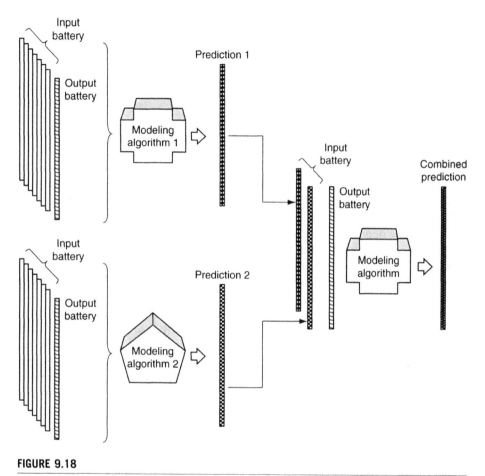

FIGURE 9.18

Combining two models.

- The fitted curve differs markedly from a straight line where it passes through the data.
- The value of the smoothed residual variance estimate is so great over some or all of the plot as to make the predictions unsatisfactory.
- You discover that an explanation is not convincing, relevant, or applicable to the business problem.

This is a problem that turns up more frequently than it should, given that most tools implement automated methods of transforming the variables of the input battery into a form more suitable for whatever underlying algorithm the miner chooses for a particular model. Although good transformation methods are available, not all tools do an equally good job of making the transformations. Because the transformations are often made invisibly and automatically, a miner may not even be particularly aware that the tool is actually modeling a different version of each variable in the input battery than that visible in the dataset.

Fortunately, the problem is relatively easy to address because the miner can reformat the data before applying the modeling tool, so that the input battery presents the variable formats in a way that is appropriate for the chosen underlying algorithm. Generally speaking, tools only reformat data that the automated transformation method recognizes as needing transformation. If the miner transforms a variable, no other transformation is needed, and the underlying algorithm models the data as presented.

Although not exactly a formatting problem, there is another issue with the variable's data format—that of missing values. Some algorithms cannot deal with missing values at all; others deal with missing values poorly; and yet others apparently have no particular problem with missing values. The importance of dealing with the issue depends on the underlying modeling algorithm. However, it turns out in practice that even algorithms that inherently aren't meant to be affected by missing values often perform better when the missing values are replaced using good imputation methods. Thus, it is a good practice to replace all missing values using well-founded imputation methods.

Most tools offer some method for replacing missing values, but many of these methods are not well founded and can do more harm than good, despite their being built into the tool. Just because they are included in the tool does not mean that they work well! There are good methods of replacing missing values, but unless the tool actually incorporates well-founded methods, missing value imputation methods have to be applied to datasets outside the tool's environment, just as, in general, with the reformatting methods.

There are three basic techniques for reformatting data, plus the not-exactly-reformatting technique of replacing missing values:

- Binning.
- Normalizing range.
- Normalizing distribution.

Apply these techniques with care, as they are not all equally applicable under all circumstances. This section looks at each technique in turn with guidelines for when each is most likely to be applicable.

Reformatting Data: Binning
Mainly, binning is a simple and straightforward technique for turning continuous variables into ordinal or categorical variables. It should be noted that ordinal and categorical variables could also sometimes be usefully binned. However, binning ordinal or categorical variables requires advanced binning tools and techniques, such as information-based binning, discussed later in this section. Numeric variables often have to be binned because tools often use underlying algorithms—decision trees and naïve Bayesian networks, for instance—that require the variables to be categorical or ordinal rather than numeric.

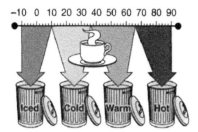

FIGURE 9.19

Binning numeric values.

Binning is so called, perhaps, because when binning a variable, various sub-ranges of values of the variable are all put together into a bin. Figure 9.19 illustrates the concept, using as an example a numeric variable measuring the temperature of coffee (in degrees Celsius.). The temperature of coffee ranges, say, from just below the freezing point of water to close to boiling. In daily conversation, we don't often discuss the temperature of coffee in terms of degrees of any temperature scale. Instead, we characterize the temperature in terms of classifications—such as iced, cold, warm, and hot—which have a generally accepted colloquial meaning and an understood subjective range of experience associated with each label. In the terms used here, this is a form of binning in which each of the categories is the bin label, and the upper and lower limits of the range of temperatures associated with each bin form what are called the *bin boundaries*. Of course, a mining tool doesn't care if the bin labels are arbitrary or meaningful, but it is good practice to make the labels as meaningful as possible.

The principle of binning is straightforward, even intuitive. However, whenever any continuous variable is binned, it's important to keep in mind that information is unavoidably lost in the binning process. All of the separate values in any bin are treated as if they were identical. All information about the distribution of values across the range of the bin is lost.

On the other hand, the lost information may be a worthwhile sacrifice in order to make the variable usable to a mining tool. And on some occasions, binning can actually remove more noise than useful information, especially if the binning is optimally done. This can sometimes result in better models, even for algorithms that could use the variables in their unbinned form. The problem is in the expression "if the binning is optimally done." Optimal binning is not necessarily straightforward.

The problem of deciding how to bin a variable is twofold: 1) discover how many bins to use, and 2) determine how best to assign values to each bin.

Assigning Bin Boundaries

One simple way to assign bin boundaries is to divide the range of the variable into a number of bins and let each bin cover its appropriate fraction of the range.

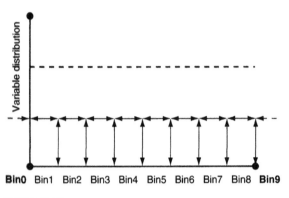

Bin0 Bin1 Bin2 Bin3 Bin4 Bin5 Bin6 Bin7 Bin8 **Bin9**

FIGURE 9.20

Equal range bins.

Figure 9.20 shows ten bins in total. Eight bins cover the range of the variable across its expected range, so each bin covers one-eighth (12.5 percent) of the entire expected range of the variable. At each extreme of the range is a bin that takes any values that fall outside the expected range of the variable. The too-large and too-small values often turn up in real-world datasets, and it's quite easy to put in a couple of catchall bins to hold any that are found. Although not shown in the figure, another bin is sometimes used for instances with missing values.

The bins in Figure 9.20 are shown across the ordered range of the variable with, say, least values on the left and greatest on the right. Each bin covers the same amount of the range of values of the variable as any other bin, and this binning arrangement is called *equal range binning*. This arrangement might work if the variables' values were distributed fairly evenly across the range of the variable, as indicated by the dashed horizontal line representing the distribution. However, most variables don't have particularly uniform distributions.

Figure 9.21 illustrates a nonuniform distribution that approximates a normal distribution. Here it's easy to see that most of the values cluster around the mean value, which is indicated by the peak of the dashed line. If equal range binning were used in this circumstance, it's easy to see that the bins around the mean would contain most of the instances, and the bins at the extremes would have very few. In the absence of any specific reason to use some other arrangement, it's been found most generally useful to have bins with fairly equal numbers of instances in each, so the bin boundaries illustrated in Figure 9.21 are adjusted to evenly balance the bin contents. This arrangement, not surprisingly, is called *equal frequency binning* because the bin boundaries are arranged so that, as much as possible, all the bins have a similar number of instances in them.

However, it's hard to know how many bins to have under either of these arrangements. Exactly where the optimum number lies is difficult to determine. Starting with 20 to 30 usually seems to work well. The key is to have enough bin categories so that the mining tool can develop a sufficient complexity of patterns

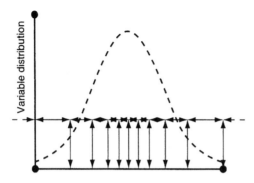

FIGURE 9.21

Equal frequency bins.

in the input battery to map to the output battery. Experimenting with adjusting the bin count and boundaries often helps with these simple binning strategies.

These are basic and fairly common methods of binning. Given a number of bins, it's fairly easy to arrange the boundaries automatically, and equal frequency is the binning method to try first. The number of bins in the input battery needs to be partly determined by the desired resolution of the output battery—more resolution calls for more bins. Binning the output battery, if needed, has to be driven by the needs of the business problem determined by the desired degree of resolution. In general, with the simple binning methods, the input battery variables should start with approximately as many bins as the output battery if the output battery is itself binned. If the output battery is left as a continuous variable, try 20 or 30 equal-frequency bins.

These are two common, simple binning methods, and although they are not optimal, mining tools usually offer at least these methods and sometimes only these methods. Or, more appropriately put, there is no justification to think that any particular arrangement of equal range, or equal frequency, bins will turn out to be optimal. Many mining tools that offer alternative binning methods often implement binning strategies that, although more complex and far less straightforward than these simple methods, are also not necessarily optimal. However, there are methods of achieving binning strategies that are nearer to optimal.

Information-Based Binning

The simple binning strategies just discussed are unsupervised strategies. That is to say, any binning of a variable is made without any reference to any other variables at all, including those in the output battery. Because a classificatory model has an output battery, it is possible to use the output battery to direct the binning of the input battery so that the binning reveals the maximum amount of information about the output battery. This, of course, would be a supervised binning strategy. Potentially, it can do a better job than the simple binning strategies because it uses information from both the input battery variable and the output battery.

Information content in variables can be measured according to the underlying theory called *information theory*. It is possible to create a binning strategy using information theory that retains in one variable the maximum amount of information about another variable. There are several ways of implementing an information-based binning strategy, but two are particularly useful.

Least information loss binning, as the name implies, creates bin boundaries that optimally retain information in the input battery variable that describes the output battery variable. This method retains any ordering present in the input battery variable and creates bin boundaries accordingly. The boundaries are placed to have neither equal frequency bins nor equal range bins, but so that the total amount of information about the output variable in all the bins is greater than any other arrangement of bin boundaries, or number of bins, provides.

Maximum information gain binning is potentially the most powerful information-based binning strategy. This is another supervised binning strategy, but in this case, the ordering of the input variable is not necessarily maintained, and input battery variable values are mapped into bins so that maximum information is gained about the output battery. For maximum information gain binning to work, it is crucial to have a dataset that fully represents the actual distribution to be modeled. Without it, this binning strategy will produce garbage. Surprisingly, it is not always possible to represent the distribution of a population, however large the sample size.

These are powerful binning strategies, but their practical implementation requires a high degree of complexity and calculation. This is easy for a computer, but totally impractical as a humanly applied technique. Optimal binning can be crucial in deriving a good model from a dataset. Unfortunately, few mining tools offer any sophisticated binning strategies, let alone optimal ones. Because binning is so important to building good models, Dorian Pyle who wrote this chapter for *Business Modeling and Data Mining* (Morgan Kaufmann, 2003) maintains a website (*www.modelandmine.com*) that offers a binning tool to address a dataset and determine the appropriate bin boundaries using several binning strategies, including those described here. Once the binning tool has discovered the bin boundaries, it's easy to set them in any mining tool that allows custom bins to be created. For readers who do not have easy access to adjust manual bin boundaries, the binning tool will also write out a binned version of any variable, or set of variables, so the miner can incorporate them into the input battery. This should allow any reader of this book with access to the Internet to experiment with different binning strategies and to discover the power, importance, and effectiveness of optimal binning.

Reformatting Data: Normalizing Ranges

Some algorithms, most notably neural networks, are highly restricted in the range of values to which they are sensitive. Many of the most popular types of neural networks require a numeric input range, including values either from −1 to +1 or from 0 to 1. For any tool implementing one of these algorithms, there's no problem whatsoever in modifying the input range of a numeric variable to match the needs of the algorithm. The tool simply scans the input battery, determines the maximum and minimum values present for all numeric variables, and rescales the input values appropriately. However, any algorithm that requires all numeric input has to deal somewhat differently with categorical or ordinal variables.

As an example, consider days of the week. A weekly cycle requires coding into two variables with values; Figure 9.22 shows them as V1 and V2. However, days of the week actually occur sequentially, one after the other from, say, Sunday through Saturday. This naturally occurring sequence of days can be numbered as, for the sake of this example, 1–7, and shown in the column headed "Seq."

When the underlying algorithm of a mining tool can take variables only in the form of numbers, it is necessary to recode any categorical or ordinal values numerically to represent either a sequence or a cycle as needed. One common practice, and one that some mining tools adopt in automated conversion of categorical variables into a numeric representation, is to simply assign numbers to categories as they are encountered in a dataset. For the sake of this example, the figure shows such a numeric assignment to the categories of day values based on their alphabetical order. This numeric assignment is shown in the column headed "Alpha" in Figure 9.22. But note that this assignment imposes an implied order on the categories. In this case, the implied order imposed doesn't match the naturally occurring sequence. (There is no reason to suppose that assigning numbers to categories in the order that they are encountered in a dataset will match any naturally occurring sequence either.)

Figure 9.23 shows that if the natural sequence were appropriately matched, the relationship between natural sequence and assigned order would be as shown in the graph on the left. However, the arbitrary alphabetic assignment results in a relationship between the natural sequence and the assigned sequence shown in the graph on the right. This assignment produces what seems to be a complex,

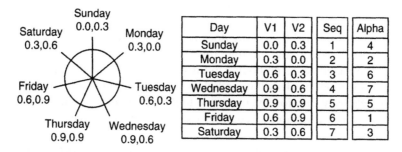

Day	V1	V2	Seq	Alpha
Sunday	0.0	0.3	1	4
Monday	0.3	0.0	2	2
Tuesday	0.6	0.3	3	6
Wednesday	0.9	0.6	4	7
Thursday	0.9	0.9	5	5
Friday	0.6	0.9	6	1
Saturday	0.3	0.6	7	3

FIGURE 9.22

Coding days of the week.

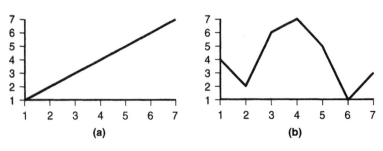

FIGURE 9.23

Different relationships for different day-of-week codings.

and certainly a nonlinear, relationship between the natural sequence and the assigned values. Because the natural sequence is the one that occurs in the real world, it is important to represent that sequential information to the model—and as simply as possible.

For the few categories used in this example, the relationship is not terribly complex, and it would be easy for any mining tool to discover and characterize it. However, when the number of categories rises, say when using stock-keeping units (SKUs) or ZIP codes, any natural ordering that exists in the real world can be made so inaccessible to a mining tool that it becomes impossible to discover any usable relationship.

The first point for any miner to note is that whenever there is a need to convert categorical and ordinal—particularly ordinal—variables to numeric representations, it is important to discover if there is a naturally occurring order or sequence for the categories and to distribute the categories in their appropriate locations in the range of the numeric representation. As is often the case when dealing with data, the rule is this: Wherever possible, look it up or dig it up rather than make it up.

This issue of discovering an appropriate ordering is obviously important to the quality of the resulting model. Yet what is to be done for categorical and ordinal variables when there is no apparent rationale for assigning numeric values?

A dataset as a whole incorporates many patterns and relationships among its variables. If a categorical variable actually does have a naturally occurring order, as is always the case for an ordinal variable, this relationship is incorporated into the structure of the relationships embodied in the dataset. It may be complex and nonobvious on inspection, but it will nonetheless still be present. Although hard for a miner, it is relatively easy for an automated tool to discover any ordinal relationship for any categorical variable in a dataset and to derive appropriate numeric labels for each category.

Assigning appropriate numeric labels, if this can be done, is far better than using an automated discovery of numeric labels. Adding appropriate numeric labels actually adds information to a dataset. When this can't be done, the automated assignment, although it doesn't actually add any information to the dataset, at least doesn't add erroneous information, which arbitrary assignment of numbers to labels almost certainly does. The arbitrary assignment simply adds noise to a dataset and may well hamper a tool's ability to discover and characterize the important and meaningful relationships that do exist. Automated discovery of appropriate numeric labels at least avoids the possibility of actively adding garbage!

Replacing an arbitrary numeric assignment of category values with those reflected out of a dataset can considerably improve a model created by an algorithm requiring all numeric representation. However, although easily accomplished, few tools are capable of discovering, let alone assigning, appropriate numeration to categories. Thus, as with binning, and for all the same reasons, a category numerating tool is available on Pyle's website.

Reformatting Data: Normalizing Distribution

The distribution of a variable describes the way that the variable's values spread themselves through the range of the variable. Some distributions are fairly familiar, such as what is known as the *normal distribution,* shown earlier in Figure 9.21. In a normal distribution, the greatest number of values occurs clustered around the mean (or average) of the distribution, with far fewer values falling at the extremes. However, it's not only numeric variables that have a distribution. Ordinal and categorical variables also have values, although they aren't numeric values, and the values usually occur with frequencies different from each other. An easy way to represent such a distribution is with a histogram, each column representing the number of instances in each class.

In spite of the similarity in name, normalizing a distribution isn't necessarily the process of making the distribution more like a normal distribution. Rather, the term means regularizing or standardizing a distribution in some way. It is possible, although unusual, to normalize categorical or ordinal distributions, although to some extent that is what is going on if one of the more advanced binning techniques is applied to such variables. Usually, it's only numeric variables that have their distributions normalized, and in this discussion, distribution normalization is confined to numeric variables.

Equal frequency binning works as well as it does in part because it is a distribution normalizing technique. Consider that any algorithm regards each of the bins as just as significant as any other bin. However, in equal frequency binning, each bin is arranged so that it contains the same number of instances as any other bin, at least insofar as it's possible to do so. This has redistributed the values in the variable so that they are uniformly spread across the range of the variable. To be sure, there are fewer values, only one value for each bin, but each bin value occurs as often as any other bin value, so the distribution is as close to uniform as this binning metric can get it. Thus, one strategy for normalizing a distribution that can work quite well is to use equal frequency binning with a high bin count (say, 101 bins), and assign each bin a value a uniform increment apart. If the chosen bin value ranges from 0 to 1, the bins would be assigned values of 0, 0.01, 0,02, 0.03 . . . 0.98, 0.99, 1.00. This strategy normalizes both the range and the distribution, of course. To normalize just the distribution, assign each bin the mean value of the instances in the bin.

Note that it is also possible to continuously remap any numeric distribution so that it is uniformly distributed across its range. "Continuous" means that there are no bins and each value is uniquely mapped to some other unique value, rather than mapped to a bin value shared by several adjoining values. Such a continuous remapping allows every different value in a distribution to participate in contributing to the model and retains all of the information that a variable has to offer. Binning always necessitates loss of information because, as already noted, all of the values in a bin, no matter how different they are from each other, are all assigned the same bin value. Few, if any, mining tools incorporate continuous distribution normalization, so Pyle has included a tool that will perform continuous remapping of numeric variables with the binning tool mentioned earlier in this section.

Why Does Distribution Normalization Work?

Consider an extreme case of skew in a distribution. Think of the series of numbers 1, 2, 3, 4, 5, 6, 7, 8, 9, 1000. This series ranges from 1 to 1000. However, almost all of the values fall in only 1 percent of this range. The value 1000 is called an *outlier* because it lies far from the bulk of other values in the series. For this example, it is a rather extreme outlier, but it may be quite impossible to say that it is an error of any sort or even an erroneous value. Quite justifiably, this might be a perfectly valid entry. For an example of a real-world situation in which such extremes occur, consider insurance claims, where most are for very small amounts but a few are huge. Or think of legal settlements. Now consider the problem for a numeric mining algorithm. To span the range, it has to encompass values from 1 to 1000, yet almost all of the values are to all intents and purposes indistinguishable from each other. If these values were binned using a 101-bin equal-range strategy, one bin at one end of the range would contain all but one of the values in it, 99 of the bins would be totally empty, and 1 bin at the other extreme of the range would contain a single instance. The mining algorithm would see only two values! (This, of course, is why equal frequency binning is preferred, because it wouldn't have this problem.)

Without binning or some other redistribution strategy, almost all numerically sensitive algorithms, when presented with this range of values, would have to scale their inputs such that this actual distribution would be indistinguishable from a dataset containing only two values. This means that any information carried by the values 1 through 9 would be effectively lost.

Intuitively, the problem is similar, although by no means as severe, whenever a distribution has some values that group together, even when the grouping is fairly benign, such as that of the normal distribution. It takes at least a great deal more complexity in any model to deal with clumping in distributions, and more complex models are far more prone to learn noise rather than the desired relationships, take longer to train, and are more difficult to understand than simpler models. So although it may be theoretically possible for a mining tool to deal with almost any distribution problem, in practice, in order to make the tool sufficiently noise-resistant, the complexity has to be limited—and so is its ability to deal with clumps and bumps in a distribution.

For such distributions as the example used here, either high-bin count, equal-frequency unsupervised binning, continuous remapping, or supervised binning handily finesses the problem by producing a variable with a distribution from which any mining tool can extract the maximum information.

Distribution Normalization in Explanatory Models

Distribution normalization can play an important role in improving the performance of classificatory models. However, it can play an even more important role in building explanatory models, particularly when using clustering and especially when using visually based clustering tools such as the SOM tool.

The problem is that when the range is broad, but most of the values are packed into some small part of the range, a couple of things seem to happen on a map. First, because color represents value, almost all of the values are represented by a single hue. Second, because at least one of the extremes has few values, the map seems to show an almost uniform hue, as if the variable had only a single value for the vast majority of the instances. Thus, meaningful patterns that might well actually exist are effectively invisible.

Figure 9.24 illustrates a variable that has a highly concentrated cluster of values with an extreme outlier. The linear, or unmodified, distribution can be seen in the left histogram, showing that almost all of the 30,000 instances have values of less than 50 but at least 1, although certainly few instances have a value of over 12,000. When mapped or clustered, this appears to show a binary variable with, as far as can be determined visually, all of the instances having a single value. Redistributing the values as shown in the right histogram spreads the values that

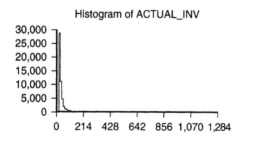
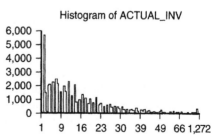

FIGURE 9.24

Redistributing variable values.

are present across the displayable range, and makes any patterns present far easier to see.

Reformatting Data: Replacing Missing Values

Replacing missing values doesn't change the format of the data. However, it's necessary in some cases, and always worthwhile, for a number of reasons. For those algorithms that cannot deal with missing values, something has to be done—the miner has no choice. Some tools automatically ignore the whole instance, and all of the values it contains, if one of them is missing. In many real-world datasets, this can make some otherwise perfectly usable datasets totally unminable as almost every instance has one value or another missing. Even for those mining algorithms that can inherently deal with missing values, empirical evidence suggests that replacing missing values with well-founded imputed values turns out to improve the quality of the resulting model. The problem, of course, is in the phrase "well-founded imputed values." It turns out that many of the missing value replacement options offered by many mining tools are actually damaging to a dataset in that they add spurious relationships, obscure existing relationships, and generally reduce model quality, sometimes severely. How does this happen?

In almost all datasets, values are not missing at random. To see that this is so in at least one real-world dataset, suppose you have a model—called the missing value check model (MVCM)—built on a dataset that, within the input battery, contains only and exclusively a characterization of which values are missing and which values are present. The fact that many of the input battery variables had interesting relationships with the output battery with only a missing/present flag indicates that the values weren't simply missing at random. Random occurrences do not form consistent patterns, and these are consistent patterns. Of course, the fact that it holds true in this one dataset is merely anecdotal evidence that missing values are not missing at random, and it is only evidence that this is true in this case. However, experience shows that in far and away the majority of cases, values turn out not to be missing at random in most datasets with missing values.

Note that if it is indeed true that values are not missing at random, they must be missing with some regularity, or pattern. Replacing missing values with any constant value, exactly as was done in the MVCM, will reveal that pattern. Now this isn't in itself a bad thing because it may well be that those patterns need to be explicated, which is why the MVCM technique calls for adding a variable describing any useful discovered relationship. The problem is how replacing missing values affects the other patterns in the dataset.

Notice that all the talk about patterns in datasets comes down to this: There is a relationship between the values that any one variable takes in any particular instance, and the values that the other variables in the same instance take. Some of these relationships might be "tighter" than others in the sense that for some variables, when one takes on certain values in an instance, it pretty much constrains another variable in the same instance to have values in a narrow range.

Some relationships might be "looser" in the sense that, when one variable takes on certain values, another might have values that still tend to range around a fair amount. But whatever the constraints on the ranges of values, a model describes no more than what the ranges are and how tight the coupling is among all of the variables in the input battery and how those relate to similar relationships in the output battery. The key here is that, to a greater or lesser extent, all of the variables change their values together and in lockstep. Whatever the patterns are, a good model needs to characterize them as clearly and accurately as possible.

It is, regrettably, a common practice to replace missing values with some constant value, such as the mean of a numeric variable or the most frequent category of a categorical. Many tools offer this as the only missing value replacement method. What happens to the dataset's relationships if some constant value is used as a replacement for a missing value?

Because there is a pattern to the way that variables' values occur in an instance, it's obvious that the pattern implies that any one variable's value is related at least somewhat to the values in the other variables. Given that such a relationship between variable values—a pattern—exists, when one value is missing, any replacement value has to take account of the other nonmissing values and find a replacement value that best fits the existing pattern so as not to add to, modify, distort, or damage it. There can be no generally good, single value that will serve in all cases. The ideal value to plug in when one is missing has to be whatever value turns out to best match the values that are present, given the relationships that exist between them. However, if some inappropriate value is used instead, the modeling tool has no choice but to incorporate that inappropriate value as a true part of the actual pattern.

Note what occurs as a result of replacing any single value. The missing value pattern discovered with the MVCM in a given variable is not a part of the inter-related pattern of that variable to the other variables. The MVCM type of relationship is a separate relationship that needs to be described separately, which is why good practices call for it to be added as a separate variable. But the first thing that any constant value replacement does is to comingle two patterns in one variable—one is the pattern defined by the interrelationships with other variable values, and the other is the MVCP-type pattern.

The second effect of using a constant value replacement is to confuse any modeling tool into thinking that a variable actually takes on specific values in relationship to all the other values when, in fact, no such relationship can possibly be justified. There is actually no reason to suppose that the replacement value is the one that would have existed had the value not been missing, and, in fact, based on the other variables' values, most of the time there's good reason to think that whatever fixed value is used is wrong!

In summary—and just considering these two effects alone, which are quite bad enough—adding any constant value as a replacement for missing values overlays the actual pattern that exists with another pattern that exists and then additionally distorts the first pattern by specifying that the variable's relationship behaves in ways that it actually doesn't. In short, missing value replacement with a constant value can utterly destroy some relationships that do exist, hide others, and make yet others inaccessible.

It should hardly be a surprise that inappropriate missing value replacement often does more harm than good, and always—*always*—reduces the quality of the best possible model. The best possible model from the damaged dataset simply isn't as good as the best possible model from the same dataset with well-founded and appropriately imputed missing value replacements.

So what should the miner do? Well, part of the answer, of course, is already accomplished, because the best practice of creating a separate variable where necessary with the MVCM retains one pattern in the dataset without comingling, and consequent obfuscation, of the two patterns just mentioned.

The other part of the answer is not to use any constant value as a replacement for missing values. The answer—the only answer that does not damage data for mining—is to use a value that takes account of all the values that are present in a given instance. In fact, there are a number of methods that work well, some more complex and theoretically well founded than others. These go by such grandiose names as "maximum likelihood missing value estimation" and "covariate imputation." In practice, the method used seems to make little difference to the final result. The difficulty, of course, is that once again, replacement of missing values is most easily accomplished by automated tools as it is impractical to manually make the necessary calculations to build the replacement algorithm. Therefore, Pyle (2003) has made available a missing value replacement tool on his website (*www.modelandmine.com*) so that the reader can explore the benefits from a good practice (that is, well-founded missing value imputation when the reader's tool of choice doesn't support it) or simply view the effect of different imputation strategies. The tool will replace missing values and provide a dynamic missing value algorithm developed from the training data for use at runtime.

9.2.4 Problem: Respecifying the Algorithm

One of the possible problems a miner might face is that the model wasn't able to characterize the relationships from the input battery to the output battery adequately. This might be indicated when the following occurs:

- There is no significant difference in naïve and mined model performance.
- The residuals appear to contain information that could be used to improve the prediction.
- The regression line fitted to the actual value versus residual XY plot is not horizontal.
- The value of the smoothed residual variance estimate is so great over some or all of the plot as to make the predictions unsatisfactory.
- You discover that an explanation is not convincing, relevant, or applicable to the business problem.

The viewpoint here is that the difficulty in improving model performance may not necessarily lie with the data but in the capabilities of the mining algorithm and the way it has been specified. Recall that an underspecified model is one in which the constraints on the algorithm were such that it didn't have enough flexibility to properly characterize the relationships in the data. An overspecified model is one that has so much flexibility that it captured not only the underlying relationships, but a lot of junk too. As with the tale of Goldilocks and the three bears, the amount of specification that's needed is "j-u-s-t r-i-g-h-t!" How is just right to be determined? The answer lies with the training and test datasets.

As a reminder, the object of modeling is to create the best model possible in the training dataset that works best in the test dataset: build in training, apply in test. If the model performs about equally in both training and test datasets, then it may—*may*—be underspecified because it's possible that it hasn't yet fully characterized the noise-free relationships. If the model performs far better in the training dataset than in the test dataset, then the model is overspecified because, so long as the datasets are properly representative; it has obviously learned noise that exists in the training dataset but not in the test dataset.

The answer to determining when the model is well-specified—not too much, not too little, but "j-u-s-t r-i-g-h-t"—is to keep improving the model until it is just overspecified, and use the immediately previous iteration just before overspecification set in. In other words, keep building more specific models in the training dataset all the time the improved models do better in the test dataset. Regardless of performance in the training dataset, as soon as a model returns worse results in the test dataset than a previous iteration of the model, use the previous iteration as the final specification level for the model.

It's well worth noting that the iterations are needed for each diagnostic test. The problem is that, strictly speaking, the diagnostic symptoms are not independent. For instance, however appropriately specified a model is under one set of circumstances, any change in, say, the dataset required to improve performance on another diagnostic test will affect the model's specificity. This implies that any change in any of the model parameters requires a total recalibration of all the others, leading to an almost endless improvement process. The practice is not so tough. Improving model performance in any one of the diagnostic areas does not usually have any dramatically detrimental impact on the other areas.

Each mining tool features a different set of knobs to twiddle to adjust the algorithm in use, even when the different mining tools employ the same basic algorithm. So although the particulars of what has to be done vary from tool to tool (and even sometimes from release to release of the same tool), what can be done with each mining algorithm incorporated in each tool is, in general, fairly easy to describe. In some tool sets, the knobs that a miner could twiddle to tune the algorithm are completely removed, in which case there's nothing to be done to adjust the algorithm. There are still some options to try. You could use a different algorithm, in the case of a multi-algorithm tool set, or you could try a different tool. As a general good practice, it is always worth having more than one algorithm to try on a dataset. Just as there is no one right answer to most problems, there is no one right mining tool, nor one right mining algorithm, for all datasets and all problems.

This section next looks at the knobs that are available to generically adjust each algorithm and presents them algorithm by algorithm. Note that the discussion here assumes that the algorithms are wrapped in tools that have eliminated most of the complexity that is involved in applying the raw algorithm to any dataset. The techniques discussed here cover only those adjustments that tool vendors often provide to allow for tuning of different algorithms. But this discussion covers only algorithms as they are embedded in tools. This section does not cover tuning and adjusting the various raw algorithms, which is a far more complex process than covered here.

Just as a reminder, don't necessarily expect to find controls in each tool that allow a miner to make these adjustments. On the other hand, this discussion does not cover all of the possible adjustments that could possibly be made to each algorithm, just the more popular ones. Some vendors offer more knobs, some vendors fewer, some none at all. The vendors' problem is how much complexity to expose; the miners' is how much flexibility is available. To discover what any individual tool offers, it's important to read the documentation and work with the help screens for each tool.

Algorithm Adjustment: Nearest Neighbor or Memory-Based Reasoning

Nearest neighbor algorithms offer only two types of basic adjustment: the number of neighbors to be considered and the method of determining the estimated value.

Adjusting the number of neighbors is fairly straightforward. The algorithm is sometimes known as k-nearest neighbor, where k stands for the number of neighbors. So one of the controls offered is sometimes simply called "k," assuming that the miner knows what it means.

Increasing k tends to make the model more resistant to noise and therefore less sensitive to learning nuance. If the model seems underspecified, try reducing k so that the model is more sensitive. If the model seems overspecified, try increasing k. All that is happening here is that with more neighbors in consideration, the estimated result is being averaged over a larger group; with fewer neighbors, it's averaged over a smaller group.

Ignoring for the moment the effect of the size of the group, the estimated value is determined by looking at the output battery values for each of the k neighbors and taking an average of them all as the estimate. In this basic method, all neighbors contribute equally to the final result. Alternatively, weight the value of each neighbor according to its distance from the instance to be estimated. With such a weighting mechanism, more distant neighbors have less effect on the estimated value than nearer ones. In general, with all neighbors equally weighted—using a simple mean—the algorithm is less sensitive than when using distance weighting. Thus, as far as neighbor weighting is concerned, if the model is underspecified, try using a distance-weighted estimate. If the model is overspecified, use equally weighted (or unweighted) estimates.

Algorithm Adjustment: Decision Trees

Decision trees split individual variables into leaves. At each leaf, the decision tree selects the best variable to split that leaf from all of the available variables. The root covers the whole dataset. At the first split, the smallest leaf cannot cover more than 50 percent of the instances in a dataset, and it may cover less than 50 percent. (Consider that if the tree makes binary splits, an equal split between the leaves would be 50/50, and it probably would not be equally balanced. A nonbinary split tree [like the SVCHAID] would have the smallest leaf cover considerably less than 50 percent.) At the split on the first-level leaf, the smallest next leaf can cover no more than 25 percent of the instances. Thus, at each level of splitting, each leaf covers a smaller and smaller amount of the dataset. Eventually the number of instances covered by any leaf becomes so small that it isn't representative of the population, and the leaves at that point are only characterizing noise.

It's an odd difference between real trees and decision trees: whereas real trees have their roots in the ground and their leaves in the air, a decision tree has its root in the air (or at least, at the top) and its leaves in the ground (or at least, at the bottom). In general, the higher up a decision tree that a leaf is located—that is, the nearer to the root—the more general it is. The further from the root that a leaf is located, the more specific (i.e., nongeneral) it is. Thus, one way to prevent trees from learning noise is to set some minimum amount of instances that a leaf must contain. If that limit is set too high, the tree will be underspecified. If the limit is set too low, the tree will be overspecified.

There are other metrics that stop trees growing in some algorithms, such as how significant each split is, with a tree not splitting below some chosen level of significance. However, all of the methods prevent the tree from growing trivial leaves that only represent noise. Some tree tools allow the miner to select leaves to merge. This allows a miner to not only steer tree growth, but also to some extent incorporate domain knowledge into the tree structure through this type of guidance. Tree tools offering this feature should be looked on more favorably than those that don't.

Whatever technique is used to adjust the specificity of decision trees, it amounts in the end to having as many leaves as possible that contain enough instances to be representative of the underlying relationships in a dataset. Too few leaves, or in other words, leaves with large numbers of instances, and the tree is underspecified because it can only represent at best the main trends and no detail of the relationships. Too many leaves, or in other words, leaves with few instances, and the tree is overspecified because it then represents too great a level of detail. The key here is to have as many representative leaves as possible so that all of the detail is captured, and to ensure that they are all truly representative to make certain that they represent real relationships, not noise.

Selecting Root Splits

Decision trees choose to split each leaf on the variable that the tree algorithm determines as providing the best split. This applies to the root just as much as to the other leaves. The SVCHAID tree algorithm used earlier can show a list of variables ranked by the order in which the tree algorithm would choose each variable to split the root (or any other leaf if desired). (See, for instance, Figure 9.4 or 9.5.) It is sometimes the case that a better-specified tree results if the second or third choice variable is chosen to split the root. It's important not to remove any variables from consideration for the other leaves, so the first or second choice candidate variables have to remain in the dataset for other leaves to be split on those variables. Thus, simply removing the variable on which the initial tree split the root from the input battery is not suggested here—just change the variable that is allowed to split the root. (Not all tree tools implement this important feature, so when using some tools, the miner may not be able to steer the tree growth in this way. Trees without this feature are of extremely limited value to a miner and should, if possible, be avoided.)

Empirically, the reason that better-specified trees result from not using the "best" split of the root is that it rearranges the tree so that the later leaves are more appropriately split and are more resistant to learning noise. Do note that a totally different tree is likely to result from using a different variable to split the root. Recall that there is no one "proper" explanation of a dataset, and there is no "correct" model of a dataset. Left to its own devices, a tree will produce an explanation or model, but this is not to be regarded as the only one, nor even necessarily the best one. The best one is the one that most appropriately meets the modeler's/miner's needs—and that may not be what the tree algorithm wants to produce when left to itself. In this case, what's needed is the best specified tree, and the controls that need twiddling are leaf size and root split.

Algorithm Adjustment: Rule Extraction
Among the features of rules, there are three that are important to specification:

- They cover some number of instances.
- They have some probability of being true.
- Each rule has a level of complexity depending on how many conditions can be included in each rule.

All these features can be adjusted to change the specificity of the model.

Rules are required to cover some minimum number of instances in the dataset. If the rules are required to cover more instances, then this will result in generating less specific rules. Contra wise, the fewer instances required as a minimum for a rule to apply to (cover), the more specific the rule.

Rules will almost certainly not be perfect. In almost all cases, there will be exceptions and counter-examples to any general rule. (These exceptions also can be very interesting in explaining a dataset.) The number of instances in which the rule is correct, divided by the number of instances to which the rule applies, correct or not, gives the accuracy (also sometimes called *probability level* or *confidence level*) of a rule. Requiring a higher minimum level of accuracy produces more general models; lowering the required minimum accuracy increases specificity.

Rules can be constructed from multiple conditions. The conditions are the "if" part of the rule. Each additional condition can be joined by logical connections such as "If . . . and . . . and . . . then . . ." This rule has three conditions. Some rule extractors—by no means all—can incorporate other logical connectors such as "or" and "not." The more conditions allowed in a rule, the more specific the rule becomes; the fewer conditions permitted, the more general the rule. Similarly, allowing more variety of logical connectors enables the resulting rules to be more specific; less variety restricts the specificity.

Algorithm Adjustment: Clustering

There are many different algorithms that perform unsupervised clustering; there are also many that perform supervised clustering. They do not work in the same manner, and so each particular algorithm will almost certainly produce a different set of clusters from the other clustering algorithms. However, and usefully for the miner, regardless of the considerable technical differences, the "knobs" appear much the same for all clustering techniques.

Clustering algorithms offer essentially two adjustments. One is the number of clusters specified by the miner. It's common that the algorithm requires the miner to select some number of clusters for the algorithm to use to cluster the data. A "good" number of clusters may not be apparent from any well-founded basis, even to a highly experienced miner. It's rather like simple binning—work with clustering, and discover what seems to work with the type of data on hand. Not a theoretically satisfactory state of affairs, but there it is. Obviously, the more clusters selected, the more specific the resulting model; the fewer clusters selected, the more general the model. This scenario is sometimes called *k-means clustering*. The *"k"* is the number of clusters (rather like *k*-nearest neighbor—data miners are apparently not an imaginative lot at naming algorithms!). The "means" part of the name is derived from the fact that clustering algorithms of this basic type work with the means (average values) of various clusters to decide which instances are included in which clusters.

The second adjustment works with a set of slightly different clustering algorithms that try to find some appropriate number of clusters, rather than having the miner choose some arbitrary number. If left to themselves, these clustering methods have a rather unfortunate habit of ending up with every instance in a separate cluster. Thus, analogously to the instance count in decision tree leaves and the instance count in extracted rules, in clustering algorithms that try to discover an appropriate number of clusters, as well as to which cluster to assign a particular instance, it's important to limit the algorithm's enthusiasm and require some minimum number of instances in each cluster discovered. Just as before, the higher the minimum, the more general the model; the lower the minimum, the more specific the model.

Algorithm Adjustment: Self-Organizing Maps

The specificity of a SOM requires a fairly straightforward adjustment—more neurons, more specificity; fewer neurons, more generality. With very few neurons, the map will be extremely general. Imagine a 10-neuron × 10-neuron map. Then compare that map to one with 500 × 500 neurons. Obviously, with more neurons, more detail shows. Adding neurons makes the map more specific in that it reveals more detailed relationships.

An overspecified SOM (too many neurons) tends to show all of the fine detail—the relationships that exist between small numbers of instances that are likely mainly noise. An underspecified SOM (too few neurons) tends to show only broad, sweeping generalities.

Note that creating a map in the training dataset and applying it to the test dataset to see if it produces similar maps (the diagnostic test for over/underspecification) works for SOMs just as well as for any other mining algorithm. However, the key is to make sure that the explanations revealed by the map are similar, not that the appearance of the two maps is approximately identical. The physical layout will almost certainly be different, but the relationships should be the same.

There is an additional way to judge the specificity of a SOM. If a SOM develops very few clusters (say, two or three), so long as the data is reasonably complex, the chances are that the SOM is underspecified. With more than 20 clusters, unless the dataset is huge, the map may well be overspecified—but even if it isn't, it may be too complex to explain (which is the whole purpose of a SOM). If the complexity is genuine, it's worth breaking the dataset into overlapping sets of variables in multiple input batteries and explaining the whole dataset, section by section. The overlapping variables in input batteries help to connect the explanations in one battery to the explanations in the next.

Although not directly related to appropriate specification of the SOM, a useful technique for improving the explanatory insight from a SOM can be normalizing distributions. (See the section titled Reformatting Data: Normalizing Distribution.) SOMs sometimes appear to be underspecified—that is, they don't show much detail in the nature of the relationships—when the difficulty actually is that the ranges of values in a variable are not presented to the SOM conveniently. Normalizing distributions often produces more insight than trying for more specification.

Algorithm Adjustment: Support Vector Machines

Support vector machines are another form of clustering (see the section titled Algorithm Adjustment: Clustering) and have many similar issues. The main specificity issues that are particular to support vector machines concern how the overlapping clusters are to be separated—and almost all clusters in real-world datasets overlap. In addition to the same "knobs" that clustering algorithms have, there is usually one that determines the "tightness" or "stiffness" of the cluster boundary. The tension really determines the curvature of the boundary between the clusters—more flexibility, more specification; less flexibility, less specification.

Essentially, the more flexible the boundary, the more easily it is able to modify each boundary to surround each cluster; but too much flexibility, and it will be cutting out relationships that do exist in the training data, but not in the test data.

Algorithm Adjustment: Linear Regression

The basic linear regression algorithm is a masterpiece of mathematic simplicity and elegance. In its basic form, it has no "knobs" at all. However, no tool applies linear regression in its basic form—usually multiple linear regression at the very least. Modifications, all of them needed, deal with all kinds of problems—the need for all numeric input, its inability to deal with missing values, and many similar problems. Most of these problems, and how to deal with them, were discussed earlier.

Linear regression inherently resists overspecification. After all, it can only represent linear relationships, and in this sense is the ultimately "stiff" fit to any dataset. It's a linear relationship or nothing. However, although the data mining interpretations of the linear regression theme still adhere to the basic premise of a linear fit, there is one control that impacts specification in some datasets.

The linear regression algorithms in mining tools are usually one of a variety of "robust" regressions. This means that they are modified to accommodate many of the problems that beset nonrobust regression. The main one that concerns specification is the presence of outliers. The problem is that data points that lie a long way from the regression plane, and are at the extremes of the range, disproportionately affect the results. Imagine it as a seesaw problem. The effect that any rider has on the seesaw depends on how near to the ends each sits—the farther out, the more effect. Riders in linear regression also get bigger (same as heavier) the farther they are from the regression line. So imagine 20 children all sitting near the pivot point of the seesaw. Moving one doesn't make any huge effect. However, sit an elephant on one end, and the elephant has more effect than all the children you care to pile on the middle of the seesaw. The same thing occurs with linear regression. The outliers can move the regression plane out of all proportion to their actual importance. This oversensitivity to a few data points (possibly only one) is an example of overspecification. The more robust a linear regression, the more general it is; the less robust the regression, the more specific.

However, an astute reader will note that normalizing the distribution (see the section titled Reformatting Data: Normalizing Distribution) in part removes the inordinate effect of outliers in any case. Robust regressions are really only needed for datasets that are not prepared as described here. When the data is prepared in accordance with good practice procedures for data mining, the robustness of the regression makes little difference. Thus, this "knob" and any others intended to affect specificity of linear regressions have little impact in adequately prepared datasets.

Algorithm Adjustment: Curvilinear Regression

The real difference between linear regression and curvilinear regression is that the seesaw referred to in the previous section is more like a piece of rope—not much good for riding. But suppose that the children, fed up with an elephant sitting on their seesaw, go off to play in the sandbox. They are scattered across the sandbox in no particular order. A stiff plank of wood, no matter how it is arranged to lie across the edges of the sandbox, probably won't come close to many of the denizens. A piece of rope, however, is flexible enough to be passed from hand to hand so that all of them can, without moving their position, hang on to it.

So much for children in sandboxes. When it comes to data points, the purpose is to find a flexible line that best characterizes any curvature that exists in the dataset. To do that, it has to pass as close as possible to all the points that represent the true curvature present in the data without being too flexible. Too much flexibility and the curve starts to represent the fluctuations that are present in the training dataset but that aren't in the test dataset—or elsewhere in the world. Too much flexibility and the curve represents noise.

The "knob" in nonlinear regression is the amount of curvature allowed in the regression curve. It may be called "degrees of freedom" or "magnitude of exponent" or "stiffness" or quite a lot of other things according to the toolmaker's whim. However, the knob simply adjusts the algorithm to allow more (or fewer) kinks, twists, bends, and curves. The more flexible the curve is allowed to be, the more specific the model; the less flexible the curvature, the less specific or more general the model.

Algorithm Adjustment: Neural Networks

Neural networks offer the ultimate in flexibility of fitting a regression curve to a dataset. Unlike curvilinear regression, if properly set, they can induce greater stiffness on some parts of the curve than on other parts. Curvilinear regression is limited to having the same degree of stiffness, or flexibility, over the whole of the curve. Exactly as with curvilinear regressions, specificity of the models produced using neural networks is accomplished by controlling the amount of flexibility allowed the curve. However, along with the additional power of neural networks goes a good deal more complexity.

Neural networks are built from artificial neurons. Conceptually, each of the input battery variables is assigned to an input neuron, and each output battery variable is assigned to an output neuron. Between the input and output neurons there may be—and almost always are—what are called *hidden neurons*. They are hidden in the sense that they are sandwiched between the input and output neurons, and like the cheese in a cheese sandwich where the slices of bread hide the cheese, so the input and output neurons hide the hidden neurons.

Hidden neurons are often arrayed in layers. A network containing one hidden layer connects all of the input neurons to one side, and all of the output neurons are connected to the other side. With more hidden layers, one layer connects to the next—so you'd have input, hidden, hidden, and output in a four-layer network. Several things contribute to the allowed flexibility of the fitted curve, but in general they all boil down to more neurons, more flexibility. The number of input and output neurons is fixed—one per variable—and can't be altered without changing the dataset. What varies is the number of hidden neurons. The number of hidden layers can alter too, of course, but that has less effect on curve flexibility and more on learning speed.

> **Rule of thumb:** Start with three layers (so one must be a hidden layer). Usually, the output is a single neuron corresponding to the single-variable output battery. Structure the hidden layer so that it has half the number of neurons as the input layer. It's a rule of thumb, and a starting point only, but in manually set networks, it often proves to be a good place to start. Many tools use automated procedures to estimate an appropriate beginning network architecture.

In general, more neurons make for a more specific model; fewer neurons make for a less specific model.

Algorithm Adjustment: Bayesian Nets

Naïve Bayesian networks look, if their architecture is drawn out, rather like neural networks. However, these networks are built of nodes, not neurons. The internal complexity of each node is different from that of neurons, but the architecture in which the nodes are arranged appears similar. Naïve Bayesian networks may have no hidden layer, so the inputs connect straight to the output. More complex Bayesian networks still may not have layers, but separate clusters of nodes cross-connected in complex ways.

As a rule of thumb, the complexity in Bayesian networks derives from both the number of nodes and the number of interconnections between the nodes. It's more the complexity of interconnections that is important; but complexity of interconnection is roughly proportional to the number of interconnections, and it is easier to count interconnections than to try more involved methods of determining complexity. Sometimes, especially when a Bayesian network is induced from a dataset, the network can be extremely complex indeed. Even there, counting nodes and interconnections seems to work well as a complexity estimate in practice.

> **Rule of thumb:** More complex networks are more likely to be overspecified than less complex networks. So more nodes, more connections, or both means more specificity. Fewer nodes, connections, or both means less specificity, thus more generality.

Algorithm Adjustment: Evolution Programming

Evolution programming produces program fragments that can be embedded into complete programs for execution. The fragments are usually more or less complex logical or mathematic statements that express the relationship between input battery and output battery. Internally, the algorithm uses populations of candidate programs that evolve using techniques analogous to mating and mutating. Most of the knobs that control the evolution process have more influence on speed of convergence (how quickly the best program fragment is discovered) than on specification of the resulting model. Of course, if the population sizes, breeding rates, mutation rates, and so on aren't appropriately set, the model might appear to be underspecified, but that is really a result of a poor learning process, not inherently in the way the model is specified. It's worth noting, though, that of the algorithms mentioned here, it is really only this one that separates the learning process from model specification. It's true that neural network algorithms also separate the learning process from model specification, but not as presented in mining tools, only in the raw algorithm. The commercially available tools implementing evolution programming, however (at least those known to the author), do expose knobs for adjusting model specification and, quite separately, controls for adjusting the learning process. Commercial tools generally don't expose controls for adjusting the learning process for other algorithms.

The model resulting from an evolution programming tool is itself a program. It has a degree of complexity that depends on how long it can be (that is, how many lines of program code it can include) and what mathematic and logical functions can be included. The longer the program, or the more the variety of functions, the greater the complexity and the higher the degree of specification. The shorter the program, or the fewer the variety of functions, the less the degree of specification. In fact, program length has far more effect on level of specification than variety of functions permitted. Program length, because it limits how many discrete program steps can be included in the final program, seems to have far more impact on specification than allowing or not allowing complex mathematic or logical structures as part of the evolved program such as sine, exclusive, or hyperbolic tangent, for instance.

Algorithm Adjustment: Some Other Algorithm

This listing of algorithms is certainly not comprehensive. There are other algorithms included in some tools that are not covered here. The author has tried to include the most popular algorithms, and those that seem to be gaining in popularity, even if not yet included in commercially available tools as of this writing. However, new algorithms are continually being invented, and even were that not the case, there are still several commercial mining tools that implement algorithms not mentioned here. Those not mentioned here are usually only implemented by a single vendor in their tool. However, at least a couple of dozen mining algorithms are commercially available at this writing but are not included here. Many of them are sufficiently similar to one of the algorithms mentioned here that they are, as far as tuning specification goes, simply different flavors of those that are already discussed. Others may seem to be sufficiently different to justify being labeled as different algorithms. However, so far, all the mining algorithms have certain broad features in common, at least as far as model specification goes.

First, all algorithms pretty much separate the learning process from the specification process. There are almost always some controls on raw algorithms—and certainly on any of the more complex raw algorithms—that tune the training or learning process and a pretty much separate set of knobs that tune the specification process. It is generally the case that when wrapped in tools, the tool vendor hides most or all of the complexity involved in the training or learning process. When complexity is exposed, it is usually for knobs to tune the specification process. This is because it turns out, in general, to be much harder to find a good automatic specification tuning process than to find a good automatic training tuning process.

All mining algorithms available in tools today can be viewed as working in one of two fundamental ways. Either they chop instances up into discrete chunks, as in decision tree leaves or clustering algorithm clusters, or they find continuous estimates, as with regressions or neural networks.

With any algorithm that chops instances into discrete chunks, adjusting a knob that decreases the minimum permitted size of the chunks always increases specificity of the resulting model. Increasing the minimum permitted chunk size decreases model specificity.

Algorithms that assemble a continuous estimate always seem to require a number of internal structures. For neural networks, it's neurons; for Bayesian networks, it's nodes and interconnections; for self-organizing maps, it's neurons; for evolution programs, it's program steps; for nonlinear regression, it's degrees of freedom; and so the list goes on. Whatever the exact nature of the internal structure, the rule of thumb is that more of it increases specificity, and less of it decreases specificity of the resulting model.

These two generalizations about chunk size and internal complexity seem to have held true so far, and there are also good theoretic grounds to support these conclusions. Thus, whatever mining algorithm is embedded in a tool, if adjustments affecting specificity are available, they will almost certainly influence, as appropriate, either chunk size or internal structural complexity. Once a miner has identified what these knobs are, adjusting them should tune the specificity of any mining algorithm in any modeling tool.

9.2.5 Problem: Insufficient Data

One of the possible problems a miner might find is that the test dataset isn't representative of the same relationships that are in the training dataset. This might be indicated when the following occurs:

- The regression line fitted to the predicted value versus residual value XY plot isn't effectively flat.
- The model's predicted values are all systematically skewed to be either higher than the actual values or lower than the actual values.
- The regression line fitted to the actual value versus predicted value XY plot is far from laying on the lower-left, upper-right diagonal.
- The value of the smoothed residual variance estimate is so great over some part of or all of the plot as to make the predictions unsatisfactory.

Having different underlying relationships in different datasets is normally a problem with shortage of data. Without sufficient data, it often happens that noise predominates because, when split into the three required datasets, there isn't enough data to truly represent the underlying relationships adequately in the separate datasets. Because it's hard to build accurate and reliable models without representative data, rule-of-thumb checks can help a miner to make sure that there is sufficient data, and that the training, test, and evaluation datasets are all also representative of the underlying structures and patterns in the data to produce accurate and reliable models. Earlier in this chapter (see the section titled Reformatting Data: Replacing Missing Values), we discussed how to check for data adequacy by building several check models. This discussion assumes that these checks have been done, and that the dataset as a whole, and the separate training, test, and evaluation datasets, passed those tests for consistency. If those tests have not been done, or if the dataset did not pass the tests, then the problem is almost certainly insufficient data—and considerably insufficient data too. To arrive at this diagnosis almost certainly means that there simply isn't enough data available for a reliable model to be discovered, the rest of this discussion notwithstanding.

If you are reading this section during model diagnosis, if the tests have not yet been done, or if the tests indicated insufficient data, stop reading and go and find more data, or accept the model as the best that can be had under the circumstances. The remainder of this section applies *only* if the earlier tests were applied and successfully passed.

Anyone who is still reading this section as a diagnostic aid rather than for general information almost certainly has a sampling problem—but it's also probably exacerbated by a variable representation problem. Dividing a source dataset into training, test, and evaluation datasets requires that each instance in the source has a proportional chance of being assigned to one of the datasets. Thus, with a 60/20/20 division, any instance has to have a 60 percent chance of being assigned to the training dataset, a 20 percent chance of being assigned to the test dataset, and a 20 percent chance of being assigned to the evaluation dataset. Simply taking the first 60 percent of a dataset as the training dataset, the next 20 percent as a test dataset, and the remainder as an evaluation dataset is a dangerous practice and is fraught with problems—even if the datasets produced this way pass the rule of thumb tests for representativeness.

The potential problem comes from the fact that often, and frequently unbeknownst to the miner, the data in a source dataset is in some sort of order. The CREDIT dataset, for instance, has all the BUYER = 1 instances first, and all the BUYER = 0 instances following. This is because of the way that the dataset was balanced in that all the BUYER = 1 records were selected first and the appropriate BUYER = 0 records were later appended to the file to achieve the needed balance. If the first 60 percent of this dataset were used for training, the test and evaluation datasets would have no BUYER = 1 responders at all.

The rule of thumb checks for representativeness do not check all of the variables in a dataset. They only work at all so long as the instances in the three datasets are indeed chosen at random from the source data. So if the three datasets were not built using random selection, rebuild them.

However, the possible problem that introduced this section—where training and test datasets are not representative of the same relationships—may be an indication that the dataset needs balancing. The fact that the relationships don't represent the same patterns in the test and training datasets only applies between input and output batteries. It's quite possible to have all of the three dataset input batteries representative of the same patterns in all datasets but find that the output battery isn't representative—which is exactly the case in the unmodified CREDIT dataset with BUYER = 1 occurring for about 1 percent of the instances. Even testing input and output batteries separately to ensure that each is representative doesn't solve the problem, because it is possible to have the input battery representative in all three datasets, the output battery representative in all three datasets, but have dissimilar relationships between input and output batteries in all three datasets. How?

In the CREDIT example, assume the input battery in all three datasets actually is fully representative of the same patterns. Testing the output battery in all three datasets would reveal only that, for the binary variable that constitutes the whole output battery, about 1 percent had the value 1 and 99 percent had the value 0, and that this was true in all three datasets. As far as possible, testing the input and output battery separately would reveal each as being representative. However, with such a low density of responders in the output battery, it is possible that the few instances that did occur would have different relationships between input and output battery in each dataset.

The only real answer is to check that the relationship between input and output batteries is similar in all three datasets—but that isn't accomplished by a rule of thumb. That calls for full-scale modeling of any relationships, which is what the miner is trying to do in constructing the model in the first place. There is no shortcut, only good modeling practice.

Thus, the possible problem that introduced the section may well be a sign that the dataset needs balancing in order to build a robust model. Failing that, rule-of-thumb checks notwithstanding, there simply may not be enough data. The rule of thumb is a guide, not a certainty, and only modeling finally discovers whether the data is in fact sufficient to define a satisfactory model. If, despite all efforts, this turns out to be the case, the only answer is to get more, or better, or more and better data.

9.2.6 Problem: Uneven Data

Another problem a miner might find is that the training and test data represent some relationships better than others. This may be indicated by some residual values that are more common than others.

An input battery of any complexity contains a huge number of relationships. The only ones of interest to a modeler are, in a classification model, those that relate to the output battery and, in an explanatory model, those that relate to the business problem. Naturally, some of the patterns in the input battery will be more indicative of output battery states than other patterns ("better correlated," to use a more technical term). One problem is that the correlation of the patterns in the input battery may change depending on various factors, such as the actual value of the input battery variable(s).

Imagine a dataset containing a single-variable input battery and a single-variable output battery. Suppose that when the values of the input battery are low in their range, the correlation is very good, but as they increase, the correlation becomes less in proportion to the magnitude of the input. What would the residuals look like? A glance back at Figure 9.17 shows what might be expected.

The correlation between two variables, which is traditionally measured over the whole of the range of both variables, usually does vary from one part of the range to another. It is possible for multivariate datasets, as the input battery almost always is, to behave this way too. However, the impact is usually more "blurred" when many variables are involved. As the patterns in one set of input battery variables lose their relevance, other patterns, perhaps in other variables, assume higher relevance.

In many datasets, the correlation between input battery and output battery turns out to be pretty even. It's still true, nonetheless, that some parts of the multivariate range will be more correlated with the output battery than other parts. It is possible for the correlation between input battery and output battery to change in "steps" rather than smoothly. When this happens (not often in practice) the residuals also tend to change in steps and to show "clumps" of common residual values.

Far more common is the situation shown in Figure 9.25, or some variant of it with more variables. In some parts of the range of data, the relationship is reasonably well defined. The problem is that in other parts there is no data to define the

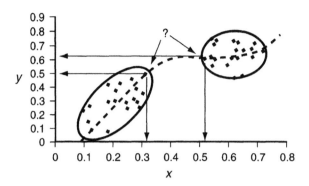

FIGURE 9.25

Ill-defined portions of a relationship.

relationship—if there is any. The dashed line indicating the relationship between about 0.50 and 0.62 on the Y axis and 0.31 and 0.52 on the X axis simply has no data defining what it might be. The mining algorithm can make a "best fit" through this area based only on the influence of the distant points where data occurs more densely. It's not that the mining algorithm made any errors in discovering how to make the best fit. The problem is that there aren't many data points around in important parts of the relationship to give much clue as to the true relationship in that area. If the test dataset contains any data points in that area, the model is not likely to have estimated the actual underlying relationship.

Now, to be sure, Figure 9.25 is an exaggeration to illustrate a point. The sorts of datasets modeled in data mining will have far more data points than those illustrated—and far more variables. However, the concept still applies. Where input battery data in its multivariate distribution clusters together, the relationships will be much better defined than in areas where the density of points is less dense. If, as often happens, the data does have such clusters, variance of the residuals will tend to increase and decrease with the density of the data in the input battery. The "patches" or clusters in the input battery will tend to be reflected as patches, or clusters, in the residuals.

Perhaps nothing can be done about the problem. Some things in life come in patches or clusters, and the data simply reflects this as a fact of life. Data miners don't always accept this as a valid excuse and do things like balancing datasets to account for it, which will work in this case too. However, before balancing a dataset, it's worth ensuring that the data as collected for mining does, in fact, reflect the full range of behaviors that the world offers and that the dataset hasn't been selectively truncated in some way. Selectively including, or not including, some instances introduces bias into a dataset, something that needs to be carefully monitored. (See Section 9.2.7 for a fuller description of bias.)

9.2.7 Problem: Estimation Bias When Mining a Model

A miner might find that the model is "biased" into preferentially producing certain predicted values. (See Section 9.2.13 about variance bias.) This may be indicated by the following:

- Patches, clumps, or clusters of residuals in the residual lines.
- The regression line fitted to the actual value versus predicted value XY plot is far from laying on the lower-left, upper-right diagonal.

Bias here is used in exactly its colloquial meaning—to lean toward, to be predisposed toward, or to favor something. In mining, therefore, a mined model is said to be *biased* when it has a tendency to produce one, or several, particular classifications. A mined model is also biased when it produces estimates that are all offset by a fixed amount, or by an amount that varies in fixed relationship to the magnitude or class of the estimate. As an example, a model choosing which of several cross-sell products to offer that predominantly chooses the same product from the selection available is biased in favor of that product. Similarly, a model to estimate the return on investment from a project that consistently underestimates the actual return by some fixed amount or by some fixed percentage is also biased. Bias in the estimates of mined models are relatively easy to address and may be produced by underspecification (see Section 9.2.4).

Although an appropriately specified model should not have any bias in its residuals (see Sections 9.1 and 9.2.4), sometimes a mining algorithm may have trouble if some of the relationships are not well represented in the data. When this is the case for the output battery, it calls for balancing the dataset; this may also work to help the model learn relationships that are important but not well represented in the source dataset.

It's worth noting that bias is a crucial issue when constructing datasets and during deployment, but these issues don't arise during mining and refining a model and are not covered here.

9.2.8 Problem: Noise Reduction

A miner might discover that to avoid learning noise, the tool was too restricted in the flexibility it was allowed when learning the relationships. This may be indicated when the following occurs:

- There is no significant difference in naïve and mined model performance.
- The mean of the residuals is not 0.
- The curve fitted to the actual value versus predicted value XY plot differs markedly from a straight line where it passes through the data.
- The value of the smoothed residual variance estimate is so great over some or all of the plot as to make the predictions unsatisfactory. (See Section 9.2.16 on noisy and irrelevant variables.)

Noise is a problem, and using an underspecified model is one technique that makes the model more noise resistant. However, finding an appropriate specification level is better than underspecifying a model just to enable it to resist learning noise. (Section 9.2.4 describes in detail how to appropriately specify a mining algorithm regardless of the level of noise in a dataset.) Nonetheless, it may be possible to increase the specificity of the mining algorithm if some of the noise present in a dataset can be reduced. The intuition here is that if some of the noise can be removed from a dataset, the model can better learn the underlying relationships without having to be as noise resistant. Naturally, any noise-removing techniques that are applied to the source dataset have to be duplicated on any runtime data during deployment, so the transformations to reduce noise have to be carried forward.

One important noise-reduction technique is missing value replacement. (See the section titled Reformatting Data: Replacing Missing Values.) Replacing missing values may allow a more specific model to be created on a dataset than before they were replaced. Replacement tends to have this noise-reducing effect even on algorithms that can handle missing values without replacement. This action also tends to reduce the variance of the residuals or, in other words, to produce more precise (or more confident) estimates, even if the specification level of the model isn't changed.

Another noise-reduction technique is binning; the supervised binning techniques for input battery variables are particularly useful. (See the section titled Reformatting Data: Binning.) Another, perhaps preferable, alternative to binning is normalizing the distribution of the input battery. (See the section titled Reformatting Data: Normalizing Distribution.) If the noise is in the output battery, equal frequency binning is a good practice, although redistribution of the output battery distribution is again a better alternative.

Manual aggregation of variable detail also sometimes works well, especially if a dataset has several aggregation levels. It's often beneficial to have variable aggregations along some common metric. For instance, aggregating hourly sales to daily, daily to weekly, or weekly to monthly (depending on the needs of the business problem) may produce better estimates. If most of the aggregation periods are monthly and sales are aggregated daily, for instance, a common aggregation period could very well reduce noise. Either convert the aggregation period to daily by taking 1/29th, 1/30th, or 1/31st of the monthly amounts as appropriate to the month, or roll up daily to monthly sales amounts. Common aggregation periods tend to introduce less noise and produce less residual variance. However, rolling up isn't a choice if the estimates needed are for short periods, say daily. The choice then is to try a "roll down" of monthly to daily.

Another noise-reduction technique that works when there are a fair number of variables in the input battery is to "bundle" groups of variables together. (This is a data miner's version of what statisticians think of as *principal curves and surfaces analysis.*) Many mining tools provide information about how well the variables correlate with each other. If the tool available doesn't provide such information, Excel will do the job, although it's more time consuming. Take bundles of variables that correlate well with each other, create a model using one bundle at a time as the input battery, and use the original output battery to build the bundle model. When all of the commonly correlated variables have been grouped into bundles, replace the bundles in a new input battery with the bundle predictions. Bring any unbundled variables forward into the combining model. This creates a composite model built from several models, with input variables feeding into bundling models, the output from which becomes the input to later combining models. Figure 9.26 illustrates this concept.

Even when well specified, it is always tough to create a model that learns the underlying relationships (called *signal*) and at the same time resists learning the spurious relationships (called *noise*) that exist in any dataset. The ideal would be to determine some sort of signal-to-noise ratio and use it to calibrate the model. Unfortunately, that is an advanced mining topic not covered here. However, one technique is to create an initial model that is as good as possible, then add the output from that model to the original input battery as another variable, and remodel the newly created input battery. The idea is that the initial model will have learned some of the signal at least. The second model can use this as a starting point and, with the initial model's output as an added feature, may be able to improve on the final output.

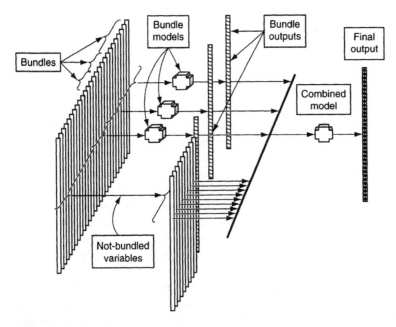

FIGURE 9.26

Combining bundles of variables to reduce noise.

9.2.9 **Problem: Categorical Correlation**

A miner might find that there are many categorical values in the input battery that all represent a similar phenomenon or phenomena. This may be indicated when the following occurs:

- The residuals histogram (and, therefore, the residuals distribution) is obviously not normal.
- The apparent ranges of actual and predicted values are different or the density of points is not uniform and not symmetrical about a diagonal line from lower left to upper right in the actual value versus predicted value XY plot.
- The curve fitted to the actual value versus predicted value XY plot differs markedly from a straight line where it passes through the data.

Categorical variables, just as with other types of variables, can carry information that is sufficiently similar to each other so that the variables seem effectively identical to the modeling tool. Age and income are typical examples of this phenomenon in many datasets. Age and income can be represented as categories, and if this were done, both age and income, on average, might very well increase together.

Sometimes there are several to many variables carrying essentially similar relationships. Many mining algorithms make what is called an *assumption of independence.* Independent variables do not have similar relationships to each other. Similarity of information content makes variables "dependent" on each other in the sense that what value one variable takes on depends on the value taken by another variable. When many variables carry similar information, some mining algorithms give undue weight to the evidence that they provide—rather as a human may be persuaded by the behavior of a crowd, even if everyone is making a mistake. For instance, if everyone read the *New York Times* and was very much influenced by the film critic, asking 100 people who all agreed that a film was excellent doesn't mean any more than the single critic's opinion if the 100 all reflect the critic's opinion. Thus, the views of the readers would be dependent on the views of the critic. It's similar with variables. In the same way that you might think that you had 100 independent reviews of a film, so the mining algorithm "thinks" it has multiple sets of evidence leaning in a particular direction. If all of the variables actually represent different expressions of the same underlying phenomenon (technically called a *latent* phenomenon), the mining algorithm may be unduly influenced by the apparent predominance of the evidence. Bundling highly correlated variables serves, in part, to overcome this tendency toward bias. (See Sections 9.2.7 and 9.2.8.)

Regardless of the desired resolution of the output, the output can't have any finer resolution than the granularity of the input battery allows. When many variables carry few categories, and particularly when the input battery variables are all highly dependent, the predicted values may be clumped into discrete groups. Perhaps, after bundling, the categories in the input battery are still too few to provide sufficient resolution for the prediction (or understanding, if the model is an explanatory one). If the input battery does have many categories, it may be that most of the categories are only sparsely represented, many of them represented by relatively few instances as a proportion of the dataset. In this case, it might be worth trying to balance the dataset carefully to better represent categories of interest. In the end, it may simply be that the data available doesn't contain relationships sufficient to provide the resolution or continuity of output needed. Then the only choice is to find data with more variability.

9.2.10 Problem: Partial Colinearities

Another possible problem is that a large number of variables in the input battery may carry similar information over parts of their range. This may be indicated when the following occurs:

- The residuals histogram (and, therefore, the residuals distribution) is obviously not normal.
- The apparent ranges of actual and predicted values are different, or the density of points is not uniform, and not symmetrical about a diagonal line from lower left to upper right in an actual value versus predicted value XY plot.
- The curve fitted to the actual value versus predicted value XY plot differs markedly from a straight line where it passes through the data.

Variables, quite naturally, vary their values over their range. However, the variance is usually not uniform over the range of the variable. This nonuniformity shows up in the variable's distribution, which in at least some sense is a description of the nonuniformity of variance of a variable. The central "hump" of the normal distribution, for instance, represents a clustering of values about the variable's mean. Glance back, for instance, at Figure 9.9. It's also possible for variables to have actual, or relative, gaps in their distributions, as shown earlier in Figure 9.25.

When individual variables exhibit such behaviors, it usually doesn't cause a problem. Even when many variables show such behaviors, it still causes little problem—unless the variables are partially dependent on each other. Perhaps for some parts of their range, the variables are somehow linked, whereas over the rest they aren't. Apart from common missing value ranges this situation is rare. However, when it does happen, it can affect the output quite severely. The correlated subranges can bias the output values so that the residuals have a far higher variance in some parts of their range than in other parts, or the residuals seem patchy in some areas as the model makes systematic errors. Distribution normalization, or possibly binning, may ameliorate this problem.

9.2.11 **Problem: Data Not Representative of the Business Problem**

A miner might face the problem of an input battery that, although it checks as representative of the population, has some parts of the output battery range represented by very few instances (records) and other parts represented by very many instances. This may be indicated when the following occurs:

- The residuals histogram (and, therefore, the residuals distribution) is obviously not normal.
- The apparent ranges of actual and predicted values are different, or the density of points is not uniform, and not symmetrical about a diagonal line from lower left to upper right in an actual value versus predicted value XY plot.
- The curve fitted to the actual value versus predicted value XY plot differs markedly from a straight line where it passes through the data.
- The value of the smoothed residual variance estimate is so great over some or all of the plot as to make the predictions unsatisfactory.

Consider a dataset in which only 1 percent of the instances were BUYER = 1. These relatively few records would be insufficient for many mining tools to adequately model. ("Adequately" only means "well enough to impact the business problem.") The answer is to balance the dataset. The reason for the rebalancing is fundamental to the process of modeling and mining. Initially, it is important to both modeler and miner for the dataset to be as unbiased as possible. Thus, the dataset should represent as true a state of the world as is possible. It is only from this beginning that the dataset can be carefully adjusted to least distort any other relationships, save those specifically balanced. This ideally results in a dataset that is still as representative of the world as possible but is more amenable to the needs of the mining tool. The reason for the balancing adjustment is that although the initial dataset may be as representative of the world as possible, it isn't necessarily representative of the business problem. Adjustment is needed to make the dataset representative of the business problem as well as of the world.

9.2.12 **Problem: Output Limiting**

A miner might discover that the tool may be clipping the output predictions. This may be indicated when the regression line fitted to the actual value versus residual XY plot is not horizontal.

Some tools limit the range of the output predictions to the range discovered during mining; some don't. The idea is, for instance, that if the minimum value in the training dataset range was 0, it makes little sense to have a predicted value of, say, −0.4. However, assuming that the model is not perfect, it will make errors, and these will naturally tend to range both above and below the actual value— including at the top and bottom of the range.

Whether or not the output limiting is important to the business problem, it will produce apparent distortion in the residuals similar to that shown earlier in Figures 9.7 and 9.8. As far as checking the residuals for systematic error is concerned, output limiting is not a problem.

9.2.13 Problem: Variance Bias

One of the problems a miner might find is that there may be a bias that affects all of the input battery variables. This may be indicated when the regression line fitted to the actual value versus residual XY plot is not horizontal.

Any discussion of sampling bias needs to look at possible ways of seeing the effects of bias on a dataset. As patterns in the input value change, it is to be expected that, with some degree of confidence, the output battery will change its value too. However, in general, regardless of the change in magnitude of either input or output battery, the distribution remains fairly constant over the whole range. Sometimes when bias is present, it may leave traces of its presence by changing distribution as magnitude changes.

Another possible result of bias that affects the output variance is that, while retaining a mean of 0, the variance is nonetheless correlated to prediction magnitude. Figure 9.17 illustrated this effect where the residual variance was low when the predicted value was at one end of its range, and it was larger when the predicted value was at the other end, and the variance at any point was proportional to the magnitude of the prediction.

Whatever is going on in the real world to produce such a change in residual variance is outside the system of variables that form the input battery. Something else changes that is biasing all of the input variables. This is a firm clue not only that better data would improve the model but also that the data might be available—or at least a clue that the phenomenon might be measurable. If it affects all, or a significant fraction, of the input battery variables so notably, it should be possible to discover what is actually producing this effect.

9.2.14 Problem: The Modeling Tool Is Broken

A broken mining tool or algorithm may be indicated by almost any untoward situation or circumstance. Mining tools or algorithms do break—but not often! Data mining tools are computer programs—pieces of software—and as with all other software, they are subject to the normal array of "features" (also known as bugs and glitches). As a miner, if you discover one of these features, just shrug your shoulders—such are the vagaries of fate. It's worth contacting the vendor with bugs and with usability feedback. As with any vendor, what your provider chooses to do about helpful feedback (and unsolicited advice from data miners) lies in the lap of the gods.

However, software bugs are not the main subject of this section. Occasionally—very, very occasionally—the tool or algorithm is fundamentally flawed. The example in this chapter illustrated in Figure 9.11, in which the tool actually fails to make predictions in part of the range where it obviously should, is certainly a flaw. Whether it is a bug or a fundamental problem greatly depends on the definition of each term and is irrelevant for the purposes of this discussion. It is a failure in algorithm or program logic that is permanently embedded in this version of the mining tool's code. A workaround won't fix it, it isn't an intermittent or transient problem, and it isn't dependent on the data that a miner chooses to model. In this case, the tool is broken and requires repair before it is again usable.

This situation really doesn't happen often. Almost all data mining tools, and certainly all of those that have been in the marketplace for some time, are not likely to be broken in the sense discussed here. Naturally, they will all have their idiosyncrasies and their unintended "features"; that is only to be expected. However, nothing is perfect, and the example discussed in this chapter is not contrived to prove a point. This example is drawn from a real business modeling and data mining project, and it illustrates a real broken mining tool.

The corrective action here is simply to use another tool. Do, of course, report the problem to the tool vendor. The point to note is that sometimes—not often, for sure, and only after conscientious checking, but sometimes—a good worker really is constrained to blame the tools!

9.2.15 **Problem: Anachronistic Variables**

Leakage from anachronistic variables may be indicated by a model making perfect, or near perfect, classifications that are not explicable as either trivial or obvious.

Anachronistic variables are a pernicious mining problem. However, they aren't any problem at all at deployment time—unless someone expects the model to work! Anachronistic variables are out of place in time. Specifically, at data modeling time, they carry information back from the future to the past. Many, perhaps even most, business classification models are outcome models—that is, they are modeling outcomes that occur later in time. For the purposes of mining, the data has an arbitrary "now" point so that the model can learn to classify the future outcomes that have, in fact, already occurred. The modeled outcomes are, of course, only in the future relative to the arbitrary "now" point. Because the dataset necessarily contains information about events that occur later than the "now" point, it's crucial to take scrupulous care that no later information leaks back.

Any future information that does leak back will be present in all three datasets, so it won't be detected until the model is deployed; performance is far from the anticipated model functioning because the needed information about the future outcome will be missing. A clue that there's temporal leakage is that the model turns out to be too good to be true. Too good to be true usually is, and perfect models are a dead giveaway. (See the section titled Reformatting Data: Normalizing Distribution.)

If any outcome classification model seems far better than reasonably expected, check carefully for anachronistic variables. Build single variable models to discover any variables that individually seem too good to be true. Think carefully about how or why they might be anachronistic. Eventually, deployment will certainly prove whether any temporal leakage occurred, but that is not the best time to discover the problem.

9.2.16 Problem: Noisy or Irrelevant Variables

Another possible problem is that the input battery contains one or more very noisy or completely irrelevant variables. This may be indicated when the following occurs:

- There is no significant difference in naïve and mined model performance.
- The residuals appear to contain information that could be used to improve the prediction.
- The value of the smoothed residual variance estimate is so great over some or all of the plot as to make the predictions unsatisfactory.
- Significant clusters are present in the input battery with a high degree of separation between them.

Noisy or totally irrelevant variables may be a problem, and they certainly are for some algorithms. The problem is not with the noise, nor the irrelevancy, but with the fact that they interfere with the algorithm's ability to discover relationships from the other variables. This may seem to be odd at first glance. If there are variables in the input battery that have some specific degree of relationship with the output battery, how is it that adding irrelevant or highly noisy variables to the input dataset prevents the mining algorithm from learning the best relationships that are present?

Consider this. If noisy or irrelevant variables do have an adverse impact, the noisiest and most irrelevant certainly should have such an impact. A variable that is all noise has to be totally irrelevant. Such a variable is one that is constructed to be purely random. If it's a binary variable, the toss of a fair coin to determine its value would produce a random variable of this sort. Other analogous techniques produce random variables of all types.

The interesting thing about random variables is that they don't look random—at least, not to human intuition. In fact, random variables are, perhaps surprisingly, guaranteed to contain patterns. The longer the random sequence, the more patterns the random variable will contain. If you have the patience, flip a fair coin 100 or more times and look at the result. What turns up has runs and sequences in it that at first sight don't look random at all. Nonetheless, random they are. However, if there are patterns, they will correlate more or less with the output battery. Algorithms that chop the dataset into smaller and smaller pieces, such as decision trees or rule extractors, will eventually come to a piece in which the apparently most suitable variable on which to split is the random variable—and from there on it's all downhill as this causes random fragmentation of the dataset.

Even some continuous estimators, such as neural networks, are distracted by the apparent, but actually spurious, patterns. In those parts of the dataset where the random variable appears to have a correlated pattern, the continuous estimator will incorporate the apparently useful pattern. Naturally, the test dataset won't have the same pattern, but learning will be halted before the model is specific enough to extract the entire pattern that is actually available. (See Section 9.2.4.)

As an aside, there are tools that are quite impervious to noisy or irrelevant variables, such as naïve Bayes. However, these algorithms pay a heavy price because they assume independence of variables, and where the variables carry redundant information they are sorely swayed. That's why one of the earlier techniques advises removing correlated variables by bundling. (See Section 9.2.8.)

Many mining tools list the variables by "importance." Be careful with this term. Variables are ranked only as they are important for a specific model. Different models of the same dataset, sometimes even with the same mining algorithm, can rate the importance of variables differently for the separate specific models. This is not to say that some variables don't carry more information than others, and it's not to say that several different models created using different algorithms won't commonly select a similar set of variables. But the importance of variables is not really something to be reported or counted on, except as they are important for a specific model in a specific dataset. At this writing, there is no generally accepted measure of importance for variables, no generally accepted method of determining importance, and no sign of one on the horizon. However, as an advanced data mining technique, it is possible to measure how much information any variable or set of variables carries about any output battery, and to define, before building any model, how good it could be at its best. But this is not a measure of importance. Importance is relative only to specific models, not to datasets.

Nonetheless, and given the caveats in the preceding paragraph, many mining tools do rate variable importance for the created model. After trying several iterations of refining a model, if it turns out that some selection of variables are consistently rated as unimportant, remove them. Recall that it is good practice to create the simplest model, and one facet of "simple" is as few variables as possible.

If an importance measure isn't available, try building several models with small but different selections of variables. Discard any variables that are commonly present in the worst models.

9.2.17 Problem: Interaction Effects

One of the possible problems a miner might find is that the tool (algorithm) selected does not inherently explore interaction effects when important interaction effects are present. This may be indicated when the following occurs:

- The curve fitted to the actual value versus predicted value XY plot differs markedly from a straight line where it passes through the data.
- The value of the smoothed residual variance estimate is so great over some or all of the plot as to make the predictions unsatisfactory.
- An explanation is not convincing, relevant, or applicable to the business problem.

Interaction effects can be crucial, and they are easy to understand. If you want to carpet a room, it's not enough to know just the length of the room, nor is it enough to know just the width of the room. Interaction between length and width gives the number of square feet of a room, and that is the information you need to buy carpet. In this example, multiplication produces the interaction effect.

Several data mining algorithms do not incorporate interaction effects into their modeling. Several other algorithms do. However, whether any algorithm does or does not incorporate interaction effects, it is useful to explicitly incorporate them where they are known. Even when an algorithm can learn interaction effects, it speeds learning and better resists noise if the interaction effect is explicitly included. (In this example, it would save the mining tool having to learn how to multiply, which is easy, but why force it to learn something that the modeler/miner already knows?)

For those algorithms that don't incorporate interaction effects, explicitly representing them in a dataset can make a crucial difference to the quality and power of the model. An easy way of representing interacting variables is to multiply them and add another variable to the input battery with the result. On the other hand, it's always worth at least checking performance using a tool with an algorithm that does incorporate interaction effects, such as neural networks. Even if the main model is, say, a decision tree, and it performs well, it's still worth checking the models against each other as a sort of "sanity check."

Better still, if the tools are available, is to explicitly check for interactions. To do that, it's worth taking a quick look at what interactions are, how they affect data and mining tools, and how to actually discover and characterize interactions in a dataset.

Variable Interactions

Interactions between variables simply means that the effect that one input variable has on the output variable changes depending on the value of some other variable. So as an example, with "Y" as the output variable and "A" and "B" as input variables, the effect that "A" has on "Y" depends on the value of "B."

All of the data mining algorithms available have different signature behaviors, capabilities, and performance. For example, decision trees don't inherently include interactions and neural networks do. Does this mean that networks are inherently better than decision trees? No! It does mean that if interactions are important, they have to be explicitly included in the input battery for any algorithm that doesn't inherently discover them. However, other algorithms that do discover such interactions still benefit from having them included. It requires greater complexity in the algorithm to discover such interactions, and without sufficient complexity, it still won't discover the interactions.

Additional complexity can itself be a problem, mainly because of these three things:

1. The increase in complexity might simply lead to the algorithm learning noise instead of the desired relationship.
2. The complexity will slow the learning, sometimes to a crawl, making discovering meaningful models a far slower process and possibly slowing learning so much that the project becomes impractical.
3. There is no easy way to determine how much complexity is enough.

However, an easy way to determine whether the data contains important interactions, and a good rule of thumb to indicate how to characterize the interactions, is through the use of interaction indicator plots (IIPs).

Interaction Indicator Plots

Using IIPs allows the miner to put the important interactions into the input dataset instead of into model complexity, even for those algorithms that could, if so configured, characterize the interactions. Understanding the interactions can make an enormous difference in explaining relationships in a dataset. For predictive models with those algorithms that don't inherently characterize such interactions, it can improve the model enormously. It might at first glance seem easy to include all of the interactions as a matter of course. However, this direction leads to a variable explosion! For a dataset with 10 variables in the input battery, and including only two interactions, say x^2 and x^3, this adds $10 \times 9 \times 2 \times 180$ additional interaction variables to the original 10. For each of the 10 variables, every one can interact with one of the other 9 (thus 10×9), and there are two possible interactions proposed (x^2 and x^3). Try it with a 20-variable input battery, and it requires 760 extra interaction variables. Not only is this variable bloat damaging to the dataset, but it's also almost certainly unnecessary because many of these interactions won't carry any useful information. The answer is to pick and choose and use only the interactions that are useful and appropriate. Understanding the use of IIPs is a place to start.

The principle underlying IIPs is straightforward. It requires all the variables to be numeric or recoded numerically using a principled recoding method if they are categorical (see the section titled Reformatting Data: Normalizing Ranges). It's convenient to normalize the range of the input variables; 0–1 is usual. In essence, an IIP plots the values of the output variable for every input variable, as influenced by every one of the other input variables in turn. Thus, for an output variable, say y, it's discovering the interaction, if any, between two input variables, say a and b, that is important.

To understand how this is done, start by considering the plot of how output varies with a single variable. When a single variable is used, the result is called a

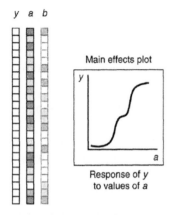

FIGURE 9.27

Main effects plot.

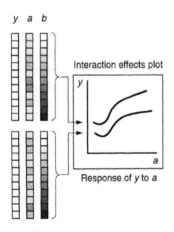

FIGURE 9.28

Interaction effects plot.

main effects plot, one of which is illustrated in Figure 9.27. It simply shows the values for the output variable *y* over its range for the values of the input variable, shown here as *a,* over its range.

Notice that in this figure variable *b* is shaded out because in a main effects plot it's only the relationship between *y* and *a* over the range of both variables that shows up. To discover if there are interactions between *a* and *b* when *y* is the output variable, the data is (at least conceptually) ordered on the variable *b* and then split into two parts with equal numbers of instances in each part, as shown in Figure 9.28.

One part of the divided dataset contains all instances of above average values of *b*, and the other part contains all of the instances of average or less value for *b*. A separate effects plot for each part of the dataset shows two plotted curves. Each curve shows the relationship between *y* and *a*. However, because the variables have been ordered and separated into two parts based on the values of *b*, if there are any differences in the relationship between *y* and *a* in the two plots, it can only be because of the change in the value of *b*, because that is all that has changed. Any differences in the relationship will show up as differences in the height or shape of the two curves. Or to put it another way, if the relationship between *y* and *a* in the two partitions is identical, the two curves will lie one on top of the other, and it would appear to be a single curve. If two curves appear, something changes in the relationship between *y* and *a* at different values of *b*. The differences can only be because *a* interacts with *b*.

The differences in shape between the two curves indicate the nature of the interaction between the two variables. Interpreting IIPs is quite straightforward after only a little familiarity. Some typical interactions are shown in Figure 9.29.

Figure 9.29 shows IIPs for three variables; *a*, *b*, and *c*. In the left IIP showing interactions of *a* with *y*, the response curves are similarly shaped and essentially parallel to each other. The interaction that is present is clearly additive because the plotted curves are at different heights. Because they are the same distance apart and the same shape, it's clear that the only difference in response for the two bands of values is that band 1 has had a constant value added to it compared to band 0. (Or conversely, band 0 has had some constant value subtracted from it compared to band 1.) In any case, the response is identical except for the addition (or subtraction) of some value. It's usually not necessary to include additive interaction explicitly in a dataset. (Also, note that in statistical terms an additive interaction is called "no interaction" and is not distinguished from the situation where the two plotted curves lie one on top of another. As far as data miners are concerned, these purely additive effects can be important and are most easily characterized as "additive interactions," statistical use notwithstanding.)

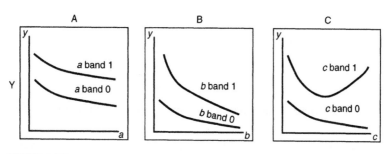

FIGURE 9.29

Typical IIPs.

The central IIP showing interactions of b with y shows that the slope of the interactions in the two bands changes, although the direction of curvature remains the same. An IIP such as this suggests that a multiplicative relationship exists in the output response between b and x. Thus, including an interaction variable created from bx in the input battery is indicated.

The right side IIP displaying interactions of c with y shows two phenomena. Not only does the slope change, but so does the direction of curvature. The slope change again suggests a multiplicative interaction, as in the interaction with b. However, the change in the direction in curvature suggests that higher degree interaction is needed too: cx^2. (Notice that on the left of this image both curves are falling. However, about the middle of the image the upper curve begins to rise while the lower curve keeps falling.)

In general, a change in slope suggests the interaction term x^1 (usually shown simply as x), and every additional curvature divergence suggests the need for an additional degree of interaction, x^2, x^3, x^4, and so on.

Figure 9.30 shows a set of IIPs for five variables, a through d in the input battery with variable Y as output. Inspection of these IIPs suggests that interaction effects ba (perhaps b^2a), da, d^2a, a^2b, and cd should be included in the input battery.

Why these particular interactions? Let's take them individually:

- The plot in row A, column B has curves that are pretty much the same shape, but diverge, or separate, in appearance from left to right. Recall that plot lines that are essentially the same shape but at different distances apart at different points in the plot show a multiplicative relationship, thus indicating that the interaction can be represented as $b \times a$, which is usually represented as ba or "b times a."

- In the same plot, row A and column B, it's possible that at the right side the curvature direction of the two plot lines are moving in different directions. Recall that a change in the direction of curvature indicates the possibility of a higher-order interaction (square, cube, and so on) with one additional power possibly needed for each change in direction. The direction change here isn't much, if it's there at all, so it's just a hint that one additional order might be useful, so this would be b^2a. But it's just a hint and probably not needed here.

- Consider the IIP in column D, row A. Notice that there is some divergence between the two plot lines. Recall that divergence points to a multiplicative interaction, so this points to da, as well as a possible change in direction of slope. If so, d^2a (that is, the square of d multiplied by a).

- Column A, row B. Is there some divergence here? Perhaps. Enough for a^2b? Perhaps.

- How about column C, row D? Looks like a multiplicative interaction because the slopes diverge, so this points to the possible need for cd.

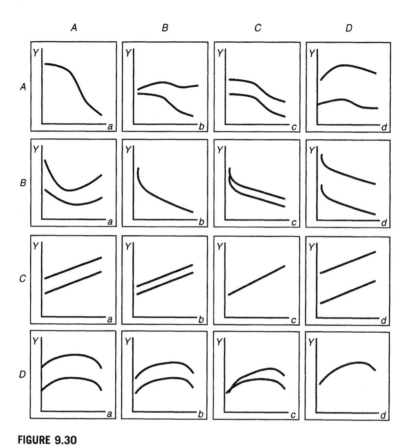

FIGURE 9.30

IIPs for five variables *a* through *d* interacting with output variable *Y.*

In practice, these plots are useful indeed. Figure 9.31 shows a screen shot from a mining tool showing some of the IIPs for the CREDIT dataset. A quick glance shows an interesting range of interactions among the variables shown. Notice that the variables BEACON and DAS (top row, second box) seem to have a multiplicative relationship. However, note carefully that DAS and BEACON (second row, left column) have a very different relationship. Why?

Keep in mind that the Y variable is actually BUYER in this set of IIPs. So the whole set shows the response of BUYER to several variables when ordered and separated based on the values of other variables. The plots show first (top row, second box) BEACON ordered by, and separated on, the variable DAS. The other IIP (second row, left column) shows the interactions for DAS ordered by and separated on BEACON. Thus, these are not symmetrical plots. DAS by BEACON cannot be expected to look anything like BEACON by DAS. Mind you, although

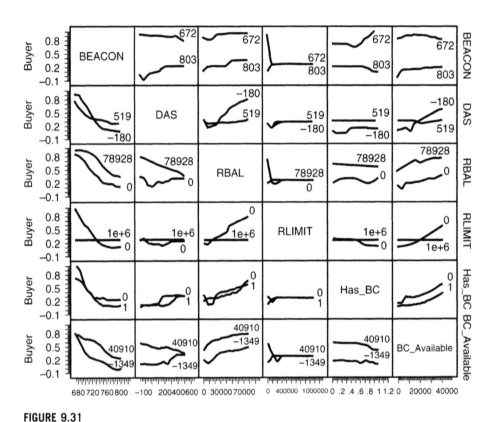

FIGURE 9.31

Interaction plots from the CREDIT dataset.

different, if there is an interaction one way, then expect an interaction of some type the other way too.

So far, so good (as Wile E. Coyote so often noted when pursuing the Road Runner). This works fine with five or six variables. It might even be tractable with ten input variables and one output variable so long as the modeler/miner has access to automated IIP tools. But with many more than ten input variables, and certainly when dealing with the many tens or hundreds of variables of most minable datasets, this is not any sort of practical solution.

Note that it is, in principle, fairly easy to automate input variable interaction detection and variable creation, including detecting the necessary degree of interaction, although few, if any, commercial data mining tools available at this writing offer such an option. Alternatively, it's also fairly simple in principle to add the necessary interaction variables to a dataset using a data preparation tool separate from the mining tool, but this too at this writing is not currently available as an option in data mining or separate data preparation tools. It's also worth noting that to do the job properly, the interaction variables created should themselves be checked for interactions. But to do all this by hand is to all intents and purposes impossible—tough for people, although computationally not much of a problem *if* it were automated.

There are noncommercial tools available that help, but short of such aids a miner has to fall back on other methods. First, go back to the business problem frame, the problem map, the cognitive map, the business process map, and the cause and effect map. In all these places, there are clues as to where variables are expected to interact and which variables they are. At least create IIPs for these variables. If there is one, use the system simulation or a process simulation and look at where the interactions occur in these simulations. Simulations allow a priori (or before the fact) determination of probable interactions.

In addition, use mining tools to discover which variables are collinear. Datasets with many variables almost certainly have large numbers of variables that are collinear or, in other words, are effectively carrying the same information as each other. Create "bundles" of collinear variables (see Section 9.2.8). Use one variable from the bundle, or a composite surrogate variable created from the bundle, to represent the bundle. This will often reduce the number of variables in a dataset to a manageable number to create IIPs, especially if an automated IIP tool is available. (It's harder if they are built "by hand" using, say, Excel, but perhaps still possible.)

The main point here is that incorporating interaction variables is essential in creating the best quality models for some algorithms and extremely useful for others. Including necessary interactions almost always improves a model and never harms it. Conversely, not including them can be very damaging. Use any means available to determine and incorporate the relevant interaction variables.

9.2.18 Problem: Insufficient Data

Sometimes the data available is limited in quantity, or instances describing specific outcomes of particular business interest represent a low proportion of the total number of instances and are insufficient to build a useful model, even with a balanced dataset, and no further data is to be had. This is indicated when no further data is available and the following is true:

- The instances (records) available are too few for modeling, and it is known that the data represents the full range of behaviors of interest in the business problem.
- Balancing the dataset to increase the relative prevalence of specific outcomes requires reducing the total size of the dataset so that it is no longer representative of the population.

The essence of this problem is that the existing instances somehow have to be increased in number to a total number large enough for modeling. The data has to somehow be increased in quantity in such a way that the expanded sample remains at least as representative of the population as the original sample.

There are a couple of approaches to expanding, or multiplying, the quantity of data, one far less technically complex than the other. Both have their benefits and problems, and neither should be used as a substitute for getting more data if possible. These are both last resort methods for use when no further data can possibly be had.

Expanding the Data

The most straightforward method of increasing the apparent amount of data is simply to duplicate the instances. Copy the original dataset and append the copy to the original. Do this several times and the result appears to be a sizable dataset. It's just the original dataset in multiple copies, of course, but this certainly increases the amount of data without introducing any changes in any of the data's other characteristics.

One problem here is that some algorithms won't really notice this as more data, simply multiple runs through the same dataset—which is true because that's what it is. In this case, this sort of expansion will not benefit the situation. Some tools are actually sensitive to the order that the instances are presented and because this expansion hasn't reordered the records, it's possible that randomly ordering the expanded records will make a difference.

However, whether reordered or not, expanding the data in this way only creates duplicates of the existing instances. Some mining algorithms are sensitive only to differences in the instances. (Imagine clustering—all of the duplicated instances fall on top of each other changing nothing about the state space at all.) Nonetheless, data expansion as described so far does help model quality with some tools. Sometimes additional benefit can be had by adding a small amount of random noise to each value. The noise has to be constructed so that, if numeric, the noise component itself has a mean of 0, or if categories, so that the modal category is still the original category. This noise added to the duplicate instances in total amounts to no change, but it makes each instance appear unique.

Multiplying the Data

A second approach to increasing the apparent amount of data, data multiplication, requires the availability of appropriate and technically more complex tools than those used for data expansion. The idea here is to determine the joint distribution of the dataset and to create random values that have the same joint distribution characteristics as the original dataset. This technique does not work if only the univariate distributions are considered, and determining a multivariate distribution requires tools specifically designed for the task.

To understand why using multivariate distributions is essential, consider the univariate distributions for two variables, labeled "Y" and "X" in two datasets, "set 1" and "set 2." Variables X and Y in both datasets are approximately normally distributed. If univariate distributions were sufficient to duplicate the datasets, both set 1 and set 2 should be identical. In both datasets, X and Y have the same range, 0–1, and the same distribution, normal.

However, suppose that the joint ranges of these variables are totally different. Of course, the dataset used to illustrate this point was specifically put together so that the individual variables had the same range and distribution in both datasets, yet none of the XY points in set 1 fall into the same space as those in set 2. This issue is precisely the same in any real-world dataset—it's the joint distribution, the multivariate distribution, that is crucial to duplicate, not the univariate distributions.

There is no substitute for having sufficient data. However, if sufficient data is positively not to be had, multiplying the data that is available by adding random instances that are similar in their total multivariate distribution to the original dataset is usually far more effective than expanding the data in the way described in the previous section.

9.3 SUMMARY

Refining the model is a crucial piece of the data mining process. Refining requires methods for checking a model's performance, insight for understanding what the checks reveal, knowledge of what applicable techniques are relevant to improve model performance, and methods for applying the techniques to modeling data, or business problems, as appropriate. This chapter walks through the methods of diagnosis to discover problems with examples and presents methods for applying the techniques. Insight and understanding come only with practice and repetition.

No matter how technically effective the model appears and no matter how well tested, the model has no value unless effectively deployed. Deployment is where the technical effort blends into meeting the business needs. Deployment is the final, utterly crucial step in effective data mining.

Social Network Analysis

The size of the Web and the reach of search engines were both increasing rapidly by late 1996, but there was growing frustration with traditional information retrieval (IR) systems applied to Web data. IR systems work with finite document collections, and the worth of a document with regard to a query is intrinsic to the document. Documents are self-contained units and are generally descriptive and truthful about their contents.

In contrast, the Web resembles an indefinitely growing and shifting universe. Recall, an important notion in classic IR, has relatively little meaning for the Web; in fact, we cannot even measure recall because we can never collect a complete snapshot of the Web. Most Web search engines present the best 10 to 20 responses on the first page, most users stop looking after the second page, and all that seems to matter is the number of relevant "hits" within the first 20 to 40 responses—in other words, the precision at low recall.

Focusing on precision is not a great help either. On one hand, Web documents are not always descriptive or truthful. Site designers use nontextual content such as images and Flash (*www.adobe.com*) to project the desired look and feel. Entire businesses are built on stuffing pages with invisible keywords to lure search engines to index pages under common queries. Often, the match between a query and a Web page can be evaluated only by looking at the link graph neighborhood of the page. On the other hand, the Web is also afflicted with the "abundance problem." For most short queries (such as "Java") there are millions of relevant responses. Most Web queries are two words long. How can we hope to identify the best 40 documents matching a query from among a million documents if documents are not self-complete and truthful?

Apart from the sheer flux and populist involvement, the most important features that distinguish hypertext from a text collection for IR research are hyperlinks. Hyperlinks address the needs of amplification, elaboration, critique, contradiction, and navigation, among others. The hyperlink graph of the Web evolves organically, without any central coordination, and yet shows rich global and local properties. Hyperlink graph information is a rich supplement to text, sometimes even beating text in terms of information quality.

Starting around 1996, a frenzy of research efforts has sought to understand the structure of the Web and to exploit that understanding for better IR. Research has proceeded in a few major directions:

- Hyperlinks were used in conjunction with text for better topic classification.

- For broad queries that elicited large response sets from keyword search engines, hyperlinks were used to estimate popularity or authority of the responses. Google is a prime example of such techniques. This chapter in large part deals with such techniques.

- Independent of specific applications, researchers made comprehensive measurements on the Web and on the reach of search engines. They formulated models of creation, modification, and destruction of nodes and links that closely predicted observed data. The last part of this chapter deals with this area.

This chapter deals with a variety of link-based techniques for analyzing social networks that enhance text-based retrieval and ranking strategies. As we shall see, social network analysis was well established long before the Web, in fact, long before graph theory and algorithms became mainstream computer science. Therefore, later developments in evolution models and properties of random walks, mixing rates, and eigensystems (Motwani & Raghavan, 1995) may make valuable contributions to social network analysis, especially in the context of the Web.

10.1 SOCIAL SCIENCES AND BIBLIOMETRY

The Web is an example of a *social network*. Social networks have been extensively researched long before the advent of the Web. Perhaps coincidentally, between 1950 and 1980, around the same time that Vannevar Bush's proposed hypermedium called *Memex* was gaining acceptance, social sciences made great strides in measuring and analyzing social networks. (See the authoritative text by Wasserman and Faust [1994] for details.)

Networks of social interaction are formed between academics by coauthoring, advising, and serving on committees; between movie personnel by directing and acting; between musicians, football stars, friends, and relatives; between people by making phone calls and transmitting infections; between countries via trading relations; between papers through citation; and between Web pages by hyperlinking to other Web pages.

Social network theory is concerned with properties related to connectivity and distances in graphs, with diverse applications like epidemiology, espionage, citation indexing, and the like. In the first two examples, one might be interested in identifying a few nodes to be removed to significantly increase average path length between pairs of nodes. In citation analysis, one may wish to identify influential or central papers.

10.1.1 **Prestige**

Using edge-weighted, directed graphs to model social networks has been quite common. With this model, it has been clear that in-degree is a good first-order indicator of *status* or *prestige*. More interestingly, as early as 1949, Seeley realized the recursive nature of prestige in a social network (Seeley, 1949, pp. 234-35):

> [W]e are involved in an "infinite regress": [an actor's status] is a function of the status of those who choose him; and their [status] is a function of those who choose them, and so ad infinitum.

Consider the node (vertex) adjacency matrix E of the document citation graph, where $E[i, j] = 1$ if document i cites document j, and zero otherwise. Every node v has a notion of prestige $p[v]$ associated with it, which is simply a positive real number. Over all nodes, we represent the prestige score as a vector $\mathbf{p}$. Suppose we want to confer to each node v the sum total of prestige of all u that links to v, thus computing a new prestige vector $\mathbf{p}'$. This is easily written in matrix notation as

$$\mathbf{p}' = E^T \mathbf{p} \tag{10.1}$$

because

$$p'[v] = \sum_u E^T[v, u] p[u]$$
$$= \sum_u E[u, v] p[u]$$

To reach a *fixpoint* for the prestige vector, one can simply start with $\mathbf{p} = (1, \ldots, 1)^T$ and turn Equation 10.1 into an iterative *assignment* $\mathbf{p} \leftarrow E^T\mathbf{p}$, interleaved with normalizing $||\mathbf{p}||_1 = \sum_u p[u]$ to 1, to avoid numeric overflow. This process will lead to a convergent solution for $\mathbf{p}$ and is called *power iteration* in linear algebra (Golub & van Loan, 1989). The convergent value of $\mathbf{p}$, the fixpoint, is called the *principal eigenvector* (i.e., the eigenvector associated with the eigenvalue having the largest magnitude) of the matrix E^T. Clearly, work by Seeley and others between 1949 and 1970 firmly established this eigen analysis paradigm. Enhancements such as an attenuation factor ($\mathbf{p}' = \alpha E^T\mathbf{p}$) are also known.

10.1.2 **Centrality**

Various graph-based notions of centrality have been proposed in the social network literature. The *distance* $d(u, v)$ between two nodes u and v in a graph without edge weights is the smallest number of links via which one can go from u to v. (One can add up the edge weights in the case of a weighted graph to derive the path length.) The *radius* of node u is $r(u) = \max_v d(u, v)$. The *center* of the graph is arg $\min_u r(u)$, the node that has the smallest radius. One may look for influential papers in an area of research by looking for papers u with small

$r(u)$, which means that most papers in that research community have a short citation path to u.

For other applications, different notions of centrality are useful. In the case of trading partners and cartels, or in the study of epidemics, espionage, or suspected terrorist communication on telephone networks, it is often useful to identify *cuts*: a (small) number of edges that, when removed, disconnect a given pair of vertices. Or one may look for a small set of vertices that, when removed (together with edges incident with them), will decompose the graph into two or more connected components.

The variations of graph-based formulations and measures that have been used in the social sciences are too numerous to cover in detail; I will conclude this section with the observation that no single measure is suited for all applications and that the repertoire of measures is already quite mature.

10.1.3 Co-citation

If document u cites documents v and w, then v and w are said to be *co-cited* by u. Documents v and w being co-cited by many documents like u is evidence that v and w are somehow related to each other. Consider again the node (vertex) adjacency matrix E of the document citation graph, where $E[i, j] = 1$ if document i cites document j, and zero otherwise. Then

$$
\begin{aligned}
(E^T E)[v, w] &= \sum_u E^T[v, u] E[u, w] \\
&= \sum_u E[u, v] E[u, w] \\
&= |\{u : (u, v) \in E, (u, w) \in E\}|
\end{aligned}
\tag{10.2}
$$

The entry (v, w) in the $(E^T E)$ matrix is the *co-citation index* of v and w and an indicator of relatedness between v and w. One may use this pairwise relatedness measure in a clustering algorithm, such as *multidimensional scaling* (MDS). MDS uses the document-to-document similarity (or distance) matrix to embed the documents represented as points in a low-dimensional Euclidean space (such as the 2D plane) while "distorting" interpoint distances as little as possible. Visualizing clusters based on co-citation reveals important social structures between and within link communities. Such studies have been performed on academic publications several years back (McCain, 1992) and later by Larson on a small collection from the Web (1996) concerning geophysics, climate, remote sensing, and ecology. A sample MDS map is shown in Figure 10.1.

10.2 PAGERANK AND HYPERLINK-INDUCED TOPIC SEARCH

Two algorithms for ranking Web pages based on links, PageRank and hyperlink induced topic search (HITS), were developed around the fall of 1996 at Stanford

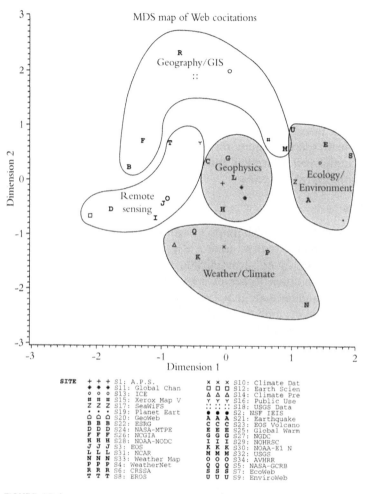

FIGURE 10.1

Social structure of Web communities concerning geophysics, climate, remote sensing, and ecology. The cluster labels are generated manually. This image is taken from Larson (1996).

University by Larry Page[1] and Sergey Brin, and at IBM Almaden by Jon Kleinberg. Both sought to remedy the "abundance problem" inherent in broad queries, supplementing precision with notions related to prestige in social network analysis.

In PageRank, each page on the Web has a measure of *prestige* that is independent of any information need or query. Roughly speaking, the prestige of a page is proportional to the sum of the prestige scores of pages linking to it. In HITS, a

---

[1] PageRank is named after Larry Page, a founder of Google.

query is used to select a subgraph from the Web. From this subgraph, two kinds of nodes are identified: *authoritative* pages to which many pages link and *hub* pages that consist of comprehensive collections of links to valuable pages on the subject.

Although there are technical differences, all three measures are defined recursively: prestige of a node depends on the prestige of other nodes, and the measure of being a good hub depends on how good neighboring nodes are as authorities (and vice versa). Both procedures involve computing eigenvectors for the adjacency matrix, or a matrix derived thereof, of the Web or a suitably relevant subgraph of the Web. In this section we will study these algorithms and take a careful look at their strengths and weaknesses.

10.2.1 PageRank

Assume for the moment that the Web graph is strongly connected—that is, from any node u there is a directed path to node v. (It is not; we come back to this issue a little later.) Consider a Web surfer clicking on hyperlinks forever, picking a link uniformly at random on each page to move on to the next page. Suppose the surfer starts from a random node in accordance with a distribution $\vec{p}_0$, with probability $p_0[u]$ of starting from node u, where $\sum_u p_0[u] = 1$. Let the adjacency matrix of the Web be E, where $E[u, v] = 1$ if there is a hyperlink $(u, v) \in E$, and zero otherwise. We overload E to denote both the edge set and its corresponding matrix.

After clicking once, what is the probability $p_1[v]$ that the surfer is on page v? To get to v, the surfer must have been at some node u with a link to v in the previous step and then clicked on the specific link that took her from u to v.

Given E, the out-degree of node u is given simply by

$$N_u = \sum_v E[u, v] \tag{10.3}$$

or the sum of the uth row of E. Assuming parallel edges (multiple links from u to v) are disallowed, the probability of the latter event given the former (i.e., being at u) is just $1/N_u$. Combining,

$$p_1[v] = \sum_{(u,v) \in E} \frac{p_0[u]}{N_u} \tag{10.4}$$

Let us derive a matrix L from E by normalizing all row-sums to one—that is,

$$L[u, v] = \frac{E[u, v]}{\sum_\beta E[u, \beta]} = \frac{E[u, v]}{N_u} \tag{10.5}$$

With L defined as previously, Equation 10.4 can be recast as

$$p_1[v] = \sum_u L[u, v] p_0[u] \tag{10.6}$$

or

$$p_1 = L^T p_0 \qquad (10.7)$$

The form of Equation 10.7 is identical to that of Equation 10.1 except for the edge weights used to normalize the degree. After the ith step, we will get

$$p_{i+1} = L^T p_i \qquad (10.8)$$

We will initially assume that nodes with no outlinks have been removed a priori. If E and therefore L are *irreducible* (i.e., there is a directed path from every node to every other node) and *aperiodic* (i.e., for all u, v, there are paths with all possible number of links on them, except for a finite set of path lengths that may be missing), the sequence (p_i), $i = 0, 1, 2, \ldots$ will converge to the principal eigenvector of L^T—that is, a solution to the matrix equation $p = L^T p$, also called the *stationary distribution* of L. The prestige of node u, denoted $p[u]$, is also called its PageRank. Note that the stationary distribution is independent of p_0.

For an infinitely long trip made by the surfer, the converged value of p is simply the relative rate at which the surfer hits each page. There is a close correspondence to the result of the "aimless surfer" model described earlier and the notion of prestige in bibliometry: a page v has high prestige if the visit rate is high, which happens if there are many neighbors u with high visit rates leading to v.

The simple surfing model does not quite suffice, because the Web graph is not strongly connected and aperiodic. An analysis of a significant portion of the Web graph (a few hundred million nodes) in 2000 showed that it is not strongly connected as a whole (Bröder et al., 2000). Only a fourth of the graph is strongly connected. Obviously, there are many pages without any outlinks, as well as directed paths leading into a cycle, where the walk could get trapped.

A simple fix is to insert fake, low-probability transitions all over the place. In the new graph, the surfer first makes a two-way choice at each node:

1. With probability d, the surfer jumps to a random page on the Web.
2. With probability $1 - d$, the surfer decides to choose, uniformly at random, an out-neighbor of the current node as before.

d is a tuned constant, usually chosen between 0.1 and 0.2. Because of the random jump, Equation 10.7 changes to

$$p_{i+1} = (1-d) L^T p_i + d \begin{pmatrix} 1/N & \cdots & 1/N \\ \vdots & \ddots & \vdots \\ 1/N & \cdots & 1/N \end{pmatrix} p_i$$

$$= \left((1-d) L^T + \frac{d}{N} \boxed{1_N} \right) p_i$$

simplifying notation,

$$= (1-d) L^T p_i + \frac{d}{N} (1, \ldots, 1)^T \qquad (10.9)$$

where N is the number of nodes in the graph. $p[u]$ is the PageRank of node u. Given the large number of edges in E, direct solution of the eigensystem is usually not feasible. A common approach is to use *power iterations* (Golub & van Loan, 1989) which involves picking an arbitrary nonzero $\mathbf{p}_0$ (often with all components set to $1/N$), repeated multiplication by $(1-d)L^T + \dfrac{d}{N}\boxed{1_N}$, and intermittent scaling $|\mathbf{p}i|$ to one. Because notions of popularity and prestige are at best noisy, numeric convergence is usually not necessary in practice, and the iterations can be terminated as soon as there is relative stability in the ordering of the set of prestige scores.

There are two ways to handle nodes with no outlink. You can jump with probability one in such cases, or you can first preprocess the graph, iteratively removing all nodes with an out-degree of zero (removing some nodes may lead to the removal of more nodes), computing the PageRanks of surviving nodes, and propagating the scores to the nodes eliminated during the preprocessing step.

In this application, the exact values of $\mathbf{p}_i$ are not as important as the ranking they induce on the pages. This means that we can stop the iterations fairly quickly. Page et al. (1998) reported acceptable convergence ranks in 52 iterations for a crawl with 322 million links.

In Google, the crawled graph is first used to precompute and store the PageRank of each page. Note that the PageRank is independent of any query or textual content. When a query is submitted, a text index is used to first make a selection of possible response pages. Then an undisclosed ranking scheme that combines PageRank with textual match is used to produce a final ordering of response URLs. All this makes Google comparable in speed, at query time, to conventional text-based search engines.

PageRank is an important ranking mechanism at the heart of Google, but it is not the only one: keywords, phrase matches, and match proximity are also taken into account, as is anchor text on pages linking to a given page. Search Engine Watch (*www.searchenginewatch.com*) reports that during some weeks in 1999, Google's top hit to the query "more evil than Satan" returned www.microsoft.com, probably because of anchor text spamming. This embarrassment was fixed within a few weeks. The next incident occurred around November 2000, when Google's top response to a rather offensive query was www.georgewbushstore.com. This was traced to *www.hugedisk.com*, which hosted a page that had the offensive query words as anchor text for a hyperlink to www.georgewbushstore.com.

Although the details of Google's combined ranking strategy are unpublished, such anecdotes suggest that the combined ranking strategy is tuned using many empirical parameters and checked for problems using human effort and regression testing. The strongest criticism of PageRank is that it defines prestige via a single random walk uninfluenced by a specific query. A related criticism is of the artificial decoupling between relevance and quality, and the ad hoc manner in which the two are brought together at query time, for the sake of efficiency.

10.2.2 **Hyperlink-Induced Topic Search**

In HITS, proposed by Kleinberg (1998), a query-dependent graph is chosen for analysis, in contrast to PageRank. Specifically, the query q is sent to a standard IR system to collect what is called a *root set R* of nodes in the Web graph. For reasons to be explained shortly, any node u that neighbors any $r \in R$ via an inbound or outbound edge—that is, $(u, r) \in E$ or $(r, u) \in E$—is included as well (E is the edge set for the Web). The additional nodes constitute the *expanded set* and, together with the root set, form the *base set* V_q. Edges that connect nodes from the same host are now eliminated because they are considered "navigational" or "nepotistic" (also see Section 10.3.1). Let us call the remaining edges E_q. We thus construct the query-specific graph $G_q = (V_q, E_q)$ (Figure 10.2). (I will drop the subscript q where clear from context.)

Kleinberg observed that as in academic literature, where some publications (typically in conferences) initiate new ideas and others consolidate and survey significant research (typically in journals or books), the Web includes two flavors of prominent or popular pages: *authorities,* which contain definitive high-quality information, and *hubs,* which are comprehensive lists of links to authorities. Every page is, to an extent, both a hub and an authority, but these properties are graded. Thus, every page u has two distinct measures of merit: its hub score $h[u]$ and its authority score $a[u]$. Collectively, scores over all nodes in G_q are written as vectors $\vec{a}$ and $\vec{h}$, with the uth vector component giving the score for node u.

As in the case of PageRank, the quantitative definitions of hub and authority scores are recursive. The authority score of a page is proportional to the sum of hub scores of pages linking to it, and conversely, its hub score is proportional to the authority scores of the pages to which it links. In matrix notation, this translates to the following pair of equations:

$$\vec{a} = E^T \vec{b} \qquad\qquad (10.10)$$

$$\vec{b} = E\vec{a} \qquad\qquad (10.11)$$

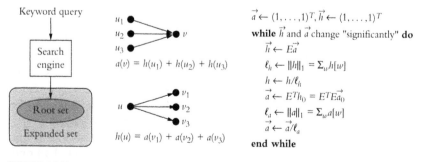

FIGURE 10.2

The HITS algorithm. l_h and *la* are L_1 vector norms.

Again, power iterations may be used to solve this system of equations iteratively, as shown in the pseudocode in Figure 10.2. When $\vec{a}$ attains convergence, it will be the principal eigenvector of $E^T E$. $\vec{b}$ will converge to the principal eigenvector of EE^T. Typically, runs with several thousand nodes and links "converge" in 20 to 30 iterations, in the sense that the rankings of hubs and authorities stabilize.

Summarizing, the main steps in HITS are as follows:

1. Send query to a text-based IR system and obtain the root set.
2. Expand the root set by radius one to obtain an expanded graph.
3. Run power iterations on the hub and authority scores together.
4. Report top-ranking authorities and hubs.

The entire process is generically called *topic distillation*. User studies (Chakrabarti et al., 1999) have shown that reporting hubs is useful over and above reporting authorities, because they provide useful annotations and starting points for users to start exploring a topic.

Bipartite subgraphs are key to the reinforcement process in HITS. Consider Figure 10.2. If in some transfer step node v_1 collects a large authority score, in the next reverse transfer, the hub u will collect a large hub score, which will then diffuse to siblings v_2 and v_3 of node v_1. Many times, such diffusion is crucial to the success of HITS, but it can be overdone. Some causes and remedies are discussed in Sections 10.3 and 10.4.

The key distinction of HITS from PageRank is the modeling of hubs. PageRank has no notion of a hub, but (Google) users seem not to regard this as a major handicap to searching, probably because on the Web, great hubs soon accumulate inlinks and thereby high prestige, thus becoming good authorities as well.

Higher-Order Eigenvectors and Clustering

If the query is ambiguous (e.g., "Java" or "jaguar") or polarized (e.g., "abortion" or "cold fusion"), the expanded set will contain a few, almost disconnected, link communities. In each community there may be dense bipartite subgraphs. In such cases, the highest-order eigenvectors found by HITS will reveal hubs and authorities in the largest near-bipartite component. One can tease out the structure and ranking within smaller components by calculating not only the principal eigenvector but also a few more. The iterations expressed in Equation 10.10 find the *principal eigenvectors* of EE^T and $E^T E$. Other eigenvectors can also be found using the iterative method. Given an $n \times n$ matrix M ($= E^T E$, say) for which we wish to find k eigenvectors, we initialize an $n \times k$ matrix X (generalizing the $n \times 1$ vector before) with positive entries. Let $X(i)$ be the ith column of X. The iterations are generalized to the steps shown in Figure 10.3 (Golub & van Loan, 1989).

Similar to Larson's study (Figure 10.1), higher-order eigenvectors can reveal clusters in the graph structure. In the a or b vector, each graph node had only one number as a representation. Thanks to using X, each node now has k hub scores and k authority scores. These should not be interpreted as just more scores

```
1: while X does not converge do
2:    X ← MX
3:    for i = 1, 2, . . . do
4:       for j = 1, 2, . . . , i − 1 do
5:          X(i) ← X(i) − (X(i) · X(j))X(i)
             {orthogonalize X(i) with regard to column X(j)}
6:       end for
7:       normalize X(i) to unit L₂ norm
8:    end for
9: end while
```

FIGURE 10.3

Finding higher-order eigenvectors in HITS using power iterations.

for ranking but as a multidimensional geometric embedding of the nodes. For example, if $k = 2$, one can plot each node as a point in the plane using its authority (or hub) score row-vector. For a polarized issue like "abortion," there are two densely linked communities on the Web, with sparse connections in between, mostly set up via eclectic hubs. A low-dimensional embedding and visualization may bring out community clustering graphically in case a query matches multiple link communities.

The Connection between HITS and Learning Style Inventory/Singular Value Decomposition

There is a direct mapping between finding the singular value decomposition (SVD) of E and the eigensystem of EE^T or E^TE. Let the SVD of E be $U\Sigma V^T$, where $U^TU = \mathbf{I}$ and $V^TV = \mathbf{I}$ and Σ is a diagonal matrix diag $(\sigma_1, \ldots, \sigma_r)$ of singular values, where r is the rank of E, and $\mathbf{I}$ is an identity matrix of suitable size. Then $EE^T = U\Sigma V^TV\Sigma U^T$ $= U\Sigma\mathbf{I}\Sigma U^T = U\Sigma^2U^T$, which implies that $EE^TU = U\Sigma^2$. Here if E is $n \times n$ with rank r, then U is $n \times r$; Σ and Σ^2 are $r \times r$. Specifically, $\Sigma^2 = \text{diag}(\sigma_1^2, \ldots \sigma_r^2)$. $U\Sigma^2$ $n \times r$ as well. If $U(j)$ is the jth column of U, we can write $EE^TU(j) = \sigma_j^2U(j)$ which means that $U(j)$ is an eigenvector of EE^T with corresponding eigenvalue σ_j^2 for $j = 1, \ldots, r$. If Σ^2 is arranged such that $\sigma_1^2 \geq \ldots \sigma_r^2$, it turns out that finding the hub scores for E is the same as finding $U(1)$, and more generally, finding multiple hubs/authorities corresponds to finding many singular values of EE^T and E^TE.

Thus, the HITS algorithm is equivalent to running SVD on the hyperlink relation (`source,target`) rather than the (`term,document`) relation to which SVD is usually applied. Recall that SVD finds us vector representations for terms and documents in "latent semantic space." As a consequence of the equivalence shown above, a HITS procedure that finds multiple hub and authority vectors also finds a multidimensional representation for nodes in a hypertext graph. We can either present the SVD representation visually to aid clustering or use one of the many clustering algorithms on this representation of documents.

10.2.3 Stochastic HITS and Other Variants

Several subsequent studies have provided deeper analysis and comparison of HITS and PageRank. I provide here several observations that improve our understanding of how these algorithms work.

HITS is sensitive to local topology. The two graphs in Figure 10.4(a) differ only in the insertion of one node (5) to turn a single edge into a chain of two edges, something that frequently happens on the Web owing to a redirection or reorganization of a site. You can verify that this edge splitting upsets the scores for HITS quite significantly, whereas it leaves PageRanks relatively unaffected. More specifically, the update equations for authorities change from the system

$$a_2 \leftarrow 2a_2 + a_4 \tag{10.12}$$

$$a_4 \leftarrow a_2 + a_4 \tag{10.13}$$

to the new system

$$a_2 \leftarrow 2a_2 + a_4 \tag{10.14}$$

$$a_4 \leftarrow a_4 \tag{10.15}$$

$$a_5 \leftarrow a_2 + a_5 \tag{10.16}$$

Thus, node 5 takes the place of node 4, the mutual reinforcement between the authority scores of nodes 2 and 4 is lost, and node 4's authority score vanishes to zero compared to those of nodes 2 and 5.

HITS needs *bipartite cores* in the score reinforcement process. Consider the graph in Figure 10.4(b): it has two connected components, each of which is a complete bipartite graph, with 2×2 and 2×3 nodes. Let us assign all hub scores to 1 and start HITS iterations. After the first iteration, each authority score in the

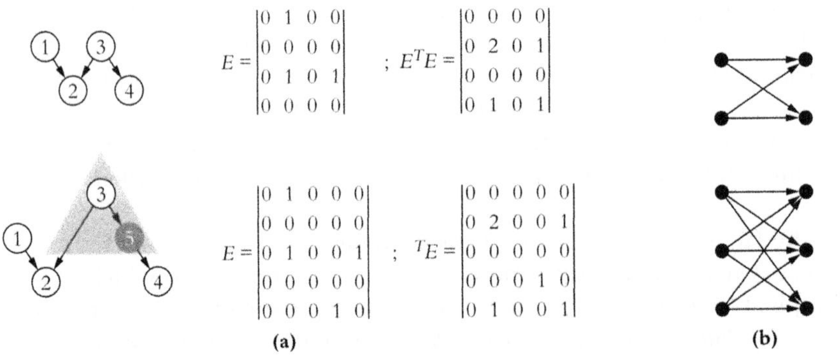

(a)   (b)

FIGURE 10.4

Minor perturbations in the graph may have dramatic effects on HITS scores (a). The principal eigenvector found by HITS favors larger bipartite cores (b).

Table 10.1 Authority Scores

Iteration	h_{small}	a_{small}	h_{large}	a_{large}
0	1	0	1	0
1a	1	2	1	3
1h	4	2	9	3
2a	4	8	9	27
2h	16	8	81	27

smaller component will be 2 and each authority score in the larger component will be 3. The scores will progress as shown in Table 10.1.

Here I ignore score scaling, because the relative magnitude of the scores illustrates the point. In general, after $i > 0$ full iterations, we can show that $a_{small} = 2^{2i-1}$ and $a_{large} = 3^{2i-1}$. Thus, their ratio is $a_{large}/a_{small} = (3/2)^{2i-1}$, which grows without bound as i increases. Thus, in the principal eigenvector, the smaller component finds absolutely no representation. In contrast, it can be verified that PageRank will not be so drastic; the random jump will ensure some positive scores for the prestige of all nodes.

Many researchers have sought to improve HITS by removing some of these anomalies. Lempel and Moran (2001) proposed a *stochastic algorithm for link structure analysis* (SALSA). The goal of SALSA was to cast bipartite reinforcement in the random surfer framework. They proposed and analyzed the following random surfer specification while maintaining the essential bipartite nature of HITS:

1. At a node v, the random surfer chooses an inlink (i.e., an incoming edge (u, v)) uniformly at random and moves to u.
2. Then, from u, the surfer takes a random forward link (u, w) uniformly at random.

Thus, the transition probability from v to w is

$$p(v,w) = \frac{1}{\text{InDegree}(v)} \sum_{(u,v),(u,w)\in E} \frac{1}{\text{InDegree}(u)} \qquad (10.17)$$

This may be regarded as the authority-to-authority transition; a symmetric formulation (follow an outlink and then an inlink) handles hub-to-hub transitions.

SALSA does not succumb to tightly knit communities to the same extent as HITS. In fact, the steady-state node probabilities of the authority-to-authority transition (assuming it is irreducible and ergodic) have a simple form:

$$\pi_v \propto \text{InDegree}(v) \qquad (10.18)$$

That is, the SALSA authority score is proportional to the in-degree. Although the sum in Equation 10.17 suggests a kind of sibling link reinforcement, the probabilities are chosen such that the steady-state node probabilities do not reflect any nonlocal prestige diffusion. It might be argued that a total absence of long-range diffusion is at the opposite extreme from HITS, and an intermediate level of reinforcement is better than either extreme.

A recent study by Ng et al. (2001) shows that HITS's long-range reinforcement is bad for *stability*: random erasure of a small fraction (say, 10 percent) of nodes or edges can seriously alter the ranks of hubs and authorities. It turns out that PageRank is much more stable to such perturbations, essentially because of its random jump step. Ng et al. propose to recast HITS as a bidirectional random walk by a "random surfer" similar to PageRank: Every timestep, with probability d, the surfer jumps to a node in the base set uniformly at random. With the remaining probability $1 - d$:

- If it is an odd timestep, the surfer takes a random outlink from the current node.
- If it is an even timestep, the surfer goes backward on a random inlink leading to the current node.

Ng et al. showed that this variant of HITS with random jumps has much better stability in the face of small changes in the hyperlink graph, and that the stability improves as d is increased. (They also showed this to be the case with PageRank.) Obviously, $d = 1$ would be most stable but useless for ranking: scores would diffuse all over. There is no recipe known for setting d based on the graph structure alone. It is clear that, at some stage, page content must be reconciled into graph models of the Web to complete the design of Web IR systems (Haveliwala, 2002).

10.3 SHORTCOMINGS OF THE COARSE-GRAINED GRAPH MODEL

Both HITS and PageRank use a coarse-grained model of the Web, where each page is a node in a graph with a few scores associated with it. The model takes no notice of either the text or the markup structure on each page. (HITS leaves the selection of the base set to an external IR algorithm.)

In real life, Web pages are more complex than the coarse-grained model suggests. An HTML page sports a tag-tree structure, which is rendered by browsers as roughly rectangular regions with embedded text and hyperlinks. Unlike HITS or PageRank, human readers do not pay equal attention to all the links on a page. They use the position of text and links (and their interpretation of the text, of course) to carefully judge where to click to continue on their (hardly random) surfing.

Algorithms that do not model the behavior of human information foragers may fall prey to many artifacts of Web authorship, which I illustrate in this section. In the next section, I will describe several enhancements to the model and algorithms that avoid such pitfalls.

10.3.1 Artifacts of Web Authorship

The central assumption in PageRank and HITS is that a hyperlink confers authority. Obviously, this holds only if the hyperlink was created as a result of editorial judgment based on the contents of the source and target pages, as is largely the case with social networks in academic publications. Unfortunately, that central assumption is increasingly being violated on the Web.

Much has changed about authoring Web pages ever since those algorithms were proposed. HTML is increasingly generated by programs, not typed in by hand. Pages are often generated from templates or dynamically from relational and semistructured databases (e.g., Zope; zope.org). There are sites designed by companies whose mission is to increase the number of search engine hits for their customers. Their common strategies include stuffing irrelevant words in pages and linking up their customers in densely connected cliques, even if those customers have nothing in common. The creation and dissemination of hypertext happens at an unprecedented scale today and is inexorably coupled with commerce and advertising. I will describe three related ways in that these authoring idioms manifest themselves.

Nepotistic Links

Kleinberg summarily discarded links connecting pages on the same host, because these links, largely authored by the same person, did not confer authority in the same sense as an academic citation, and could therefore be regarded as "nepotistic."[2]

Soon after HITS was published, Bharat and Henzinger (Bharat & Henzinger, 1998) found that the threat of nepotism was not necessarily limited to same-site links. Two-site nepotism (a pair of websites endorsing each other) was on the rise. In many trials with HITS, they found two distinct sites h_1 and h_2, where h_1 hosted a number of pages u linking to a page v on h_2, driving up $a(v)$ beyond what may be considered fair.

Two-host nepotism can also happen because of Web infrastructure issues, for example, in a site hosted on multiple servers such as *www.yahoo.com* and *dir12.yahoo.com*, or the use of the relative URLs with regard to a base URL specified with the <a base=...> HTML construct. If it is a simple case of mirroring, algorithms can generally be developed to fix the problem, but deliberate nepotism also exists on the Web.

---

[2]Page et al. do not discuss nepotistic links in their paper.

Clique Attacks

Over time, two-host nepotism evolved into multihost nepotism, thanks to the culture of professional Web-hosting and "portal" development companies. It is now surprisingly common to encounter query response pages with elaborate navigation bars that have links to other sites with *no* semantic connection, just because these sites are all hosted by a common business. I show one example in Figure 10.5, but the Web has plenty of such pages and sites.[3] These sites form a densely connected graph, sometimes even a completely connected graph, which led me to name the phenomenon a "clique attack."

Sometimes members of the clique have URLs sharing substrings, but they may map to different Internet protocol (IP) addresses. It is not easy to judge from the graph alone whether the clique is a bona fide, content-inspired link community, or has been created deliberately. An example of a clique attack is shown in Figure 10.6. Both HITS and PageRank can fall prey to clique attacks, although by tuning d in PageRank, the effect can be reduced.

Mixed Hubs

Another problem with decoupling the user's query from the link-based ranking strategy is that some hubs may be *mixed* without any attempt on the part of the hub writer to confound a search engine. Technically, this is hard to distinguish from a clique attack, but it probably happens even more frequently than clique attacks. For example, a hub u containing links relevant to the query "movie awards" may also have some links to movie production companies. If a node v_1 relevant to movie awards gains authority score, the HITS algorithm (see Figure 10.2) would diffuse the score through u to a node v_2, which could be a movie production company homepage. Another example, in the form of a section of links about "Shakespeare" embedded in a page about British and Irish literary figures in general, is shown in Figure 10.7. Mixed hubs can be a problem for both HITS and PageRank, because neither algorithm discriminates between outlinks on a page. However, a system (such as Google) using PageRank may succeed at suppressing the ill effects by filtering on keywords at query time.

10.3.2 Topic Contamination and Drift

The expansion step in HITS was meant to increase recall and capture a larger graph G_q, which was subjected to eigen analysis. Why was this needed? Here is one reason. As of late 1996, the query "browser" would fail to include Netscape's Navigator and Communicator pages, as well as Microsoft's Internet Explorer page in the root set, because at that time these sites avoided a boring description like "browser" for their products. However, millions of pages included blurbs such as

---

[3]Although these sites might disappear with time, I will give some more examples: *www.411web.com*, *www.depalma-enterprises.com*, *www.cyprus-domains.com*, and *www.usa.worldweb.com*.

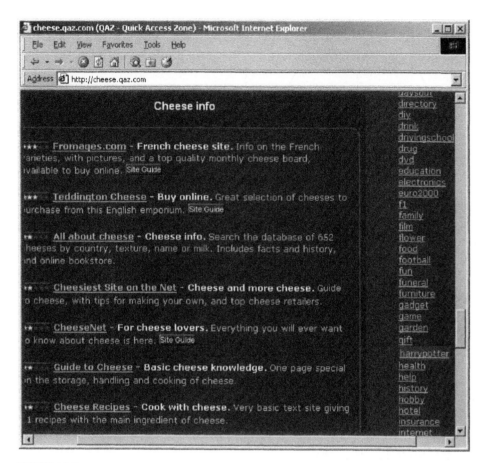

FIGURE 10.5

Hyperlinks generated from templates in navigation bars do not reflect content-based editorial judgment and often implement "clique attacks" that foil HITS-like algorithms. There are only a handful of links related to *cheese* on this page, but there are more than 60 nepotistic links going to different hosts from ads.qaz.com through women.qaz.com.

"this page is best viewed with a frames-capable *browser* such as . . ." and linked to these authoritative browser pages.

Conversely, sometimes good authorities would be included in the root set, but hubs linking to them might not be adequately represented in the root set for HITS to be able to estimate reliable authority scores for the former pages. The radius-1 expansion step of HITS would include nodes of both categories into the expanded graph G_q. Thus, the expansion step in HITS is primarily a recall-enhancing device. However, this boost in recall sometimes comes at the price of precision.

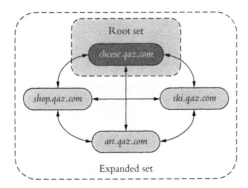

FIGURE 10.6

How a clique attack takes over link-based rankings.

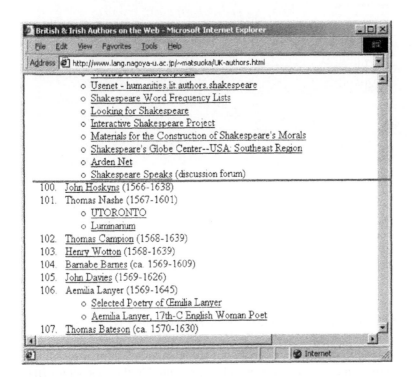

FIGURE 10.7

A mixed hub on British and Irish authors with one section dedicated to Shakespeare.
(The horizontal line has been added by hand to demarcate the section.)

Consider a set of topics such as proposed by Yahoo!, and for simplicity assume that each Web page belongs to exactly one topic. Experimental evidence (Chakrabarti, van den Berg, & Dom, 1999; Davison, 2000) suggests that there is locality of content on the Web—that is, if a page is about cycling, following an outlink is more likely to lead to a page about cycling as well, compared to sampling a page uniformly at random from the Web. (The probability that the latter action will get us a page with a specific topic c is the fraction of pages in the Web belonging to topic c.)

This locality works in a very short radius, however. The probability of a page linking to another page of the same topic falls short of one for nontrivial topics, and the more specific the topic is, the smaller is this probability. Within a small number of links, the probability that all nodes have the same topic as the starting point vanishes rapidly.

Expansion by a single link was the maximum that could usually be tolerated by HITS; at radius two, most of the pages would be off-topic and the output of HITS would be largely unsatisfactory. (Indefinite graph expansion with HITS would make it degenerate to a PageRank-like scoring system with no connection to any specific query.) Even at radius one, severe contamination of the root set may occur, especially if pages relevant to the query are often linked to a broader, more densely linked topic. For example, at one time[4] the graph G_q corresponding to the query "movie awards" included a large number of movie company pages such as MGM and Fox, together with a number of hubs linking to them more densely than the subgraph that contained pages related to Oscar, Cannes, and so on. As a result, the hub and authority vectors have large components concentrated in nodes about movies rather than movie awards.

The preceding example is one of *topic generalization*. Another possible problem is that of *topic drift*. For example, pages on many topics are within a couple of links of sites like Netscape, Internet Explorer, and Free Speech Online. Given the popularity of these sites, HITS (and PageRank) runs the danger of raising these sites to the top once they enter the expanded graph. Drift and contamination can sometimes be purposefully engineered, as in Figure 10.5. In effect, a Trojan horse page connected to a large clique can overwhelm any purely graph-based analysis (as in Figure 10.6).

An ad hoc fix is to list known *stop-sites* that would be removed from the expanded graph, but this could have undesirable effects, as the notion of a "stop-site" is often context-dependent. For example, for the query "java," *www.java.sun.com* is a highly desirable site, whereas for a narrower query like "swing," it may be considered too general.

Topic contamination may affect both HITS and PageRank. The top results from HITS may drift away from the query. The PageRank of irrelevant nodes may become unduly large because of membership or proximity to dense subgraphs.

---

[4]Both the Web and HITS have undergone significant evolution, so these specific anecdotes may be transient, although similar examples abound.

Again, a system (such as Google) using PageRank as one of many scores in ranking may be able to avoid problems by using a suitable relative weighting of scores.

10.4 ENHANCED MODELS AND TECHNIQUES

In this section we will consider hyperlink information in conjunction with text and markup information, model HTML pages at a finer level of detail, and propose enhanced prestige ranking algorithms.

The models that we have discussed thus far offer simple and elegant representations for hypertext on the Web. Consequently, the mature fields of graph theory and matrix algebra can then be brought to bear. As we observed in the previous section, such simple graph models break down in a variety of ways. This section offers solutions to some of the problems with the simplistic models.

10.4.1 Avoiding Two-Party Nepotism

Bharat and Henzinger (1998) invented a simple and effective fix for two-site nepotism (the B&H algorithm). They observed that ascribing one unit of voting power to each page pointing to a given target may be too extreme, especially if those source pages are all on the same website. They proposed that a *site*, not a page, should be the unit of voting power. Therefore, if it is found that k pages on a single host link to a target page, these edges are assigned a weight of $1/k$. This is unlike HITS, where all edges have unit weight.

This modification changes E from a zero–one matrix to one with zeros and positive real numbers. However, EE^T and E^TE remain symmetric, and the rest of the HITS computation goes through as before. In particular, all eigenvectors are guaranteed to be real, and higher-order vectors can be used to identify clusters and link-based communities. Bharat and Henzinger evaluated the weighted scheme with the help of volunteers, who judged the output to be superior to unweighted HITS.

Although it is easy to modify the PageRank formulation to take edge weights into account, it is not publicly known if the implementation of PageRank in Google uses edge weights to avoid two-party (or other forms of) nepotism. Another idea worth experimenting with is to model pages as getting endorsed by *sites*, not single pages, and compute prestige for sites as well, represented by some sort of aggregated supernodes.

Although the B&H edge-weighting scheme reduces the problems of two-host nepotism, multihost nepotism is harder to isolate from a genuinely authoritative Web community. We shall study one approach to reducing that problem in Section 10.4.4.

10.4.2 Outlier Elimination

Bharat and Henzinger (1998) observed that keyword search engine responses are largely relevant to the query (even if they are not of the highest quality or popularity). It is the indiscriminate expansion of links that is mostly responsible for contaminating the expanded graph. They devised a content-based mechanism to reduce contamination and resulting drift. Before performing the link expansion, they computed the term vectors of the documents in the root set (using the Term Frequency, Inverse Document Frequency [TFIDF] model) and the centroid μ of these vectors. When the link expansion was performed, any page v that was "too dissimilar" to the centroid μ (i.e., the cosine between the vector representation of v and μ was too small) was discarded, and HITS-like iterations were performed only over the surviving pages.

In HITS, expansion to a radius more than one could be disastrous. Outlier elimination in the B&H algorithm has quite a stabilizing effect on graph expansion, especially if the relevant root set is large. One may envisage a system that continues indefinite expansion and keeps pruning outliers in the vector space. However, the centroid *will* gradually drift, even if much more slowly than in HITS, and eventually the expanded set will bear little relevance to the query.

10.4.3 Exploiting Anchor Text

There is a simple if crude way in which the initial mapping from a keyword query to a root set followed by the graph expansion can be folded into a single step, in fact, one that does not involve power iterations. Consider each page in the root set not as a single node in a graph but as a nested graph that is a chain of "micronodes." Each micronode is either a textual token or an outbound hyperlink. Tokens that appear in the query are called *activated*. (Assume for simplicity that the query has no negated token and a phrase is a compound token.)

Prepare a map from URLs to integer counters, initialized to all zeros. Pick a positive integer k. Consider all outbound URLs that are within a distance of k links of any activated node. Increment the counter associated with the URL once for every activated node encountered. Finally, sort the URLs in decreasing order of their counter values and report the top-rated URLs. The procedure, called *Rank-and-File* (Chakrabarti and Dom, 1998), is illustrated in Figure 10.8. Note that only the root set is required for the analysis.

With some tuning of k, the answers from Rank-and-File are astonishingly good for many broad queries. Note that although pages outside the root set are not fetched (and this makes the method substantially faster than HITS or B&H), URLs outside the root set are being rated. In effect, this method is like spreading an activation from terms to neighboring links.

Just like HITS may return better results than those obtained by sorting by indegree, the simple one-step procedure above can be improved by bringing

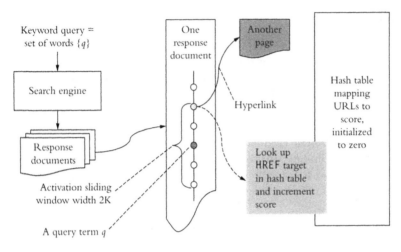

FIGURE 10.8

A simple ranking scheme based on evidence from words near anchors.

power iterations back into it. The simplest way to do this is to tweak the edge weights in the graph on which power iterations are performed. In HITS, all edges have unit weight. Taking the cue from Rank-and-File, we can increase the weights of those hyperlinks whose source micronodes are "close" to query tokens. This is how the Clever[5] project and search system (Chakrabarti et al., 1999) combined HITS and Rank-and-File.

Another modification is to change the shape of the activation window. In Rank-and-File, the activation window used to be a zero-one or rectangular window of width $2k$. Instead, we can make the activation window *decay* continuously on either side of a query token.[6] The activation level of a URL v from page u can be the sum of contributions from all query terms near the HREF to v on u.

The decay is an attempt to reduce authority diffusion, which works reasonably well, even though mixed hubs often have sharp section boundaries. For example, a personal bookmark hub may have a series of sections, each with a list of URLs with corresponding annotations. A query term matching terms in the first annotation of section i may activate the last few URLs in section $(i - 1)$. The heuristics in Clever work reasonably well, partly because not all multisegment hubs will encourage systematic drift toward a fixed topic different from the query topic.

A stock of queries with preranked answers and a great deal of human effort is necessary to make the best choices and tune all the parameters. This was indeed the case with the Clever project; three or four researchers spent a few hours per week over a year running experiments and inspecting results for anomalies.

---

[5]*Clever* was intended to be an acronym for *client-side eigenvector enhanced retrieval.*
[6]Negated terms can be used for the keyword search, but there seems to be no clear way to use them in the activation step.

10.4.4 Exploiting Document Markup Structure

Here I sketch the key transitions in modeling Web content that characterize the discussion thus far in this chapter.

HITS. Each page is a node without any textual properties. Each hyperlink is an edge connecting two nodes with possibly only a positive edge weight property. Some preprocessing procedure outside the scope of HITS chooses what subgraph of the Web to analyze in response to a query.

B&H algorithm. The graph model is as in HITS, except that nodes have additional properties. Each node is associated with a vector-space representation of the text on the corresponding page. After the initial subgraph selection, the B&H algorithm eliminates nodes whose corresponding vectors are far from the typical vector computed from the root set.

Rank-and-File. This replaced the hubs-and-authorities model with a simpler one. Each document is a linear sequence of tokens. Most are terms, some are outgoing hyperlinks. Query terms *activate* nearby hyperlinks. No iterations are involved.

Clever. A page is modeled at two levels. The coarse-grained model is the same as in HITS. At a finer grain, it is a linear sequence of tokens as in Rank-and-File. Proximity between a query term on page *u* and an outbound link to page *v* is represented by increasing the edge's weight *(u, v)* in the coarse-grained graph.

All these models are approximations to what HTML-based hypermedia really is. Figure 10.9 shows a more faithful view. HTML pages are characterized by tag-trees, also called the *document object model* (DOM). DOM trees are interconnected by regular HREFs. (For simplicity, I remove location markers indicated by a # sign from URLs, which occurs in a very small fraction of search engine responses. Thus, all HREF targets are DOM tree roots.) I will call this the *fine-grained model*.

Segmenting Document Object Model Trees

Upon encountering the pages shown in Figures 10.5 or 10.7, a human surfer will have no problem in focusing on links appearing in zone(s) relevant to his interest and avoiding links in other zones. For uniformity, clique attack and mixed hubs will be collectively called *multitopic pages* in this section.

We can name at least two kinds of clues that help users identify relevant zones on a multitopic page. An obvious one is text. In Figure 10.5, the term "cheese" occurs in only a limited area, and likewise for "Shakespeare" in Figure 10.7. The other clue to a zone's promise is its density of links to relevant sites known to the user. I will focus on textual clues for the rest of this discussion.

Perhaps the first idea that comes to mind is to give preferential treatment to document object model subtrees where query terms occur frequently. This scheme will not work well for some queries, even if we could somehow define what "frequently" means. For example, for the query "Japanese car maker," DOM sub-

```
<html> ... <body> ...
<table ...>
<tr><td>
        <table ...>
        <tr><td><a href="http://art.gaz.com">art</a></td></tr>
        <tr><td><a href="http://ski.gaz.com">ski</a></td></tr>...
        </table>
</td></tr>
<tr><td>
        <ul>
        <li><a href="http://www.fromages.com">Fromages.com</a>
        French cheese ... </li>
        <li><a href="http://www.teddingtoncheese.co.uk">Teddington...</a>
        Buy online...</li>
        ...
        </ul>
</td></tr>
</table>...
</body></html>
```

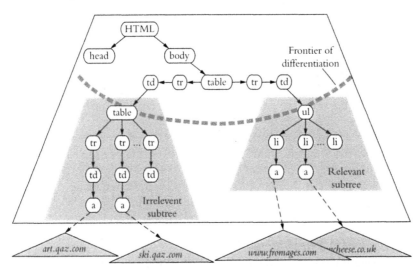

FIGURE 10.9

Characterization of hypertext as a collection of interconnected trees. The HTML tag-tree of a multitopic hub can be segmented into relevant and irrelevant subtrees.

trees with links to *www.honda.com* and *www.toyota.com* rarely use any of the three query words; they instead use just the names of the companies, such as "Honda" and "Toyota." Therefore, depending on direct syntactic matches between query terms and the text in DOM subtrees can be unreliable.

One idea from the B&H algorithm comes to our aid. Even though query terms are difficult to find near good links, the centroid of the root set features "Honda" and "Toyota" with large weights. Figure 10.10 shows similar examples. Therefore, to estimate the relevance of a DOM subtree rooted at node u with regard to a

sushi: sushi, japanese, restaurant, page, bar, rice, roll
gardening: garden, home, plants, information, organic, click
bicycling: bike, bicycle, page, site, ride, tour, new, sports
alcoholism: alcohol, treatment, drug, addiction, recovery, abuse
blues: blues, site, festival, jazz, music, new, society

FIGURE 10.10

Despite a few Web-specific words ("click," "site") and mild generalizations ("drug"), the largest components of root set centroid vectors are extremely intuitive.

query, we can simply measure the vector-space similarity (like B&H) between the root set centroid and the DOM subtree's text, associating u with this score.

For a multitopic page (such as the one in Figure 10.5, shown as a DOM in Figure 10.9), what kind of pattern can we expect to see in these scores? If we already knew the frontier of differentiation in Figure 10.9, we would expect the irrelevant subtree (containing the clique attack or nepotistic links) to have a small score and the subtree related to cheese to have a larger score. Above the frontier, these scores would be averaged out somewhat because of the cosine measure (the Jaccard measure may do the same). The score at the page's root in Figure 10.9 would be in between the scores at the relevant subtree root and irrelevant subtree root. By the same token, relevant subtree root descendants will also have scores distributed both above and below the subtree root score. So what is special about the frontier?

To answer this question, we need a generative model for the text embedded in the DOM tree. Atomic blocks of text occur only at some leaves in the DOM tree (e.g., between <A> and </A> or between <P> and </P>); we consider these *micro-documents*. Each internal node represents a collection of microdocuments, those that appear as leaves in the subtree rooted at that internal node. We can use any of the generative models to characterize the distribution of terms in a collection of microdocuments. Such a generic term distribution is represented as Φ.

Let the term distribution over all microdocuments over all Web pages in V_q be Φ_0. One may imagine a "superroot" node whose children are the DOM roots of all Web pages in V_q. Then Φ_0 is the term distribution associated with this super-root. Smaller sets of microdocuments about specific topics will have term distributions different from Φ_0. Subtrees concerning different topics in a multitopic page are expected to have somewhat different term distributions.

Given a DOM subtree with root node u, we can greedily decide if it is "pure" or "mixed" by comparing some cost measure for the following two options:

1. The tree T_u rooted at u is pure, and a single term distribution Φ_u suffices to generate the microdocuments in T_u with large probability. In this case, we *prune* the tree at u.

2. u is a point of *differentiation* (see Figure 10.9), and each child v of u has a different term distribution Φ_v from which the microdocuments in their corresponding subtrees were generated. In this case, we *expand* the tree at u.

We can start this process at the root and continue expansion until no further expansion is profitable as per the cost measure, as shown in Figure 10.11.

1: **Input:** DOM tree of an HTML page
2: initialize frontier F to the DOM root node
3: **while** local improvement to code length possible **do**
4:     pick from F an internal node u with children $\{v\}$
5:     find the cost of pruning at u (see text)
6:     find the cost of expanding u to all v (see text)
7:     **if** expanding is better **then**
8:         remove u from F
9:         insert all v into F
10:   **end if**
11: **end while**

FIGURE 10.11

Greedy DOM segmentation using MDL.

As with applications of the *minimum description length* (MDL) principle, we can devise a model cost and data cost to drive the search for the frontier. The model cost at DOM node u is the number of bits needed to represent the parameters of Φ_u, denoted $L(\Phi_u)$, which is encoded with regard to some *prior* distribution Π on the parameters, approximately $-\log \Pr(\Phi_u|\Pi)$. The data cost at node u is the cost of encoding all the microdocuments in the subtree T_u rooted at u with regard to the model Φ_u at u, approximately

$$-\sum_{d \in T_u} \log \Pr(d|\Phi_u)$$

Fine-Grained Topic Distillation

We will now integrate the segmentation step described before into a HITS/B&H-style topic-distillation algorithm.

There is a certain asymmetry between how people interpret hubs and authorities, despite the symmetric formulation of HITS. A good authority page is expected to be dedicated in its entirety to the topic of interest, whereas a hub is acceptable if it has a reasonable number of links relevant to the topic of interest, even if there are some irrelevant links on the page. The asymmetry is reflected in hyperlinks: Unless used as navigational aids, hyperlinks to a remote host almost always point to the DOM *root* of the target page.[7]

We will use DOM segmentation to contain the extent of authority diffusion between co-cited pages (like v_1 and v_2 in Figure 10.2) through a multitopic hub u. If we believe that u should be segmented into unrelated regions, we should represent u not as a single node but with one node for each segmented subtree of u, which will have the desirable effect of *disaggregating* the hub score of u, preventing the relevant portion of hub scores from reinforcing the putative authorities linked from irrelevant regions of the hub DOM tree. For example, in Figure 10.9, two nodes would be created, one for the unwanted subtree and one for the

---

[7]To be fair, authors avoid linking to internal regions of pages also because the HREF will break if the author of the target pages removes the <a name...> marker.

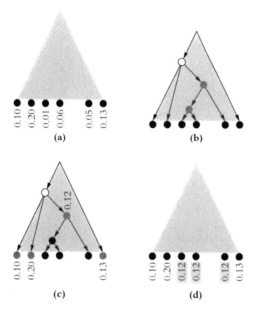

FIGURE 10.12

To prevent unwanted authority diffusion, we aggregate hub scores along the frontier nodes (no complete aggregation up to the DOM root) followed by propagation to the leaves. Initial values of leaf hub scores are indicated (a). Must-prune nodes are marked (b). Frontier microhubs accumulate scores (c). Aggregate hub scores are copied to leaves (d).

favored subtree. We expect that the latter will take an active role in reinforcing good authorities, whereas the former's score will dwindle in comparison. Figure 10.12 illustrates this step.

The complete algorithm is given in Figure 10.13. We allow only the DOM tree roots of root set nodes to have a nonzero authority score when we start, unlike HITS and B&H, which set all scores to positive numbers. We believe that positive authority scores should diffuse out from the root set only if the connecting hub regions are trusted to be relevant to the query. Accordingly, the first half-iteration implements the $\mathbf{h} \leftarrow E\mathbf{a}$ transfer.

For the transfer steps, the graph represented by E does not include any internal nodes of DOM trees. The new steps **segment** and **aggregate** are the only steps that involve internal DOM nodes. Therefore, only DOM roots have positive authority scores, and only DOM leaves (corresponding to HREFs) have positive hub scores.

I have focused on text-based DOM segmentation, but I said near the beginning of Section 10.4.4 that outlinks to known authorities can also help us segment a hub. Specifically, if all large leaf hub scores are concentrated in one subtree of a hub DOM, we may want to limit authority reinforcement to this subtree. At the end of an $\mathbf{h} \leftarrow E\mathbf{a}$ transfer step, we could use only the leaf hub scores (instead of

```
1: collect Gq for the query q
2: construct the fine-grained graph from Gq
3: set all hub and authority scores to zero
4: for each page u in the root set do
5:     locate the DOM root ru of u
6:     set aru = 1
7: end for
8: while scores have not stabilized do
9:     perform the h ← Ea transfer
10:    segment hubs into "microhubs"
11:    aggregate and redistribute hub scores
12:    perform the a ← ETh transfer
13:    normalize |a|
14: end while
```

FIGURE 10.13

Fine-grained topic distillation. Note that the vertex set involved in E includes only DOM roots and leaves and *not* other internal nodes. Internal DOM nodes are involved only in the steps marked **segment** and **aggregate**.

text) to segment the hub DOMs. The general approach to DOM segmentation remains unchanged; we only have to propose a different Φ and Π. When only hub score–based segmentation is used in Figure 10.13, let us call the resulting algorithm DOMHITS. We can also combine clues from text and hub scores (Chakrabarti, Joshi, & Tawde, 2001). For example, we can pick the shallowest frontier or we can design a joint distribution combining text and hub scores. Let us call such an algorithm DOMTextHITS. We discuss the performance of DOMHITS and DOMTextHITS in the next section.

10.5 EVALUATION OF TOPIC DISTILLATION

The huge success of Google speaks for itself, but then, Google today is much more than just PageRank alone. From the perspective of controlled, reproducible research experiments, it is extremely difficult to evaluate HITS, PageRank, and similar algorithms in quantitative terms, at least until benchmarks with the extent, detail, and maturity of IR benchmarks are constructed. Currently the evaluation seems largely based on an empirical and subjective notion of authority. As one example of the subjective nature of the formulation, there is no upfront reason why conferral of authority ought to be linear, or even compoundable. In this section I will discuss a few papers that have sought to measure, using human effort or machine learning techniques, the efficacy of various algorithms for social network analysis applied to the Web.

10.5.1 HITS and Related Algorithms

Kleinberg's original paper (1998) and a follow-up experience report (Gibson, Kleinberg, & Raghavan, 1998) describe a number of experiments with HITS. HITS has been found reasonably insensitive to the exact choice of the root set. This property was tested by picking a root set with 200 nodes and iterating HITS 50 times to derive the "ground truth" set of ten hubs and ten authorities, which we may call $C_{10}(200, 50)$, in general, $C_{10}(r, i)$ for r root set pages and i iterations. Figure 10.14 shows the size of intersections between $C_{10}(200, 50)$ and $C_{10}(r, i)$ for $r = 25, 50, 100, 200$ and $i = 1, 3, 10, 50$ for six topics.

One may also use different search engines to generate the root set. A 1998 study by Bharat and Bröder (1998) showed that the portions of the Web covered by major search engines have small overlap. When seeded from different search engines (AltaVista, Infoseek, and Excite) the principal communities (i.e., the communities corresponding to the largest eigenvalue) discovered by HITS were different. Ng et al.'s study (2001) of the stability of HITS corroborates this observation. However, the principal community found using one search engine was often found as a nonprincipal community (corresponding to some other eigenvalue) using another search engine. Another way to perturb the root set is to ask the query in different languages, for example, "astrophysics" and "astrophysique." The top authorities in the principal community for the query "astrophysics" were found to largely overlap with the top authorities in a nonprincipal community for the query "astrophysique."

There are two recent careful empirical evaluations of the efficacy of various link-based ranking strategies. Amento et al. (Amento, Terveen, & Hill, 2000) chose five queries that corresponded to broad topics in Yahoo! They used Yahoo! to assemble the root set. Some of the rank orderings used were as follows:

- *PR*. PageRank as computed over the expanded graph (not large crawls of the Web).
- *HITS*. HITS with B&H edge weights, as described in Section 10.4.1.
- *IN*. The number of sites that link to this site, computed on a coarse site-level graph.

Forty volunteers ranked URLs, which were then used to judge the quality of these orderings. Amento et al. first confirmed that there were large, significant correlations (in the range of 0.6 to 0.8) between the rankings produced by the volunteers, indicating that consistent notions of quality exist. (Otherwise the other measurements would have been pointless.)

From volunteer input, it was found that about a 0.32 fraction of all documents were of high quality, the precision at rank 5 is about 0.75, and the precision at rank 10 about 0.55 using the various link-based rankings, which were all comparable in performance. The correlation between the various ranking methods is shown in Table 10.2. Of course, these numbers do not mean that the notion of "all links are not equal" underlying the HITS family of algorithms is invalidated. The queries and communities experimented with were quite different (compare the topics in Figure 10.14 with those in Table 10.2), as were the times of experimentation (1997 and 2000).

Surprisingly, a simple scoring heuristic called *NumPages* performed quite close to the link-based strategies. NumPages simply set the score of page u to the

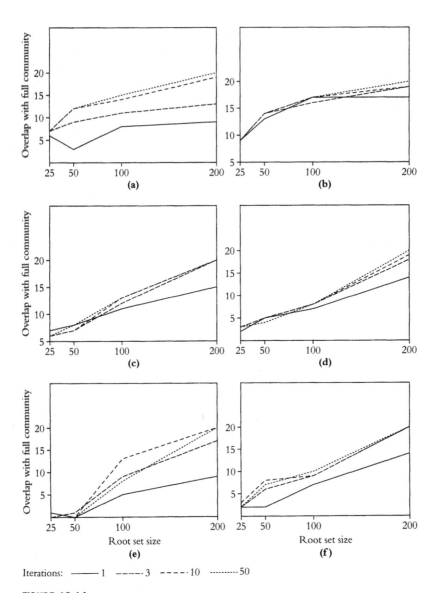

FIGURE 10.14

For six test topics HITS shows relative insensitivity to the root-set size r and the number of iterations i: (a) Harvard, (b) cryptography, (c) English literature, (d) skiing, (e) optionization, and (f) operations research. In each case, the y-axis shows the overlap between the top ten hubs and top ten authorities (20 pages total) and the "ground truth" obtained by using $r = 200$ and $i = 50$.

Table 10.2 Authority Rank Correlation across Different Ranking Strategies Shows Broad Agreement

Topic	IN and HITS	IN and PR	HITS and PR
Babylon 5	0.97	0.93	0.90
Buffy	0.92	0.85	0.70
Simpsons	0.97	0.99	0.95
Smashing Pumpkins	0.95	0.98	0.92
Tori Amos	0.97	0.92	0.88
Spearman average	0.96	0.93	0.87
Kendall average	0.86	0.83	0.75

number of pages published on the host serving the page u, which is a rough indication of how extensive the site is on the topic of the query. This measure was surprisingly strongly correlated with authority scores.

The second user study has been conducted by Singhal and Kaszkiel (2001). The National Institute of Standards and Technology (trec.nist.gov) organizes an annual IR competition called the Text REtrieval Conference (TREC). Since 1998, TREC has added a "Web Track" featuring 500,000 to 700,000 pages from a 1997 Web crawl collected by the Internet Archive (Hawking et al., 2000) and real-life queries collected from commercial search engine logs. TREC personnel assesses the top 1000 results returned by competition participants to generate precision scores. The goal in this competition is not to compile a collection of high-quality links about a topic, but to locate the obvious page/site from a keyword description. Although this task is not directly comparable to topic distillation, the results of the study are instructive, the main result being that link-based ranking strategies decisively beat a state-of-the-art IR system on Web workloads (Figure 10.15).

10.5.2 Effect of Exploiting Other Hypertext Features

Clever (Chakrabarti et al., 1999) was evaluated using 26 queries first used in the *Automatic Resource Compilation* (ARC) system (Chakrabarti et al. 1998) and later by Bharat and Henzinger (1998). Clever, Yahoo!, and AltaVista were compared. AltaVista and Clever directly used the query as shown in Figure 10.16. For Yahoo!, the query was mapped manually to the best-matching leaf category. The top ten pages were picked from AltaVista, the top five hubs and authorities were picked using Clever, and ten random URLs were picked from Yahoo!. These were rated as bad, fair, good, and fantastic by 37 volunteers, with good and fantastic ratings regarded as relevant. Clever won in 50 percent of the queries; Clever and Yahoo!

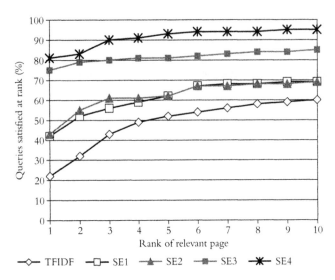

FIGURE 10.15

Link-based ranking beats a traditional text-based IR system by a clear margin for Web workloads. One hundred queries were evaluated. The *x* axis shows the smallest rank where a relevant page was found, and the *y* axis shows how many out of the 100 queries were satisfied at that rank. A standard TFIDF ranking engine is compared with four well-known Web search engines (Raging Search, Lycos, Google, and Excite). Their respective identities have been withheld in this chart by Singhal and Kaszkiel (2001).

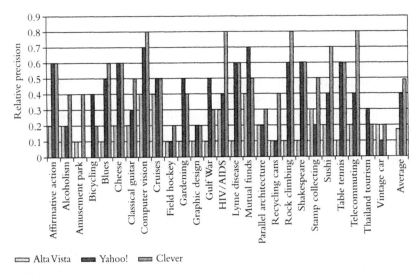

FIGURE 10.16

In studies conducted in 1998 over 26 queries and 37 volunteers, Clever reported better authorities than Yahoo!, which in turn was better than AltaVista. Since then, most search engines have incorporated some notion of link-based ranking.

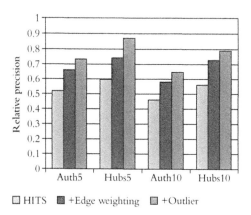

FIGURE 10.17

B&H improves visibly beyond the precision offered by HITS. ("Auth5" means the top five authorities were evaluated.) Edge weighting against two-site nepotism already helps, and outlier elimination improves the results further.

tied in 38 percent of the queries; Yahoo! won in 19 percent of the queries; and AltaVista never beat the others.[8]

Experiments based on the same query collection were also used for evaluating the B&H topic system, again using volunteer input. Results shown in Figure 10.17 show relative precision for HITS, HITS enhanced with edge weights to fight two-host nepotism, and this in turn enhanced with outlier elimination (documents with similarity better than median to the centroid of the base set were retained). Significant improvements are seen in the precision judgments.

DOMHITS and DOMTextHITS show visible resistance to topic drift as compared to HITS (Chakrabarti, Joshi, & Tawde, 2001). These experiments did not depend on volunteers. Instead, the following strategy was used:

1. The Open Directory from dmoz.org (a topic taxonomy like Yahoo!) was massaged to form a classification system with about 250 classes covering most major topics on the Web, together with at least 1000 sample URLs per topic.

2. A text classifier called Rainbow was trained on these classes.

3. A few topics (`/Arts/Music/Styles/classical/Composers`, `/Arts/Visual_Arts`, `/Business/Human_Resources`, and `/Computers/Security`) were chosen from the complete set for experimentation. For each topic chosen, 200 URLs were sampled at random from the available examples to form the root set.

4. HITS, DOMHITS, and DOMTextHITS were run starting from each of these root sets.

---

[8]Results today are likely to differ; since our experiments, most search engines appear to have incorporated some link-based ranking strategy.

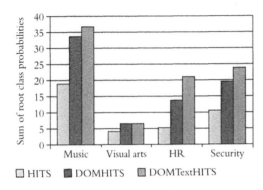

FIGURE 10.18

Top authorities reported by DOMTextHITS have the highest probability of being relevant to the Open Directory topic whose samples were used as the root set, followed by DOMHITS and finally HITS. This means that topic drift is smallest in DOMTextHITS.

5. For each class/topic c, the top 40 authorities, excluding pages already in the root set, were submitted to the Rainbow classifier. For each such document d, Rainbow returned a Bayesian estimate of $\Pr(c|d)$, the posterior probability that document d was generated from (i.e., is relevant to) topic c.

6. By linearity of expectation, $\sum_d \Pr(c|d) = \sum_d E([d \in c]) = E(\sum_d [d \in c])$ is the expected number of authorities relevant to c—a measure of "staying on topic."

Figure 10.18 shows that across the topic, DOMTextHITS is more resistant to topic drift than DOMHITS, which is more resistant than HITS. How do DOMHITS and DOMTextHITS resist drift? Figure 10.19 shows the number of DOM nodes pruned (that is, judged to be on the frontier) and expanded in the first few iterations of the while-loop in Figure 10.13 (using DOMHITS). Two queries are shown. For the first query, "bicycling," there is no danger of drift, and the number of pruned nodes increases quickly, whereas the number of expanded nodes falls. This means that DOMHITS accepts a large number of pages as pure hubs. For the other query, "affirmative action," there is a clique attack from popular software sites owing to a shareware of that name. In this case, the number of expanded nodes keeps increasing with subsequent iterations, meaning that DOMHITS rightly suspects mixed hubs and expands the frontier until they reach leaf DOM nodes, suppressing unwanted reinforcement.

10.6 MEASURING AND MODELING THE WEB

So far in this chapter we have discussed a variety of techniques for analyzing the Web graph and exploiting it for better searches. Most of these techniques depend implicitly on *locality* in various guises, for example, textual similarity, link neigh-

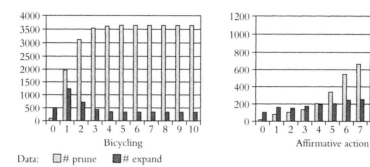

FIGURE 10.19

The number of nodes pruned versus expanded may change significantly across iterations of DOMHITS, but it stabilizes within 10 to 20. For base sets where there is no danger of drift, there is a controlled induction of new nodes into the response set owing to authority diffusion via relevant DOM subtrees. In contrast, for queries that led HITS/B&H to drift, DOMHITS continued to expand a relatively larger number of nodes in an attempt to suppress drift.

borhoods, and page structure. Furthermore, although actions such as adding or removing pages, terms, and links are local, they can be characterized by very robust global properties.

Early works on the theory of random graphs (with a fixed number of nodes n) have studied various properties such as the number of connected components and vertex connectivity under simple edge creation models, a common one being that each of the $n(n-1)$ potential edges is materialized with a fixed probability p. It is hardly surprising that these models are not suitable for the Web: the Web graph was obviously not created by materializing edges independently at random.

10.6.1 Power-Law Degree Distributions

One of the earliest regularities in Web structure to be measured and modeled has been the *degree distribution* of pages, both in-degree and out-degree. To a first approximation, Web page degree follows the *power-law distribution:*

$$\Pr(\text{out-degree is } k) \propto 1/k^{a_{out}} \qquad (10.19)$$

$$\Pr(\text{in-degree is } k) \propto 1/k^{a_{in}} \qquad (10.20)$$

This property has been preserved modulo small changes in a_{out} and a_{in} as the Web has grown, and this has been experimentally verified by a number of people.

It is easy to fit data to these power-law distributions, but that does not explain how largely autonomous page and link creation processes can end up producing such a distribution. An early success in this direction came from the work of

Barabási and Albert (1999). They proposed that the graph (let it be undirected to simplify the following discussion) continually adds nodes to increase in size, as is eminently the case with the Web. They also proposed a key property in their model called *preferential attachment*, which dictates that a new node is linked to existing nodes not uniformly at random, but with higher probability to existing nodes that already have large degree, a "winners take all" scenario that is not far removed from reality in most social networks.

The graph starts with m_0 nodes. Time proceeds in discrete steps. In each step, one node is added. This new node u comes with a fixed number of m edges ($m \leq m_0$), which connect to nodes already existing in the graph. Suppose at this timestep an existing node v is incident on d_v existing edges. Associate v with a probability $p_v = d_v / \sum_w d_w$, where w ranges over all existing nodes. Node u makes m choices for neighbors. For each trial, node v is chosen with probability p_v.

If this system evolves for t timesteps, the resulting graph has $m_0 + t$ nodes and mt edges, and therefore the total degree over all nodes is $2mt$. Let us approximate the degree $k_i(t)$ of node i at timestep t as a continuous random variable. Let $k_i(t)$ be shorthand for $E(k_i(t))$. At time t, the infinitesimal expected growth rate of k_i is $m \times \dfrac{k_i}{2mt} = \dfrac{k_i}{2t}$, by linearity of expectation. Thus, we can $\partial k_i / \partial t = k_i / 2t$, which leads to the solution

$$k_i(t) = m\sqrt{\frac{t}{t_i}} \tag{10.21}$$

by enforcing the boundary condition $k_i(t_i) = m$.

Next let us find the number of nodes i at time t that have $k_i(t) > k$ for some fixed k. For $k_i(t) > k$ to be true, we need $t_i < m^2 t / k^2$, and therefore the fraction of nodes that satisfies this condition is $\dfrac{m^2 t}{(m_0 + t)k^2}$ because the total number of nodes is $m_0 + t$ at this time. Approximating k to be a continuous variable as well, and differentiating with regard to k, we get that the fraction of nodes having expected degree k is roughly

$$-\frac{\partial}{\partial k}\frac{m^2 t}{(m_0 + t)k^2} = \frac{2m^2 t}{(m_0 + t)k^3} \tag{10.22}$$

This establishes the power law with an exponent of three. If the system runs for a long time ($t \rightarrow \infty$), the degree distribution of the resulting graph becomes independent of m_0, the only arbitrary parameter in the model.

Exponents from Web measurements differ from 3; they range between 2.1 and 2.5 (Figure 10.20). One reason could be that the simple linear model for probability of attachment may not be accurate. Power-law degree distributions have been confirmed by a number of other measurements, such as by Bröder and others (2000).

Closer inspection of additional data showed that the pure power-law model does not fit well for low values of k. It appeared that winners did not quite take

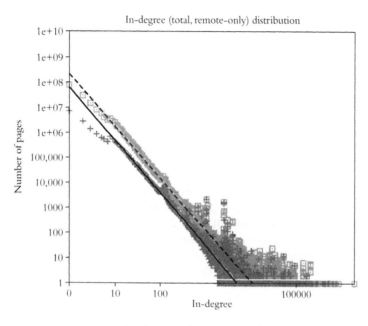

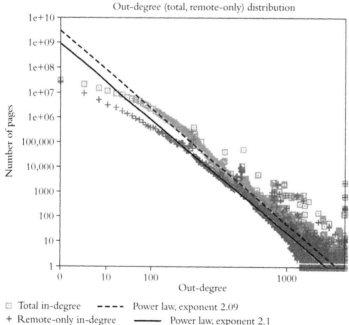

□ Total in-degree   ▪ ▪ ▪ ▪ Power law, exponent 2.09

+ Remote-only in-degree ────── Power law, exponent 2.1

FIGURE 10.20

The in- and out-degree of Web nodes closely follow power-law distributions, except at low degrees.

all—the degree distribution actually has a peak at a modest value of k. The preferential attachment model described here does not explain this phenomenon.

A refinement that has been found to improve the fit is the following two-choice behavior in generating links: With some probability d, newly generated node will link uniformly at random to an existing node. With probability $(1 - d)$, the earlier preferential attachment rule is followed. Basically, the mixing parameter d gives as-yet unpopular pages a chance to eventually attain prominence.

10.6.2 The "Bow Tie" Structure and Bipartite Cores

In November 1999, Bröder et al. (2000) mapped a large Web crawl containing more than 200 million nodes to expose the large-scale structure of the Web graph as having a central, strongly connected core (SCC); a subgraph (IN) with directed paths leading into the SCC, a component (OUT) leading away from the SCC, and relatively isolated tendrils attached to one of the three large subgraphs. These four regions were each about a fourth the size of the Web, which led the authors to call this the "bow tie" model of the Web (Figure 10.21). They also measured

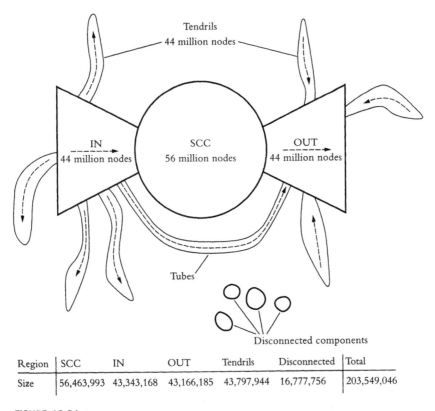

Region	SCC	IN	OUT	Tendrils	Disconnected	Total
Size	56,463,993	43,343,168	43,166,185	43,797,944	16,777,756	203,549,046

FIGURE 10.21

The Web as a bow tie (Bröder et al., 2000).

interesting properties like the average path lengths between connected nodes and the distribution of in- and out-degree. Follow-up work by Dill et al. (2001) showed that subgraphs selected from the Web as per specific criteria (domain restriction, occurrence of keyword, etc.) also appear to often be bow tie–like, although the ratio of component sizes varies somewhat. There are no theories predicting the formation of a bow tie in a social network, unlike power-law degree distributions. We do not even know if the bow tie will be the most prominent structure in the Web graph 10 years from now.

Kumar et al. (1999) wrote programs to search a large crawl of the Web for bipartite cores (e.g., those that take an active role in topic-distillation algorithms). They discovered tens of thousands of bipartite cores and empirically observed that a large fraction are in fact topically coherent. A small bipartite core is often an indicator of an emerging topic that may be too fine-grained to be cataloged manually into Web directories.

10.6.3 Sampling Web Pages at Random

Many of the measurements discussed in this section involve sampling the Web. The precision of some of the estimated parameters clearly depends on the uniformity of the sample obtained.

We must be careful how we define "sampling from the Web," because the Web has dynamic pages generated in response to an unlimited number of possible queries or an unlimited variety of browser cookies. The Web also has malicious or accidental "spider traps," which are infinite chains and trees of pages generated by a combination of soft links, CGI scripts, and Web server mappings. Clearly, we need to settle on a finite graph before we can measure the quality of a sample.

As a result of an ongoing race, Web crawlers do a good job of avoiding such pitfalls while collecting pages to index, although this may mean that they leave out some safely indexable pages. We may use this notion of a public, indexable subset of the Web as our universe and consider sampling in the context of this universe. This is not a precise characterization either, because the Web is not strongly connected, and therefore what ground a crawler can cover depends on the starting point.

To make progress without getting bogged down by the technicalities described here, let us set up the problem from a perspective of a fixed crawling strategy, starting from a fixed set of pages. Assume for simplicity that the Web does not change while the crawl completes. At the end of the crawl, the crawler may output the set of all URLs crawled. From this set, a URL may be readily sampled uniformly at random. The key question is, can a URL be sampled uniformly at random without undertaking a full crawl?

Why is uniform sampling of URLs from the Web of interest? I will propose a few applications. Sampling may be used to quickly and approximately answer aggregate queries about the Web, such as "What fraction of Web pages are in the `.co.jp` domain?" Answering such a question may help balance crawling load across a distributed team of crawlers. Assuming one has a reasonably reliable classifier for a given topic taxonomy such as Yahoo! one may ask what fraction of Web pages belongs to each of the topics. This may be useful for channeling effort toward cataloging topics for that the taxonomy is underrepresented in proportion to the Web. Such measurements can be extended to links. One may sample links and classify the two endpoints to estimate how often a page related to one topic links to a page on another topic. Clusters of densely connected topics may be used to redesign or reorganize topic taxonomies. In the rest of this section, we will study a progression of ideas for uniform sampling from the Web.

PageRank-Like Random Walk

One way to approximate a random sample is to implement a suitable random walk on the graph to be crawled. If the graph satisfies certain properties, a random walk is guaranteed to visit nodes at a rate that quickly approaches the stationary distribution of prestige given in Equation 10.7, forgetting any effects of the starting point with high probability.

Henzinger et al. (2000) and others have proposed to use the "random surfer" notion underlying PageRank (see Section 10.2.1) directly to derive random samples. Recall the transition matrix L used there, and also recall the uniform jump to avoid getting trapped somewhere in the Web graph. The uniform jump can be modeled as a simple *jump matrix* $J = \frac{1}{N}\boxed{1_N}$, where $N = |V|$. As we discussed before, the random surfer uses J with probability d and L with the remaining probability $1 - d$. Thus, as in Equation 10.9,

$$\mathbf{p}_{i+1} = \left(dJ + (1-d)L^T\right)\mathbf{p}_i \qquad (10.23)$$

or

$$p_{i+1}[v] = \frac{d}{|V|} + (1-d)\sum_{(u,v)\in E}\frac{p_i[u]}{N_u}$$

Because all elements of J are positive and $0 < d < 1$, $(dJ + (1 - d)L^T)$ represents an irreducible and aperiodic Markovian transition process with a unique, well-defined stationary distribution that is the principal eigenvector of $(dJ + (1 - d)L^T)$.

Unfortunately, in an actual implementation of the random surfer, there is no way to jump to a random node in V, because that is the problem we are trying to solve! Henzinger et al. approximate the jump by running 1000 walks at the same time that use a pooled collection of URLs visited thus far to implement the jump. This introduces what is called the *initial bias*, which tends to keep the surfer closer to the starting set of URLs than would be the case if a truly random jump were possible.

The basic approach here is to first run a random walk for some time, then sample from the page set thus collected. For any page v,

$$\Pr(v \text{ is sampled}) = \Pr(v \text{ is crawled})\Pr(v \text{ is sampled}|v \text{ is crawled}) \qquad (10.24)$$

We must set Pr(v is sampled | v is crawled) in a way such that Pr(v is sampled) is the same for all v. To do this, we need to first estimate Pr(v is crawled).

Let the steady-state PageRank vector corresponding to Equation 10.23 be $\mathbf{p}^*$. In a sufficiently long walk that visits w nodes in all, we would expect node v to be visited $w\,p^*[v]$ times. Even much shorter walks of about $\sqrt{|V|}$ hops, if limited to the SCC of the Web, are also expected to suffice. Most nodes will appear at most once in short walks of length at most $\sqrt{|V|}$. (This is similar to the claim that you need about $\sqrt{365}$ people in a party before you get two people with the same birthday.) Under this assumption, we can approximate

$$\begin{aligned} \Pr(v \text{ is crawled}) &= E(\text{number of times } v \text{ is visited}) \\ &= wp^*[v] \end{aligned} \tag{10.25}$$

From Equations 10.24 and 10.25, it is clear that we must set

$$\Pr(v \text{ is sampled}|v \text{ is crawled}) \propto 1/p^*[v] \tag{10.26}$$

Again, we cannot know $\mathbf{p}^*$ and must approximate it. The simple solution is to use the actual *visit ratio* of each page—that is, the number of visits to each page divided by the walk length. This is not perfect, because the visit ratio is discrete and has large jumps compared to the smallest PageRank values.

Given the approximations and biases involved, how can we evaluate the quality of such sampling algorithms? Because we cannot hope to "know" the whole Web graph, it is best to generate a finite, unchanging, artificial graph that resembles the Web graph in some important properties (such as degree distribution). Now one can sample from this graph and thus generate, say, a sampled degree distribution. Comparing this with the true degree distribution will give an indication of the uniformity of the algorithm. In fact, any property can be arbitrarily assigned to each node (such as two colors, red and blue) and the sample properties compared with the global properties (e.g., fraction of red nodes).

Henzinger et al. generated synthetic graphs with controlled in- and out-degree distributions and compared the true degree distributions with those derived from their sampling algorithms. The results, presented in Figure 10.22, show negligible deviations for out-degree distribution and small deviations for in-degree distribution. They also explore a number of applications of random sampling, such as estimating the fraction of URLs in various top-level domains and estimating search engine coverage.

Random Walk on a Regular Graph

The probability "inversion," Equation 10.26, is problematic with a large number of nodes that are never visited during short walks. In an attempt to reduce this problem, Bar-Yossef and others (2000) sought to alter the graph in such a way that a sufficiently long random walk leads *directly* to a uniform sample.

It is easy to see that a vector with all elements set to $1/|V|$ is an eigenvector for the adjacency matrix of an undirected graph where every node has the same

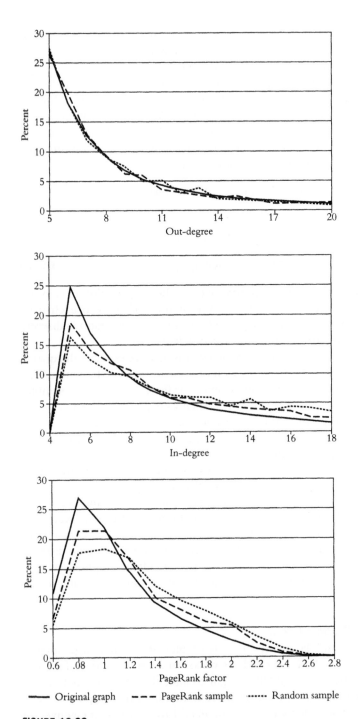

FIGURE 10.22

Random walks based on PageRank give sample distributions close to the true distribution used to generate the graph data, in terms of out-degree, in-degree, and PageRank.

degree. It also turns out that this is the principal eigenvector (Golub & van Loan, 1989). Therefore, if only the Web graph were undirected and regular (i.e., all nodes have the same degree), we would be done.

Bar-Yossef et al. forced these two properties to roughly hold for the graph they walk, in the following manner. First, when making a transition from one node u to the next, candidates are considered not only from out-neighbors of u but also in-neighbors of u. (This can be done by a "backlink" query interface, provided by many search engines.) Thus, the Web graph is in effect rendered undirected. Second, the degree of all nodes is equalized by adding $N_{max} - N_v$ *self-loops* to node v, where N_{max} is the maximum degree.

You may immediately protest that using a search engine to find backlinks voids a previously stated goal. This criticism is valid, but for many applications, including crawling, an older crawl is available to approximately answer the backlink queries. That the backlink database is incomplete and out of date introduces yet other biases into the strategy, requiring empirical checks that their effects are mild. The "ideal" walk (if the backlink database were complete and up to date) and the realistic implementation WebWalker are shown in Figure 10.23. The key modification is that WebWalker maintains its own in- and out-neighbor list for each node, and this must not be modified once created, even if new paths are found to nodes as the crawl proceeds. It turns out that, like Henzinger's random walk, WebWalker also needs a random jump to take it out of tight cycles and cliques (Berg, 2001), but for simplicity this is not shown in the pseudocode.

```
1: Ideal Random Walk:
2: pick starting node
3: for given walk length do
4:     consider current node v on the walk
5:     self-loop at v a random number of times,
           which is distributed geometrically with mean 1 − N_v/N_max
6:     pick the next node uniformly at random from in- and out-neighbors of v
7: end for
```

```
1: WebWalker:
2: pick start node u and set I_u = O_u = ∅
3: for given walk length do
4:     consider current node v on the walk
5:     if v has not been visited before then
6:         get in-neighbors of v using a search engine
7:         get out-neighbors of v by scanning for HREFs
8:         add new neighbors w to I_v and O_v only if w has not been visited already
9:     end if
10:    self-loop at v as in the Ideal Random Walk
11:    pick the next node uniformly at random from I_v ∪ O_v
12: end for
```

FIGURE 10.23

Random walks on regular graphs derived from the Web graph.

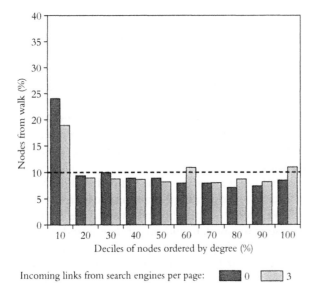

Incoming links from search engines per page: ▮ 0 ▢ 3

FIGURE 10.24

Random walks performed by WebWalker give reasonably unbiased URL samples; when sampled URLs are bucketed along degree deciles in the complete data source, close to 10 percent of the sampled URLs fall into each bucket.

As with the PageRank-based random walk, one can stage sampling problems where the answer is known. Bar-Yossef et al. used a real Web crawl with between 100 and 200 million nodes collected by Alexa Internet (*www.alexa.com*) in 1996. They sorted the nodes in that crawl by degree and computed the deciles of the degree distribution. Next they performed a random walk on this graph and collected the samples into buckets according to the same deciles. If the sample is unbiased, each bucket should have about one-tenth of the pages in the sample. Figure 10.24 shows that this is the case except for some bias toward high-degree nodes, which is expected.

10.7 RESOURCES

An in-depth treatment of social network theory dating from the 1950s and before the growth of the Web can be found in the classic text by Wasserman and Faust (1994). Larson (1996) and Pirolli, Pitkow, and Rao (1996) discuss document clustering based on combinations of text and link attributes. In the context of the Web, hyperlink-based authority rating systems were first reported by Page and Brin (1998) and Page et al. 1998) and Kleinberg (1998). Carriere and Kazman proposed an early system for visual searching and ranking using hyperlinks (1997). Kleinberg's (1999) HITS system was improved by a number of research efforts, such as Clever, and topic distillation (Bharat & Henzinger, 1998).

Gibson and others (1998) studied convergence properties of HITS, as well as graph clusters identified by multiple eigenvectors output by HITS. Barabási and Albert were among the first to analyze the degree distribution of the Web graph and propose models to explain it Barabási and Albert (1999). Later work by Pennock and others (1996) showed that winners do not take all; a slight modification to the model of Barabäsi and Albert shows a much better fit to Web data.

Kumar and others (1999) have proposed alternative models that explain the power-law degree distribution. Bharat and Bröder (1998) were among the first to consider sampling Web pages systematically to find the sizes of and overlaps in the crawl graphs collected by major search engines. The PageRank-based sampling technique is a result of the work of Henzinger and others (2000). The regular graph sampling idea results from the work of Bar-Yossef and others (2000).

References

Amento, B., L. G. Terveen, and W. C. Hill. Does "authority" mean quality? Predicting expert quality ratings of Web documents. *SIGIR*, pp. 296-303. ACM, 2000.

Bar-Yossef, Z., A. Berg, S. Chien, J. Fakcharoenphol, and D. Weitz. Approximating aggregate queries about Web pages via random walks. *Proceedings of the 26th International Conference on Very Large Databases (VLDB)*, pp. 535-544, 2000.

Barabási, A.-L., and R. Albert. Emergence of scaling in random networks. *Science*, 286:509-512, 1999.

Berg, A. Random jumps in Web Walker. Personal communication, April 2001.

Bharat, K., and A. Bröder. A technique for measuring the relative size and overlap of public Web search engines. *Proceedings of the 7th World Wide Web Conference (WWW7)*, 1998.

Bharat, K., and M. R. Henzinger. Improved algorithms for topic distillation in a hyperlinked environment. *Proceedings of the 21st International ACM SIGIR Conference on Research and Development in Information Retrieval*, pp. 104-111, August 1998.

Blum, A., and T. M. Mitchell. Combining labeled and unlabeled data with co-training. *Computational Learning Theory*, pp. 92-100, 1998.

Brin, S., and L. Page. The anatomy of a large-scale hypertextual Web search engine. *Proceedings of the 7th World Wide Web Conference (WWW7)*, 1998.

Bröder, A., R. Kumar, F. Maghoul, P. Raghavan, S. Rajagopalan, R. Stata, A. Tomkins, and J. Wiener. Graph structure in the Web: Experiments and models. *WWW9*, pp. 309-320, Amsterdam, May 2000.

Bush, V. As we may think. *The Atlantic Monthly*, July 1945.

Carriere, J., and R. Kazman. WebQuery: Searching and visualizing the Web through connectivity. *WWW6*, pp. 701-711, 1997.

Chakrabarti, S., and B. E. Dom. Feature diffusion across hyperlinks. U.S. Patent No. 6,125,361, April 1998. IBM Corp.

Chakrabarti, S., B. Dom, D. Gibson, J. Kleinberg, P. Raghavan, and S. Rajagopalan. Automatic resource compilation by analyzing hyperlink structure and associated text. *Proceedings of the 7th World Wide Web Conference (WWW7)*, 1998.

Chakrabarti, S., B. E. Dom, S. R. Kumar, P. Raghavan, S. Rajagopalan, A. Tomkins, D. Gibson, and J. Kleinberg. Mining the Web's link structure. *IEEE Computer*, 32(8):60-67, 1999.

Chakrabarti, S., M. M. Joshi, and V. B. Tawde. Enhanced topic distillation using text, markup tags, and hyperlinks. *SIGIR*, vol. 24, New Orleans, September 2001.

Chakrabarti, S., M. van den Berg, and B. Dom. Focused crawling: A new approach to topic-specific Web resource discovery. *Computer Networks*, 31:1623-1640, 1999. First appeared in the 8th International World Wide Web Conference, Toronto, May 1999.

Davison, B. D. Topical locality in the Web. *Proceedings of the 23rd Annual International Conference on Research and Development in Information Retrieval (SIGIR 2000)*, pp. 272-279, Athens, July 2000.

Gibson, D., J. M. Kleinberg, and P. Raghavan. Inferring Web communities from link topology. *ACM Conference on Hypertext*, pp. 225-234, 1998.

Golub, G. H., and C. F. van Loan. *Matrix Computations.* Johns Hopkins University Press, 1989.

Haveliwala, T. H. Topic-sensitive PageRank, *WWW*, pp. 517-526, Honolulu, May 2002.

Hawking, D., E. Voorhees, N. Craswell, and P. Bailey. Overview of the TREC-8 Web track. In E. Voorhees and D. Harman (eds.), *Proceedings of the 8th Text Retrieval Conference (TREC-8)*, NIST Special Publication 500-246:131-150, 2000.

Henzinger, M. R., A. Heydon, M. Mitzenmacher, and M. Najork. On near-uniform URL sampling. *WWW9*, Amsterdam, May 2000.

Kleinberg, J. M. Authoritative sources in a hyperlinked environment. *Proceedings of ACM-SLAM Symposium on Discrete Algorithms*, 1998. Also appears as IBM Research Report RJ10076(91892).

Kumar, S. R., P. Raghavan, S. Rajagopalan, and A. Tomkins. Trawling the Web for emerging cyber-communities. *WWW8/Computer Networks*, 31(11-16):1481-1493, 1999.

Larson, R. Bibliometrics of the World Wide Web: An exploratory analysis of the intellectual structure of cyberspace. *Annual Meeting of the American Society for Information Science*, 1996.

Lempel, R., and S. Moran. SALSA: The stochastic approach for link-structure analysis. *ACM Transactions on Information Systems (TOIS)*, 19(2):131-160, April 2001.

McCain, K. W. Core journal networks and cocitation maps in the marine sciences: Tools for information management in interdisciplinary research. In D. Shaw (ed.), *Proceedings of the 55th ASIS Annual Meeting*, pp. 3-7, Medford, NJ, 1992.

Motwani, R., and P. Raghavan. *Randomized Algorithms.* Cambridge University Press, 1995.

Ng, A., A. Zheng, and M. Jordan. Stable algorithms for link analysis. *Proceedings of the 24th Annual International ACM SIGIR Conference*, New Orleans, September 2001.

Page, L., S. Brin, R. Motwani, and T. Winograd. The PageRank citation ranking: Bringing order to the Web. Unpublished manuscript, 1998.

Pennock, D. M., G. W. Flake, S. Lawrence, C. L. Giles, and E. J. Glover. Winners don't take all: Characterizing the competition for links on the Web. *Proceedings of the National Academy of Science*, 2000.

Pirolli, P., J. Pitkow, and R. Rao. Silk from a Sow's Ear: Extraction Usable Structures from the Web. *ACM CHI*, 1996.

Seeley, J. R. The net of reciprocal influence: A problem in treating sociometric data. *Canadian Journal of Psychology*, 3:234-240, 1949.

Singhal, A., and M. Kaszkiel. A case study in Web search using TREC algorithms. *WWW10*, Hong Kong, May 2001.

Wasserman, S., and K. Faust. *Social Network Analysis: Methods and Applications.* Cambirdge University Press, 1994.

Index

Printed and bound by CPI Group (UK) Ltd, Croydon, CR0 4YY

03/10/2024

01040314-0009